Knowledge Management

An Interdisciplinary Perspective

Series on Innovation and Knowledge Management

Series Editor: Suliman Hawamdeh *(University of North Texas)* **ISSN: 1793-1533**

---

*Published**

Vol. 5 Creating Collaborative Advantage Through Knowledge and Innovation
edited by Suliman Hawamdeh *(University of Oklahoma)*

Vol. 6 Knowledge Management: Innovation, Technology and Cultures
edited by Christian Stary *(Johannes Kepler University, Austria)*, Franz Barachini *(Vienna University of Technology, Austria)* and Suliman Hawamdeh *(University of Oklahoma, USA)*

Vol. 7 Knowledge Management: Competencies and Professionalism
edited by Suliman Hawamdeh *(University of Oklahoma, USA)*, Kimberly Stauss *(University of Arkansas, USA)* and Franz Barachini *(Vienna University of Technology, Austria)*

Vol. 8 Managing Knowledge for Global and Collaborative Innovations
edited by Samuel Chu *(The University of Hong Kong)*, Waltraut Ritter *(Knowledge Dialogues, Hong Kong)* and Suliman Hawamdeh *(University of Oklahoma, USA)*

Vol. 9 Governing and Managing Knowledge in Asia (2nd Edition)
edited by Thomas Menkhoff *(Singapore Management University,* Singapore), Hans-Dieter Evers *(University of Bonn, Germany)* and Chay Yue Wah *(SIM University, Singapore)*

Vol. 10 The Dynamics of Regional Innovation: Policy Challenges in Europe and Japan
edited by Yveline Lecler *(University of Lyon, France)*, Tetsuo Yoshimoto *(Ritsumeikan University, Japan)* and Takahiro Fujimoto *(University of Tokyo, Japan)*

Vol. 11 Knowledge Management: An Interdisciplinary Perspective
by Sajjad M. Jasimuddin *(Aberystwyth University, UK)*

*The complete list of the published volumes in the series can be found at http://www.worldscibooks.com/series/sikm_series.shtml.

Series on Innovation and Knowledge Management - Vol. 11

Knowledge Management

An Interdisciplinary Perspective

Sajjad M Jasimuddin
Aberystwyth University, UK

World Scientific

NEW JERSEY • LONDON • SINGAPORE • BEIJING • SHANGHAI • HONG KONG • TAIPEI • CHENNAI

Published by

World Scientific Publishing Co. Pte. Ltd.
5 Toh Tuck Link, Singapore 596224
USA office: 27 Warren Street, Suite 401-402, Hackensack, NJ 07601
UK office: 57 Shelton Street, Covent Garden, London WC2H 9HE

British Library Cataloguing-in-Publication Data
A catalogue record for this book is available from the British Library.

Series on Innovation and Knowledge Management — Vol. 11
KNOWLEDGE MANAGEMENT
An Interdisciplinary Perspective

ISBN-13 978-981-4271-22-6
ISBN-10 981-4271-22-5

In-house Editor: Wanda Tan

Typeset by Stallion Press
Email: enquiries@stallionpress.com

Printed in Singapore.

To my beloved parents, A. K. M. Aftabuddin and Kohinoor Dilara Aftab. You have been such a strong beacon of guiding light for me for so long. You are treasured blessings. Rest in peace.

Preface

Despite being a relatively young discipline, knowledge management has grown dramatically in size and influence over the past two decades. Its widespread usage as a task of major consulting firms is phenomenal. The notion of knowledge management has become increasingly important in our ever-changing global environment due to an increased awareness of the significance of knowledge in an organization's success. The main focus of knowledge management practice has been on why and how an organization discovers and deploys its knowledge. In the 21st century, an organization's ability to discover and deploy actionable knowledge faster than its competitors is regarded as a powerful source of competitive advantage. The footprints of knowledge management can now be found as a top business agendum.

The motivation for this book comes from the recognition that too many scholars from many different disciplines have discussed and used knowledge management. Throughout this book, the notion of knowledge management and its relationship with other related disciplines is explored.

Early academic discussions about the concept of knowledge management date back to the 1980s. In line with this, research done by Beckman (1999)[1] suggests that Karl Wiig was the first scholar to coin the term "knowledge management" in 1986 at an International Labour

[1] The details for this and other references cited in the Preface can be found in the Bibliography.

Organization (ILO) conference in Switzerland. However, an issue of the journal *Public Administration Review* (Vol. 35, Iss. 6, 1975) could be thought to be one of the earliest contributions to the knowledge management field (Gu, 2004).

From its beginnings as a fad in the information management discipline, the knowledge management field has progressed significantly. There has been a tremendous surge of research and practice over the last 10 years in this area. Substantial academic output is evidenced by the rapid growth of both the knowledge management communities (e.g., Information and Knowledge Management Society) and the journals associated with knowledge management (e.g., *Journal of Knowledge Management*, *Journal of Information & Knowledge Management*, *Knowledge Management Research & Practice*, *Knowledge and Process Management*).

There are a number of reasons that prompt me to write a book on knowledge management. Interest in knowledge management education has never been greater. Evidence now shows that many students are pursuing their doctoral research in various issues of knowledge management. Similarly, knowledge management is being more frequently added as a course in the business curriculum. It is also observed that a rapidly increasing number of modules on knowledge management at graduate and postgraduate levels have been offered by the higher education institutions (e.g., Aberystwyth University, Aston University, Cranfield University, University of East Anglia, University of Leeds, Lancaster University, University of Manchester, University of Warwick) over the past five years.

Accompanying the growth in institutional provision has been an equally impressive growth in the number of books devoted to the various aspects of knowledge management (e.g., Al-Hawamdeh, 2003; Dierkes *et al.*, 2001; Awad and Ghaziri, 2004; Becerra-Fernandez *et al.*, 2004; Choo, 1998; Davenport and Prusak, 1998; Despres and Chauvel, 2000; Desouza, 2005; Easterby-Smith and Lyles, 2003; Gamble and Blackwell, 2001; Hawryszkiewycz, 2009; Hislop, 2005; Holsapple, 2003; Jashapara, 2004; Lehaney *et al.*, 2004; Leonard-Barton, 1995; Liebowitz, 1999b; Malhotra, 2000b; Morey *et al.*, 2002; Mertins *et al.*, 2003; McNabb, 2007; Newell *et al.*, 2002a;

Schwartz, 2006b; Tiwana, 2002; Wiig, 1993). While such contributions are invariably welcomed, most writers are preoccupied with discussing the basics of knowledge management and how it can be operationalized.

It is noted that scholars from various disciplines have attempted to explore the unexplored areas within knowledge management and exploit them to fit into their own areas of study. So far, we have not discovered the linkage between knowledge management and disciplines such as information management, strategic management, organizational learning, human resource management and innovation management. There is a tendency among scholars from these disciplines to claim ownership. This book aims to identify the issues that seem to clarify the notion of a discipline — for example, "information management" with respect to "knowledge management" — in order to provide fresh insights into the interdisciplinary field of knowledge management.

This book attempts to provide some insights on knowledge management, explaining it as an interdisciplinary field so as to establish the argument that this field is not grounded in a specific discipline. In particular, this book will look at a number of issues that successfully bridge the linkage of knowledge management with information management, strategic management, organizational learning and innovation management. It can be argued that high potential for synergies between knowledge management and other disciplines seems obvious, given the many interrelations and dependencies between these fields. The book intends to help readers understand how knowledge management and the other related disciplines can fit together on the apparent synergies between them.

This book is considered to be a stand-alone volume. Specifically, the text is intended to explain the role of knowledge management and present a thorough review of the relevant literature from an interdisciplinary perspective. The book follows a traditional sequencing of topics, and contains 11 chapters in total. An overview of the key issues to be addressed along with an outline of the book are given below.

Chapter 1 sets the scene for knowledge in an organizational context, which is at the center of the knowledge management discipline. A discussion about what knowledge is from a philosophical point of view and alternative perspectives on organizational knowledge will be furnished. Knowledge, information and data are sometimes used interchangeably in the management and information systems literature; an attempt will be made to reduce the confusion between these constructs using a knowledge hierarchy. Since knowledge is regarded as the key resource of sustainable competitive advantage for an organization, the increasingly significant role of organizational knowledge will be elaborated.

Chapter 2 reviews the key issues that constitute the notion of knowledge management and discusses various facets of the knowledge management process. The importance, for a firm, of managing organizational knowledge to gain a competitive advantage will be explained.

Chapter 3 takes the opportunity to address some of the unresolved operational issues regarding knowledge management. The diverse opinions on the definition of knowledge management will be identified, and then the various debates and perspectives on knowledge management and its related activities will be discussed. Questions such as whether knowledge management is grounded in a specific discipline or a multidisciplinary field, who owns the field, whether it is a universal paradigm or a management fad, and whether it has a technical-centric or social-centric view, will be addressed.

Chapter 4 focuses on various theories surrounding organizational knowledge that are widely cited in the relevant literature. However, the existing theories have overlooked the role of knowledge extracted from external sources. An attempt is thus made to identify gaps in the theories of organizational knowledge and then propose an alternative view of knowledge typology based on its sources.

Chapter 5 presents an overview of the features of the knowledge economy, along with those of agrarian and industrial economies. Moreover, various categories of organizations based on knowledge intensity will be expanded so as to clarify the terms "knowledge-based organization", "knowledge-intensive firm", "professional service firm" and "knowledge-creating company".

Chapter 6 attempts to outline the origin of knowledge management in order to establish the argument that the knowledge management field is not derived from a single discipline. Rather, it is grounded in several established disciplines.

Chapter 7 concentrates on the themes and concepts associated with information management, including its origin and strategic role in an organization, so as to understand its connection with knowledge management. The chapter then reviews scholars' views on the relationship between knowledge management and information management. An attempt is made to identify the relevant factors in order to shed some light on the nature of their association.

Chapter 8 pays attention to the notion of organizational learning, and clarifies the current status of organizational learning concepts through a discussion on its origin, properties and role to enhance and sustain an organization's competitive advantage. The chapter then describes the contradictory views of scholars to address whether knowledge management is a forerunner of organizational learning or vice versa. Accordingly, the similarities and differences between the two subjects are discovered by highlighting the key factors that help to establish a positive link between them.

Chapter 9 focuses on the concept of strategic management and explores its relationship with knowledge management. The historical development of strategic management, the key topics of strategic management research and its role in organizations are elaborated. A cross-fertilization of ideas between strategic management and knowledge management can be found when reviewing the relevant scholars' views on their association. Several variables are used to understand the relationship between the two disciplines that will provide valuable insights into this linkage issue.

Chapter 10 emphasizes the notion of innovation management so as to establish its connection with knowledge management. The chapter starts with a discussion about various definitions and perspectives of innovation management to reduce any confusion. Moreover, its typology and role in enhancing the competitive advantage of an organization over that of its rivals are discussed. The chapter also identifies some key areas relating to the innovation management discipline. The conflicting views of scholars on the connection between innovation management and knowledge management are highlighted.

Finally, the factors that help to determine whether knowledge management facilitates innovation management or vice versa are elaborated.

Chapter 11 looks into the future of knowledge management, taking a critical perspective on the way in which knowledge management is implemented. Knowledge management holds great promise; however, the success of knowledge management in achieving its stated objectives varies. It is essential to identify the issues and challenges related to knowledge management, particularly its implementation. The purpose of the final chapter of this book is to take stock of some of the major points raised in the preceding chapters. This chapter will address certain knowledge management challenges, and offer suggestions for future work that may help additional progress.

Knowledge Management: An Interdisciplinary Perspective is intended for students taking knowledge management courses at the higher education level as well as practitioners who have not taken such courses. It will also be useful for a range of scholars and professionals in other disciplines. This book has been written to set a new standard for knowledge management books.

The reader will find a tight, integrated flow of topics from chapter to chapter. Specifically, each chapter is well organized, with topics flowing logically within each section and each chapter, having thorough explanations and complete coverage of each topic that is introduced, and drawing on a solid theoretical base. The graphics presented will provide a road map, giving readers an advantage in learning about the complex and changing field of knowledge management, and thereby making it easier for readers from different academic backgrounds to learn the material so that they can apply it in their respective careers.

Sajjad M. Jasimuddin
Aberystwyth University, UK

Contents

List of Abbreviations

ABS	Association of Business Schools, UK
AOM	Academy of Management
APQC	American Productivity and Quality Center
BAM	British Academy of Management
BPR	business process re-engineering
CAD	computer-aided design
CEO	chief executive officer
CIO	chief information officer
CKO	chief knowledge officer
COP	community of practice
CSCW	computer-supported collaborative work
DfEE	Department for Education and Employment, UK
DTI	Department of Trade and Industry, UK
HICSS	Hawaii International Conference on System Sciences
IBM	International Business Machines
ICAM	International Conference on Advances in Management
ICT	information and communication technology
ILO	International Labour Organization
IM	information management
IO	industrial organization
IT	information technology
JIT	just-in-time
KBO	knowledge-based organization
KBV	knowledge-based view
KCC	knowledge-creating company

KE	knowledge economy
KIF	knowledge-intensive firm
KM	knowledge management
KMS	knowledge management systems
MBA	Master of Business Administration
OECD	Organisation for Economic Co-operation and Development
PC	personal computer
PSF	professional service firm
QC	quality circle
R&D	research and development
RAE	Research Assessment Exercise, UK
RBV	resource-based view
SECI	socialization, externalization, combination and internalization
SMS	Strategic Management Society
STA	socio-technical approach
SWOT	strengths, weaknesses, opportunities and threats
TQM	total quality management
VRIN	valuable, rare, inimitable and non-substitutable

List of Tables

List of Figures

Acknowledgments

"It could be said of me that in this book I have only made up a bunch of other men's flowers, providing of my own only the string that ties them together."

Michel de Montaigne (1533–1592)
French moralist and essayist

In line with Montaigne's statement, I have created a book that is a bouquet of other scholars' "flowers" as I have brought together the leading ideas, concepts, frameworks and theories surrounding the knowledge management field. I believe I have successfully arranged them in a way that each complements the 'beauty' and 'fragrance' of others. In particular, the specific management studies discussed cover the subject areas of knowledge management, information management, strategic management, organizational learning and innovation management.

I am grateful to Suliman Al-Hawamdeh for his encouragement and support in creating this book.

I also want to thank the team at World Scientific, particularly the editors Sandhya Venkatesh and Wanda Tan Hui Ping, for working so hard to publish the book.

Finally, I would like to express my high gratitude to my family (Shakila, Saad and Ziyad) for their tolerance and unwavering support.

Chapter 1

Knowledge in an Organizational Context

Knowledge Objectives

After studying this chapter, you should be able to:

- Provide a basic introduction of organizational knowledge;
- Discuss the notion of knowledge from a philosophical perspective;
- Differentiate between the three constructs — data, information and knowledge;
- Explain the emerging views of knowledge from a knowledge management perspective; and
- Describe the significance of knowledge in contemporary organizations.

1.1 Introducing the Chapter

Organizational knowledge is the core component that is widely discussed in the emerging interdisciplinary discourse of knowledge management. Over the last 20 years, many issues within the knowledge management domain have received much attention among researchers and practitioners. However, research on the concept of knowledge itself is not new. Since time immemorial, knowledge has been regarded as an important topic of study as it draws from a wide range of disciplines. In the emerging knowledge-based society, one of the key areas that appears to be involved in knowledge management is organizational knowledge. It is evident that the concept of organizational knowledge has received much attention in the knowledge management literature. The idea of organizational knowledge is at the center of all the themes and issues surrounding knowledge management, which will be explained in detail throughout subsequent chapters of this book.

Scholars have contributed a lot to develop and popularize the concept of organizational knowledge. Among them are such notables as Peter Drucker, Daniel Bell, Thomas Davenport, Laurence Prusak, Peter Senge, Dorothy Leonard-Barton, Michael Polanyi, Ikujiro Nonaka, Hirotaka Takeuchi, J. C. Spender and Frank Blackler, all of whom stress the growing importance of organizational knowledge. In the 21st century, knowledge has become a key concern for organizations.

In this very first chapter, I will present the basic notion and process of organizational knowledge and its importance so as to establish the argument that knowledge is a strategic source of sustainable competitive advantage for an organization, be it a private organization or a public enterprise, a government organization or a non-governmental organization. A fuller description of its definitions will also be provided.

Organizational knowledge itself is an eclectic topic. Spender (2008) supports this view, arguing that knowledge remains a curiously elusive topic. There are contradictory views regarding the origin of knowledge. This book will introduce a model of the disciplinary roots of knowledge management that will help to illustrate the dynamic relationships in line with the debate on the notion of knowledge.

This chapter will demonstrate the link between the notion of knowledge and an organization, and is structured as follows. Section 1.2 starts with a discussion about what knowledge is from a philosophical point of view. Various definitions of organizational knowledge given by management scholars will be elaborated in Section 1.3. There is confusion between knowledge, information and data; these constructs are sometimes used interchangeably in the management and information systems literature. It is important to clarify whether knowledge, information and data are the same or different. With this in mind, Section 1.4 focuses on a knowledge hierarchy relating to these constructs (i.e., knowledge, information and data). There are various perspectives on knowledge in organizations. Section 1.5 focuses on two alternative perspectives in order to help the reader understand different types of knowledge. Since organizational knowledge is regarded as the key resource of sustainable competitive advantage for organizations, the increasingly significant role of organizational knowledge is outlined in Section 1.6. The chapter ends with a concluding summary in Section 1.7.

1.2 The Notion of Knowledge from a Philosophical Perspective

Interest and concern have been expressed about the source, nature and quality of knowledge since the time of great philosophers like Socrates, Plato and Aristotle (Hazlett *et al.*, 2005). According to Sveiby (1997), the concept of knowledge traditionally falls in the area of epistemology (i.e., the philosophical study of the nature of knowledge and how it is created). The majority of knowledge management scholars tend to focus on organizational knowledge with respect to its hierarchy and typology (Jasimuddin, 2005). Nevertheless, there is a growing awareness of the way in which organizations manage and nurture their knowledge. In recent times, organizational knowledge has emerged at the center of the knowledge management discourse (Drucker, 1993; Bell, 1973; Toffler, 1990; Grant, 1996).

It can be argued that, in the emerging knowledge-based society, it will be easier to conceptualize and utilize organizational knowledge if various themes and issues associated with the notion of knowledge can be clarified and explained. In this regard, the knowledge management literature includes a number of distinctions between different forms of knowledge. For example, Tiwana (2002, p. 65) classifies knowledge using four key dimensions:

(i) type (i.e., technological knowledge, business knowledge or environmental knowledge);
(ii) focus (i.e., operational knowledge or strategic knowledge);

(iii) complexity (i.e., explicit knowledge or tacit knowledge); and
(iv) perishability over time (i.e., low perishable knowledge or high perishable knowledge).

Several management scholars (e.g., Polanyi, 1962; Nonaka and Takeuchi, 1995; Spender, 1996; Blackler, 1995) have contributed to the development of theories of organizational knowledge in the relevant management literature. While existing theories of organizational knowledge from a management perspective will be elaborated in Chapter 4, this section will explain the notion of knowledge from a philosophical perspective.

As mentioned earlier, the term "knowledge" itself as a concept is not new in the relevant academic and philosophical literature. Newell *et al.* (1999, p. 3) state that "definitions and debates about the nature of knowledge have appeared in philosophical literature since the classical Greek period". The word "knowledge" derives from the Greek word *episteme.* The first philosophical definition of knowledge given by the great philosopher Plato described the concept of knowledge as "justified true belief". *Collins English Dictionary* (2000) defines knowledge as "the facts, feelings, or experiences known by a person or group of people". Marr *et al.* (2003) give a comprehensive picture, arguing that philosophers have debated the definition of knowledge for ages. In line with this, several other scholars (e.g., Hislop, 2005; Jashapara, 2004) argue that the discussions and debates associated with knowledge have occupied the minds of philosophers for ages. Specifically, Marr *et al.* (2003) argue that philosophers — most notably Aristotle (1998), Descartes (1996), Locke (1998), Kant (1999), Hegel (1997), Wittgenstein (1953) and Heidegger (1962) — have debated the definition of knowledge for centuries. Likewise, Jashapara (2004) provides a comprehensive categorization of philosophers who view knowledge differently under two groups:

- The *idealist* philosophers (e.g., Plato, Descartes, Kant, Hegel, Husserl, Heidegger and Sartre), who think of knowledge as an entity within an individual's mind; and

- The *empirical* philosophers (e.g., Aristotle, Locke, Hume, Peirce, James, Dewey and Wittgenstein), who view knowledge as evolving from an individual's senses.

As noted earlier, the great Greek philosopher Plato defined knowledge as "justified true belief", which is widely cited in the knowledge management literature. The fact is that Plato brought issues like perception and true judgment in order to address the definition of knowledge. Although Plato's definition of knowledge is widely accepted by scholars, such a definition is still under widespread discussion and sometimes criticism (Gettier, 1963). For example, Gettier (1963) — in his legendary three-page article, "Is Justified True Belief Knowledge?" — attempted to overturn the thousand-year-old definition of knowledge (i.e., "justified true belief") postulated by Plato. This corresponds well with Nonaka (1994), who admits that the history of philosophy can be regarded as a never-ending search for the meaning of knowledge. Similarly, Boyett and Boyett (2001) conclude by saying that it is easy to discuss knowledge, but it is very difficult to find a comprehensive definition of knowledge. It is worth mentioning that this book concentrates on organizational knowledge within the knowledge management discipline, as will be reflected in the rest of the book.

1.3 Organizational Knowledge Defined

It is not surprising that there are diverse views of what knowledge is. In this regard, Hlupic *et al.* (2002) rightly comment that there are differences in the understanding of the term "knowledge" as well as its dimensions. Tsoukas and Vladimirou (2001) state that the notion of organizational knowledge is "much talked about but little understood". Parallel to this, Newell *et al.* (2002, p. 3) argue that "knowledge is an intrinsically ambiguous and equivocal term". Since defining organizational knowledge is difficult, probably hundreds of definitions of knowledge could be found in the relevant literature.

Despite this fact, Lin and Wu (2005) assert that information becomes knowledge when it is interpreted by individuals, given a context, and anchored into the beliefs and commitments of individuals. For Kanter (1999), knowledge is power for decision making and execution. Leonard and Sensiper (1998) see knowledge as information that is pertinent, actionable and based on some experience process. Nonaka and Takeuchi (1995, p. 58) define knowledge as a dynamic human process of justifying personal belief toward the "truth". This corresponds well with Davenport and Prusak (1998, p. 5), who provide a comprehensive definition of knowledge as "a fluid mix of framed experience, values, contextual information, and expert insight that provides a framework for evaluating and incorporating new experiences and information".

However, several researchers (e.g., Machlup, 1980; Alavi and Leidner, 1999; Blackler, 1995; Spender, 1996; Connell *et al.*, 2003) claim that knowledge is a catalyst for useful actions and decisions. Similarly, others (e.g., Gao *et al.*, 2008; Tiwana, 2001; von Krogh *et al.*, 2000) contend that knowledge should relate to action. Machlup (1980), for instance, argues that the kind of knowledge that is important for business is practical knowledge. Reflecting this view, Bourdreau and Couillard (1999) contend that knowledge is a driving force for action and a sphere of influence for professionals.

Tiwana (2002, p. 37) repeats the definition, stating that "knowledge is actionable information. Actionable refers to the notion of relevant and being available in the right place at the right time, in the right context, and in the right way so that anyone (not just the producer) can bring it to bear on decisions being made every minute". Similarly, drawing on Plato's definition, Alavi and Leidner (1999) strongly argue that knowledge is justified personal belief that increases an individual's capacity to take effective action. Furthermore, Alavi and Leidner (2001, p. 109) state:

> Knowledge is ... the result of cognitive processing triggered by the inflow of new stimuli. ... [I]nformation is converted to knowledge once it is processed in the mind of individuals and knowledge becomes information once it is articulated and presented in the form of text, graphics, words, or other symbolic forms.

A common theme here is the fact that knowledge is linked to the capacity for action. In line with this, several other scholars (chiefly, Drucker, 1992; Kanter, 1999; Sveiby, 1997; Nonaka and Takeuchi, 1995; Mahlitta, 1996; Vail, 1999) define knowledge as the decision and power to act. Nonaka and Takeuchi (1995), for example, contend that knowledge should relate to action. Table 1.1 depicts organizational knowledge definitions provided by various management scholars.

Borrowing from the definition of knowledge postulated by Plato and by Alavi and Leidner, the definition of organizational knowledge that will be used throughout this book is of interpreted organizational information which is processed from data (i.e., facts and events) that helps organizational members to take purposeful actions and make decisions so as to accomplish their assigned tasks — what Machlup (1980) calls practical knowledge.

Table 1.1 presents some representative definitions of knowledge. This demonstrates that there is no commonly accepted definition of knowledge (Hofer-Alfeis and van der Spek, 2002) because, as noted earlier, it is difficult to define knowledge (Gamble and Blackwell, 2001). Blackler (1995, p. 1032) rightly comments that knowledge is multi-faceted and complex, and therefore is very hard to define. Indeed, the fact that this subject has been studied by several disciplines and from different approaches is an obvious illustration of the lack of consensus. This corresponds well with Hlupic *et al.*'s (2002) comment that "a possible reason for the vagueness and ambiguity in the definition of organizational knowledge seems to be that the word 'knowledge' means different things to different people who are coming from different academic and philosophical backgrounds".

Furthermore, Hlupic *et al.* (2002) identify several factors that help to understand why it is extremely difficult to define knowledge. These factors include:

- *The intangible nature of knowledge.* Knowledge itself is very much intangible in nature. Since knowledge is not tangible, it appears as an extremely complex concept to define.

Table 1.1 Organizational Knowledge Defined

Authors	Definitions
Bourdreau and Couillard (1999)	A driving force for action and a sphere of influence for professionals
Buckley and Carter (2000)	"Structured information", which does not characterize the simpler "information"
Davenport and Prusak (1998)	A fluid mix of framed experience, values, contextual information, and expert insight that provides a framework for evaluating and incorporating new experiences and information
Galup *et al.* (2002)	Inseparable information in context
Kanter (1999)	Power for decision making and execution
Leonard and Sensiper (1998)	Information that is pertinent, actionable and based on some experience
Lin and Wu (2005)	Information that becomes knowledge when it is interpreted by individuals, given a context, and anchored into the beliefs and commitments of individuals
Mahlitta (1996)	Information for action
Nonaka and Takeuchi (1995)	A dynamic human process of justifying personal belief toward the "truth"
Plato (1992)	Justified true belief
Polanyi (1962, 1966)	An activity which is better described as a process of knowing
Tiwana (2002)	In the business context, nothing but actionable information
Tsoukas and Vladimirou (2001)	The set of collective understandings embedded in a firm, which enable it to put its resources to particular uses
Vail (1999)	A value-adding tool for organizations

- *The subjective and eclectic nature of knowledge.* The difficulty with the definition of knowledge is compounded even further because knowledge itself is believed to be a subjective and eclectic field.
- *The emerging rather than established field of knowledge.* Organizational knowledge is treated as an emerging topic in the management field rather than an established one. As a result, the difficulty with definitions is even further felt.

1.4 Knowledge Hierarchy

Not only is it difficult to explain what organizational knowledge is, but there is also confusion in understanding data and information in line with the notion of organizational knowledge. The question of whether data, information and knowledge have a similar meaning remains unresolved. Numerous attempts have been made to link knowledge with data and information. A number of researchers (e.g., Frappaolo, 1997; KPMG, 1999) argue that the terms "data", "information" and "knowledge" have a very similar meaning. Other scholars (e.g., Wiig, 1993; Nonaka, 1994; Court, 1997; Davenport and Prusak, 1998; Blumentritt and Johnston, 1999; Buckley and Carter, 2000; Alter, 1996; Tobin, 1996; van der Spek and Spijkervet, 1997; Bouthillier and Shearer, 2002; Beckman, 1999) contend that knowledge differs from information and data. For example, Bouthillier and Shearer (2002) state that the distinctions drawn between the related concepts of data, information and knowledge need to be examined in order to differentiate knowledge management from other well-established disciplines, particularly information management.

As far as the definitions of data and information are concerned, several authors (e.g., Davenport and Prusak, 1998; Drucker, 1998; Tiwana, 2002; Buckley and Carter, 2000) argue that they are less contentious and relatively straightforward compared to the definition of knowledge. Reflecting this view, Davenport and Prusak (1998) see data as a structured record of transactions within an organization. Specifically, Davenport and Prusak (1998, p. 2) define data "as a set of discrete, objective facts about events" and suggest that "in an organizational context, data is most usefully described as structured records of transactions". Davenport and Prusak (1998, p. 3) continue to describe information as "a message, usually in the form of a document or an audible or visible communication". Drucker (1998) supports this view, postulating that "[i]nformation is data endowed with relevance and purpose" (p. 5).

In attempting to link knowledge and information, Tiwana (2002, p. 37) claims that "knowledge in the business context is nothing but *actionable information*. Knowledge allows for making predictions, casual associations, or predictive decisions about what to do — unlike information, which simply gives us the facts". Moreover, several other authors draw distinctions between data, information and knowledge. Drucker (1999), for instance, contends that information is data with attributes of relevance and purpose. Information is, above all, context-based. According to the American Productivity and Quality Center (1996), knowledge is information that has value. Buckley and Carter (2000, pp. 57–58) state: "Information is 'interpreted data', with meaning not possessed by simple data, and knowledge is 'structured information' ... which does not characterise the simpler 'information'".

Likewise, Alavi and Leidner (2001) suggest that data are combined to create information, while information is combined to create knowledge. Similarly, Tiwana (2002, p. 37) argues that knowledge "is formed in and shared between individual and collective minds. It does not grow out of databases but evolves with experience, successes, failures, and learning over time". In their classic book, *Working Knowledge*, Davenport and Prusak (1998) provide a thorough discussion of the distinctions between data, information and knowledge, suggesting that "data are simply facts, which then become information by the addition of meaning, while knowledge originates in peoples' heads, drawing on information which is transformed and enriched by personal experience".

On the other hand, Walters (2000) argues that knowledge is neither data nor information, though it is related to both. Knowledge is information made actionable (Mahlitta, 1996), or information made actionable in a way that adds value to the enterprise

(Vail, 1999). In this context, Jashapara (2005) points out that knowledge rather than information has become the critical resource, as knowledge workers provide the driving force for innovation and productivity improvements in goods and services. Al-Hawamdeh (2002) succinctly elaborates the distinction between knowledge and information as thus:

> Knowledge embodied in books and journals does not necessarily translate into useful and usable knowledge unless it is read, manipulated and communicated from one person to another. In other words, knowledge can only reside in the minds of people and the minute it leaves the human mind, it is information. However, not all types of knowledge can be codified and captured. Knowledge in the form of skills and competencies can only be transferred from one person to another through interaction. Information management on the other hand deals with knowledge that can be captured, processed and managed.

Likewise, Nonaka and Takeuchi (1995, p. 58) make the following observations about knowledge and information: "First, knowledge, unlike information, is about beliefs and commitment. Knowledge is a function of a particular stance, perspective, or intention. Second, knowledge, unlike information, is about action. ... And third, knowledge, like information, is about meaning. It is context specific and relational". They actually consider knowledge as "a dynamic human process of justifying personal belief toward the 'truth'".

It can be concluded that, although the terms "data", "information" and "knowledge" can be used with a similar meaning, knowledge also differs from information and data. It is helpful to view data, information and knowledge as separate constructs that are linked sequentially. Parallel to this, Zins (2006) contends that data, information and knowledge are viewed as sequential. There are many dimensions in explaining the relationship among them.

Several other scholars (e.g., Beckman, 1999; Nissen *et al.*, 2000; Davenport and Prusak, 1998; Tuomi, 1999) attempt to resolve the issue by organizing knowledge, information and data into a hierarchy. Each level in the hierarchy builds on the one below it, so data are required to create information and information is required to create knowledge. Most researchers agree on the fact that data occupy the lowest level in the knowledge hierarchy, while knowledge is above data and information. Walters (2000), for example, reports that the differences between data, information and knowledge are often a matter of degree. However, Tuomi (1999) proposes a reverse hierarchy (knowledge–information–data), arguing that "data emerge only after we have information, and that information emerges only after we already have knowledge" (p. 103); therefore, "the hierarchy of data–information–knowledge should be turned the other way around. Data emerge last — only after there is knowledge and information available" (p. 107).

Extending Tuomi's concept of a reversed hierarchy, Nissen (2002) proposes a two-dimensional knowledge hierarchy model. Using the vertical axis to represent action ability and the horizontal axis to represent volume, Nissen concludes that knowledge is the most actionable level but the rarest, whereas data are the least actionable level but have the greatest volume. As he puts it:

> [T]he transferor of knowledge could indeed view the hierarchy … where knowledge is necessary to produce information, which in turn is necessary for creating data that is conveyed (e.g., via paper, network, speech, observable action). However, the receiver of knowledge would view the hierarchy in the opposite perspective … where data are placed into context to become information, and information that enables action becomes knowledge. [Nissen, 2002, p. 253]

In the existing literature, considerable similarity of opinions among scholars on the relationship between data, information and knowledge is detected. For example, the list of stock prices displayed on a commercial screen is data; information is the meaningful data that are extracted for the prices of various stocks; and finally knowledge is the processed information that helps one to make decisions regarding stock investments, taking into account other relevant information and data such as stock price, company profile, industry information, portfolio risk and availability of funds. Likewise, Wilson (1996, p. 34) explains the relationship between the three constructs using the following practical example:

> For instance, if you are standing on the platform at Paddington Station waiting to go to Oxford, you may consult a time table (data) to look up the departure time of the next train (information). Then you may look at your watch to see what time it is (more information) and subtract this time from the departure time so that you know how long you have to wait (knowledge). Along with other knowledge of the options open to you, you can then decide what there is time for: enough only to board the train? ... or to buy a newspaper first? ... or to sit down and wait with newspaper, coffee and bun? (decision and action).

These constructs can be viewed as a hierarchy of increasing meaning, depth and relevance to action, as depicted in Figure 1.1. In line with this, Zack (1999, p. 46) also provides a conceptual analysis on the differences between data, information and knowledge:

> Data represent observations or facts out of context that are, therefore, not directly meaningful. Information results from placing data

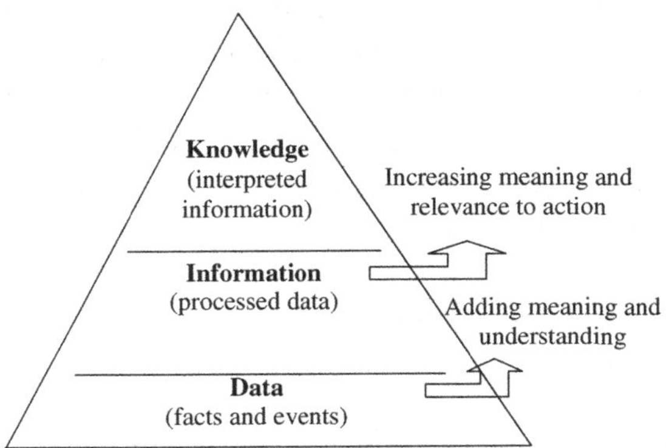

Figure 1.1 Data–Information–Knowledge Hierarchy

> within some meaningful context, often in the form of a message. Knowledge is that which we come to believe and value on the basis of the meaningfully organized accumulation of information (messages) through experience, communication, or interference.

It is to be noted that the knowledge hierarchy depicts the transformation of knowledge, in which data is converted to information and information is converted to knowledge. This corresponds well with Nissen (2002), who argues that data are placed in context to create information and that information which becomes actionable is knowledge.

Following our discussion on the knowledge hierarchy, the perspectives on organizational knowledge and its related activities will be addressed next.

1.5 Perspectives on Knowledge in Organizations

Before moving on to the discussion about the role of knowledge in organizations, an essential starting point is to mention the emerging views associated with the notion of organizational knowledge. Several scholars (Empson, 1999, 2001; Newell *et al.*, 2002) have come forward with various perspectives on knowledge in organizations in order to help us understand different types of knowledge. For example, Newell *et al.* (2002) explain the notion of knowledge from two different viewpoints, that is, the structural perspective and the processual perspective. According to them, the structured viewpoint suggests that knowledge is a discrete, objective, largely cognitive entity, while the processual perspective views knowledge as rooted in action and social practice.

Likewise, Empson (2001) discusses two alternative perspectives on organizational knowledge:

- knowledge as an asset; and
- knowing as a process.

Empson (2001) identifies several dimensions in order to discuss the perspectives on knowledge. These dimensions help to understand the two broad alternative perspectives on knowledge. These dimensions surrounding the perspectives include:

- purpose of research;
- disciplinary foundations;
- underlying paradigm;
- epistemological assumption;
- models of knowledge; and
- main levels of analysis.

Table 1.2 shows the six dimensions provided by Empson (2001) in discussing the two distinctive perspectives on knowledge in organizations.

Table 1.2 Alternative Perspectives on Knowledge in Organizations

Dimensions	Knowledge as an Asset	Knowing as a Process
Purpose of research	Normative — to identify valuable knowledge and to develop effective mechanisms for managing knowledge within organizations	Descriptive — to understand how knowledge is created, articulated, disseminated and legitimated within organizations
Disciplinary foundations	Economics	Sociology
Underlying paradigm	Functionalist	Interpretive
Epistemological assumption	Knowledge as an objectively definable commodity	Knowledge as a social construct
Models of knowledge	Exchanges of knowledge among individuals are governed by an implicit market within organizations	Knowledge is disseminated and legitimated within organizations through an ongoing process of interaction among individuals
Main levels of analysis	Organization and its knowledge base	Individual in social context

Source: adapted from Empson (2001, p. 813).

Moreover, Jakubik (2007) provides complementary views of knowledge, based on a review of the extant knowledge management literature. Her framework represents the four major views of knowledge together and their relationships. These complementary views of knowledge entail the ontological, epistemological, commodity and community views. Her analysis of various perspectives of knowledge are displayed below:

- *The ontological view of knowledge.* "Ontology studies the nature of phenomena, in this case 'knowledge'. Objectivity and subjectivity in the ontological sense are predicates of entities (brute facts, e.g., 'river', 'mountain', or institutional facts, e.g., 'company', 'marriage') and they describe the modes of existence. Knowledge is the products of the individual mind and it is subjective in the ontological sense."
- *The epistemological view of knowledge.* "The epistemological view of knowledge is a scientific, philosophical view of the nature of knowledge itself. Knowledge is an institutional fact because it requires human institutions (e.g., language) for its existence. ... We can make objective and subjective statements about knowledge. For those who believe that knowledge can be acquired, shared, knowledge is 'explicit' (knowledge is a more objective concept) and for those who believe that knowledge needs to be personally experienced, knowledge is 'tacit' (knowledge is a more subjective concept)."
- *The commodity view of knowledge.* "The commodity view of knowledge is a managerial approach to knowledge, where knowledge is understood as a static organizational resource as a commodity. This entitative view of knowledge has an epistemologically objective assumption, i.e., 'knowledge is an objectively definable commodity'. In the knowledge management literature, the commodity view of knowledge is also referred to as the 'product-centered' approach, the 'content-centered' or as the 'codification' approach."
- *The community view of knowledge.* "The community or social view of knowledge assumes that knowledge is not static, but rather a

> dynamic concept and that it is created in social interactions: 'knowledge is a social construct'. This approach is also referred to as the 'process-centered' approach. The processual view of knowledge is interpretive and it focuses on individuals in a social context."

Jakubik (2007) successfully illustrates in her framework how different views and types of knowledge prescribed by knowledge management scholars are related to each other, further claiming that "the ontological (reality), epistemological (science), commodity (managerial), and the community (social construct) views of knowledge are not mutually exclusive views, but rather they are complementary to each other" (see Figure 1.2).

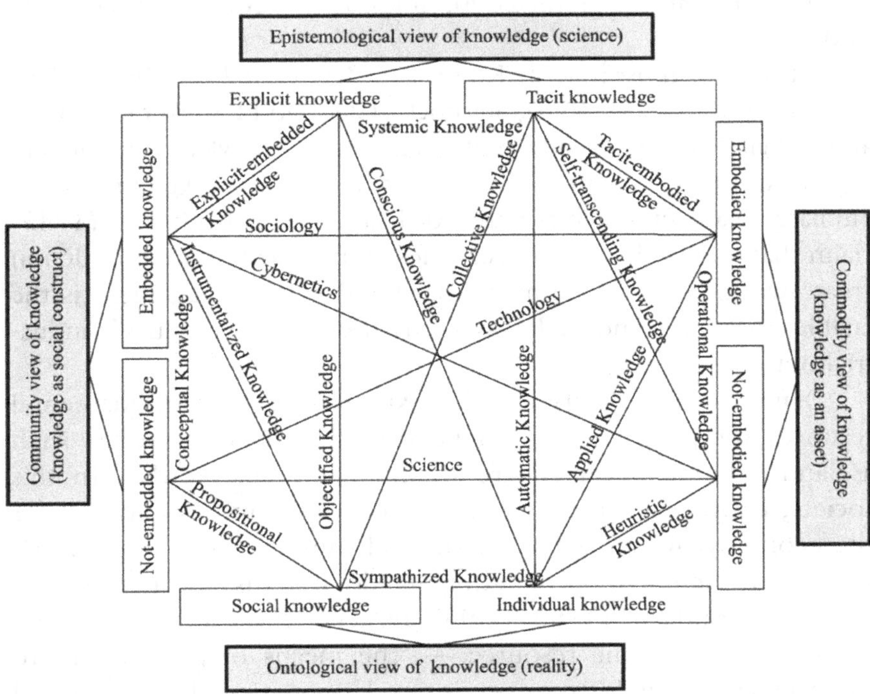

Figure 1.2 Emerging Views of Knowledge

Source: adapted from Jakubik (2007).

Although there are still many unresolved issues regarding our understanding of knowledge, academics and practitioners are focusing much more attention towards comprehending the role of knowledge in organizational success. This will be dealt with next.

1.6 The Role of Knowledge in an Organizational Context

The role played by knowledge in an organization has been receiving growing recognition in the management literature (e.g., Bell, 1979; Hayes-Roth *et al.*, 1983; Toffler, 1990; Drucker, 1992, 1993; Brown and Duguid, 1998; Nonaka and Takeuchi, 1995; Choo, 1996, 1998; Binney, 2001; Jasimuddin *et al.*, 2005; Hsieh *et al.*, 2009; Spender, 1996; Wang-Cowham, 2008; Grant, 1996; Teece *et al.*, 1997; Kogut and Zander, 1992; Prahalad and Hamel, 1990; Argote and Ingram, 2000; Singh *et al.*, 2008; Bhagat *et al.*, 2002).

Scholars — most notably Kogut and Zander (1992), Bell (1979), Prahalad and Hamel (1990), Starbuck (1992) and Drucker (1993) — argue that, in a post-industrial society, the knowledge within an organization is the main source of its competitive advantage. Similarly, academics such as Earl (2001) and Hayes-Roth *et al.* (1983) claim that knowledge is a source whose refinement and reproduction create wealth, and furthermore that knowledge management is the enabler that turns knowledge as a crucial input into a valuable industrial output.

Drucker (1992) argues that knowledge is a fundamental resource for people, while conventional production factors such as land, labor and capital are secondary. In his words, "In this society, knowledge is the primary resource for individuals and for the economy overall. Land, labor, and capital — the economist's traditional factors of production — do not disappear, but they become secondary" (1992, p. 95). Drucker continues by arguing, "The basic economic resource — 'the means of production' to use the economist's term — is no longer capital, nor natural resources (the economist's 'land'), nor labor. It is ... knowledge" (1993, p. 8).

This point is also underscored by Quinn (1992, p. 241), who puts it thus:

> With rare exceptions, the economic and producing power of a modern corporation lies more in its intellectual and service capabilities than in its hard assets — land, plant and equipment. ... Virtually all public and private enterprises — including most successful corporations — are becoming dominantly repositories and coordinators of intellect.

This view is an extension of that of Toffler (1990), who recognizes the fact that, in a knowledge-based society, knowledge is the source of the highest-quality power. Many other scholars (e.g., Grant, 1996; Baden-Fuller and Pitt, 1996; Nonaka and Takeuchi, 1995; Hendriks, 2001) also emphasize the role of knowledge in organizations. Or, stated differently, organizational knowledge is one of the main, strategically significant resources that eventually leads to the generation of competitive advantage for firms. In explaining its role in an organization, Tsoukas and Vladimirou (2001, p. 976) claim that "organizational knowledge is the capability members of the organization have developed to draw distinctions in the process of carrying out their work, in particular concrete contexts, by enacting sets of generalizations whose application depends on historically evolved collective understanding".

Likewise, Hamel and Prahalad (1991) maintain that an organization's value stems from knowledge and competencies which are embedded in people. This coincides with the development of the knowledge-based theory of the firm, as postulated by Grant (1997), who argues that the transition from an industrial society to a knowledge-based society has led to an increasing focus on knowledge as the most important resource for organizations. Reflecting this view, the UK Department for Education and Employment (2000, p. 4) asserts, "Knowledge is crucial because at the cutting edge of innovation in the new economy are knowledge producers: universities and businesses whose fundamental products are the ideas and research which provide the engine for change in goods and services".

In fact, it could be argued that an organization's knowledge is the strategic resource in intelligent decision making (Tversky and Kahneman, 1981), forecasting (Rowe and Wright, 1999), planning (Buckley and Carter, 2000) and intuitive judgment (Tiwana, 2002). Marquardt (1996, p. 129) further elaborates on this, commenting:

> Knowledge has become more important for organizations than financial resources, market position, technology, or any other company asset. Knowledge is seen as the main resource used in performing work in an organization. The organization's traditions, culture, technology, operations, systems, and procedures are all based on knowledge and expertise. Employees need knowledge to increase their abilities to improve products and services to provide quality service to clients and consumers.

In connection with this, Choo (1996) identifies three critical reasons underlying the utilization of knowledge within an organization:

(i) to make strategic decisions;
(ii) to make sense of changes in its external environment; and
(iii) to create new knowledge.

Managing organizational knowledge has recently emerged as a critical concern for organizations. Due to an organization's ability to explore and exploit knowledge for its benefit, the popularity of the knowledge management field has increased tremendously. Knowledge assets have emerged as the tools with which today's organizations need to function in order to gain competitive advantage. That is why all organizations have started viewing themselves as knowledge-intensive firms (which will be discussed in Chapter 5) and have adopted knowledge management approaches in every business functional area and corporate action. The next chapter will elaborate on the notion of knowledge management.

1.7 Concluding Summary

Knowledge is considered the most critical resource of an organization in the emerging knowledge-based society. One key area that appears to be involved in knowledge management is the idea of organizational knowledge, which will be evident throughout the book. This chapter has addressed the notion of knowledge, its philosophical aspects, its relationship with the two related concepts of data and information, and various perspectives on knowledge within the knowledge management field. The word "knowledge" itself is a subject with many different meanings and interpretations. Since knowledge management is a relatively new discipline of the 1990s, there is no consensus in the relevant management literature regarding the definition of organizational knowledge.

There is still a debate about what we mean by the term "organizational knowledge". Due to its popularity, several scholars have produced definitions of knowledge. Some scholars (e.g., Drucker, 1992; Kanter, 1999; Alavi and Leidner, 1999; Sveiby, 1997; Nonaka and Takeuchi, 1995; Mahlitta, 1996; Vail, 1999; Leonard and Sensiper, 1998; Bourdreau and Couillard, 1999; Gao *et al.*, 2008; Tiwana, 2001; von Krogh *et al.*, 2000; Davenport and Prusak, 1998; Tiwana, 2002; Connell *et al.*, 2003) define knowledge as the decision and power to act. An essential starting point is to mention the working definition of organizational knowledge that is used throughout this book: the interpreted organizational information which is processed from data (i.e., facts and events) that helps organizational members to take purposeful actions and make decisions in order to accomplish their assigned tasks and thereby gain competitive advantage.

Although the terms "data", "information" and "knowledge" can be used with a similar meaning, knowledge does differ from information and data. While data are facts and events, information is processed data, and finally organizational knowledge is interpreted organizational information that actually helps people to take purposeful actions and make decisions. This chapter has also briefly looked at the hierarchy of knowledge around these three concepts.

Research on organizational knowledge within the knowledge management field has a legacy that spans over 20 years, with more recent exponential growth. However, as suggested earlier, a diversity of perspectives have been used to look at organizational knowledge issues. The theoretical underpinnings of these perspectives are based on the organizational knowledge framework developed by Jakubik (2007).

Having viewed the phenomenon from four different perspectives, Jakubik (2007) offers a comprehensive picture of organizational knowledge. It is worth mentioning that a pluralistic stance is taken when it comes to discussing organizational knowledge, which falls somewhere between the rather divergent perspectives while recognizing the contradictions.

There is no doubt that there has recently been recognition that knowledge is an important strategic component for organizational survival. There is an agreement about the importance of the knowledge available for current and future use. As mentioned previously, the notion of organizational knowledge helps to enhance an organization's sustainable competitive advantage. Consequently, the concept of knowledge has received much interest in management literature over the last decade or so. This chapter has helped to acquaint readers, be they researchers or managers, with the notion of knowledge and the role of knowledge in organizations.

Apparently, knowledge seems to be a long-lasting phenomenon because academics and practitioners from various disciplines are showing an interest in pursuing research and practice surrounding the topic. Scholars, irrespective of their backgrounds, argue that knowledge is the key resource of the knowledge-based era. A good number of management theorists have contributed to the discussion of organizational knowledge, stressing the growing importance of knowledge as a strategic resource for organizations.

There is still a debate about various aspects of organizational knowledge and its link to the emerging interdisciplinary field of knowledge management. Nevertheless, this chapter has focused on understanding what knowledge is from an organizational perspective, and contrasted knowledge to other concepts such as data and information. Despite the fact that numerous practical questions and challenges concerning organizational knowledge remain unanswered and demand research, knowledge is emerging as one of the vital organizational resources of the firm and there is a growing awareness of the way organizations manage knowledge. The next chapter will focus on the various aspects of the emerging interdisciplinary notion of knowledge management.

Further Reading

Arikan, A. T. (2009). Interfirm knowledge exchanges and the knowledge creation capability of clusters. *Academy of Management Review*, 34(4), October, 658–676.

Marouf, L. and Doreian, P. (2010). Understanding information and knowledge flows as network processes in an oil company. *Journal of Information and Knowledge Management*, 9(2), 105–118.

McKinney, E. H. Jr. and Yoos, C. J. II (2010). Information about information: a taxonomy of views. *MIS Quarterly*, 34(2), June, 329–344, A1–A5.

Melkas, H. and Harmaakorpi, V. (2008). Data, information and knowledge in regional innovation networks: quality considerations and brokerage functions. *European Journal of Innovation Management*, 11(1), 103–124.

Tsai, W. and Wu, C.-H. (2010). Knowledge combination: a cocitation analysis. *Academy of Management Journal*, 53(3), June, 441–450.

References

Alavi, M. and Leidner, D. (1999). Knowledge management systems: emerging views and practices from the field. In *Proceedings of the 32nd Hawaii International Conference on System Sciences* (pp. 1–11).

Alavi, M. and Leidner, D. (2001). Knowledge management and knowledge management systems: conceptual foundations and research issues. *MIS Quarterly*, 25(1), 107–136.

Al-Hawamdeh, S. (2002). Knowledge management: re-thinking information management and facing the challenge of managing tacit knowledge. *Information Research* (online journal), 8(1), available at http://informationr.net/ir/8-1/paper143.html/.

Alter, S. (1996). *Information Systems: A Management Perspective*, 2nd ed. Menlo Park, CA: Benjamin/Cummings Publishing.

American Productivity and Quality Center (1996). *Knowledge Management: Consortium Benchmarking Study Final Report*. Houston, TX: APQC International Benchmarking Clearinghouse.

Argote, L. and Ingram, P. (2000). Knowledge transfer: a basis for competitive advantage in firms. *Organizational Behavior and Human Decision Processes*, 82(1), 150–169.

Aristotle (1998). *The Metaphysics*. H. Lawson-Tancred, trans. London: Penguin Books.

Baden-Fuller, C. and Pitt, M. (1996). The nature of innovating strategic management. In C. Baden-Fuller and M. Pitt (eds.), *Strategic Innovation* (pp. 3–42), London: Routledge.

Beckman, T. J. (1999). The current state of knowledge management. In J. Liebowitz (ed.), *Knowledge Management Handbook* (pp. 1–22), Boca Raton, FL: CRC Press LLC.

Bell, D. (1973). *The Coming of Post-Industrial Society.* Harmondsworth: Penguin.

Bell, D. (1979). Thinking ahead: communication technology — for better or for worse. *Harvard Business Review*, 57(3), May/June, 20–42.

Bhagat, R., Kedia, B., Harverston, P. and Triandis, H. (2002). Cultural variations in the cross-border transfer of organizational knowledge: an integrative framework. *Academy of Management Review*, 27(2), 204–221.

Binney, D. (2001). The knowledge management spectrum — understanding the KM landscape. *Journal of Knowledge Management*, 5(1), 33–42.

Blackler, F. (1995). Knowledge, knowledge work and organizations: an overview and interpretation. *Organization Studies*, 16(6), 1021–1046.

Blumentritt, R. and Johnston, R. (1999). Towards a strategy for knowledge management. *Technology Analysis & Strategic Management*, 11(3), 287–300.

Bourdreau, A. and Couillard, G. (1999). Systems integration and knowledge management. *Information Systems Management*, 16(4), 24–32.

Bouthillier, F. and Shearer, K. (2002). Understanding knowledge management and information management: the need for an empirical perspective. *Information Research* (online journal), 8(1), available at http://informationr.net/ir/8-1/paper141.html/.

Boyett, J. H. and Boyett, J. T. (2001). *The Guru Guide to the Knowledge Economy.* New York: Wiley.

Brown, J. and Duguid, P. (1998). Organizing knowledge. *California Management Review*, 40(3), 90–111.

Buckley, P. J. and Carter, M. J. (2000). Knowledge management in global technology markets: applying theory to practice. *Long Range Planning*, 33, 55–71.

Choo, C. W. (1996). The knowing organization: how organizations use information to construct meaning, create knowledge and make decisions. *International Journal of Information Management*, 16(5), 329–340.

Choo, C. W. (1998). *The Knowing Organization: How Organizations Use Information to Construct Meaning, Create Knowledge and Make Decisions.* New York: Oxford University Press.

Collins English Dictionary (2000). Glasgow: HarperCollins Publishers.

Connell, N. A. D., Klein, J. H. and Powell, P. L. (2003). It's tacit knowledge but not as we know it: redirecting the search for knowledge. *Journal of the Operational Research Society*, 54, 140–152.

Court, A. W. (1997). The relationship between information and personal knowledge in new product development. *International Journal of Information Management*, 17(2), 123–138.

Davenport, T. H. and Prusak, L. (1998). *Working Knowledge: How Organizations Manage What They Know*. Boston, MA: Harvard Business School Press.

Descartes, R. (1996). *Meditations on First Philosophy*. J. Cottingham, ed. and trans. Cambridge: Cambridge University Press.

Drucker, P. F. (1992). The new society of organizations. *Harvard Business Review*, 70(5), 95–104.

Drucker, P. F. (1993). *Post-Capitalist Society*. New York: HarperCollins.

Drucker, P. F. (1998). The coming of the new organization. In *Harvard Business Review on Knowledge Management* (pp. 1–19), Boston, MA: Harvard Business School Press.

Drucker, P. F. (1999). *Management Challenges for the 21st Century*. Oxford: Butterworth-Heinemann.

Earl, M. J. (2001). Knowledge management strategies: toward a taxonomy. *Journal of Management Information Systems*, 18(1), 215–233.

Empson, L. (1999). Books — knowledge management: in search of the philosophers' stone. *Business Strategy Review*, 10(2), 67–71.

Empson, L. (2001). Introduction: knowledge management in professional service firms. *Human Relations*, 54(7), 811–817.

Frappaolo, C. (1997). Finding what's in it. *Document World*, 2(5), September/October, 23–30.

Galup, S. D., Dattero, R. and Hicks, R. C. (2002). Knowledge management systems: an architecture for active and passive knowledge. *Information Resources Management Journal*, 15(1), 22–27.

Gamble, P. and Blackwell, J. (2001). *Knowledge Management: A State of the Art Guide*. London: Kogan Page.

Gao, F., Li, M. and Clarke, S. (2008). Knowledge, management, and knowledge management in business operations. *Journal of Knowledge Management*, 12(2), 3–17.

Gettier, E. L. (1963). Is justified true belief knowledge? *Analysis*, 23(6), 121–123.

Grant, R. M. (1996). Prospering in dynamically-competitive environments: organizational capability as knowledge integration. *Organization Science*, 7, 375–387.

Grant, R. M. (1997). The knowledge-based view of the firm: implications for management practice. *Long Range Planning*, 30(3), 450–454.

Hamel, G. and Prahalad, C. K. (1991). Corporate imagination and expeditionary marketing. *Harvard Business Review*, 69(4), 81–92.

Hayes-Roth, F., Waterman, D. A. and Lenat, D. B. (1983). An overview of expert systems. In F. Hayes-Roth, D. A. Waterman and D. B. Lenat (eds.), *Building Expert Systems*, Reading, MA: Addison-Wesley.

Hazlett, S., McAdam, R. and Gallagher, S. (2005). Theory building in knowledge management: in search of paradigms. *Journal of Management Inquiry*, 14(1), 31–42.

Hegel, G. W. F. (1997). *On Art, Religion, and the History of Philosophy*. J. G. Gray, ed. Cambridge, MA: Hackett Publishing.

Heidegger, M. (1962). *Being and Time*. J. Macquarrie and E. Robinson, trans. New York: Harper & Row.

Hendriks, P. H. J. (2001). Many rivers to cross: from ICT to knowledge management systems. *Journal of Information Technology*, 16(2), 57–72.

Hislop, D. (2005). *Knowledge Management in Organizations*. Oxford: Oxford University Press.

Hlupic, V., Pouloudi, A. and Rzevski, G. (2002). Towards an integrated approach to knowledge management: 'hard', 'soft' and 'abstract' issues. *Knowledge and Process Management*, 9(2), 90–102.

Hofer-Alfeis, J. and van der Spek, R. (2002). The knowledge strategy process — an instrument for business owners. In T. H. Davenport and G. J. B. Probst (eds.), *Knowledge Management Case Book*, 2nd ed. (pp. 24–39), Erlangen, Germany: Publicis/Wiley.

Hsieh, P. J., Lin, B. and Lin, C. (2009). The construction and application of knowledge navigator model (KNM): an evaluation of knowledge management maturity. *Expert Systems with Applications*, 36(2), Part 2, 4087–4100.

Jakubik, M. (2007). Exploring the knowledge landscape: four emerging views of knowledge. *Journal of Knowledge Management*, 11(4), 6–19.

Jashapara, A. (2004). *Knowledge Management: An Integrated Approach*. Essex: Prentice Hall.

Jashapara, A. (2005). The emerging discourse of knowledge management: a new dawn for information science research? *Journal of Information Science*, 31(2), 136–148.

Jasimuddin, S. M. (2005). Knowledge of external sources' knowledge: new frontiers to actionable knowledge. In M. A. Rahim and R. T. Golembiewski (eds.), *Current Topics in Management*, Vol. 10 (pp. 39–50), New Brunswick, NJ: Transaction Publishers.

Jasimuddin, S. M., Klein, J. H. and Connell, C. (2005). The paradox of using tacit and explicit knowledge: strategies to face dilemmas. *Management Decision*, 43(1), 102–112.

Kant, I. (1999). *Critique of Pure Reason*. P. Guyer and A. W. Wood, eds. and trans. Cambridge: Cambridge University Press.

Kanter, J. (1999). Knowledge management, practically speaking. *Information Systems Management*, 16(4), Fall, 7–15.

Kogut, B. and Zander, U. (1992). Knowledge of the firm, combinative capabilities, and the replication of technology. *Organization Science*, 3(3), 383–397.

KPMG (1999). *The Power of Knowledge — A Business Guide to Knowledge Management*. London: KPMG Consulting.

Leonard, D. and Sensiper, S. (1998). The role of tacit knowledge in group innovation. *California Management Review*, 40, 112–132.

Lin, C. and Wu, C. (2005). A knowledge creation model for ISO 9001:2000. *Total Quality Management*, 16(5), 657–670.

Locke, J. (1998). *An Essay Concerning Human Understanding*. A. S. Pringle-Pattison and D. Collinson, eds. Ware, Hertfordshire: Wordsworth Editions Ltd.

Machlup, F. (1980). *Knowledge: Its Creation, Distribution, and Economic Significance*. Princeton, NJ: Princeton University Press.

Mahlitta, J. (1996). Smarten up! *Computerworld*, 29(23), 84–87.

Marquardt, M. (1996). *Building the Learning Organization: A Systems Approach to Quantum Improvement and Global Success*. New York: McGraw-Hill.

Marr, B., Gray, D. and Neely, A. (2003). Why do firms measure their intellectual capital? *Journal of Intellectual Capital*, 4, 441–464.

Newell, S., Robertson, M., Scarbrough, H. and Swan, J. (2002). *Managing Knowledge Work*. Basingstoke: Palgrave Macmillan.

Newell, S., Swan, J., Galliers, R. and Scarbrough, H. (1999). The intranet as a knowledge management tool? Creating new electronic fences. In M. Khosrowpour (ed.), *Proceedings of the Information Resources Management Association International Conference, "Managing Information Technology Resources in Organizations in the Next Millennium"*.

Nissen, M. (2002). An extended model of knowledge-flow dynamics. *Communications of the Association for Information Systems*, 8, 251–266.

Nissen, M., Kamel, M. and Sengupta, K. (2000). Integrated analysis and design of knowledge systems and processes. *Information Resources Management Journal*, 13(1), 24–43.

Nonaka, I. (1994). A dynamic theory of organizational knowledge creation. *Organization Science*, 5(1), 14–37.

Nonaka, I. and Takeuchi, H. (1995). *The Knowledge-Creating Company: How Japanese Companies Create the Dynamics of Innovation*. Oxford: Oxford University Press.

Plato (1992). *Theaetetus*. B. Williams, ed., M. J. Levett, trans. and M. Burnyeat, rev. Cambridge, MA: Hackett Publishing.

Polanyi, M. (1962). *Personal Knowledge: Towards a Post-Critical Philosophy*. Chicago, IL: University of Chicago Press.

Polanyi, M. (1966). *The Tacit Dimension*. London: Routledge.

Prahalad, C. K. and Hamel, G. (1990). The core competition of the corporation. *Harvard Business Review*, 68(3), 79–91.

Quinn, J. B. (1992). *Intelligent Enterprise: A Knowledge and Service Based Paradigm for Industry*. New York: The Free Press.

Rowe, G. and Wright, G. (1999). The Delphi technique as a forecasting tool: issues and analysis. *International Journal of Forecasting*, 15, 353–375.

Singh, M. D., Kant, R. and Narain, R. (2008). Knowledge management practices: a sectoral analysis. *International Journal of Innovation and Learning*, 5(6), 683–710.

Spender, J. C. (1996). Making knowledge the basis of a dynamic theory of the firm. *Strategic Management Journal*, 17(Special Issue), 45–62.

Spender, J. C. (2008). Organizational learning and knowledge management: whence and whither? *Management Learning*, 39(2), 159–176.

Starbuck, W. H. (1992). Learning by knowledge-intensive firms. *Journal of Management Studies*, 29(6), 713–740.

Sveiby, K. E. (1997). *The New Organizational Wealth: Managing and Measuring Knowledge-Based Assets*. San Francisco, CA: Berrett-Koehler Publishers.

Teece, D. J., Pisano, G. and Shuen, A. (1997). Dynamic capabilities and strategic management. *Strategic Management Journal*, 18(7), 509–533.

Tiwana, A. (2001). *Knowledge Management: E-Business and Customer Relationship Management Applications*. Upper Saddle River, NJ: Prentice Hall.

Tiwana, A. (2002). *The Knowledge Management Toolkit: Orchestrating IT, Strategy and Knowledge Platforms*, 2nd ed. Upper Saddle River, NJ: Prentice Hall.

Tobin, D. (1996). *Transformational Learning: Renewing Your Company Through Knowledge and Skills*. New York: John Wiley & Sons.

Toffler, A. (1990). *Powershift: Knowledge, Wealth and Violence at the Edge of the 21st Century*. New York: Bantam Books.

Tsoukas, H. and Vladimirou, E. (2001). What is organisational knowledge? *Journal of Management Studies*, 38(7), 973–993.

Tuomi, I. (1999). Data is more than knowledge: implications of the reversed knowledge hierarchy for knowledge management and organizational memory. *Journal of Management Information Systems*, 16(3), 103–117.

Tversky, A. and Kahneman, D. (1981). The framing of decisions and the psychology of choice. *Science*, 211, 453–458.

UK Department for Education and Employment (2000). *Opportunity for All: Skills for the New Economy*. London: DfEE.

Vail, E. F. (1999). Mapping organizational knowledge. *Knowledge Management Review*, 8(May/June), 10–15.

van der Spek, R. and Spijkervet, A. (1997). Knowledge management: dealing intelligently with knowledge. In J. Liebowitz and L. Wilcox (eds.), *Knowledge Management and Its Integrative Elements* (pp. 31–60), Boca Raton, FL: CRC Press.

von Krogh, G., Ichijo, K. and Nonaka, I. (2000). *Enabling Knowledge Creation: How to Unlock the Mystery of Tacit Knowledge and Release the Power of Innovation*. New York: Oxford University Press.

Walters, D. (2000). Virtual organisations: new lamps for old. *Management Decision*, 38(6), 420–436.

Wang-Cowham, C. (2008). HR structure and HR knowledge transfer between subsidiaries in China. *The Learning Organization*, 15(1), 26–44.

Wiig, K. M. (1993). *Knowledge Management Foundations: Thinking About Thinking — How People and Organizations Create, Represent, and Use Knowledge*. Arlington, TX: Schema Press.

Wilson, D. A. (1996). *Managing Knowledge*. Oxford: Butterworth-Heinemann.

Wittgenstein, L. (1953). *Philosophical Investigations*. G. E. M. Anscombe, trans. Oxford: Basil Blackwell.

Zack, M. H. (1999). Managing codified knowledge. *Sloan Management Review*, 40(4), 45–58.

Zins, C. (2006). Redefining information science: from "information science" to "knowledge science". *Journal of Documentation*, 62(4), 447–461.

Chapter 2

Strategic Role of Knowledge Management

Knowledge Objectives

After studying this chapter, you should be able to:

- Provide a basic introduction of knowledge management;
- Highlight the key terms used in the study of knowledge management;
- Describe the major topics associated with knowledge management;
- Elaborate on the knowledge management process; and
- Explain the importance of knowledge management in organizations.

2.1 Introducing the Chapter

Knowledge management is a multidisciplinary paradigm and is gradually emerging as a fully fledged discipline. Birkinshaw (2001) supported this assertion almost a decade ago, contending that knowledge management is evolving as a discipline filled with concepts, principles, frameworks and numerous theories. In fact, knowledge management has grown to be pervasive. It could even be argued that the knowledge management field is not optional anymore. The notion of knowledge management has attracted an enormous amount of attention from various organizations, be they private organizations or public enterprises, military command or civil service centers, educational institutions or business firms. A survey of chief executive officers (CEOs) of American corporations revealed that knowledge management is regarded as one of the most important trends in the 21st-century corporate environment, surpassed only by the concept of globalization (MacGillivray, 2003). In recent years, organizations have paid more and more attention to knowledge management (Chase, 1997, 2006; Shariq, 1997; de Pablos, 2002).

There are many reasons for an individual, be they a researcher or a practitioner, to explain why knowledge management is considered an increasingly important area of study and practice. For example, managers tend to explore and exploit organizational knowledge so as to make better decisions. It is worth mentioning that giant corporations such as Dow Chemical, Hewlett-Packard, Accenture, Cable & Wireless, DaimlerChrysler, Ernst & Young, Ford, Unilever and Siemens were pioneers in developing knowledge management initiatives. Against this backdrop, students have been recently showing an interest to understand the notion of knowledge management in order to use it in an organizational setting. Therefore, knowledge management is currently emerging as a very prominent field of study, and universities across the world are now offering new courses on knowledge management. Al-Hawamdeh (2005), for example, took a balanced and practical approach while developing a graduate program in knowledge management at Nanyang Technological University in Singapore.

Scholars have contributed enormously in developing and popularizing the knowledge management field. A number of management theorists have contributed to its evolution. Among the most notable pioneers are Karl Wiig, Thomas Davenport, Laurence Prusak, Peter Senge, Dorothy Leonard-Barton, John Edwards, Heather Smith, James McKeen, Ikujiro Nonaka and Hirotaka Takeuchi, all of whom stress the growing importance of knowledge as a strategic resource for organizations. The following sections will concentrate on various aspects of the emerging interdisciplinary discourse of knowledge management.

I will start with a brief discussion on the various facets and current situation of the knowledge management field in order to clarify concepts and help the reader understand its strategic importance. There are many issues surrounding knowledge management. Section 2.2 elaborates on the relevant topics that constitute knowledge management. The fact is that knowledge management itself is a subject with many different meanings and interpretations; there is no consensus in the relevant management literature regarding its definition. Section 2.3 will demonstrate various definitions of knowledge management given by management theorists. Although early academic discussions about the concept of knowledge management date back to the 1990s, there is still much debate regarding the knowledge management process. Section 2.4 will briefly discuss the various facets of the knowledge management process. The strategic role of knowledge management as a source of competitive advantage for organizations is addressed in Section 2.5. Finally, the chapter ends with a conclusion in Section 2.6.

2.2 Relevant Topics Associated with Knowledge Management

This section provides a description of the fundamental concepts of knowledge management. As a starting point, an understanding of the topics surrounding knowledge management is necessary in order to clarify its current status. In the meantime, knowledge management has been widely regarded as a strategic issue of management research. Before moving on to the definitions provided by theorists, the topics that constitute the knowledge management discipline will be discussed.

During the last 20 years, and especially during the last decade, the various areas of knowledge management have received adequate attention in both academic and research circles. Figure 2.1 illustrates the majority of the topics found in the relevant literature associated with knowledge management. Most of the knowledge management research tends to focus on four key issues that appear to be involved in knowledge management: knowledge typology, knowledge transfer,

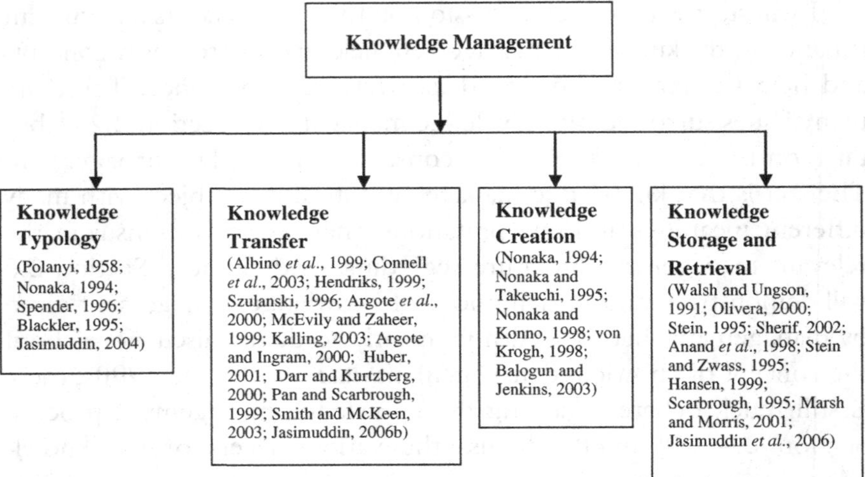

Figure 2.1 The Relevant Topics of Knowledge Management

Source: adapted from Jasimuddin (2006a).

knowledge creation and knowledge storage (Jasimuddin, 2006a). These topics are detailed below.

2.2.1 *Organizational Knowledge and Its Typology*

As mentioned in the previous chapter, organizational knowledge itself is at the center of all themes and issues surrounding the knowledge management field. By definition, organizational knowledge is interpreted information (i.e., processed data) that helps members of an organization to take purposeful actions so as to perform their assigned tasks properly.

Although the study of the notion of knowledge is not new, in recent times scholars have realized that knowledge is now considered the most critical resource of an organization (Drucker, 1993; Bell, 1973; Toffler, 1990; Grant, 1996). As discussed in the previous chapter, knowledge is one of the crucial production factors or means in terms of an organization's capacity to survive and, hence, gain a sustainable competitive advantage. This coincides with the development of the "knowledge-based society", as postulated by Drucker (1992), who argues that, in a knowledge-based society, knowledge is the primary resource whereas the economist's traditional factors of production (i.e., land, labor and capital) become secondary.

In fact, organizational knowledge is the key issue of the knowledge management discipline. This has been widely acknowledged in the relevant management literature (Hsieh *et al.*, 2009; Spender, 1996; Drucker, 1993; Wang-Cowham, 2008; Grant, 1996; Teece *et al.*, 1997; Kogut and Zander, 1992; Prahalad and Hamel, 1990; Argote and Ingram, 2000; Singh *et al.*, 2008; Bhagat *et al.*, 2002). Furthermore, several knowledge management scholars (e.g., Polanyi, 1958; Nonaka, 1994; Spender, 1996; Blackler, 1995; Jasimuddin *et al.*, 2005a; Empson, 2001) address the debates and perspectives on organizational knowledge and its related activities, including its importance, as well as its typology within the existing theories of knowledge. Most knowledge management scholars (e.g., Toffler, 1990; Drucker, 1992; Brown and Duguid, 1998; Nonaka and Takeuchi, 1995; Choo, 1996; Binney, 2001; Jasimuddin *et al.*, 2005b) argue that the role played by knowledge management in an organization has been receiving growing recognition.

2.2.2 *Knowledge Transfer*

Knowledge transfer is important both within an organization, i.e., an intra-organizational environment (Szulanski, 2000; Kalling, 2003; van den Hooff and van Weenen, 2004; O'Dell and Grayson, 1999; Osterloh and Frey, 2000), and between different organizations, i.e., an inter-organizational environment (Albino *et al.*, 1998; Powell *et al.*, 1996; McEvily and Zaheer, 1999). In particular, knowledge transfer between individuals and departments within an organization is considered to be a crucial task in modern business (van den Hooff and van Weenen, 2004; O'Dell and Grayson, 1998).

A number of researchers (Argote, 1999; Davenport and Prusak, 1998; Grant, 1996; van Wijk *et al.*, 2008; Hendriks, 1999; Szulanski, 2000; Kalling, 2003; Argote and Ingram, 2000; Easterby-Smith *et al.*, 2008; Hansen, 1999; Stenmark, 2000; Inkpen, 1996;

Haldin-Herrgard, 2000; Barachini, 2009) within the knowledge management field have shown considerable interest in the notion of knowledge transfer. More specifically, the issues with regard to knowledge transfer that have been widely researched include:

- factors that facilitate and inhibit knowledge transfer (Szulanski, 1996; McDermott and O'Dell, 2001; Smith and McKeen, 2003; Argote and Ingram, 2000; Hendriks, 1999; Kalling, 2003; van den Hooff and van Weenen, 2004); and
- the knowledge transfer process (Szulanski, 1996; Huber, 1991; Pan and Scarbrough, 1999).

Several researchers (e.g., Szulanski, 1996; Kalling, 2003; van den Hooff and van Weenen, 2004; O'Dell and Grayson, 1998; Osterloh and Frey, 2000) argue that an organization's success can be based on its ability to transfer knowledge from one organizational unit to another. Realizing the significance of knowledge transfer, Holtshouse (1998, p. 277) suggests that "study on how knowledge can be transferred between knowledge contributors and seekers" is one of the three priority areas for further knowledge management research.

2.2.3 *Knowledge Creation*

Knowledge creation is another important research topic in the knowledge management field. Despite the fact that knowledge creation is a relatively recent topic within the knowledge management discourse, a growing body of empirical evidence indicates that knowledge creation is crucial. Indeed, knowledge generators are at the cutting edge of innovation, as they provide the engine for change in processes and products (Nonaka, 1994; Nonaka and Takeuchi, 1995; Nonaka and Konno, 1998; von Krogh, 1998; Balogun and Jenkins, 2003).

In their seminal book, *The Knowledge-Creating Company*, Nonaka and Takeuchi (1995) point out that interactions between various types of knowledge available in an organization lead to the creation of new knowledge. Thus, they propose a dynamic model of knowledge creation, popularly termed the SECI model — socialization, externalization, combination and internalization. Knowledge creation embraces a continual dialogue between explicit and tacit knowledge, which eventually boosts the creation of new ideas and knowledge.

2.2.4 *Knowledge Storage*

Viewing knowledge as a crucial resource, organizations recognize the value of knowledge storage for present and future use. Knowledge storage is an important strategic topic of knowledge management, as it helps to understand how organizational knowledge is stored and retrieved for present and future (re)use in problem solving or decision making.

Many scholars (e.g., Walsh and Ungson, 1991; Olivera, 2000; Stein, 1995; Sherif, 2002; Anand *et al.*, 1998; Stein and Zwass, 1995; Hansen, 1999; Scarbrough, 1995; Marsh and Morris, 2001; Jasimuddin *et al.*, 2006) recognize the need for and advantages of knowledge storage. The storage of knowledge is an important part of knowledge management, as it helps to ensure the availability of the right knowledge to the right people at the right time. Stein (1995), for example, suggests that a better understanding of knowledge storage can assist organizations in solving problems through the utilization of stored knowledge. In this regard, Walsh and Ungson (1991, pp. 73–74) point out that the storage of knowledge has three critical roles to play within an organization:

(i) An informational role, i.e., contributing to decision making;
(ii) A controlling role, i.e., monitoring present activities to ensure that previous mistakes are not being repeated (and thus minimizing transaction costs); and
(iii) A political role, i.e., influencing the actions of others resulting from the control of knowledge.

However, there are many other issues surrounding knowledge management that have yet to be explored. Although various areas of knowledge management have received much attention during the past few decades, one very important issue that has been missed or relatively neglected is the linkage of knowledge management with other established disciplines such as information management, organizational learning, strategic management and innovation management. Such a study may help to draw a clearer picture of the disciplinary roots of knowledge management. For now, only some isolated descriptions of the background of knowledge management are available. This is supported by Moffett *et al.* (2003), for example, who argue that "there are many areas within the knowledge management domain that have remained unexplored. One of such areas is the origin of knowledge management".

We will see in Chapters 3 and 6 that knowledge management is a multidisciplinary paradigm and is not grounded in a specific subject. Knowledge management draws from a wide range of disciplines. As a result, there are contradictory views regarding the genesis of knowledge management. It is observed that knowledge management research has been advanced and enriched by bringing diverse perspectives, concepts and topics of inquiry into the knowledge management field. There is no doubt that knowledge management is an interdisciplinary field and is slowly emerging as a fully fledged discipline.

The disciplinary roots of knowledge management will be addressed in full detail in Chapter 6. For the remainder of this chapter, I will explain the notion and process of knowledge management as well as its importance. A fuller description of the definitions of knowledge management can be found in the next section.

2.3 Knowledge Management Defined

The knowledge management concept is difficult to comprehend by reference to its topics alone. Instead, knowledge management can be better understood when its definitions provided by theorists are gathered, which is the focus of this section. Many attempts have been made to define knowledge management, as shown in Table 2.1. Thus far, no consensus has emerged even on a core definition of knowledge management. Many scholars (e.g., Lopez *et al.*, 2004; Earl, 2001; Chauvel and Despres, 2002) have admitted that defining the concept

Table 2.1 Selected Definitions of Knowledge Management

Authors	Definitions
Awad and Ghaziri (2004, p. 28)	The process of gathering and making use of a firm's collective expertise wherever it resides — on paper, in databases or in people's heads
Bassi (1997, p. 25)	The process of creating, capturing and using knowledge to enhance organizational performance
Becerra-Fernandez *et al.* (2004, p. 372)	The activities involved in discovering, capturing, sharing and applying knowledge in terms of resources, documents and people skills, so as to enhance, in a cost-effective fashion, the impact of knowledge on the unit's goal achievement
Beckman (1999)	The formalization of and access to experience, knowledge and expertise to create new capabilities, enable superior performance, encourage innovation and enhance customer value
Beijerse (1999)	The achievement of organizational goals through the strategy-driven motivation and facilitation of knowledge workers to develop, enhance and use their capability to interpret data and information (by using available sources of information, experience, skills, culture, character, personality, feelings, etc.) through a process of giving meaning to these data and information
Bergeron (2003)	A deliberate, systematic business optimization strategy that selects, distills, stores, organizes, packages and communicates information essentials to the business of a company in a manner that improves employee performance and corporate competitiveness
Bhatt (2001)	A process of knowledge creation, validation, presentation, distribution and application
Bounfour (2003)	A set of procedures, infrastructures, technical and managerial tools, designed towards creating, sharing and leveraging information and knowledge within and around organizations
Brooking (1997)	An activity which is concerned with strategy and tactics to manage human-centered assets
Davenport *et al.* (1998)	Attempts to do something useful with knowledge to accomplish organizational objectives through the structuring of people, technology and knowledge content

(*Continued*)

Table 2.1 (*Continued*)

Authors	Definitions
DeJarnett (1996)	Knowledge creation, which is followed by knowledge interpretation, knowledge dissemination and use, and knowledge retention and refinement
Frappaolo and Toms (1999)	A tool set for the automation of deductive or inherent relationships between information objects, users and processes
Heavin and Neville (2006, p. 626)	The capture, storage, dissemination and creation of organizational knowledge as a means of creating competitive advantage
Hibbard (1997)	The capture of an organization's collective expertise wherever it resides — in people's heads, in databases or on paper — and the distribution of such expertise wherever it can produce the biggest returns
Hult (2003)	The organized and systematic process of generating and disseminating information, and selecting, distilling and deploying explicit and tacit knowledge, to create unique value that can be used to achieve a competitive advantage in the marketplace by an organization
Huysman and de Wit (2000)	The support of knowledge sharing
Jashapara (2004, p. 309)	The effective learning processes associated with the exploration, exploitation and sharing of human knowledge (tacit and explicit) that use the appropriate technology and cultural environments to enhance an organization's intellectual capital and performance
Jasimuddin *et al.* (2006, p. 875)	A discipline that promotes an integrated approach to identifying, capturing, storing, retrieving and transferring an organization's knowledge so as to enhance its competitive advantage
Jones (2003)	An integrated, systematic approach to identify, manage and share all of the department's information assets, including databases, documents, policies and procedures, as well as previously unarticulated expertise and experience resident in individual officers
Laudon and Laudon (2000)	The process of systematically and actively managing and leveraging the stores of knowledge in an organization

(*Continued*)

Table 2.1 (*Continued*)

Authors	Definitions
Lehaney *et al.* (2004)	The systematic organization, planning, scheduling, monitoring and deployment of people, technology and environment, with appropriate targets and feedback mechanisms, under the control of a public- or private-sector concern and undertaken by such a concern to facilitate explicitly and specifically the creation, retention, sharing, identification, acquisition, utilization and measurement of information and new ideas in order to achieve strategic aims, such as improved competitiveness or improved performance, subject to financial, legal, resource, political, technical, cultural and societal constraints
Liebowitz and Wilcox (1997)	The ability of organizations to manage, store, value and distribute knowledge
Macintosh (1996)	The identification and analysis of available and required knowledge, and the subsequent planning and control of actions to develop knowledge assets so as to fulfill organizational objectives
Malhotra (1998)	Organizational processes that seek a synergistic combination of the data and information processing capacity of information technologies, and the creative and innovative capacity of human beings; it caters to the critical issues of organizational adaptation, survival and competence in the face of increasingly discontinuous environmental change
Martinez (1998, p. 89)	The encouragement among individuals to communicate their knowledge by creating environments and systems for capturing, organizing and sharing knowledge throughout the company
McNabb (2007, p. 285)	The creation and subsequent management of an organizational culture that encourages knowledge to be created, shared, learned, enhanced, organized and used for the benefit of the organization and its stakeholders
Newman and Conrad (2000, p. 11)	A discipline that seeks to improve the performance of individuals and organizations by maintaining and leveraging the present and future value of knowledge assets
O'Dell (1997)	The application of systematic approaches to find, understand and use knowledge to create value

(*Continued*)

Table 2.1 (*Continued*)

Authors	**Definitions**
O'Dell and Grayson (1998)	A strategy to be developed in a firm to ensure that knowledge reaches the right people at the right time, and that those people share and use the information to improve the organization's functioning
O'Leary (1998)	The formal management of knowledge for facilitating the creation, access and reuse of knowledge, typically using advanced technology
Quintas *et al.* (1997, p. 387)	The process of continually managing knowledge of all kinds to meet existing and emerging needs, to identify and exploit existing and acquired knowledge assets, and to develop new opportunities
Snowden (1999, p. 63)	The identification, optimization and active management of intellectual assets, either in the form of explicit knowledge held in artifacts or as tacit knowledge possessed by individuals or communities
Tiwana (2002, p. 371)	The management of organizational knowledge for creating business value and generating a competitive advantage
Tsoukas and Vladimirou (2001, p. 973)	The dynamic process of turning an unreflective practice into a reflective one by elucidating the rules guiding the activities of the practice, by helping to give a particular shape to collective understandings, and by facilitating the emergence of heuristic knowledge
van der Spek and Spijkervet (1997)	The explicit control and management of knowledge within an organization aimed at achieving the company's objectives
Wiig (1997)	The systematic creation and use of knowledge to maximize an organization's knowledge-related effectiveness and returns on its knowledge assets and to renew them constantly
Zuckerman and Buell (1998, p. 81)	The strategic application of collective company knowledge and know-how to build profits and market share; knowledge assets — both ideas and concepts as well as know-how — are created through the computerized collection, storage, sharing and linking of corporate knowledge pools

of knowledge management is difficult. Earl (2001, p. 215) rightly comments, "Just like knowledge itself, knowledge management is difficult to define". Moreover, the understanding of the knowledge management phenomenon remains fragmented and contested.

Several comprehensive reviews have appeared, but they also fail to provide a concrete, universally accepted definition of knowledge management. Among the most notable of these are Awad and Ghaziri (2004), Becerra-Fernandez *et al.* (2004), DeJarnett (1996), Hibbard (1997), Jashapara (2004), McNabb (2007), Newman and Conrad (2000), Snowden (1999) and Wiig (1997). Wiig (1997), for example, views knowledge management as the systematic creation and utilization of knowledge to maximize the knowledge-related effectiveness of an organization; DeJarnett (1996) sees knowledge management as the process of creating, interpreting, disseminating, applying, preserving and refining knowledge; and Hibbard (1997) defines knowledge management as the capture of an organization's collective expertise wherever it resides — in people's heads, in databases or on paper — and the distribution of such expertise wherever it can produce the biggest returns. Moreover, Davenport *et al.* (1998) define knowledge management as a process of collecting, distributing and efficiently using the knowledge resource. However, Snowden (1999, p. 63) gives a broader definition, saying that "knowledge management can be defined as the identification, optimization, and active management of intellectual assets, either in the form of explicit knowledge held in artifacts or as tacit knowledge possessed by individuals or communities".

The differences in the understanding of the term "knowledge management" stem from the fact that it could be understood from various different dimensions. While attempting to explain why it is difficult to define knowledge management, Lopez *et al.* (2004) states: "This is due to the fact that this subject has been studied by several disciplines and from different approaches". Therefore, it is not surprising that there are diverse views of what knowledge management is. As an obvious illustration of this lack of consensus, Table 2.1 presents some representative definitions of knowledge management, which supports Chauvel and Despres's (2002) argument that "[t]here is no homogeneous definition for knowledge management because different disciplines contribute to the field of knowledge management".

While reviewing 18 different definitions surrounding knowledge management, Hlupic *et al.* (2002) identify possible factors for the vagueness and ambiguity in defining knowledge management. One of these factors lies with its key issue, i.e., the notion of organizational knowledge itself, which has already been elaborated in the previous chapter (see Section 1.3). As a result, knowledge management means different things to different people. More specifically, Hlupic *et al.* (2002, p. 92) mention several reasons that help to explain why defining knowledge management is so difficult. These reasons are displayed below:

- *Extremely complex concept.* Knowledge management deals with knowledge, which is very intangible and complex in nature. As a result, knowledge management is an extremely difficult concept to explain.
- *Eclectic nature of the field.* Knowledge management is considered a subjective rather than objective concept. Therefore, the difficulty of defining knowledge management is compounded due to the eclectic nature of the field.
- *Emerging discipline.* Knowledge management is yet to be considered a well-established discipline because the subject is still an emerging field. The difficulty in finding a concrete, universally accepted definition of knowledge management is thus even further magnified.

Therefore, it is not surprising that there are diverse views of what knowledge management is. The wide range of definitions reflects the fact that the majority of scholars working in the knowledge management field come from a wide range of disciplines, such as psychology, management science, organizational science, sociology, strategy, production engineering, etc. (Nonaka and Takeuchi, 1995).

In this regard, Jashapara's (2005) appraisal of the definitions of knowledge management is worth mentioning. Jashapara (2005) concludes that the different dimensions used in defining knowledge management have been brought together into an integrated, interdisciplinary perspective. According to him, some definitions of knowledge management come from a strong information systems perspective, while others borrow from a human resources perspective, and a few adopt a strategic management perspective. Thus, knowledge management is multidisciplinary, and combines both theory and practice. As Scarbrough (1996) comments, "The sprawling and eclectic literature and the ambiguity and definitional problems ... allow different groups to project their own interests and concerns onto it".

Despite the differences in the definition of knowledge management, however, it seems that there is one common parameter throughout the different definitions: its role in organizational effectiveness and competitiveness. In other words, another way to better understand the notion of knowledge management is by reference to its process. The knowledge management process will be dealt with next.

2.4 Knowledge Management Process

Numerous attempts have been made to explain the knowledge management process. Scholars have suggested different activities with respect to the knowledge management process, including the creation, transfer and sharing of knowledge. The different ways of generating, creating and transferring knowledge across different levels of an organization have been widely discussed as the knowledge management process (Badaracco, 1991; Nonaka and Takeuchi, 1995; Sanchez and Heene, 1997). In fact, the knowledge management process may be fragmented and divided into various subphases. This section discusses the major activities and processes associated with knowledge management: knowledge acquisition, knowledge creation, knowledge storage, knowledge transfer and knowledge application.

Interestingly, knowledge management entails various activities such as the acquisition, creation and exploitation of organizational knowledge. As with the definitions of knowledge management, attempts to explain its components are numerous. While discussing the knowledge management process, Hult (2003), for example, mentions the inbound side and the outbound side of the knowledge management process, which are described below:

- The inbound side of the knowledge management process refers to knowledge creation, which focuses on the "generation and dissemination of information, developing a shared understanding of the information, filtering shared understandings into degrees of potential value, and storing viable wisdom within the confines of an accessible organizational mechanism". According to Hult (2003), "a critical part of the inbound KM [knowledge management] process is the transformation of information into knowledge, a phenomenon that takes place at various places in the process but is the most pronounced at the shared understanding and filtering stages".
- On the other hand, the outbound side of the knowledge management process is all about the deployment of organizational knowledge so as to achieve the goal of sustainable competitive advantage.

Scholars (e.g., Hislop, 2005; Jashapara, 2004; Macintosh, 1996; Metaxiotis and Psarras, 2006; Siemieniuch and Sinclair, 1999; Ruggles, 1998) note that there are some activities within knowledge management that are useful to focus on in developing a knowledge management strategy. Macintosh (1996) contends that the success or failure of companies depends on how well they use the knowledge management process. According to Metaxiotis and Psarras (2006), the knowledge management process consists of four key stages, namely knowledge identification and capture, knowledge sharing, knowledge application, and knowledge creation. Similarly, Jashapara (2004, p. 5) describes five activities of the knowledge management process: discovering, generating, evaluating, sharing and leveraging knowledge. Macintosh (1996) argues that the knowledge management process incorporates activities such as the development, preservation and application of knowledge.

Siemieniuch and Sinclair (1999) state that the knowledge management process allows organizations to generate, disseminate and remove core knowledge, according to current and future requirements. Moreover, Oluic-Vukovic (2001) outlines five steps in the knowledge processing chain: gathering, organizing, refining, representing and disseminating organizational knowledge. Likewise, Ruggles (1998) identifies three main types of activities:

- knowledge generation, involving the creation of new ideas and new patterns;
- knowledge codification; and
- knowledge transfer, ensuring the exchange of knowledge between individuals and departments.

Similarly, the knowledge management process developed by KPMG (1998) — and also cited in Alavi (1997) — is comprised of six stages:

(i) acquisition (collecting, synthesizing and interpreting information from diverse sources, both external and internal);
(ii) indexing (developing classification schemes);
(iii) filtering (screening information for its importance);
(iv) linking (connecting related information);
(v) distribution; and
(vi) application.

None of these knowledge management frameworks is broad enough to allow for a complete analysis of the organizational knowledge management process. Nevertheless, the generic activities surrounding knowledge management are discussed next.

2.4.1 *Acquisition of Organizational Knowledge*

The acquisition of knowledge is an important phase in the knowledge management process. Many authors (e.g., Straker *et al.*, 2009; Inkpen, 1998, 2000; McCall *et al.*, 2008; Kogut, 1988) address the issue of knowledge acquisition. Knowledge resides both inside and outside an organization. It is available in organizational members' heads and storage bins, in both tacit and explicit forms. Knowledge acquisition is the first task in the knowledge management process so as to identify the source of knowledge and gather it for use.

2.4.2 *Creation of Organizational Knowledge*

Knowledge is created through the interaction between tacit and explicit knowledge — what Nonaka and Takeuchi (1995) call the SECI (socialization, externalization, combination and internalization) model of knowledge creation. Knowledge is developed through social interactions, using the four modes of knowledge creation. In fact, knowledge generation is best understood by focusing on micro-level interactions between individuals within an organization (Jakubik, 2007).

It is evident in the popular SECI model (Nonaka and Takeuchi, 1995) that three of the four phases in knowledge creation — socialization, externalization and combination — involve social interaction among organizational members. A knowledge-creating company seems to believe in an open system, whereby knowledge is constantly exchanged both within and outside the organization (Nonaka and Takeuchi, 1995). Similarly, referring to the importance of creating new knowledge, Nonaka (1998, p. 22) argues:

> In an economy where the only certainty is uncertainty, the one sure source of lasting competitive advantage is knowledge. When markets shift, technologies proliferate, competitors multiply, and products become obsolete almost overnight, successful companies are those that consistently create new knowledge, disseminate it widely throughout the organization, and quickly embody it in new technologies and products. These activities define the "knowledge-creating" company, whose sole business is continuous innovation.

Knowledge creation is not only based on the internal relationships with members of an organization, but also depends on the relationships with clients, suppliers, alliance members and even competitors (Dawson, 2000). In this regard, Balogun and Jenkins (2003, p. 247) comment along similar lines: "For organisational transformation to occur, an organisation's members need to evolve new tacit knowledge about the way they interact both with each other and external stakeholders, and how they coordinate their activities".

2.4.3 *Storage of Organizational Knowledge*

The preservation of knowledge is a major building block in implementing knowledge management, so as to make organizational knowledge available for re-use and for the creation of new knowledge. This is reflected by Douglas (2002, p. 74), who adds that "knowledge that is in the head of a person has limited value, while the value of knowledge can increase exponentially when it is networked, stored, and reused, and quickly integrated into business practices and processes". This view is an extension of that of Gray and Chan (2000, p. 13), who put it thus: "[K]nowledge that is created but not stored in a repository, that is either simply forgotten or passed on to a user directly without being recorded, represents a waste of resources, because a prospective user will have to solve old problems again".

Knowledge that is transferred among organizational members is likely to be more useful than that retained by an individual. Moreover, if such transferred knowledge is stored and retained in a repository so that other members of the organization could access or retrieve it for future use, then it seems to be more useful. However, not all organizational knowledge can or should be preserved and retained in a knowledge repository. If the knowledge is tacit in form, it will be very difficult to articulate and store it. If irrelevant knowledge is stored, then the knowledge repository will be filled with garbage. Therefore, efforts should be made to ensure that current, relevant and correct knowledge is stored in the knowledge repository, and is also retrievable from the repository. In addition, other knowledge that is old and irrelevant must be removed from the knowledge repository from time to time.

2.4.4 *Transfer of Organizational Knowledge*

Another important component of the knowledge management process is knowledge transfer. Barrett *et al.* (2004, p. 1) contend that a major emphasis of an organization's activities is placed on the knowledge transfer process, which is increasingly seen as crucial to organizational success and growth. To date, two important perspectives on knowledge transfer have been revealed. Most researchers in the knowledge management discourse tend to either view knowledge transfer as "an act of transmission and reception" or think of it in terms of "a process of reconstruction".

Davenport and Prusak (1998) argue that knowledge transfer involves both the transmission of information to a recipient and the absorption of information from one person (or group) to another person (or group). This coincides with Hendriks (1999, p. 92), who gives a broader view of knowledge transfer:

> Knowledge sharing is something else than but related to communication. ... To learn something from someone else, i.e., to share his or her knowledge, an act of reconstruction is needed. It takes knowledge to acquire knowledge and, therefore, to share knowledge. Knowledge sharing presumes a relation between at least two parties, one that possesses knowledge and the other that acquires knowledge. The first party should communicate its knowledge, consciously and willingly or not, in some form or other (either by acts, by speech, or in writing, etc.). The other party should be able to perceive these expressions of knowledge, and make sense of them (by imitating the acts, by listening, by reading the book, etc.). Two sub-processes make up the process of knowledge sharing.

In line with this, several other researchers — most notably Bender and Fish (2000), Albino *et al.* (1998) and Kalling (2003) — theorize the knowledge transfer process in terms of an operational level of analysis (the information system), a conceptual level of analysis (the interpretative system), or a combination of both. From an operational point of view, knowledge transfer is a communication process with information-processing activities, in which a contributor can transfer knowledge to a prospective user through information flows conveyed by an appropriate medium (Albino *et al.*, 1998;

Kalling, 2003); whereas from the conceptual viewpoint, knowledge transfer is strictly connected to the concept of the learning organization (Gilbert and Cordey-Hayes, 1996; Huber, 1991; Steensma, 1996; Albino *et al.*, 1998).

2.4.5 *Application of Organizational Knowledge*

Knowledge management is not just about the exploration of knowledge. Rather, all efforts of knowledge, including knowledge exploration, are actually geared towards its exploitation in an organization. It is noted that the investment made by an organization for knowledge management initiatives is huge; if transferred knowledge or stored knowledge is not utilized properly, it spells a total loss for the organization. Against this backdrop, it can be said that, on the whole, knowledge management implementation has not been successful. Thus, it is important to utilize the right knowledge in the right place at the right time, immediately after exploring it from the right source.

As demonstrated above, several authors (Holsapple and Jones, 2004; Watson, 2003; Webb, 1998) propose different activities of knowledge management. In this regard, Beckman (1999) rightly comments that all of these activities are frequently concurrent, repetitive and sometimes not sequential. These phases may be fragmented and divided into various subphases. This section has attempted to discuss the major tasks of the knowledge management process. However, while there are still many unresolved issues regarding our understanding of the implementation of the knowledge management process, academics and practitioners are paying much more attention to comprehending the role of knowledge management in organizations. This will be dealt with next.

2.5 The Role of Knowledge Management in Organizations

This section takes a closer look at the importance of knowledge management, explaining why such a topic is seen as a vehicle to organizational effectiveness. In the emerging knowledge-based society, knowledge management has become a key concern in organizations. Managing organizational knowledge has recently emerged as a critical task for organizations. Its popularity has increased tremendously due to its ability to explore and exploit knowledge for the benefit of organizations. Knowledge is clearly an invaluable asset for an organization (see Section 1.6). By looking at the definitions produced by knowledge management scholars as depicted in Table 2.1, it makes sense to conceptualize the critical role of knowledge management for the survival and growth of an organization. It is evident that many scholars are working on the knowledge management topic because it is important for the survival of organizations.

According to Davenport and Grover (2001), knowledge management was first developed in organizations that are basically selling knowledge: professional services as well as research and development firms. With the passage of time, though, knowledge management has quickly been moving into other industries and organizations, including manufacturing, financial services, government offices, educational institutions and military organizations.

The role played by the knowledge management field in an organization has been receiving growing recognition in the management literature (e.g., Toffler, 1990; Drucker, 1992; Brown and Duguid, 1998; Nonaka and Takeuchi, 1995; Choo, 1996; Binney, 2001; Jashapara, 2005; Jasimuddin *et al.*, 2005a). Several scholars — most notably Despres and Hiltrop (1995), Neef (1999) and Beckman (1999) — argue that, in the "post-industrial" society, knowledge management is critical for organizational growth and survival. Quintas *et al.* (1997) see along similar lines, stating that knowledge management is a continuous process of managing knowledge to meet existing and emerging needs, and to identify and exploit existing and acquired knowledge assets. As a result, managing knowledge has become a crucial function of organizations.

This view is an extension of that of Jashapara (2005), who recognizes that knowledge management practices seem to deliver a competitive advantage for organizations in the private sector and improve service quality in the public sector. Reflecting this view, KPMG (1999) asserts that knowledge management represents a systematic and organized approach to use, store and exchange knowledge in order to increase companies' output and performance. Similarly, the American Productivity and Quality Center (2004) postulates that knowledge management is equivalent to the processes necessary for knowledge identification, documentation and influence in order to make an organization competitive.

On the other hand, Wiig (1997) views knowledge management as the systematic creation and use of knowledge to maximize the knowledge-related effectiveness of an organization. Parallel to this, Hibbard (1997) argues that knowledge management helps to capture an organization's collective expertise and distribute the expertise wherever it can produce the biggest returns.

It is observed from the relevant literature that the benefits derived from knowledge management initiatives are many. As mentioned earlier, several scholars (e.g., Davenport and Prusak, 1998; Grant and Baden-Fuller, 2004; Jasimuddin *et al.*, 2005a) argue that knowledge management helps to improve sustainable competitive advantage, while others (e.g., McAdam and McCreedy, 2000) consider it a competitive necessity. As time passes, one thing that has become obvious is that knowledge management is critical to organizational survival (Beckman, 1999).

More specifically, one of the goals of knowledge management initiatives is to facilitate the product innovation of an organization. Petrash (1996) maintains that knowledge management ensures the availability of "the right knowledge to the right people at the right time", so that the best decisions and right actions can be taken at the optimum time. In connection with this, Sutton (2001, p. 80) contends that the management of knowledge seems to have two core objectives:

(i) To improve the exploitation of the knowledge resources of an enterprise; and
(ii) To protect the knowledge resources of an enterprise.

The potential benefits of knowledge management are apparent. Accordingly, Hlupic *et al.* (2002) argue that knowledge management gives organizations the operational ability to:

- Identify, appreciate and respond to strengths, weaknesses, opportunities and threats;
- Act, assimilate feedback and react in these arenas simultaneously;
- Develop the capacity to operate in real-time environments; and
- Understand and create "real" value as determined and perceived by the ultimate consumers.

Furthermore, KPMG (1999) describes knowledge management goals and provides a list of benefits derived from its application, which are mentioned below:

- Supporting innovation, the generation of new ideas and the exploitation of the organization's thinking power;
- Capturing insight and experience to make them available when, where and by whom required;
- Making it easy to find and re-use sources of know-how and expertise, whether they are recorded in a physical form or held in someone's mind;
- Fostering collaboration and knowledge sharing, as well as continual learning and improvement;
- Improving the quality of decision making and other intelligent tasks; and
- Understanding the value and contribution of intellectual assets, and increasing their worth, effectiveness and exploitation.

By reviewing the extant literature, Hazlett *et al.* (2005) also provide a comprehensive picture of the role of knowledge management in organizations:

> In recent years, however, managers from a variety of disciplines have come to view KM as the new "serious issue" in business (Bushko and Raynor, 1998; Martiny, 1998). Alvesson and Karreman (2001)

> suggest that KM is "not merely some passing fad, but is in the process of establishing itself as a new aspect of management and organization and as a new form of expertise". KM can be considered a competitive necessity (McAdam and McCreedy, 2000; Brusoni *et al.*, 2001), a strategic resource (Cabrera and Cabrera, 2002; Earl, 1994), or the source of competitive advantage (Empson, 1999; Nonaka, 1991).

It is observed that knowledge management is assuming a greater role in all types of organizations (e.g., private firms, educational institutions, public enterprises, military establishments, hospitals, government and non-governmental organizations). In particular, knowledge management has been implemented in giant companies around the world, including Accenture, Cable & Wireless, DaimlerChrysler, Ernst & Young, Ford, Hewlett-Packard, Siemens, Unilever and Xerox (Luen and Al-Hawamdeh, 2001; MacGillivray, 2003). For example, ShareNet, the knowledge managemet system used by Siemens' Information and Communication Networks division, is a global knowledge-sharing intranet that serves as an instrument to transfer and leverage existing knowledge, so as to create new knowledge in a division based in one part of the world and make it available for re-use by its employees elsewhere. The main task of knowledge management is to ensure accessibility of the right knowledge at the right time in the right form.

Like in the practitioners' front, the knowledge management field has been receiving much attention in the academics' front. A good number of journals are being published to disseminate the results of research conducted in the various aspects of knowledge management. Although formal research in the knowledge management area has been observed in mainstream information systems journals, the renaissance is mainly seen in the creation of journals surrounding knowledge management and in the devotion of special issues of several top scholarly journals to the knowledge management topic. Several special issues of management journals (e.g., *British Journal of Management* 15(S1), 2004; *Decision Sciences* 34(2), 2003; *Management Science* 49(4), 2003; *MIS Quarterly* 26(3), 2002; *Organization Science*

13(3), 2002; *Journal of Management Studies* 38(7), 2001; *Journal of Management Information Systems* 18(1), 2001; *European Journal of Information Systems* 10(2), 2001; *Journal of Strategic Information Systems* 9(2/3), 2000; *International Journal of Human-Computer Studies* 51(3), 1999; *California Management Review* 40(3), 1998; *Expert Systems with Applications* 13(1), 1997; *Long Range Planning* 30(3), 1997; *Strategic Management Journal* 17(S1), 1996) are devoted to the concepts associated with knowledge management.

Over the past few decades, 21 peer-reviewed research journals have surfaced to address major aspects of knowledge management as a primary focus. Burden's (2000) knowledge management bibliography, which encompasses both research and industry publications, cites over 900 books and 8,000 articles devoted to the field (as cited in Schwartz, 2006). Since knowledge management has emerged as a tool with which today's organizations need to function using knowledge assets, almost every establishment has started to view itself as a knowledge-intensive organization and has adopted knowledge management approaches in all business actions.

Hence, it can be argued that knowledge management is no longer a fad. That is why Davenport and Grover (2001, p. 3) claim that "it is becoming increasingly clear that knowledge management is here to stay". Today, there seems to be little doubt that knowledge management is not a fad or fashion; the fact is that knowledge management has emerged as a fundamental concept in the knowledge-based society. Moreover, both practitioners and academics alike agree that knowledge management is an important area of management research and practice, as well as an interesting area of academic debate. However, some of the important areas of knowledge management are still subject to debate. The next chapter will set out the various controversial and debatable issues that warrant further discussion.

2.6 Concluding Summary

This chapter has attempted to acquaint readers with the notion of knowledge management. Knowledge management, a relatively new discipline of the 1990s, is all about the discovery and deployment of organizational knowledge so as to gain an edge in the marketplace. Managing organizational knowledge is being increasingly recognized as a critical strategic task for organizations. The successful implementation of knowledge management initiatives helps organizations achieve the goal of sustainable competitive advantage. This chapter has highlighted the key areas that constitute the knowledge management discipline. The majority of knowledge management research is focused on topics such as knowledge typology, knowledge transfer, knowledge creation, and knowledge storage and retrieval.

Scholars from many different backgrounds have contributed much to develop and popularize the knowledge management field by organizing conferences and by publishing academic and professional journals. Although this chapter has concentrated on various aspects of the emerging interdisciplinary discourse of knowledge management, there is still a debate about what we mean by the term "knowledge management". In its most general sense, knowledge management can be defined as managing organizational knowledge in a way that helps organizations enhance their sustainable competitive advantage. Numerous attempts have been made to define knowledge management (see Table 2.1). However, it is difficult to define this concept, and there is no universally accepted definition. This is likely due to the fact that this subject has been studied by scholars belonging to various disciplines and from different approaches; thus, the word "knowledge management" means different things to different scholars. That is a possible reason for the vagueness and ambiguity in defining knowledge management.

Nevertheless, one common theme is that managing knowledge is linked to the capacity for action. Therefore, the definition of knowledge management that is used throughout this book refers to the effective and efficient discovery and deployment of organizational knowledge so as to enhance an organization's sustainable competitive advantage.

The knowledge management process consists of various stages, which are frequently concurrent, repetitive and sometimes not sequential. The various activities of knowledge management have been identified and mentioned by researchers, but no consensus has emerged even on a core knowledge management process. Rather, various approaches and understandings associated with the knowledge management process remain in play.

It has been argued in this chapter that knowledge management is more than a fad. Apparently, knowledge management seems to be a long-lasting phenomenon, as evident in the increasing attention shown by academics and practitioners from various different disciplines, such as information systems, human resources, strategic management and organizational theory. It is observed that the meanings and features of knowledge management reflect the researchers' respective disciplinary backgrounds and specific ontological assumptions.

There is no doubt that recently there has been greater recognition that managing knowledge is important for organizational survival. The successful implementation of knowledge management seems to enhance an organization's sustainable competitive advantage. The potential benefits of knowledge management are apparent. As a result, much attention is being focused on research in knowledge management.

Numerous practical questions and challenges concerning knowledge management still remain unanswered and warrant further research; these will be discussed in detail in the final chapter of this book. Nonetheless, the present chapter has addressed some of the unresolved operational issues related to knowledge management. To support knowledge management initiatives, organizations need to acknowledge the role of various disciplines that have contributed to the development of knowledge management. The focus of this book is to establish the relationships of knowledge management with other disciplines such as information management, organizational learning, innovation management and strategic management. This chapter has described the basic issues relating to knowledge management itself; the debates in the knowledge management field will be dealt with in the next chapter.

Further Reading

Ho, C.-T. (2009). The relationship between knowledge management enablers and performance. *Industrial Management & Data Systems*, 109(1), 98–117.

Jasimuddin, S. M., Connell, C. and Klein, J. H. (2008). Understanding organizational memory. In M. E. Jennex (ed.), *Knowledge Management: Concepts, Methodologies, Tools, and Applications* (pp. 171–178), London: IGI Global.

Jasimuddin, S. M. and Zhang, Z. (2011). Transferring stored knowledge and storing transferred knowledge. *Information Systems Management*, 28(1), 84–94.

Ma, Z. and Yu, K.-H. (2010). Research paradigms of contemporary knowledge management studies: 1998–2007. *Journal of Knowledge Management*, 14(2), 175–189.

Ranjan, J. (2008). Knowledge management in business schools. *Journal of Information and Knowledge Management*, 7(1), 55–62.

Reus, T. H., Ranft, A. L., Lamont, B. T. and Adams, G. L. (2009). An interpretive systems view of knowledge investments. *Academy of Management Review*, 34(3), July, 382–400.

Salmador, M. P. and Bueno, E. (2007). Knowledge creation in strategy-making: implications for theory and practice. *European Journal of Innovation Management*, 10(3), 367–390.

Sun, P. (2010). Five critical knowledge management organizational themes. *Journal of Knowledge Management*, 14(4), 507–523.

Zhang, Z. and Jasimuddin, S. M. (2008a). Toward a strategic framework of mobile knowledge management. *Knowledge and Process Management*, 15(2), 87–96.

Zhang, Z. and Jasimuddin, S. M. (2008b). Pricing strategy of online knowledge market: the analysis of Google Answers. *International Journal of E-Business Research*, 4(1), 55–68.

References

Alavi, M. (1997). *KPMG Peat Marwick U.S.: One Giant Brain*. Boston, MA: Harvard Business School.

Albino, V., Garavelli, A. C. and Schiuma, G. (1998). Knowledge transfer and inter-firm relationships in industrial districts: the role of the leader firm. *Technovation*, 19, 53–63.

Al-Hawamdeh, S. (2005). Designing an interdisciplinary graduate program in knowledge management. *Journal of the American Society for Information Science and Technology*, 56(11), 1200–1206.

Alvesson, M. and Karreman, D. (2001). Odd couple: making sense of the curious concept of knowledge management. *Journal of Management Studies*, 38(7), 995–1018.

American Productivity and Quality Center (2004). Linking knowledge to innovation and bottom line benefits. *Strategic Direction*, 20(2), 28–30.

Anand, V., Manz, C. and Glick, W. H. (1998). An organizational memory approach to information management. *Academy of Management Review*, 23(4), 796–809.

Argote, L. (1999). *Organizational Learning: Creating, Retaining and Transferring Knowledge*. Norwell, MA: Kluwer.

Argote, L. and Ingram, P. (2000). Knowledge transfer: a basis for competitive advantage in firms. *Organizational Behavior and Human Decision Processes*, 82(1), 150–169.

Argote, L., Ingram, P., Levine, J. M. and Moreland, L. (2000). Knowledge transfer in organizations: learning from the experience of others. *Organizational Behavior and Human Decision Processes*, 82(1), 1–8.

Awad, E. M. and Ghaziri, H. M. (2004). *Knowledge Management*. Singapore: Pearson.

Badaracco, J. (1991). *The Knowledge Link: Competitive Advantage Through Strategic Alliances*. Boston, MA: Harvard Business School Press.

Balogun, J. and Jenkins, M. (2003). Re-conceiving change management: a knowledge-based perspective. *European Management Journal*, 21(2), 247–257.

Barachini, F. (2009). Cultural and social issues for knowledge sharing. *Journal of Knowledge Management*, 13(1), 98–110.

Barrett, M., Cappleman, S., Shoib, G. and Walsham, G. (2004). Learning in knowledge communities: managing technology and context. *European Management Journal*, 22(1), 1–11.

Bassi, L. (1997). Harnessing the power of intellectual capital. *Training & Development*, 51(12), 25–30.

Becerra-Fernandez, I., Gonzalez, A. and Sabherwal, R. (2004). *Knowledge Management: Challenges, Solutions, and Technologies*. Upper Saddle River, NJ: Pearson/Prentice Hall.

Beckman, T. J. (1999). The current state of knowledge management. In J. Liebowitz (ed.), *Knowledge Management Handbook* (pp. 1–22), Boca Raton, FL: CRC Press LLC.

Beijerse, R. (1999). Questions in knowledge management: defining and conceptualising a phenomenon. *Journal of Knowledge Management*, 3(2), 94–109.

Bell, D. (1973). *The Coming of Post-Industrial Society*. Harmondsworth: Penguin.

Bender, S. and Fish, A. (2000). The transfer of knowledge and the retention of expertise: the continuing need for global assignments. *Journal of Knowledge Management*, 4(2), 125–137.

Bergeron, B. (2003). *Essentials of Knowledge Management*. Hoboken, NJ: John Wiley & Sons.

Bhagat, R., Kedia, B., Harverston, P. and Triandis, H. (2002). Cultural variations in the cross-border transfer of organizational knowledge: an integrative framework. *Academy of Management Review*, 27(2), 204–221.

Bhatt, G. D. (2001). Knowledge management in organizations: examining the interaction between technologies, techniques, and people. *Journal of Knowledge Management*, 5(1), 68–75.

Binney, D. (2001). The knowledge management spectrum — understanding the KM landscape. *Journal of Knowledge Management*, 5(1), 33–42.

Birkinshaw, J. (2001). Why is knowledge management so difficult? *Business Strategy Review*, 12(1), 11–18.

Blackler, F. (1995). Knowledge, knowledge work and organizations: an overview and interpretation. *Organization Studies*, 16(6), 1021–1046.

Bounfour, A. (2003). The IC-dVAL approach. *Journal of Intellectual Capital*, 4(3), 396–413.

Brooking, A. (1997). The management of intellectual capital. *Long Range Planning*, 30(3), 364–365.

Brown, J. and Duguid, P. (1998). Organizing knowledge. *California Management Review*, 40(3), 90–111.

Brusoni, S., Prencipe, A. and Pavitt, K. (2001). Knowledge specialization, organizational coupling, and the boundaries of the firm: why do firms know more than they make? *Administrative Science Quarterly*, 46(4), 597–621.

Burden, P. R. (2000). *Knowledge Management: The Bibliography*. Medford, NJ: Information Today, Inc.

Bushko, D. and Raynor, M. (1998). Knowledge management: new directions for IT (and other) consultants. *Journal of Management Consulting*, 10(2), November, 67–68.

Cabrera, A. and Cabrera, E. F. (2002). Knowledge-sharing dilemmas. *Organization Studies*, 23(5), 687–710.

Chase, R. (1997). The knowledge-based organization: an international survey. *Journal of Knowledge Management*, 1(1), 38–49.

Chase, R. (2006). A decade of knowledge management. *Journal of Knowledge Management*, 10(1), 1–6.

Chauvel, D. and Despres, C. (2002). A review of survey research in knowledge management: 1997–2001. *Journal of Knowledge Management*, 6(3), 207–223.

Choo, C. W. (1996). The knowing organization: how organizations use information to construct meaning, create knowledge and make decisions. *International Journal of Information Management*, 16(5), 329–340.

Connell, N. A. D., Klein, J. H. and Powell, P. L. (2003). It's tacit knowledge but not as we know it: redirecting the search for knowledge. *Journal of the Operational Research Society*, 54, 140–152.

Darr, E. D. and Kurtzberg, T. R. (2000). An investigation of partner similarity dimensions on knowledge transfer. *Organizational Behavior and Human Decision Processes*, 82(1), 28–44.

Davenport, T. H., De Long, D. W. and Beers, M. C. (1998). Successful knowledge management projects. *Sloan Management Review*, Winter, 43–57.

Davenport, T. H. and Grover, V. (2001). Special issue: knowledge management. *Journal of Management Information Systems*, 18(1), 3–4.

Davenport, T. H. and Prusak, L. (1998). *Working Knowledge: How Organizations Manage What They Know*. Boston, MA: Harvard Business School Press.

Dawson, R. (2000). *Developing Knowledge-Based Client Relationships: The Future of Professional Services*. Boston: Butterworth-Heinemann.

de Pablos, P. O. (2002). Knowledge management and organizational learning: typologies of knowledge strategies in the Spanish manufacturing industry from 1995 to 1999. *Journal of Knowledge Management*, 6(1), 52–62.

DeJarnett, L. (1996). Knowledge the latest thing. *Information Strategy: The Executive's Journal*, 12(2), 3–5.

Despres, C. and Hiltrop, J. M. (1995). Human resource management in the knowledge age: current practice and perspectives on the future. *Employee Relations*, 17(1), 9–23.

Douglas, P. H. (2002). Information technology is out — knowledge sharing is in. *Journal of Corporate Accounting and Finance*, 13(4), 73–77.

Drucker, P. F. (1992). The new society of organizations. *Harvard Business Review*, 70(5), 95–104.

Drucker, P. F. (1993). *Post-Capitalist Society*. New York: HarperCollins.

Earl, M. J. (1994). Knowledge as strategy: reflections on Skandia International and Shorko Films. In C. Ciborra and T. Jelassi (eds.), *Strategic Information Systems: A European Perspective* (pp. 53–69), Chichester: John Wiley & Sons Ltd.

Earl, M. J. (2001). Knowledge management strategies: toward a taxonomy. *Journal of Management Information Systems*, 18(1), 215–233.

Easterby-Smith, M., Lyles, M. A. and Tsang, E. W. K. (2008). Inter-organizational knowledge transfer: current themes and future prospects. *Journal of Management Studies*, 45(4), 677–690.

Empson, L. (1999). Books — knowledge management: in search of the philosophers' stone. *Business Strategy Review*, 10(2), 67–71.

Empson, L. (2001). Introduction: knowledge management in professional service firms. *Human Relations*, 54(7), 811–817.

Frappaolo, C. and Toms, W. (1999). Knowledge management: from terra incognita to terra firma. In J. W. Cortada and J. A. Woods (eds.), *The Knowledge Management Yearbook 1999–2000* (pp. 381–388), Boston, MA: Butterworth-Heinemann.

Gilbert, M. and Cordey-Hayes, M. (1996). Understanding the process of knowledge transfer to achieve successful technological innovation. *Technovation*, 16(6), 301–312.

Grant, R. M. (1996). Prospering in dynamically-competitive environments: organizational capability as knowledge integration. *Organization Science*, 7, 375–387.

Grant, R. M. and Baden-Fuller, C. (2004). A knowledge accessing theory of strategic alliances. *Journal of Management Studies*, 41(1), 61–84.

Gray, P. H. and Chan, Y. E. (2000). Integrating knowledge management practices through a problem-solving framework. Working Paper WP 00-03, Queen's Centre for Knowledge-Based Enterprises, Kingston, Ontario, Canada.

Haldin-Herrgard, T. (2000). Difficulties in diffusion of tacit knowledge in organizations. *Journal of Intellectual Capital*, 1(4), 357–365.

Hansen, M. T. (1999). The search–transfer problem: the role of weak ties in sharing knowledge across organizational subunits. *Administrative Science Quarterly*, 44(1), 82–111.

Hazlett, S., McAdam, R. and Gallagher, S. (2005). Theory building in knowledge management: in search of paradigms. *Journal of Management Inquiry*, 14(1), 31–42.

Heavin, C. and Neville, K. (2006). Mentoring knowledge workers. In D. G. Schwartz (ed.), *Encyclopedia of Knowledge Management* (pp. 621–626), Hershey, PA: Idea Group Reference.

Hendriks, P. (1999). Why share knowledge? The influence of ICT on the motivation for knowledge sharing. *Knowledge and Process Management*, 6(2), 91–100.

Hibbard, J. (1997). Knowing what we know. *InformationWeek*, 653, October 20, 46–64.

Hislop, D. (2005). *Knowledge Management in Organizations.* Oxford: Oxford University Press.

Hlupic, V., Pouloudi, A. and Rzevski, G. (2002). Towards an integrated approach to knowledge management: 'hard', 'soft' and 'abstract' issues. *Knowledge and Process Management*, 9(2), 90–102.

Holsapple, C. W. and Jones, K. (2004). Exploring primary activities of the knowledge chain. *Knowledge and Process Management*, 11(3), 155–174.

Holtshouse, D. (1998). Knowledge research issues. *California Management Review*, 40(3), 277–280.

Hsieh, P. J., Lin, B. and Lin, C. (2009). The construction and application of knowledge navigator model (KNM): an evaluation of knowledge management maturity. *Expert Systems with Applications*, 36(2), Part 2, 4087–4100.

Huber, G. P. (1991). Organizational learning: the contributing processes and the literatures. *Organization Science*, 2(1), 88–115.

Huber, G. P. (2001). Transfer of knowledge in knowledge management systems: unexplored issues and suggested studies. *European Journal of Information Systems*, 10, 72–79.

Hult, G. T. M. (2003). An integration of thoughts on knowledge management. *Decision Sciences*, 34(2), 189–195.

Huysman, M. and de Wit, D. (2000). Knowledge management in practice. In J. Edwards and J. Kidd (eds.), *Proceedings of the Knowledge Management Conference (KMAC 2000)*, July 17–18, Birmingham, UK.

Inkpen, A. (1996). Creating knowledge through collaboration. *California Management Review*, 39(1), 123–140.

Inkpen, A. (1998). Learning and knowledge acquisition through international strategic alliances. *Academy of Management Executive*, 12(4), 69–80.

Inkpen, A. (2000). Learning through joint ventures: a framework of knowledge acquisition. *Journal of Management Studies*, 37(7), 1019–1043.

Jakubik, M. (2007). Exploring the knowledge landscape: four emerging views of knowledge. *Journal of Knowledge Management*, 11(4), 6–19.

Jashapara, A. (2004). *Knowledge Management: An Integrated Approach.* Essex: Prentice Hall.

Jashapara, A. (2005). The emerging discourse of knowledge management: a new dawn for information science research? *Journal of Information Science*, 31(2), 136–148.

Jasimuddin, S. M. (2004). Critical assessments of emerging theories of organizational knowledge. Paper presented at the Academy of Management (AOM) Conference, New Orleans, August.

Jasimuddin, S. M. (2006a). Knowledge transfer: a review to explore conceptual foundations and research agenda. In L. Moutinho, G. Hutcheson and P. Rita (eds.), *Advances in Doctoral Research in Management*, Vol. 1 (pp. 3–20), Singapore: World Scientific.

Jasimuddin, S. M. (2006b). Towards an integrated framework of knowledge transfer. Unpublished PhD dissertation, University of Southampton, Southampton, UK.

Jasimuddin, S. M., Connell, C. and Klein, J. H. (2005a). The challenges of navigating a topic to a prospective researcher: the case of knowledge management research. *Management Research News*, 28, 62–76.

Jasimuddin, S. M., Connell, C. and Klein, J. H. (2006). Understanding organizational memory. In D. G. Schwartz (ed.), *Encyclopedia of Knowledge Management* (pp. 870–875), Hershey, PA: Idea Group Reference.

Jasimuddin, S. M., Klein, J. H. and Connell, C. (2005b). The paradox of using tacit and explicit knowledge: strategies to face dilemmas. *Management Decision*, 43(1), 102–112.

Jones, D. (2003). Knowledge management and technical communication: a convergence of ideas and skills. Available at https://faculty.washington.edu/markh/tc400/.

Kalling, T. (2003). Organization-internal transfer of knowledge and the role of motivation: a qualitative case study. *Knowledge and Process Management*, 10(2), 115–126.

Kogut, B. (1988). Joint ventures: theoretical and empirical perspectives. *Strategic Management Journal*, 9, 319–332.

Kogut, B. and Zander, U. (1992). Knowledge of the firm, combinative capabilities, and the replication of technology. *Organization Science*, 3(3), 383–397.

KPMG (1998). *Knowledge Management Research Report 1998.* London: KPMG Consulting.

KPMG (1999). *The Power of Knowledge — A Business Guide to Knowledge Management.* London: KPMG Consulting.

Laudon, K. C. and Laudon, J. P. (2000). *Management Information Systems: Organization and Technology in the Networked Enterprise*, 6th ed. Englewood Cliffs, NJ: Prentice Hall.

Lehaney, B., Clarke, S., Coakes, E. and Jack, G. (2004). *Beyond Knowledge Management.* London: Idea Group Inc.

Liebowitz, J. and Wilcox, L. (eds.) (1997). *Knowledge Management and Its Integrative Elements.* Boca Raton, FL: CRC Press.

Lopez, S. P., Peon, J. M. M. and Ordas, C. J. V. (2004). Managing knowledge: the link between culture and organizational learning. *Journal of Knowledge Management*, 8(6), 93–104.

Luen, T. W. and Al-Hawamdeh, S. (2001). Knowledge management in the public sector: principles and practices in police work. *Journal of Information Science*, 27, 311–318.

MacGillivray, A. (2003). Knowledge management education at Royal Roads University. *Competitive Intelligence Magazine*, 6(4), 37–40.

Macintosh, A. (1996). Position paper on knowledge asset management. Artificial Intelligence Applications Institute, University of Edinburgh, Scotland.

Malhotra, Y. (1998). Business process redesign: an overview. *IEEE Engineering Management Review*, 26(3), Fall, 27–31.

Marsh, C. H. and Morris, E. C. (2001). Corporate memory and technical communicators: a relationship with a new urgency. In *Proceedings of the IEEE International Professional Communication Conference 2001 (IPCC 2001)* (pp. 379–389).

Martinez, M. (1998). The collective power of employee knowledge. *HR Magazine*, 43(2), 88–94.

Martiny, M. (1998). Knowledge management at HP Consulting. *Organizational Dynamics*, 27(2), 71–78.

McAdam, R. and McCreedy, S. (2000). A critique of knowledge management: using a social constructionist model. *New Technology, Work and Employment*, 15(2), 155–168.

McCall, H., Arnold, V. and Sutton, S. G. (2008). Use of knowledge management systems and the impact on the acquisition of explicit knowledge. *Journal of Information Systems*, 22(2), Fall, 77–101.

McDermott, R. and O'Dell, C. (2001). Overcoming cultural barriers to sharing knowledge. *Journal of Knowledge Management*, 5(1), 76–85.

McEvily, B. and Zaheer, A. (1999). Bridging ties: a source of firm heterogeneity in competitive capabilities. *Strategic Management Journal*, 20, 1133–1156.

McNabb, D. E. (2007). *Knowledge Management in the Public Sector — A Blueprint for Innovation in Government.* New York: M.E. Sharpe.

Metaxiotis, K. and Psarras, J. (2006). Analysing the value of knowledge management leading to innovation. *International Journal of Knowledge Management Studies*, 1(1/2), 79–89.

Moffett, S., McAdam, R. and Parkinson, S. (2003). An empirical analysis of knowledge management applications. *Journal of Knowledge Management*, 7(3), 6–26.

Neef, D. (1999). Making the case for knowledge management: the bigger picture. *Management Decision*, 37(1), 72–78.

Newman, B. and Conrad, K. W. (2000). A framework for characterizing knowledge management methods, practices, and technologies. The Knowledge Management Theory Papers, Knowledge Management Forum, West Richland, WA.

Nonaka, I. (1991). The knowledge-creating company. *Harvard Business Review*, 69(6), 96–104.

Nonaka, I. (1994). A dynamic theory of organizational knowledge creation. *Organization Science*, 5(1), 14–37.

Nonaka, I. (1998). The knowledge-creating company. In *Harvard Business Review on Knowledge Management* (pp. 21–45), Boston, MA: Harvard Business School Press.

Nonaka, I. and Konno, N. (1998). The concept of 'ba': building a foundation for knowledge creation. *California Management Review*, 40(3), 40–54.

Nonaka, I. and Takeuchi, H. (1995). *The knowledge-Creating Company: How Japanese Companies Create the Dynamics of Innovation.* Oxford: Oxford University Press.

O'Dell, C. (1997). A current review of knowledge management best practices. Presented at the "Conference on Knowledge Management and the Transfer of Best Practices", Business Intelligence, London.

O'Dell, C. and Grayson, C. J. (1998). If only we knew what we know: identification and transfer of internal best practices. *California Management Review*, 40, 154–174.

O'Dell, C. and Grayson, C. J. Jr. (1999). Knowledge transfer: discover your value proposition. *Strategy & Leadership*, 27(2), 10–15.

O'Leary, D. (1998). Knowledge management systems: converting and connecting. *IEEE Intelligent Systems and Their Applications*, 13(3), 30–33.

Olivera, F. (2000). Memory systems in organizations: an empirical investigation of mechanisms for knowledge collection, storage and access. *Journal of Management Studies*, 37(6), 811–832.

Oluic-Vukovic, V. (2001). From information to knowledge: some reflections on the origin of the current shifting towards knowledge processing and further perspective. *Journal of the American Society for Information Science and Technology*, 52, 54–61.

Osterloh, M. and Frey, B. S. (2000). Motivation, knowledge transfer, and organizational forms. *Organization Science*, 11(5), 538–550.

Pan, S. L. and Scarbrough, H. (1999). Knowledge management in practice: an exploratory case study. *Technology Analysis & Strategic Management*, 11(3), 359–374.

Petrash, G. (1996). Dow's journey to a knowledge value management culture. *European Management Journal*, 14(4), 365–373.

Polanyi, M. (1958). *Personal Knowledge: Towards a Post-Critical Philosophy.* London: Routledge & Kegan Paul.

Powell, W. W., Koput, K. W. and Smith-Doerr, L. (1996). Interorganizational collaboration and the locus of innovation: networks of learning in biotechnology. *Administrative Science Quarterly*, 41(1), 116–145.

Prahalad, C. K. and Hamel, G. (1990). The core competition of the corporation. *Harvard Business Review*, 68(3), 79–91.

Quintas, P., Lefrere, P. and Jones, G. (1997). Knowledge management: a strategic agenda. *Long Range Planning*, 30(3), 385–391.

Ruggles, R. (1998). The state of the notion: knowledge management in practice. *California Management Review*, 40(3), 80–89.

Sanchez, R. and Heene, A. (1997). Reinventing strategic management: new theory and practice for competence-based competition. *European Management Journal*, 15(3), 303–317.

Scarbrough, H. (1995). Blackboxes, hostages and prisoners. *Organization Studies*, 16(6), 991–1019.

Scarbrough, H. (1996). *The Management of Expertise.* London: Macmillan.

Schwartz, D. G. (2006). Preface: knowledge management as a layered multidisciplinary pursuit. In D. G. Schwartz (ed.), *Encyclopedia of Knowledge Management* (pp. 1–4), Hershey, PA: Idea Group Reference.

Shariq, S. Z. (1997). Knowledge management: an emerging discipline. *Journal of Knowledge Management*, 1(1), 75–82.

Sherif, K. (2002). Barriers to adoption of organizational memories: lessons from industry. In S. Barnes (ed.), *Knowledge Management Systems* (pp. 210–221), London: Thomson Learning.

Siemieniuch, C. E. and Sinclair, M. A. (1999). Organizational aspects of knowledge lifecycle management in manufacturing. *International Journal of Human-Computer Studies*, 51, 517–547.

Singh, M. D., Kant, R. and Narain, R. (2008). Knowledge management practices: a sectoral analysis. *International Journal of Innovation and Learning*, 5(6), 683–710.

Smith, H. A. and McKeen, J. D. (2003). Instilling a knowledge-sharing culture. Working Paper WP 03-11, Queen's Centre for Knowledge-Based Enterprises, Kingston, Ontario, Canada.

Snowden, D. (1999). A framework for creating a sustainable knowledge management program. In J. W. Cortada and J. A. Woods (eds.), *The Knowledge Management Yearbook 1999–2000* (pp. 52–64), Boston, MA: Butterworth-Heinemann.

Spender, J. C. (1996). Making knowledge the basis of a dynamic theory of the firm. *Strategic Management Journal*, 17(Special Issue), 45–62.

Steensma, H. K. (1996). Acquiring technological competencies through inter-organizational collaboration: an organizational learning perspective. *Journal of Engineering and Technology Management*, 12, 267–286.

Stein, E. W. (1995). Organization memory: review of concepts and recommendations for management. *International Journal of Information Management*, 15(1), 17–32.

Stein, E. W. and Zwass, V. (1995). Actualizing organizational memory with information systems. *Information Systems Research*, 6, 85–117.

Stenmark, D. (2000). Turning tacit knowledge tangible. In *Proceedings of the 33rd Hawaii International Conference on System Sciences (HICSS)*, Hawaii.

Straker, I., Ison, S., Humphreys, I. and Francis, G. (2009). A case study of functional benchmarking as a source of knowledge for car parking strategies. *Benchmarking*, 16(1), 30–46.

Sutton, D. C. (2001). What is knowledge and can it be managed? *European Journal of Information Systems*, 10, 80–88.

Szulanski, G. (1996). Exploring internal stickiness: impediments to the transfer of best practice within the firm. *Strategic Management Journal*, 17, 27–43.

Szulanski, G. (2000). The process of knowledge transfer: a diachronic analysis of stickiness. *Organizational Behavior and Human Decision Processes*, 82(1), 9–27.

Teece, D. J., Pisano, G. and Shuen, A. (1997). Dynamic capabilities and strategic management. *Strategic Management Journal*, 18(7), 509–533.

Tiwana, A. (2002). *The Knowledge Management Toolkit: Orchestrating IT, Strategy and Knowledge Platforms*, 2nd ed. Upper Saddle River, NJ: Prentice Hall.

Toffler, A. (1990). *Powershift: Knowledge, Wealth and Violence at the Edge of the 21st Century*. New York: Bantam Books.

Tsoukas, H. and Vladimirou, E. (2001). What is organizational knowledge? *Journal of Management Studies*, 38(7), 973–993.

van den Hooff, B. and van Weenen, F. D. L. (2004). Committed to share: commitment and CMC use as antecedents of knowledge sharing. *Knowledge and Process Management*, 11(1), 13–24.

van der Spek, R. and Spijkervet, A. (1997). Knowledge management: dealing intelligently with knowledge. In J. Liebowitz and L. Wilcox (eds.), *Knowledge Management and Its Integrative Elements* (pp. 31–60), Boca Raton, FL: CRC Press.

van Wijk, R., Jansen, J. J. P. and Lyles, M. A. (2008). Inter- and intra-organizational knowledge transfer: a meta-analytic review and assessment of its antecedents and consequences. *Journal of Management Studies*, 45(4), 830–853.

von Krogh, G. (1998). Care in knowledge creation. *California Management Review*, 40(3), 133–153.

Walsh, J. P. and Ungson, G. R. (1991). Organizational memory. *Academy of Management Review*, 16(1), 57–91.

Wang-Cowham, C. (2008). HR structure and HR knowledge transfer between subsidiaries in China. *The Learning Organization*, 15(1), 26–44.

Watson, I. (2003). *Applying Knowledge Management: Techniques for Building Corporate Memories*. San Francisco, CA: Morgan Kaufmann.

Webb, S. P. (1998). *Knowledge Management: Linchpin of Change — Some Practical Guidelines*. London: ASLIB.

Wiig, K. M. (1997). Knowledge management: where did it come from and where will it go? *Expert Systems with Applications*, 13(1), 1–14.

Zuckerman, A. and Buell, H. (1998). Is the world ready for knowledge management? *Quality Progress*, 31(6), 81–84.

Chapter 3

Debates in the Knowledge Management Field

Knowledge Objectives

After studying this chapter, you should be able to:

- Demonstrate the contradictory views surrounding knowledge management;
- Identify diverse opinions on the notion of organizational knowledge;
- Provide an argument that knowledge management is not a management fad;
- Address the controversy over the origins of knowledge management;
- Explain who owns the knowledge management field; and
- Critically evaluate the perspectives on knowledge management.

3.1 Introducing the Chapter

Research in the knowledge management field has a legacy that spans over 20 years, with more recent exponential growth. A diversity of perspectives can be found when looking at the issues surrounding knowledge management. There seems to be an ongoing debate (at least for some time) on several knowledge management issues. This chapter will deal with the contradictory views on various aspects of knowledge management. For example, there are differing opinions regarding its disciplinary roots. Several scholars argue that the field has its origins in a number of related disciplines, i.e., the field draws from a wide range of disciplines. Moreover, many organizations have found that tensions exist between its implementation and the progression of change. Another serious debate that seems to remain is the question of whether knowledge management is a universal paradigm or a fad.

Ever since Karl Wiig first mentioned knowledge management, there has been continued academic and practitioners' interest in its research and practice. It is evident that knowledge management plays a large role in all types of organizations, including the world's giant companies. Over the years, it has evolved into a discipline complete with concepts, principles, frameworks and theories. Meanwhile, new courses in universities across the world have been developed and launched to educate people so that they can implement it in their respective organizational settings.

Practitioners and academics alike agree that knowledge management is a well-established area of academic debate. However, the understanding of the phenomenon itself remains fragmented and contested. Thus, the debates and dilemmas surrounding the subject have tended to attract an enormous amount of attention from researchers. Moreover, the theoretical perspectives on knowledge management continue to diverge.

In the previous two chapters of this book, the notions of organizational knowledge and knowledge management, as well as their philosophical and practical aspects, were explained. The aim of this chapter is to provide a stimulating debate on the unresolved issues. In particular, this chapter will address the debates and perspectives on knowledge management (and its related activities).

It is observed that there is no clear-cut answer while addressing the key unresolved issues. There are contradictory views on whether knowledge management is a universal paradigm or a management fad, on its disciplinary roots and origins, and on its perspectives (i.e., technical vs. social). While reviewing and synthesizing the scholarly work on knowledge management, it is found that knowledge management has received increased attention over the decades among academics and practitioners across a broad range of subjects. In some cases, well-established disciplines such as information management and strategic management, from where the various academics and practitioners come, are found to be closely related to knowledge management. This makes it difficult to separate knowledge management from these disciplines. The chapter will also focus on whether knowledge management is an emerging paradigm. In addition, some other important knowledge management topics that are still in debate will also be addressed.

The confusion over the unresolved issues will be addressed one by one in the following sections. It should be noted that the present chapter tackles some of the unresolved operational issues of knowledge management; however, there are still numerous practical questions and challenges concerning knowledge management that remain unanswered and demand research. Section 3.2 discusses the debates and perspectives surrounding organizational knowledge and its related activities. Section 3.3 identifies and discusses the diverse opinions on the definition of knowledge management. In terms of the origins of knowledge management, there is some controversy in that scholars from many different disciplines tend to claim ownership over the notion of knowledge management. With this in mind, Section 3.4 explains whether knowledge management is grounded in a specific discipline or a multidisciplinary field, and also addresses the question of who owns it. There is no consensus regarding the claim that knowledge management is a new field with its own research base; this has further brought out the confusion and contradictory views around the question of whether the field is simply another fad or fashion. Section 3.5 provides an argument that knowledge management is a universal paradigm rather than a management fad. There is also confusion and debate around whether the subject is technology-driven or has a social focus. Section 3.6 critically examines whether knowledge management is technical-centric or social-centric, or a bit of both. The chapter ends with a concluding summary in Section 3.7.

3.2 Lack of a Homogeneous Definition for Organizational Knowledge

There has been continued academic interest among scholars in the concept of organizational knowledge, as was evidenced in Chapter 1. Consequently, there is much debate in the literature on what constitutes knowledge and on its perspectives. Countless comprehensive discussions on the notion of organizational knowledge have appeared. However, the understanding of the phenomenon itself remains fragmented and contested. Moreover, theoretical perspectives on the concept of organizational knowledge continue to diverge. As a result, extracting a clear-cut definition of organizational knowledge is very difficult. More specifically, there is no homogeneous definition for organizational knowledge. This is due to the fact that different disciplines have contributed to the notion of knowledge. Several researchers (e.g., Sveiby, 1997; Phillips and Patrick, 2000) point out that there are differences in the interpretation of the term "organizational knowledge". Some scholars place emphasis on the individual, whereas the focal point for other academics is the organization.

Another factor that creates confusion is that there are many different ways through which organizational knowledge can be managed. It could also be said that a possible reason for the vagueness and ambiguity in defining organizational knowledge is the word "knowledge" itself. The term "organizational knowledge" means different things to different people. Furthermore, there is confusion between knowledge, information and data, which are sometimes used interchangeably in the management literature as already discussed in Chapter 1. In this regard, Spender (2002) proposes two approaches to viewing knowledge within the knowledge management field:

(i) Knowledge and information are seen as interchangeable, in which knowledge can always be transformed into information and all knowledge can be made explicit; and
(ii) Knowledge cannot be viewed as totally explicit, as there is a social (including tacit) component to it.

Tsoukas and Vladimirou (2001) argue that the notion of organizational knowledge is "much talked about but little understood". Debates continue to remain regarding the notion of knowledge. Nevertheless, a growing consensus now seems to be emerging that differentiates the three constructs — data, information and knowledge — within a knowledge hierarchy, in which organizational knowledge is best understood as actionable knowledge that helps in making organizational decisions.

3.3 Lack of a Universal Definition for Knowledge Management

Despite the business benefits of adopting a knowledge management initiative, there is much debate in the literature on what constitutes knowledge management. Research on knowledge management has a legacy that spans over two decades, with more recent exponential growth in its research and application. Knowledge management is now widely viewed as crucial to ensuring the growth and survival of an organization. Academics and managers from a variety of backgrounds have come to view knowledge management as the new "serious issue" in business (Bushko and Raynor, 1998; Martiny, 1998). But to many researchers and practitioners, the question of what knowledge management really is remains unclear.

It is evident from the definitions given by scholars that they define the notion of knowledge management from a diversity of perspectives. For example, Davenport *et al.* (1998) define knowledge management as the process of collecting, distributing and efficiently using the knowledge resource; while Bounfour (2003) sees knowledge management as a set of procedures, infrastructures, and technical and managerial tools that is designed towards creating, sharing and leveraging knowledge within and around organizations. Therefore, defining the concept of knowledge management is seriously difficult. No consensus has emerged even on a core definition of knowledge management in any particular research. It could be said that there is no homogeneous definition for knowledge management

(Lopez *et al.*, 2004; Chauvel and Despres, 2002). This is largely due to the fact that different disciplines have contributed to the subject.

The confusion that surrounds knowledge management definitions can be attributed to its evolution. As we will see in the next section, knowledge management is multidisciplinary and many of the terms used to describe its activities have actually been adapted from other disciplines. The knowledge management field has been studied by several disciplines. Such increased interest across a wide variety of disciplines has made it difficult to find a comprehensive definition of knowledge management. It is noticeable that the chosen characteristics and meanings of knowledge management reflect the researchers' respective disciplinary backgrounds. This, therefore, leads to disputes and difficulties in defining what knowledge management is.

Furthermore, the many different ways through which organizational knowledge can be viewed also creates confusion over its meaning. As a result, there are diverse opinions regarding the knowledge management field. Against this background, Wilson (2002a) shows his reservations on the existence of knowledge management, arguing that knowledge management is little more than a repackaged form of information management. As he puts it, "Information and knowledge are synonymous and there is very little philosophical introspection on the nature of knowledge and how such conceptions may impact on individuals and organizations".

Knowledge management has received increased attention over the last decade or so among academics and practitioners across a broad range of subjects. The next section will address the debate over whether knowledge management is derived from a wide variety of disciplines.

3.4 Knowledge Management: A Multidisciplinary Subject or a Specific Ideology?

There is confusion around the origin of knowledge management, centered on the debate over whether knowledge management is derived from a single discipline. During the past few decades, various areas of knowledge management have received much attention. However, there are a few important issues surrounding it that have been found to be missing or relatively neglected. One such area is its genesis, i.e., its disciplinary roots. Those isolated descriptions on its background that are available sometimes create confusion. This section addresses the controversy regarding the origins of knowledge management and who owns the knowledge management field.

We know that the benefits derived from knowledge management initiatives are many. Nevertheless, there is still much debate in the literature on whether the field is originated from a single discipline. As revealed from the relevant literature, this debate surrounding the notion of knowledge management can be attributed to its genesis — that is, the question of whether knowledge management is derived from a wide range of disciplines. Most knowledge management scholars agree that the knowledge management field is not drawn from a single discipline; rather, it is found that many of the terms used to describe knowledge management activities have been adapted from other disciplines. Although these terms have distinctly different meanings among those scholars who use them, they are often used interchangeably (Chase, 2006; Hicks *et al.*, 2006).

In the existing literature, there are contradictory opinions regarding the genesis of knowledge management. Reflecting this view, Lopez *et al.* (2004) postulate that the knowledge management subject has been studied by several disciplines and from different approaches. Against this background, this section attempts to partially fill that gap by providing a stimulating debate on its origin and development.

The confusion that surrounds knowledge management can be attributed to its evolution. The genesis of the knowledge management field can be traced back to the end of the 20th century. Beckman (1999), for example, asserts that Karl Wiig first coined the "knowledge management" concept in 1986 at an International Labour Organization (ILO) conference held in Switzerland; whereas other scholars argue that the research and practice of knowledge management has grown rapidly since the 1990s, driven by economic, technological and social trends in the knowledge-driven economy. Gu (2004), however, argues that knowledge management research can be traced back to the mid-1970s. Gu (2004, pp. 171–172) provides evidence for this by citing the works that were "authored by four pioneers respectively affiliated to institutions of higher learning in the United States, published in *Public Administration Review* Vol. 35, Iss. 6, 1975", which can be thought to be the earliest contributions to the field of knowledge management.

In some cases, other disciplines are very closely linked to the knowledge management field, thus making it difficult to separate them. For example, organizational learning and knowledge management are closely related; indeed, the latter seems to be a part of the former, and vice versa. This has further brought out the controversy regarding its genesis. Lopez *et al.* (2004) argue that knowledge management has been studied by several disciplines and from different approaches. According to Hazlett *et al.* (2005), two of the main disciplines that have contributed to the knowledge management discourse are information systems and management.

The fact is that scholars from various disciplines are exploring unexplored areas within the knowledge management field and exploiting them to fit into their own areas of study. At the same time, researchers from several disciplines are also attempting to claim ownership of the field. Put another way, divergent views on various aspects of knowledge management inevitably result in differences of opinion about its ownership. This is well reflected by Hazlett *et al.* (2005), who comment that the study of knowledge management has revealed an apparent dichotomy between those scholars from an information systems background and those from a management background. Resonating with this view, Jashapara (2005) argues that knowledge management is becoming a dominant part of the wider management and information systems discourses.

It is found that many different disciplines have played a role in providing fresh insights into the emerging field of knowledge management. Hence, knowledge management is interdisciplinary in nature. In other words, it is an emerging, multidisciplinary paradigm that will eventually become a fully fledged discipline. One common theme that is found today among both practitioners and academics alike is that they recognize knowledge management as an important area of management research and practice, as well as a well-established area of academic debate. Moreover, knowledge management is an eclectic field rather than grounded in a specific ideology. As Hazlett *et al.* (2005) postulate, "the development of knowledge management theory and praxis continues to involve a wide range of disciplines and contributors, each bringing their respective experiences, beliefs, and practices". This is supported by Argote (2005), who contends that understanding knowledge management does not fall neatly into one discipline. Since knowledge management draws from a wide range of disciplines, Chapters 6–10 will address the question of what disciplines this discourse draws on, and will also explore their linkages.

3.5 Knowledge Management: A Universal Paradigm or a Management Fad?

It is evident that many scholars are working on the knowledge management topic because the field has an organizational implication, i.e., ensuring the sustainable competitive advantage of an organization. In many cases, knowledge management can be considered as the latest management panacea for organizational effectiveness. As mentioned earlier, knowledge is the single most important production factor that enhances an organization's capacity to survive and ensure its sustainable competitive advantage in the knowledge-based society. While managing organizational knowledge is being increasingly recognized as a critical strategic task for organizations, the question remains whether knowledge management has become a fully fledged field or is still simply a management fad.

Today, questions still arise over whether knowledge management is a fad or fashion. That is why several researchers — most notably Ponzi and Koenig (2002), Scarbrough and Swan (2001), Hlupic *et al.* (2002) and Wilson (2002b) — have attempted to explore whether knowledge management is just another passing fad, like various management concepts such as total quality management (TQM), just-in-time (JIT), quality circle (QC) and business process reengineering (BPR). Al-Hawamdeh (2002) points out that many people wonder whether knowledge management is here to stay or is just another consultancy fad like many other management techniques.

Reflecting this view, Hlupic *et al.* (2002) state that, although other management techniques (*viz.*, TQM, QC, BPR, JIT) have flourished in the management literature for several decades, as time goes by some of these concepts have been found to be particularly controversial in practice, with multiple instances of failed implementation (Hammer and Champy, 1993).

In many cases, knowledge management is still discussed as a fashionable concept or fad. Many scholars (e.g., Swan *et al.*, 1999; Raub and Ruling, 2001; Scarbrough and Swan, 2001) address this debate by referring to a number of insights derived from the management fashion literature (e.g., Abrahamson, 1996). Drawing on Abrahamson's features of a management fashion, five indicators surrounding knowledge management are identified: the number of journal articles and books published, the number of conferences and workshops organized, the number of knowledge management gurus and consultants that have emerged, the level of interest shown by consulting firms to use knowledge management for their clients, and the extent of labeling "knowledge management" for the purpose of sales promotion. These features identifying a fad will help us decide whether the notion of knowledge management will turn into another fashion or not, and are discussed below:

- *Articles and books.* Since the 1990s, there has been a growing popularity in terms of the number of published articles and books on knowledge management. Over the past few decades, 21 peer-reviewed research journals have surfaced in academic and practitioner circles to address major aspects of knowledge management as a primary focus, as shown in Table 3.1. Moreover, several special issues of top scholarly management journals have been devoted to the topic of knowledge management. In addition, Burden (2000) has developed a bibliography, encompassing both research and industry publications, that cites over 900 books and 8,000 articles devoted to the knowledge management field (cited in Schwartz, 2006).
- *Conferences and workshops.* Conferences and seminars focusing on knowledge management are organized very frequently by

Table 3.1 A List of Journals on Knowledge Management

Journal Title (in alphabetical order)	Year Launched (frequency)	Publisher
1. *Electronic Journal of Knowledge Management*	2003 (biannually)	Academic Conferences International Limited
2. *ICFAI Journal of Knowledge Management*	2003 (quarterly)	ICFAI University Press
3. *International Journal of Applied Knowledge Management*	2008 (quarterly)	International Management Journals
4. *International Journal of Knowledge and Learning*	2005 (quarterly)	Inderscience
5. *International Journal of Knowledge and Systems Science*	2010 (quarterly)	IGI Global
6. *International Journal of Knowledge, Culture and Change Management*	2005 (bimonthly)	Common Ground Publishing
7. *International Journal of Knowledge Management*	2005 (quarterly)	IGI Global
8. *International Journal of Knowledge Management in Tourism and Hospitality*	2009 (quarterly)	Inderscience
9. *International Journal of Knowledge Management Studies*	2006 (quarterly)	Inderscience
10. *International Journal of Nuclear Knowledge Management*	2004 (quarterly)	Inderscience
11. *Journal of Information & Knowledge Management*	2002 (quarterly)	World Scientific
12. *Journal of Knowledge Management*	1997 (bimonthly)	Emerald
13. *Journal of Knowledge Management Practice*	1998 (quarterly)	The Leadership Alliance Inc.
14. *Journal of Organizational Knowledge Management*	2010 (quarterly)	IBIMA Publishing

(*Continued*)

Table 3.1 (*Continued*)

Journal Title (in alphabetical order)	Year Launched (frequency)	Publisher
15. *Journal of Universal Knowledge Management*	2005 (quarterly)	Universal Journal Series
16. *Knowledge and Innovation: Journal of the KMCI*	2000 (quarterly)	KMCI
17. *Knowledge and Process Management*	1997 (quarterly)	Wiley
18. *Knowledge Management for Development Journal*	2005 (3 issues per year)	KM4Dev
19. *Knowledge Management Research & Practice*	2003 (quarterly)	Palgrave Macmillan
20. *Knowledge Management Review*	2010 (quarterly)	Melcrum
21. *VINE: The Journal of Information and Knowledge Management Systems*	1971 (quarterly)	Emerald

academics and business organizations every year. Over the past two decades, a good number of conferences, workshops and doctoral colloquiums (e.g., the Knowledge Management Doctoral Consortium, held by the Queen's School of Business) have been launched to address the knowledge management field as a primary focus. Table 3.2 depicts representative conferences that focus exclusively on knowledge management. Furthermore, top-tier management conferences (e.g., International Conference on Advances in Management (ICAM), British Academy of Management (BAM) Conference, Hawaii International Conference on System Sciences (HICSS)) have also incorporated knowledge management by devoting a separate track to it.

- *Emerging knowledge management gurus and consultants.* The growing number of knowledge management gurus and consultants has become apparent. Karl Wiig was one of the earliest proponents of the notion of knowledge management. Other

Table 3.2 A Selected List of Conferences on Knowledge Management

Conference Title (in alphabetical order)
1. ACM Conference on Information and Knowledge Management
2. Australian Conference on Knowledge Management and Intelligent Decision Support
3. European Conference on Knowledge Management
4. Hawaii International Conference on System Sciences
5. IBIMA Conference on Knowledge Management and Innovation
6. International Conference on Knowledge Engineering and Knowledge Management
7. International Conference on Knowledge Management and Information Sharing
8. International Conference on Knowledge Management and Knowledge Economy
9. International Conference on Knowledge Management and Knowledge Technologies
10. International Conference on Knowledge Management in Asia Pacific
11. International Conference on Practical Aspects of Knowledge Management
12. Iranian Knowledge Management Conference
13. Knowledge Management Aston Conference

scholars like Suliman Al-Hawamdeh, Nick Bontis, Rory L. Chase, Steve Clarke, N. A. D. Connell, Mark Easterby-Smith, John Edwards, Murray E. Jennex, William R. King, Jonathan H. Klein, W. B. Lee, Dorothy Leonard-Barton, Jay Liebowitz, Mark Nissen, Harry Scarbrough, Dave Snowden, Michael Stankosky, Harry Tsoukas and Anthony Wensley have contributed much in developing and popularizing the knowledge management field. In particular, the topics surrounding knowledge management noticeably captured the attention of managers when Nonaka and Takeuchi (1995) as well as Davenport and Prusak (1998) attempted to make popular the concept of knowledge management in their books, *The Knowledge-Creating Company* and *Working Knowledge*, respectively.

- *Greater interest by consulting firms.* The widespread usage of knowledge management is an important task of major consulting firms. Reflecting this view, Davenport and Grover (2001) argue that knowledge management was first developed in industries that basically sell knowledge: professional services. To put it differently, knowledge management has emerged as a tool with which today's organizations attempt to ensure the utilization of organizational knowledge. That is why almost all organizations have started to view themselves as knowledge-intensive firms and have adopted knowledge management approaches in every business action. Management consulting firms, research groups, media agencies and software development firms are all good examples of knowledge-creating companies, which place a great deal of effort towards the successful implementation of knowledge management. Ernst & Young's Center for Business Innovation and IBM (International Business Machines) Consulting Services are typical examples of knowledge-creating companies that always come up with new knowledge and new ways of doing things.

- *Labeling of "knowledge management" for business promotion.* It appears that most companies have started to realize the increasing importance of the "knowledge management" label for commercial purposes. In fact, many organizations have simply re-badged various information management tools and now call them "knowledge management" tools in an attempt to jump on the bandwagon of contemporary thinking (Swan *et al.*, 1999) and to generate quick profits.

The above discussion shows that knowledge management does have Abrahamson's (1996) features of a management fashion. However, just because such a field seems to have the features of a fashion does not mean that it is nothing more than a fad. The survey findings of KPMG (1998) report that only 2% of respondents considered knowledge management to be a fad that would soon be forgotten. Likewise, Davenport and Grover (2001) argue that the implementation of knowledge management is no longer limited to those industries that basically sell knowledge, namely professional services as well as research and development (R&D) firms; rather, it has quickly been used in many other industries, including manufacturing enterprises, financial services, government agencies, medical service providers and military organizations.

Scholars — most notably Jashapara (2005) and Stankosky (2005) — nicely explain why knowledge management is not purely a fad. Stankosky (2005), for instance, argues that fads normally hang around for five years; if a discourse sustains its popularity for more than five years, then there is less likelihood that it will fall under the category of a fad. Similarly, Jashapara (2005) postulates that, with respect to a fashion, after rapid growth in its popularity for five years, the annual article count would peak and then decline rapidly. However, this is really not the case for knowledge management. Evidence shows that the rapid growth in popularity in this field is still continuing, and that its annual article count is maintaining a peak and there is no sign of decline in the foreseeable future. Having emerged as a relatively new discipline of the 1990s, Jashapara (2005) provides evidence that knowledge management has passed the five-year mark and has actually been in existence for at least 20 years. Stankosky (2005) also stresses that knowledge management is certainly not a fad because the knowledge-based economy is here to stay:

> Knowledge management has been in existence for at least 10 years. The evidence shows that knowledge management has passed the five-year mark and is becoming a dominant part of the wider management and information systems discourse. Hence it is to be argued that knowledge management is not just a fad. [Stankosky, 2005]

Therefore, knowledge management has emerged as a fundamental concept in the knowledge-based society. Researchers (e.g., Wiig, 1997; Ruggles, 1997; Buckley and Carter, 2000; Davenport and Grover, 2001) have explained that the subject is more than just a new fad. Wiig (1997), for example, notes that knowledge management is far from being a narrow management initiative or fad, such as TQM or BPR. This corresponds well with Hull's (2000, p. 49) comment that "the phenomenon is not merely some passing fad, but is in the process of establishing itself as a new aspect of management and organisations and a new form of expertise" (also cited in Alvesson and Karreman, 2001, p. 995).

Jashapara (2005) observes that there is a common agreement among scholars that knowledge management has enjoyed phenomenal growth since 1997. Hence, it is argued that knowledge management is not just a fad. That is why Davenport and Grover (2001, p. 3) conclude by claiming that "it is becoming increasingly clear that knowledge management is here to stay". In this regard, McKinlay (2002) contends that the debate surrounding knowledge management is dominated by uncritical prescription and critical abstraction. Knowledge management cannot simply be dismissed as a passing fad. Today, no one treats knowledge management as a fad or fashion; rather, knowledge management is viewed as an important area of theoretical and applied management research, and will remain a well-established area of academic debate.

3.6 Perspectives on Knowledge Management: A Technical-Centric or Social-Centric View?

Another area of discussion and debate surrounding knowledge management is related to the perspectives on knowledge management. It is noted that perspectives on knowledge management have tended to attract an enormous amount of attention among scholars. To date, it seems that two major perspectives on knowledge management have emerged. The existing research and empirical efforts in knowledge management usually focus on one of two broad categories: (i) technical issues, or (ii) human and organizational issues. These perspectives are referred to as the technical view of knowledge management and the social view of knowledge management, respectively, which will be discussed next.

The technical view of knowledge management has been labeled variously as the cognitive perspective (Swan *et al.*, 1999), the engineering perspective (Markus, 2000), or the "knowledge management as technology" camp (Alvesson and Karreman, 2001). Conversely, the alternative perspective — i.e., the social view of knowledge management — has been labeled differently as the community perspective (Swan *et al.*, 1999), the cultivation perspective (Markus, 2000), or the "knowledge management as people" camp

Table 3.3 Alternative Approaches to Knowledge Management

	Approaches	
	Technical	**Social**
Paradigm	Knowledge is objectifiable (abstracted from context).	Knowledge is socially constructed (situated in the societies).
Function	The main function of knowledge management is to make tacit knowledge explicit, and to transfer and re-use it across different locations.	The primary function of knowledge management is to transfer and apply tacit knowledge through social networking, and to create new knowledge.
Social Ties	The development of social ties is less important in transferring explicit knowledge.	The development of strong social ties is crucial to transfer tacit knowledge.
Technology	Technology is crucial to capture and transfer knowledge.	Technology is not crucial to transfer knowledge between individuals.
Strategy	The codification strategy is important for the transfer of knowledge.	The personalization strategy is important for the transfer of knowledge.

Note: compiled from Swan *et al.* (1999), Alvesson and Karreman (2001), Markus (2000), Swan and Scarbrough (2001), and Sorensen and Lundh-Snis (2001).

(Alvesson and Karreman, 2001). The basic assumptions of these perspectives are shown in Table 3.3.

A significant proportion of the contemporary literature suggests that the mechanisms used to manage organizational knowledge can be classified into two dominant groups based on the tacit/explicit dichotomy. Focusing on knowledge as a category, two very different mechanisms in order to manage knowledge have emerged — what can be called social and technical mechanisms. This view is an extension of that of Hansen *et al.* (1999). They contend that the personalization strategy is an approach whereby knowledge is closely tied to the organizational members; there is no doubt that people develop tacit knowledge and share it through direct person-to-person interactions. Contrarily, in the codification strategy, knowledge is codified and stored in databases; such knowledge is explicit in form, as it can be accessed and used easily by any member of the organization. These perspectives, i.e., the social side and the technical side of knowledge management, will be discussed in turn.

3.6.1 *Perspectives on Knowledge Management: The Social-Centric View*

Having identified and discussed the two main perspectives of knowledge management, our focus now moves to socially driven knowledge management. In the majority of the knowledge management literature, researchers (e.g., Davenport and Prusak, 1998; Lam, 1997; Storey and Barnett, 2000; Nonaka and Takeuchi, 1995; Brown and Duguid, 1998; Lave and Wenger, 1991; Argote, 1999) suggest that active, direct communication between individuals plays a large role in managing their knowledge.

3.6.2 *Perspectives on Knowledge Management: The Technical-Centric View*

Many scholars — most notably Scarbrough *et al.* (1999), Storey and Barnett (2000), Alavi and Leidner (2001), Bhatt (2001), Newell *et al.* (1999), Broendsted and Elkjaer (2001), and Huber (2001) — contend that technology plays a central role in the management of an organization's knowledge. Information and communication technology (ICT) makes the transmission of explicit knowledge, which is in words, easier. This is supported by the work of Carbonara (2005), who argues that such mechanisms have the capability to transfer a vast array of knowledge as well as reduce the space and time barriers. Resonating with this view, Loeb *et al.* (1998) observe that technology-assisted tools enable coordination across geography and time, and logically integrate knowledge spreading all over the world.

From the above discussion, it is said that most researchers in this field tend to either view knowledge management as a social issue or think of it in terms of a technical perspective. There are strengths and weaknesses in both viewpoints. Nevertheless, as observed earlier, there is a general agreement in the literature that knowledge management can be implemented through either social mechanisms or technical mechanisms. The perspective that combines both the social and technical aspects of knowledge management will be elaborated next.

3.6.3 *Combined Approach to Knowledge Management: The Socio-Technical Approach*

It is argued that the characteristics of tacit knowledge make knowledge management difficult to implement successfully (Leonard and Sensiper, 1998; Roberts, 2000). Since tacit knowledge is hard to articulate, the only way through which such knowledge can be managed is by social mechanisms. On the other hand, in seeking to manage the explicit knowledge activities, organizations have turned to technology as an enabling media. However, Dixon (2000) warns against overemphasizing technology in managing knowledge, arguing that the use of technology to replace face-to-face conversations will only bring limited success.

To overcome such difficulties, several scholars (Gupta and Govindarajan, 2000; Jasimuddin, 2008; Tsoukas, 1996; Boiral, 2002) argue that viewing knowledge management from a socio-technical approach (STA) will resolve the debate. As mentioned earlier, there are strengths and weaknesses in both approaches. Although face-to-face interaction seems to be more efficient and effective in certain situations, such interaction is not possible all the time with a colleague who works in another country. Thus, overemphasizing one approach at the expense of the other may lead to a situation in which the organization loses its competitive edge.

The majority of scholars working on this area have advocated that tacit knowledge and explicit knowledge are inseparable. Jasimuddin *et al.* (2005), for instance, contend that the relationship between the two can be likened to the portions of an iceberg above and below the waterline: the exposed explicit knowledge is supported, or given meaning, by the hidden tacit knowledge. The position of knowledge on the tacit–explicit continuum is determined by its tacit–explicit mix.

By a socio-technical approach, researchers mean a combination of the social side of knowledge management and the technical aspects of knowledge management. There are some researchers (Scarbrough, 1999; McAdam and McCreedy, 2000; Desouza and Evaristo, 2003; Swan and Scarbrough, 2001; Pan and Scarbrough, 1999) who also give isolated descriptions about the importance of combining the social and technical mechanisms, arguing that both mechanisms of knowledge are inseparable. Hence, there is a strong argument in favor of the socio-technical approach to knowledge management.

Although we have discussed several unresolved issues surrounding knowledge management, we cannot claim that the above discussions have completely resolved the debate. Rather, this chapter has shed some light to partially resolve the controversies surrounding knowledge management. Therefore, it seems that the debate will remain an ongoing discussion for the time being.

3.7 Concluding Summary

Knowledge management has appeared as an important area of research and practice. In the wake of the emergence of the knowledge society, the most strategic resource for an organization is knowledge. Recently, there has been recognition that managing knowledge is important for organizational survival. The successful implementation of knowledge management will enhance an organization's sustainable competitive advantage. The fact is that knowledge management has emerged as a fundamental issue in the knowledge-based society. This chapter has addressed some of the unresolved operational issues of knowledge management. Numerous practical questions and challenges concerning knowledge management still remain unanswered and require further research; nonetheless, this chapter has acquainted readers with the various unresolved issues of knowledge management.

In essence, knowledge management emphasizes the importance of knowledge for organizations and its pivotal role in achieving competitive advantage. A wide variety of disciplines and perspectives on knowledge management have yielded different dimensions and meanings. Since the notion of knowledge management has very diverse academic and practical roots, practitioners find it difficult to understand what knowledge management is and how the challenges it presents can best be tackled. Furthermore, such divergent views have inevitably led to differences of opinion about its ownership.

The controversy over the origins and development of knowledge management still exists. The debate is centered on whether knowledge management is derived from a single discipline or from a wide range of disciplines. Similarly, there is no consensus regarding the claim that knowledge management is a new field with its own research base. Moreover, there is much debate in the literature on what constitutes knowledge management perspectives, and theoretical perspectives on knowledge management continue to diverge.

This chapter has given researchers and managers a clearer picture of knowledge management. After tackling the basic issues relating to organizational knowledge and knowledge management, the chapter has provided a stimulating discussion on the origin of knowledge management. Knowledge management is shown to be an eclectic field rather than grounded in a specific ideology, and draws from a wide range of disciplines.

Furthermore, it is argued that knowledge management is not just a fad. Scholars state that fads normally hang around for five years, but evidence shows that knowledge management has passed the five-year mark. In fact, it has been in existence for at least 20 years, and is becoming a dominant part of the wider management and information systems discourse. Knowledge management seems to be a long-lasting phenomenon because academics and practitioners from various different disciplines, such as information systems, human resources, strategic management and organizational theory, are showing an increasing interest in it. Due to its popularity, it is right to say that knowledge management is more than just a fad.

The perspectives on knowledge management are far from being well articulated in the relevant literature; and this is compounded by the confusion around the various concepts, namely, the technical and social aspects of knowledge management. Debates have focused on the divergent perspectives of knowledge management, and the dilemma regarding whether knowledge management is best understood as a technical-centric or social-centric phenomenon is still unresolved. In spite of these diverse opinions as identified earlier in the literature, the field of knowledge management has developed quickly over the last decade. The perspective that combines both the social side and the technical side of knowledge management has been discussed in this chapter. A pluralistic stance seems to be appropriate, which falls somewhere between the rather divergent perspectives while recognizing the contradictions.

Although this chapter has addressed a number of questions of interest surrounding knowledge management, the understanding of some of the issues still remains fragmented and contested. Nevertheless, this chapter has given insightful managers and researchers a useful starting point to examine this research in more detail, as a means of guidance for implementing knowledge management initiatives in their own organizations. The controversies and debates surrounding knowledge management discussed in this chapter will also greatly improve managers' understanding of how various disciplines have contributed to the development of knowledge management, and will provide some conceptual depth in order to enable managers to develop better approaches to addressing knowledge management problems.

This chapter does not claim to close the debate on the various issues relating to knowledge management; rather, my humble purpose has been to highlight those unresolved issues. Numerous practical questions and challenges concerning knowledge management remain unanswered and demand research. One such issue is the source of knowledge. Most of the literature on knowledge management focuses on the knowledge available within an organization. However, when we talk about the management of organizational knowledge, we should mean managing the knowledge available both within and outside an organization. The next chapter will discuss the existing theories of organizational knowledge postulated by management scholars, along with addressing various sources (e.g., endogenous and exogenous) of organizational knowledge.

Further Reading

Abrahamson, E. and Fairchild, G. (1999). Management fashion: lifecycles, triggers, and collective learning processes. *Administrative Science Quarterly*, 44, 708–740.

Coakes, E., Amar, A. D. and Granados, M. L. (2010). Knowledge management, strategy, and technology: a global snapshot. *Journal of Enterprise Information Management*, 23(3), 282–304.

Cooper, V. A. and Lichtenstein, S. (2010). Supporting knowledge transfer in web-based managed IT support. *Journal of Systems and Information Technology*, 12(2), 140–160.

Jasimuddin, S. M. and Zhang, Z. (2009). The symbiosis mechanism for effective knowledge transfer. *Journal of the Operational Research Society*, 60(5), 706–716.

Mayfield, M. (2010). Tacit knowledge sharing: techniques for putting a powerful tool in practice. *Development and Learning in Organizations*, 24(1), 24–26.

Migdadi, M. M. (2009). A knowledge-centered culture as an antecedent of effective knowledge management at information technology centers in the Jordanian universities. *Journal of Systems and Information Technology*, 11(2), 89–116.

Revilla, E., Rodríguez-Prado, B. and Prieto, I. (2009). Information technology as knowledge management enabler in product development: empirical evidence. *European Journal of Innovation Management*, 12(3), 346–363.

Thomas, J. C., Kellogg, W. A. and Erickson, T. (2001). The knowledge management puzzle: human and social factors in knowledge management. *IBM Systems Journal*, 40(4), 863–884.

References

Abrahamson, E. (1996). Management fashion. *Academy of Management Review*, 21(1), 254–285.

Alavi, M. and Leidner, D. (2001). Knowledge management and knowledge management systems: conceptual foundations and research issues. *MIS Quarterly*, 25(1), 107–136.

Al-Hawamdeh, S. (2002). Knowledge management: re-thinking information management and facing the challenge of managing tacit knowledge. *Information Research* (online journal), 8(1), available at http://informationr.net/ir/8-1/paper143.html/.

Alvesson, M. and Karreman, D. (2001). Odd couple: making sense of the curious concept of knowledge management. *Journal of Management Studies*, 38(7), 995–1018.

Argote, L. (1999). *Organizational Learning: Creating, Retaining and Transferring Knowledge*. Norwell, MA: Kluwer.

Argote, L. (2005). Reflections on two views of managing learning and knowledge in organizations. *Journal of Management Inquiry*, 14, 43–48.

Beckman, T. J. (1999). The current state of knowledge management. In J. Liebowitz (ed.), *Knowledge Management Handbook* (pp. 1–22), Boca Raton, FL: CRC Press LLC.

Bhatt, G. D. (2001). Knowledge management in organizations: examining the interaction between technologies, techniques, and people. *Journal of Knowledge Management*, 5(1), 68–75.

Boiral, O. (2002). Tacit knowledge and environmental management. *Long Range Planning*, 35, 291–317.

Bounfour, A. (2003). The IC-dVAL approach. *Journal of Intellectual Capital*, 4(3), 396–413.

Broendsted, J. and Elkjaer, B. (2001). Information technology as a fellow player in organizational learning. In *Proceedings of the 9th European Conference on Information Systems (ECIS 2001)*, June 27–29, Bled, Slovenia.

Brown, J. and Duguid, P. (1998). Organizing knowledge. *California Management Review*, 40(3), 90–111.

Buckley, P. J. and Carter, M. J. (2000). Knowledge management in global technology markets: applying theory to practice. *Long Range Planning*, 33, 55–71.

Burden, P. R. (2000). *Knowledge Management: The Bibliography.* Medford, NJ: Information Today, Inc.

Bushko, D. and Raynor, M. (1998). Knowledge management: new directions for IT (and other) consultants. *Journal of Management Consulting*, 10(2), November, 67–68.

Carbonara, N. (2005). Information and communication technology and geographical clusters: opportunities and spread. *Technovation*, 25(3), 213–222.

Chase, R. (2006). A decade of knowledge management. *Journal of Knowledge Management*, 10(1), 1–6.

Chauvel, D. and Despres, C. (2002). A review of survey research in knowledge management: 1997–2001. *Journal of Knowledge Management*, 6(3), 207–223.

Davenport, T. H., De Long, D. W. and Beers, M. C. (1998). Successful knowledge management projects. *Sloan Management Review*, Winter, 43–57.

Davenport, T. H. and Grover, V. (2001). Special issue: knowledge management. *Journal of Management Information Systems*, 18(1), 3–4.

Davenport, T. H. and Prusak, L. (1998). *Working Knowledge: How Organizations Manage What They Know*. Boston, MA: Harvard Business School Press.

Desouza, K. C. and Evaristo, J. R. (2003). Global knowledge management strategies. *European Management Journal*, 21(1), 62–67.

Dixon, N. (2000). *Common Knowledge: How Companies Thrive by Sharing What They Know*. Boston, MA: Harvard Business School Press.

Gu, Y. (2004). Global knowledge management research: a bibliometric analysis. *Scientometrics*, 61, 171–190.

Gupta, A. K. and Govindarajan, V. (2000). Knowledge management's social dimension: lessons from Nucor Steel. *Sloan Management Review*, Fall, 71–80.

Hammer, M. and Champy, J. (1993). *Reengineering the Corporation*. New York: HarperBusiness.

Hansen, M. T., Nohria, N. and Tierney, T. (1999). What's your strategy for managing knowledge? *Harvard Business Review*, 77(2), 106–116.

Hazlett, S., McAdam, R. and Gallagher, S. (2005). Theory building in knowledge management: in search of paradigms. *Journal of Management Inquiry*, 14(1), 31–42.

Hicks, R. C., Dattero, R. and Galup, S. D. (2006). The five-tier knowledge management hierarchy. *Journal of Knowledge Management*, 10(1), 19–31.

Hlupic, V., Pouloudi, A. and Rzevski, G. (2002). Towards an integrated approach to knowledge management: 'hard', 'soft' and 'abstract' issues. *Knowledge and Process Management*, 9(2), 90–102.

Huber, G. P. (2001). Transfer of knowledge in knowledge management systems: unexplored issues and suggested studies. *European Journal of Information Systems*, 10, 72–79.

Hull, R. (2000). Knowledge management and the conduct of expert labour. In C. Prichard *et al.* (eds.), *Managing Knowledge* (pp. 49–68), Basingstoke: Macmillan Press Ltd.

Jashapara, A. (2005). The emerging discourse of knowledge management: a new dawn for information science research? *Journal of Information Science*, 31(2), 136–148.

Jasimuddin, S. M. (2008). A holistic view of appropriate knowledge management strategy. *Journal of Knowledge Management*, 12(2), 57–66.

Jasimuddin, S. M., Klein, J. H. and Connell, C. (2005). The paradox of using tacit and explicit knowledge: strategies to face dilemmas. *Management Decision*, 43(1), 102–112.

KPMG (1998). *Knowledge Management Research Report 1998.* London: KPMG Consulting.

Lam, A. (1997). Embedded firms, embedded knowledge: problems in collaboration and knowledge transfer in global cooperative ventures. *Organization Studies*, 21(3), 487–513.

Lave, J. and Wenger, E. (1991). *Situated Learning: Legitimate Peripheral Participation.* Cambridge: Cambridge University Press.

Leonard, D. and Sensiper, S. (1998). The role of tacit knowledge in group innovation. *California Management Review*, 40, 112–132.

Loeb, K. A., Rai, A., Ramaprasad, A. and Sharma, S. (1998). Design, development and implementation of a global information warehouse: a case study at IBM. *Information Systems Journal*, 8, 291–311.

Lopez, S. P., Peon, J. M. M. and Ordas, C. J. V. (2004). Managing knowledge: the link between culture and organizational learning. *Journal of Knowledge Management*, 8(6), 93–104.

Markus, M. L. (2000). Knowledge management. Presented at the Warwick Business School Seminar Series, University of Warwick, Coventry, UK.

Martiny, M. (1998). Knowledge management at HP Consulting. *Organizational Dynamics*, 27(2), 71–78.

McAdam, R. and McCreedy, S. (2000). A critique of knowledge management: using a social constructionist model. *New Technology, Work and Employment*, 15(2), 155–168.

McKinlay, A. (2002). The limits of knowledge management. *New Technology, Work and Employment*, 17(2), 76–88.

Newell, S., Swan, J., Galliers, R. and Scarbrough, H. (1999). The intranet as a knowledge management tool? Creating new electronic fences. In M. Khosrowpour (ed.), *Proceedings of the Information Resources Management Association International Conference, "Managing Information Technology Resources in Organizations in the Next Millennium".*

Nonaka, I. and Takeuchi, H. (1995). *The Knowledge-Creating Company: How Japanese Companies Create the Dynamics of Innovation.* Oxford: Oxford University Press.

Pan, S. L. and Scarbrough, H. (1999). Knowledge management in practice: an exploratory case study. *Technology Analysis & Strategic Management*, 11(3), 359–374.

Phillips, N. and Patrick, K. (2000). Knowledge management perspectives, organizational character and cognitive style. In J. Edwards and J. Kidd (eds.), *Proceedings of the Knowledge Management Conference (KMAC 2000)*, July 17–18, Birmingham, UK.

Ponzi, L. and Koenig, M. E. D. (2002). Knowledge management: another management fad? *Information Research* (online journal), 8(1), available at http://informationr.net/ir/8-1/paper145.html/.

Raub, S. and Ruling, C. (2001). The knowledge management tussle — speech communities and rhetorical strategies in the development of knowledge management. *Journal of Information Technology*, 16(2), 113–130.

Roberts, J. (2000). From know-how to show-how? Questioning the role of information and communication technologies in knowledge transfer. *Technology Analysis & Strategic Management*, 12(4), 429–443.

Ruggles, R. (1997). *Knowledge Management Tools*. Boston, MA: Butterworth-Heinemann.

Scarbrough, H. (1999). Knowledge as work: conflicts in the management of knowledge workers. *Technology Analysis and Strategic Management*, 11(1), 5–16.

Scarbrough, H. and Swan, J. (2001). Explaining the diffusion of knowledge management: the role of fashion. *British Journal of Management*, 12(1), 3–12.

Scarbrough, H., Swan, J. and Preston, J. (1999). *Knowledge Management: A Literature Review*. London: Institute of Personnel and Development.

Schwartz, D. G. (2006). Preface: knowledge management as a layered multi-disciplinary pursuit. In D. G. Schwartz (ed.), *Encyclopedia of Knowledge Management* (pp. 1–4), Hershey, PA: Idea Group Reference.

Sorensen, C. and Lundh-Snis, U. (2001). Innovation through knowledge codification. *Journal of Information Technology*, 16, 83–97.

Spender, J. C. (2002). Knowledge, uncertainty, and an emergency theory of the firm. In C. W. Choo and N. Bontis (eds.), *The Strategic Management of Intellectual Capital and Organizational Knowledge* (pp. 149–162), New York: Oxford University Press.

Stankosky, M. A. (ed.) (2005). *Creating the Discipline of Knowledge Management: The Latest in University Research*. Oxford: Elsevier Butterworth-Heinemann.

Storey, J. and Barnett, E. (2000). Knowledge management initiatives: learning from failure. *Journal of Knowledge Management*, 4(2), 145–156.

Sveiby, K. E. (1997). *The New Organizational Wealth: Managing and Measuring Knowledge-Based Assets*. San Francisco, CA: Berrett-Koehler Publishers.

Swan, J., Newell, S., Scarbrough, H. and Hislop, D. (1999). Knowledge management and innovation: networks and networking. *Journal of Knowledge Management*, 3, 262–275.

Swan, J. and Scarbrough, H. (2001). Editorial. *Journal of Information Technology*, 16(2), 49–55.

Tsoukas, H. (1996). The firm as a distributed knowledge system: a constructionist approach. *Strategic Management Journal*, 17(Special Issue), 11–25.

Tsoukas, H. and Vladimirou, E. (2001). What is organizational knowledge? *Journal of Management Studies*, 38(7), 973–993.

Wiig, K. M. (1997). Knowledge management: where did it come from and where will it go? *Expert Systems with Applications*, 13(1), 1–14.

Wilson, T. D. (2002a). *Knowledge Management Review: The Practitioner's Guide to Knowledge Management*. Chicago, IL: Melcrum Publishing.

Wilson, T. D. (2002b). The nonsense of 'knowledge management'. *Information Research* (online journal), 8(1), available at http://informationr.net/ir/8-1/paper144.html/.

Chapter 4

The Sources of Organizational Knowledge

Knowledge Objectives

After studying this chapter, you should be able to:

- Describe the theories of organizational knowledge proposed by knowledge management theorists;
- Identify the gaps in the existing theories of organizational knowledge;
- Explore the sources of organizational knowledge;
- Explain the role of external sources of knowledge in an organization; and
- Address an alternative theory of organizational knowledge.

4.1 Introducing the Chapter

There are various theories of organizational knowledge that have been postulated by organizational theorists. The existing theories are based on various dimensions which are used in developing the typologies of organizational knowledge. The typologies of knowledge evolved from the existing organizational knowledge theories within the knowledge management literature will be discussed in this chapter. However, one dimension of organizational knowledge that has been relatively neglected in these theories is the exogenous sources of knowledge. It is pragmatic to accommodate and thereby adjust external sources of knowledge with an organization's own knowledge. With this aim in mind, an alternative typology of knowledge will also be prescribed, focusing on the various sources of knowledge, which is the main focus of this chapter.

In fact, another way of looking at the notion of organizational knowledge is through its source. The source of knowledge is an important dimension of organizational knowledge typology. That is, the sources of knowledge help to categorize organizational knowledge into two broader types of knowledge in an organization: endogenous knowledge and exogenous knowledge. Before an alternative typology of knowledge is discussed, the existing theories of organizational knowledge will first be explained.

This chapter is organized in the following manner. Scholars have proposed various theories of knowledge, based on many different dimensions, that have been widely cited in other relevant literature on knowledge management; these dimensions include degree of tacitness, organizational level and location of knowledge. Section 4.2 will briefly discuss the extant theories of organizational knowledge. Unfortunately, these theories concentrate their discussion of knowledge on the knowledge that is available within an organization. The existing theories address organizational knowledge in terms of the knowledge that is created and available inside an organization, but overlook the role of knowledge from external sources. Section 4.3 will attempt to identify gaps in the theories of organizational knowledge postulated by knowledge management scholars, explaining the role of various sources of organizational knowledge (including exogenous knowledge). An alternative view of organizational knowledge typology based on the sources of knowledge will be prescribed in Section 4.4. The chapter ends with some concluding remarks in Section 4.5.

4.2 Existing Theories of Organizational Knowledge

Contemporary knowledge management scholars have paid much attention to the notion of organizational knowledge (see Chapter 1), and have developed various theories of organizational knowledge. Pioneers such as Polanyi (1962), Nonaka and Takeuchi (1995), Spender (1996), and Blackler (1995) have proposed theories of knowledge that have been widely cited in other relevant literature on knowledge management. These scholars categorically point out that the concept of knowledge traditionally falls in the area of epistemology. More recently, though, computer science, cognitive psychology, pedagogy and information theory have also made substantial contributions to the field (Sveiby, 1994). In fact, the theories of knowledge postulated by management gurus reflect the significance of organizational knowledge. Before the various dimensions — namely sources — of organizational knowledge are elaborated, this section will look at the existing typologies of organizational knowledge from different perspectives.

4.2.1 *Polanyi's Theory of Knowledge*

Michael Polanyi, a chemist and philosopher, defines knowledge as an activity. According to Polanyi (1962, 1966), knowledge is better described as a process of knowing, arguing that all knowledge is either tacit or rooted in tacit knowledge. Michael Polanyi is a regularly quoted contributor to the epistemological debate (Sveiby, 1997; Nonaka and Takeuchi, 1995; Zuboff, 1988), with his seminal explanation of the distinction between explicit knowledge and tacit knowledge.

It is noted that Polanyi's theory of knowledge is widely used in the knowledge management literature, as Polanyi was the first to describe the notion of tacit knowledge in his book, *Personal Knowledge* (Polanyi, 1958). He suggests that the knowledge which is articulated and expressed is only a small part of the whole body of knowledge. Tacit knowledge is constructed and created from people's understanding and experiences in the world. Polanyi strongly believes that tacit knowledge is the foundation of all knowledge. As a result, such knowledge eventually forms the basis for explicit knowledge. Viewing tacit knowledge as "in-dwelling", Polanyi (1966, p. 4) claims, "I shall consider human knowledge by starting from the fact that we can know more than we can tell".

According to Polanyi (1958), tacit knowledge is embedded in the human brain and is not easy to articulate or transfer. He cites the example of a skater who can skate beautifully but cannot explain how he or she manages to skate the way he or she does. On the other hand, explicit knowledge can be easily articulated and codified, and thereby is easier to understand, store and transfer for present and future use. Sveiby (1996, p. 380) identifies the bases of Polanyi's concept of knowledge as follows:

- True discovery cannot be accounted for by a set of articulated rules (or algorithms);
- Knowledge is public and also, to a very great extent, personal — that is, knowledge is constructed by people, and therefore contains emotions or "passion"; and
- Knowledge that underlines the explicit knowledge is more fundamental, i.e., all knowledge is either tacit or rooted in tacit form.

It is evident from the relevant knowledge management literature that "knowledge", as we know it, has been built on the classic work of Polanyi. In fact, Polanyi's work is drawn from Plato's philosophical definition of knowledge as "justified true belief". Emphasizing knowledge as an activity, Polanyi describes it as both static "knowledge" and dynamic "knowing". Polanyi's distinction between explicit knowledge and tacit knowledge has been extremely influential on the work of most knowledge management scholars, including Nonaka (1994), Spender (1996) and Blackler (1995). However, it is worth mentioning that Polanyi's writings did not attract much attention until Nonaka (1998) revived an interest in it over three decades later in a research paper entitled "The Knowledge-Creating Company", based on Nonaka and Takeuchi's (1995) seminal work of the same name. This will be discussed in turn.

4.2.2 *Nonaka's Theory of Knowledge*

Acknowledging Polanyi (1966) as his source for stating the difference between explicit knowledge and tacit knowledge, Nonaka (1994) points out that interactions between various types of existing knowledge lead to the creation of new knowledge. As mentioned earlier, Lin and Wu (2005) argue that information becomes knowledge when it is interpreted by organizational members, given a context, and anchored into the beliefs and commitments of individuals.

Nonaka (1991) contends that tacit knowledge and explicit knowledge are mutually complementary entities. Both types of knowledge interact with one another and may be transformed from one type to another through individual or collective knowledge-creating activity processes. In their seminal book, *The Knowledge-Creating Company*, Nonaka and Takeuchi (1995) establish a dynamic model of knowledge creation popularly termed the SECI model. Knowledge creation embraces a continual dialogue between explicit and tacit knowledge, which boosts the creation of new ideas. The SECI framework hypothesizes four different modes of knowledge conversion — socialization, externalization, combination and internalization (see Figure 4.1):

- *Socialization*. Socialization is the process of sharing experiences among members of an organization, and is often done through observation, imitation and practice. The socialization process helps

From \ **To**	Tacit Knowledge	Explicit Knowledge
Tacit Knowledge	Socialization	Externalization
Explicit Knowledge	Internalization	Combination

Figure 4.1 Knowledge Creation Model

Source: adapted from Nonaka (1994).

to create tacit knowledge. This is the first phase in the knowledge conversion process, in which the actors involved in the knowledge creation process share their knowledge, ideas and experiences. Or, put another way, the socialization process is all about the transformation from tacit knowledge to tacit knowledge.

- *Externalization.* Externalization is the process of articulating tacit knowledge and turning it into an explicit form. For example, such a process occurs when an employee writes down a report after attending a meeting with other organizational members. Therefore, the externalization process is the conversion of tacit knowledge to explicit knowledge.
- *Combination.* Combination is the process of assembling the existing explicit knowledge available in written form to create new explicit knowledge. Nonaka and Takeuchi (1995, p. 67) argue that "this mode of knowledge conversion (combination) involves combining different bodies of explicit knowledge". Such a process occurs, for instance, when an organizational member produces a written report based on several other written documents of the organization. Or, stated differently, the combination process is the creation of new explicit knowledge using existing explicit knowledge.
- *Internalization.* Internalization is the process of converting explicit knowledge to tacit knowledge. For example, such a process occurs after a member of an organization reads a written report about an event in the organization, thereby mentally combining it with his (her) previous experience. In the words of Nonaka and Takeuchi (1995, p. 69), "documentation helps individuals internalize what they experienced, thus enriching their tacit knowledge". Hence, the internalization process is the transformation of explicit knowledge to tacit knowledge.

According to Nonaka and Takeuchi (1995), knowledge creation is a spiraling process of interactions between tacit knowledge and explicit knowledge, leading to the creation of new ideas and knowledge through four different modes of knowledge conversion. They focus on a continuous dialogue between tacit knowledge and explicit knowledge so as to create organizational knowledge. They further argue that, although the individual on a basic level generates new knowledge, the organization does play a great role in articulating and storing that knowledge. Nonaka and Takeuchi (1995) actually label each phase of the SECI model as sympathized knowledge, conceptual knowledge, systemic knowledge and operational knowledge, respectively.

Nonaka and Takeuchi's (1995) *The Knowledge-Creating Company* achieved the highest rank in terms of citation number in 1995 in the top knowledge management publications (Serenko and Bontis, 2004). However, their SECI model is not free from limitations. Li and Gao (2003), for example, raise concerns about the SECI model, stating that "considering most cases for the model mainly came from certain Japanese manufacturing companies that more or less relates to assembly lines, it is necessary to be cautious when the model is extended for a broader application" (p. 6).

Furthermore, the combination mode of the SECI model focuses on the assembling of different bodies of explicit knowledge available in written form to create new explicit knowledge. It could be argued that, if a writer does not possess tacit knowledge, it will be very difficult for him (her) to produce a useful report by relying only on the explicit knowledge which is in written form. In this context, the example of students submitting a coursework (assignment) seems relevant. After making use of the guidelines and materials provided by a lecturer, consulting with other classmates, and borrowing published materials from various sources, the students will hand in their coursework; but among them, only a very few students will get a distinction (i.e., above 70%) for their assignment. So, within the combination mode of the SECI framework, there is some element of internalization and externalization processes as well. That is, each phase of the SECI model is not isolated; rather, all of the phases are connected.

Nevertheless, Nonaka and Takeuchi's (1995) description of the "knowledge-creating" organization provides a useful starting point for theorizing about how an individual's personal knowledge can be transformed into organizational knowledge that has value to the organization. Moreover, Nonaka *et al.* (2000) propose a knowledge-creating process consisting of three elements:

- the SECI process;
- *ba*, the shared context for knowledge creation; and
- knowledge assets, the bases of knowledge-creating processes.

4.2.3 *Spender's Theory of Knowledge*

Another theory of organizational knowledge that appears to be similar, in some respects, to Nonaka's has been suggested by Spender (1994, 1996). Viewing the organization as a dynamic, knowledge-based activity system, Spender argues that knowledge can be held either by an individual or collectively in an organization, and can also be manifested tacitly or codified explicitly. He further suggests the creation of four types of organizational knowledge, as illustrated by the two-by-two matrix in Figure 4.2. More specifically, Spender's types of knowledge include automatic knowledge, collective knowledge, conscious knowledge and objectified knowledge:

- Automatic knowledge — tacit knowledge held by the individual (i.e., personal knowledge);

	Individual	**Social**
Explicit	Conscious	Objectified
Tacit	Automatic	Collective

Figure 4.2 Types of Organizational Knowledge

Source: adapted from Spender (1996).

- Collective knowledge — tacit knowledge held by the organization (i.e., communities of practice);
- Conscious knowledge — explicit knowledge held by the individual; and
- Objectified knowledge — explicit knowledge held by the organization.

Spender (2002) also proposes two approaches to viewing knowledge within the knowledge management field, which are as follows:

- In the first approach to viewing knowledge, knowledge and information are seen as interchangeable, meaning knowledge can always be transformed into information. If this is the case, all knowledge can be made explicit.
- On the other hand, the second approach to knowledge views that knowledge cannot be totally explicit, as there is a social component to it.

In other words, Spender (2002, p. 151) distinguishes the two approaches as "one in which knowledge is conceived to be ultimately objectifiable, understandable in a scientific sense, and a second, less explored domain wherein the term knowledge is considered to extend beyond that which can never be objectified or otherwise made explicit".

Spender actually proposes a "pluralistic epistemology" in seeking to capture the different types of knowledge that an organization can make use of. Spender's (1996) typology of knowledge studies the interplay between tacit and explicit knowledge at the individual and social levels. It is observed that such a theory of knowledge appears to be an expansion of Nonaka's theory of knowledge.

4.2.4 *Blackler's Theory of Knowledge*

Synthesizing Nonaka's and Spender's views on knowledge in an organization, Blackler (1995) maintains that knowledge can be analyzed as an activity process. According to Blackler, organizational knowledge is mediated, situated, provisional, pragmatic and contested. He acknowledges that the concept of knowledge is complex, arguing that its relevance to organizational theory has been insufficiently developed. To this end, Blackler (1995) sets out a framework that includes five types of knowledge used by an organization, contending that knowledge resides in bodies, routines, dialogues, brains and symbols. Thus, Blackler classifies knowledge into five groups, which include embodied knowledge, embedded knowledge, encultured knowledge, embrained knowledge and encoded knowledge. In particular, Blackler explains organizational knowledge in the following ways:

- *Embodied knowledge.* Knowledge that resides in the hands of the individuals of an organization is called embodied knowledge. An example of such knowledge is the expertise of a craftsperson rooted in action.
- *Embedded knowledge.* Knowledge that resides in the systematic routines of a firm is referred to as embedded knowledge. Typically, this kind of knowledge comprises the systematic relationship between technology, roles, formal procedures and emergent routines.
- *Encultured knowledge.* Knowledge that is collective, performed every day, and embedded in the form of a community of practice (COP) is termed encultured knowledge. Such knowledge is closely linked to the process of achieving shared meanings resulting from interaction, and is shaped collectively.
- *Embrained knowledge.* Knowledge that resides in the brains of organizational members is labeled embrained knowledge. Such knowledge is linked to the conceptual skills and cognitive abilities of people.
- *Encoded knowledge.* Knowledge that can be easily communicated by signs and symbols among the employees of a firm is called encoded knowledge. Such knowledge takes the form of books, manuals and codes of practice.

Moreover, Blackler's framework suggests that there are four different types of organizations in which different forms of knowledge dominate. These types of organizations are mentioned below:

- Expert-dependent organizations (professional bureaucracy such as a hospital);

- Knowledge-routinized organizations (machine bureaucracy such as a traditional factory);
- Communication-intensive organizations (adhocracy innovation-mediated production); and
- Symbolic-analyst-dependent organizations (knowledge-intensive firms such as a software consultancy).

As discussed above, Polanyi (1962), Nonaka and Takeuchi (1995), Spender (1996), and Blackler (1995) have proposed various theories of knowledge that have been widely cited in other relevant literature on knowledge management. Their theories are based on many different dimensions, notably the degree of tacitness, organizational level and location. The next section will identify gaps in the existing theories of organizational knowledge and its related activities, and thereby address a new way of looking at the notion of organizational knowledge.

4.3 Gaps in Theories of Organizational Knowledge

Having reviewed various typologies of knowledge derived from existing organizational knowledge theories within the knowledge management literature in the previous section, it could be argued that these theories address organizational knowledge insofar as it refers to the knowledge that is created and available inside an organization. However, by concentrating their discussion on the knowledge that is available exclusively within an organization, these theories have overlooked the role of knowledge gathered from external sources. Therefore, one important dimension is found to be missing. Newell *et al.* (2002, p. 4) support this, commenting that the existing frameworks attempt to "explain the process by which knowledge is created and the way in which knowledge is used within an organization".

In other words, exogenous sources of knowledge have been relatively neglected in the existing theories. The fact is that most theorists of organizational knowledge — particularly Nonaka and Takeuchi (1995), Spender (1996) and Blackler (1995) — have paid less attention to the role of external forces as vital sources of knowledge.

Grant (2006), for example, argues that access to a broad knowledge base through external learning is crucial in a dynamic environment, for it helps to increase the flexibility and, therefore, performance of the organization.

Reflecting this view, Dawson (2000) stresses that knowledge creation is not solely based on the internal relationships among the members of an organization; rather, it also very much depends on the relationships with stakeholders who reside outside the organization, such as clients, suppliers, alliance members and even competitors. In this context, it could be argued that, with respect to the establishment of a joint venture, one of the motivations of the partner companies is the opportunity to acquire knowledge from each other. Similarly, it is evident that third-sector organizations gather knowledge from other organizations, including patrons and other stakeholders. So, organizations need to extend their knowledge management efforts across the firm boundary (Peña, 2002; Seufert *et al.*, 1999). Parallel to this, Balogun and Jenkins (2003, p. 247) add, "For organisational transformation to occur, an organisation's members need to evolve new tacit knowledge about the way they interact both with each other and external stakeholders, and how they coordinate their activities".

Most authors (e.g., Balogun and Jenkins, 2003; Dawson, 2000; Dyer and Singh, 1998; Gulati, 1999; Werr *et al.*, 2009) recognize that knowledge existing outside a firm's boundaries may be critical to firm success. It is not sufficient to collect, share and use the knowledge available within an organization. Knowledge about customers and other external stakeholders — along with internal stakeholders — also needs to be acquired, learnt, shared and used. Werr *et al.* (2009) stress that knowledge is increasingly residing outside the formal boundaries of the single organization, and thus call for collaboration across formal organizational boundaries. This will help to secure access to, acquire and utilize knowledge which is essential for the survival of an organization.

For example, customers and suppliers often provide an essential source of ideas and knowledge in the knowledge-creating process in order to create new knowledge about new demands, processes and products. A supplier of automobile parts to Honda has to pay close attention to its customers' needs so as to supply the right components in line with the requirements of Honda's products. In fact, both customers and suppliers are involved in the early stages of product development at Honda. Generally speaking, a company that intends to lead an industry must take the knowledge coming from other stakeholders (such as customers and suppliers) very seriously and assess its potential.

Unfortunately, the reality is that our understanding of knowledge collected and used across organizational boundaries is still rather limited (Beesley, 2004; Uzzi and Lancaster, 2003). This section will highlight the importance of external knowledge through the categorization of organizational knowledge based on sources of knowledge.

4.3.1 *Sources of Organizational Knowledge*

The important point here is that knowledge is possessed by people both inside and outside an organization. As a result, "source-based knowledge" can be incorporated as an alternative dimension of organizational knowledge. Organizations need to extract and utilize knowledge gathered from both internal and external sources.

By internal source of knowledge, we mean the knowledge available within an organization that resides in its members. The knowledge that is created, transferred and made available for use among organizational members is called endogenous knowledge. Lowendahl (1997), for example, argues that organizations — particularly knowledge-intensive firms — rely heavily on expert knowledge, embedded in intangible products and services, to compete. In line with this, Edvinsson and Sullivan (1996) also emphasize the use of employees' knowledge as a source of competitive advantage for organizations. It appears that such organizations derive their profits from the commercialization of knowledge created by their employees.

On the other hand, external source of knowledge refers to the knowledge that is available outside the firm's boundary. That is, the knowledge that resides in customers, suppliers and competitors — other than the organization's own knowledge — is called exogenous knowledge. Empson (2001), for example, emphasizes the role of clients' knowledge which resides outside the organization. In particular, Empson (2001) contends that "professional service firms rely upon two main forms of knowledge: technical knowledge and the knowledge of their clients". Likewise, Probst (1998, p. 23) categorizes knowledge under several important channels:

- Knowledge held by other firms (i.e., rival firms);
- Stakeholders' knowledge (i.e., suppliers, customers); and
- Experts' knowledge (i.e., employees).

It is essential to take into account exogenous sources of knowledge in order to exploit knowledge in an organization. The role of external sources of organizational knowledge will be discussed in turn.

4.3.2 *The Role of External Sources of Organizational Knowledge*

As opposed to the understanding of internal knowledge, several scholars (e.g., Dyer and Singh, 1998; Gulati, 1999; Jasimuddin, 2004) point out that knowledge from external sources is essential to a firm's success. Jasimuddin (2004), for example, argues that knowledge existing outside a firm's boundaries plays a significant role in knowledge creation, or at least in shaping the existing knowledge to make it more useful and actionable. Desouza *et al.* (2005) shed some light on why an organization needs to gather knowledge from external sources — particularly knowledge from various stakeholders, namely suppliers, business partners, customers, government and regulatory bodies, academia, and competitors — other than its own employees.

It is evident that the knowledge held by an organization is an outcome not only of the interaction among its own employees, but also of the interactions between endogenous forces (e.g., organizational employees) and exogenous forces (e.g., customers, suppliers, competitors). In this regard, McAdam and McCreedy (2000) question how knowledge can be restricted to within the factory while it is socially constructed. Parallel to this, Andreu and Sieber (2006, p. 173) assert, "Competitive forces put pressure on firms not only to streamline their business processes, but also to be able to incorporate relevant knowledge from the environment". Desouza *et al.* (2005) support this view, arguing that external sources of knowledge are crucial for organizations to be competitive in the current and future market.

4.3.3 *The Organizational Knowledge of Various Stakeholders Outside an Organization*

Depending on the industry in which an organization operates, some sources of external knowledge may carry more weight than others (Desouza *et al.*, 2005). For instance, suppliers provide the raw materials, work-in-progress components or finished parts of a car, which an organization then uses as automobile parts during the assembly and manufacturing of a car. Therefore, it comes as no surprise that the knowledge of suppliers is an important ingredient to Honda's operations, which involve listening to the suppliers about inventions and innovations in automobile parts such as the brakes or the gearbox. No organization can possibly be self-sufficient in the various activities needed to deliver customer value. This section will describe various stakeholders — customers, suppliers, competitors, academics and corporate partners — who are based outside an organization's boundary, and whose knowledge is crucial for its success and growth.

Customers. All businesses' survival and growth depend upon actual customers' satisfaction. An organization cannot expect to be successful if it fails to adequately meet its customers' requirements. As a result, successful organizations are those that design, build and price a product in consultation with potential customers. Today, the success of an organization very much depends on understanding its potential customer needs and expectations, and working accordingly. Organizations must actively seek such knowledge out in order to be better prepared to carry out product enhancements and innovations. Sometimes, customers may know a product better than the organization that produces it; as such, they represent a viable source of knowledge.

In order to leverage customer knowledge, it is important to understand what is meant by customer knowledge. Knowledge from customers can be defined as the insights, ideas, thoughts and information an organization may grab from its customers. These insights can be about current products and services, customers' tastes, preferences and future needs, and ideas for product innovations. Knowledge from customers is concerned more with eliciting their novel ideas and feedback. Product innovations stem from end users and customers of the products, and not from within organizational quarters (Thomke and von Hippel, 2002).

Suppliers. Suppliers' knowledge is an important ingredient to an organization's operations, for they provide raw materials, work-in-progress or finished goods. For example, a supplier of automobile parts to Toyota or Ford is an expert in the calibration of such parts. After collecting knowledge from suppliers, organizations must use it to improve existing products. Moreover, suppliers are not just in charge of providing physical products such as nuts and bolts; in the consulting service industry, suppliers provide ideas, insights, advice, etc., which are intangible in nature. Suppliers can be said to possess deep knowledge in their respective domains. Organizations can also use their suppliers' knowledge as an avenue to interact with other members of the value chain. A well-established organization is usually one that hosts an annual conference to gather its suppliers for discussions about forthcoming innovations, and thereby grab their knowledge and novel ideas.

Competitors. Organizations also collect knowledge from their competitors. Today, competing organizations tend to cooperate for mutual benefits. Take the example of the strategic engagement between two classic rivals: Amazon and Borders. Amazon, the pioneer online retailer, started out as an online bookseller (Desouza *et al.*, 2005). Its competitors were traditional bookstores like Borders and Barnes & Noble. After failing to compete adequately with Amazon, Borders decided to forge an alliance with the Internet giant through a marketing and distribution agreement. As a result, Amazon shared its technical expertise with Borders. Such a strategic alliance helped Borders manage its book inventory system and establish a dominant presence on the Internet; while Amazon could gain access to Borders' customer base, which Borders had acquired through tireless efforts over decades. Given that Borders has recently filed for bankruptcy, the question remains whether the formation of such a strategic alliance was a wise decision in this case (which is beyond the scope of this book). Nevertheless, it is evident that competitors normally have different areas of strengths and weakness, and that one's weakness may be another's strength; thus, gaining knowledge about this can be beneficial. Such knowledge can be used to improve the positioning of one's products and services, or to forge successful alliances.

Academia. Academia, particularly business and engineering science schools, represents a viable external source of knowledge for business organizations. Researchers at educational and research institutions generate new knowledge on a constant basis. Much of it is made available via working papers, research reports, discussions and panel presentations, conferences, meetings, symposiums and industry–academic collaborations. Researchers and scholars work on cutting-edge problems and have greater slack for experimentation, and are better at knowledge generation than the private sector. Many of their studies take a global perspective of the problems, and hence the knowledge generated is widely applicable to any business belonging to a given industry or facing a similar problem. Academics have the advantage of being neutral in their analyses and can access wider data points than what is available to a private organization. Academic knowledge must be tapped by seeking explicit and tacit sources. Explicit sources of knowledge include databases that house academic journals and other outlets that disseminate research results. Tacit knowledge is gained by interacting with academicians via listening to presentations, inviting academicians as consultants, and organizing industry–academia collaborative efforts.

Business partners. Building coalitions is one way to get competitors to collaborate, wherein each organization provides a piece of its strength, which will hopefully counter another member organization's weakness and make the coalition stronger. An organization must interact with various business partners, including suppliers, office equipment manufacturers, technology providers, legal firms, logistics and distribution centers, advertising houses, etc. Each of these entities provides the organization with goods or services of value that enable it to be more effective and efficient in meeting its objectives. Like suppliers, business partners have deep knowledge in their own areas of focus, as this represents their bread and butter. The organization must look to these partners for knowledge about their better internal operations. For a hospital, business partners may have cutting-edge insights on new sanitary products and disinfectants. A manufacturing firm can turn to logistics giants like FedEx to help it chart out effective distribution and logistic mechanisms. In the same vein, a manufacturing firm can contact Dentsu Inc., a marketing house, for help with product promotion and advertising materials.

From the above discussion, it is clear that knowledge can be looked at from different angles, i.e., through various external sources. Therefore, it can be said that the source of knowledge — i.e., endogenous knowledge or exogenous knowledge — is an important dimension of organizational knowledge typology. As noted earlier, the knowledge that resides in customers, suppliers and competitors is called exogenous knowledge. It is essential to adjust external sources of knowledge with an organization's own knowledge. Indeed, Eisenhardt and Santos (2002) argue that organizations in the knowledge economy need to generate dynamic capabilities that rely on combining internal competencies with the know-how of external entities. This discussion on external sources of organizational knowledge helps us to explore another form of classifying organizational knowledge. Hence, an alternative view of organizational knowledge typology will be discussed in turn.

4.4 Alternative View of Knowledge Typology

Knowledge is possessed by people both inside and outside an organization. Given the pivotal importance of exogenous knowledge, it is remarkable that the existing literature has only attracted little and rather fragmented research interest on sources of external knowledge (e.g., Hoerem *et al.*, 1996; Tsoukas, 1996; Petrash, 1996; Bailey and Clarke, 2001; Empson, 2001; Desouza *et al.*, 2005).

Drawing on insights from the extant knowledge management literature, an alternative classification of organizational knowledge is proposed. The alternative theory of organizational knowledge is based on the interactions between the roles of internal forces and external forces of organizational knowledge, which can be called "knowledge by sources". This perspective is considered by observing that several researchers (e.g., McAdam and McCreedy, 2000; Hoerem *et al.*, 1996; Tsoukas, 1996; Bailey and Clarke, 2001) have taken into account, albeit not explicitly, the importance of knowledge from other sources.

Given the significance of exogenous knowledge, four categories of organizational knowledge based on two dimensions — tacitness of knowledge and source of knowledge — can be shown as a two-by-two matrix. These categories of organizational knowledge include endogenous–tacit knowledge, endogenous–explicit knowledge, exogenous–tacit knowledge and exogenous–explicit knowledge, as depicted in Figure 4.3. Each of the quadrants implies a different type of knowledge in either personalized or codified form:

- *Endogenous–tacit knowledge.* Such knowledge remains in the hands and brains of organizational members, and is somewhat difficult to articulate and codify. A classic example of such knowledge is the skills, expertise and experiences of the employees who work in an organization.

	Tacit Knowledge	**Explicit Knowledge**
Endogenous Source	Organizational members' skills Craftspersons' expertise Employees' experiences	Manuals Codes of practice Formal routines and procedures
Exogenous Source	Suppliers' experiences Customers' ideas Competitors' next useful move Researchers' experiences	Suppliers' design manuals Customers' regulatory guidelines Competitors' products and patents Researchers' articles

Figure 4.3 Source-Based Knowledge Model

Source: adapted from Jasimuddin (2005).

- *Endogenous–explicit knowledge.* Such knowledge is codifiable and available in an organization. Organizational members may write down what they know and do, or write a report after attending a meeting, either by themselves or with other colleagues within the organization. This knowledge includes the manuals and codes of practice of a firm.
- *Exogenous–tacit knowledge.* Knowledge that is neither codified nor available within the employees of an organization falls under this category. It resides in the brains of people who are located outside the organization. This kind of knowledge seems to be very hard to gather, articulate, codify and leverage. Such knowledge includes suppliers' experiences, customers' ideas and competitors' next possible useful move.
- *Exogenous–explicit knowledge.* Such knowledge takes an articulated form but does not reside within the firm's own boundary. Rather, such knowledge is available outside the organization in explicit form. This knowledge is closely linked to suppliers' manuals, customers' requirements and competitors' patents.

This typology of organizational knowledge makes a distinction between endogenous knowledge and exogenous knowledge. An organization has limited control over the behavior of external stakeholders. External knowledge sources can range from highly explicit to highly tacit sources. It is argued that endogenous–explicit knowledge seems to be the easiest type of knowledge to acquire and manage because such knowledge is available within an organization in explicit form, whereas exogenous–tacit knowledge seems to be the most difficult to acquire and manage because such knowledge resides outside the organization's boundary in tacit form. Figure 4.4 provides an overall picture of organizational knowledge typologies covering a wide variety of dimensions postulated by various commentators who have focused mainly on the knowledge of organizational members (i.e., endogenous knowledge), along with an alternative view of organizational knowledge that emphasizes exogenous knowledge in addition to endogenous knowledge.

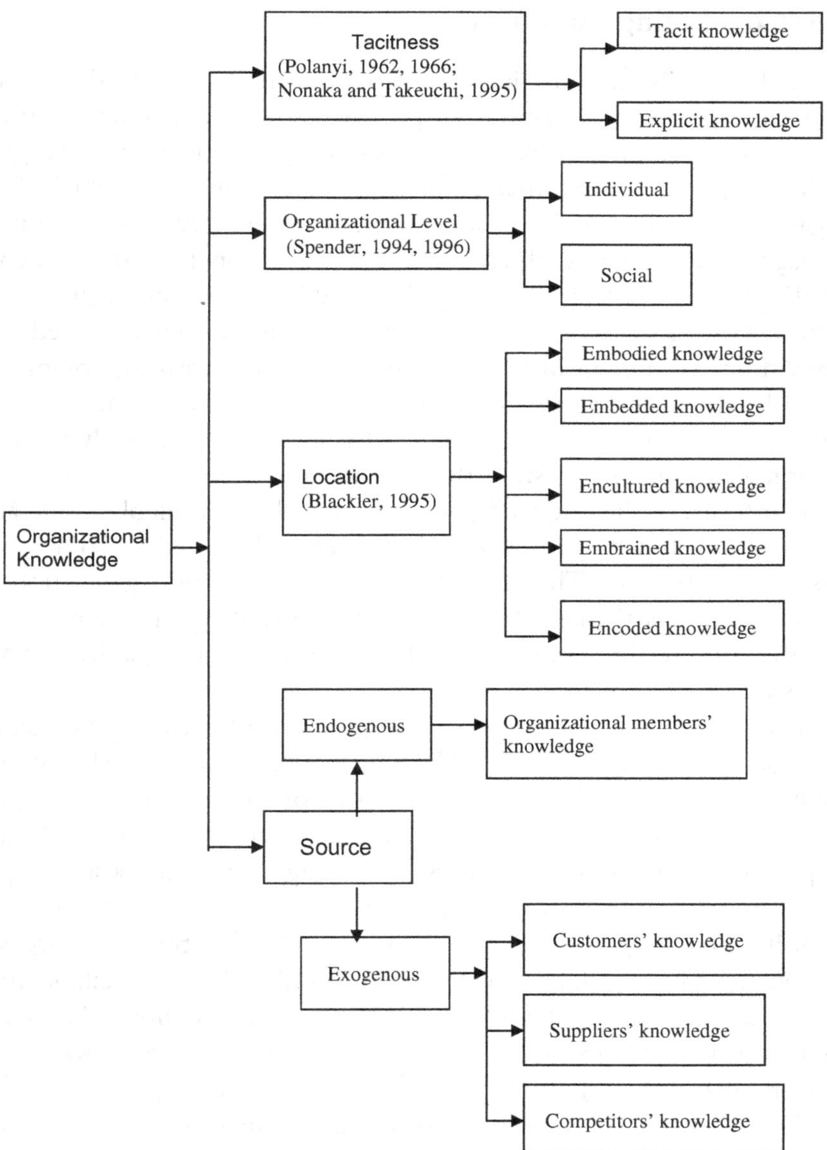

Figure 4.4 Typologies of Organizational Knowledge

4.5 Concluding Summary

Since the 1990s, various theories of organizational knowledge have been developed. This chapter has provided some interesting insights into the nature, dimensions and sources of organizational knowledge. It is widely recognized that employees' knowledge is a vehicle for organizations' competitive advantage. Contemporary knowledge management scholars such as Polanyi (1962), Nonaka and Takeuchi (1995), Spender (1996), and Blackler (1995) have proposed theories of knowledge that have been widely cited. Their theories are based on many different dimensions, notably the degree of tacitness, organizational level and location. However, these authors have concentrated their discussion on the knowledge that is available exclusively within an organization. The existing theories address organizational knowledge in terms of the knowledge that is created and available inside an organization, but have overlooked the role of knowledge from various external sources. The fact is that most theorists of organizational knowledge — particularly Nonaka, Spender and Blackler — have paid less attention to the role of external forces outside an organization as vital sources of knowledge.

Knowledge is actually possessed by people both inside and outside an organization. Against this backdrop, "source-based knowledge" is incorporated as an alternative dimension of organizational knowledge. Source-based knowledge can take various forms, such as employees' knowledge, customers' knowledge, suppliers' knowledge and competitors' knowledge. Organizations need to extract and exploit knowledge from both internal and external sources. Endogenous knowledge is created, transferred and made available for use within organizational members; while exogenous knowledge is all about the knowledge that resides in customers, suppliers and competitors (other than the organization's own knowledge).

By discussing the typologies of organizational knowledge based on various dimensions postulated by organizational theorists, along with an alternative typology of knowledge, this chapter has helped readers understand the role of both endogenous and exogenous sources of knowledge for an organization's success.

Further Reading

Alryalat, H. and Al Hawari, S. (2008). Towards customer knowledge relationship management: integrating knowledge management and customer relationship management process. *Journal of Information and Knowledge Management*, 7(3), 145–157.

Dimitrova, V., Kaneva, M. and Gallucci, T. (2009). Customer knowledge management in the natural cosmetics industry. *Industrial Management & Data Systems*, 109(9), 1155–1165.

Kasabov, E. (2010). The compliant customer. *MIT Sloan Management Review*, 51(3), Spring, 18–19.

References

Andreu, R. and Sieber, S. (2006). External and internal knowledge in organizations. In D. G. Schwartz (ed.), *Encyclopedia of Knowledge Management* (pp. 173–179), Hershey, PA: Idea Group Reference.

Bailey, C. and Clarke, M. (2001). Managing knowledge for personal and organisational benefit. *Journal of Knowledge Management*, 5(1), 58–68.

Balogun, J. and Jenkins, M. (2003). Re-conceiving change management: a knowledge-based perspective. *European Management Journal*, 21(2), 247–257.

Beesley, L. G. (2004). Multi-level complexity in the management of knowledge networks. *Journal of Knowledge Management*, 8(3), 71–100.

Blackler, F. (1995). Knowledge, knowledge work and organizations: an overview and interpretation. *Organization Studies*, 16(6), 1021–1046.

Dawson, R. (2000). *Developing Knowledge-Based Client Relationships: The Future of Professional Services*. Boston: Butterworth-Heinemann.

Desouza, K. C., Awazu, Y. and Jasimuddin, S. M. (2005). Utilizing external sources of knowledge. *Knowledge Management Review*, 8(1), 16–19.

Dyer, J. H. and Singh, H. (1998). The relational view: cooperative strategy and sources of interorganizational competitive advantage. *Academy of Management Review*, 23(4), 660–679.

Edvinsson, L. and Sullivan, P. (1996). Developing a model for managing intellectual capital. *European Management Journal*, 14(4), 356–364.

Eisenhardt, K. M. and Santos, F. M. (2002). Knowledge-based view: a new theory of strategy? In A. Pettigrew, H. Thomas and R. Whittington (eds.), *Handbook of Strategy and Management* (pp. 139–164), London: Sage.

Empson, L. (2001). Fear of exploitation and fear of contamination: impediments to knowledge transfer in mergers between professional service firms. *Human Relations*, 54(7), 839–862.

Grant, R. M. (2006). The knowledge-based view of the firm. In D. O. Faulkner and A. Campbell (eds.), *The Oxford Handbook of Strategy* (pp. 203–231), New York: Oxford University Press.

Gulati, R. (1999). Network location and learning: the influence of network resources and firm capabilities on alliance formation. *Strategic Management Journal*, 20(5), 397–420.

Hoerem, T., von Krogh, G. and Roos, J. (1996). Knowledge-based strategic change. In G. von Krogh and J. Roos (eds.), *Managing Knowledge: Perspectives on Cooperation and Competition* (pp. 116–136), London: Sage.

Jasimuddin, S. M. (2004). Critical assessments of emerging theories of organizational knowledge. Paper presented at the Academy of Management (AOM) Conference, New Orleans, August.

Jasimuddin, S. M. (2005). Knowledge of external sources' knowledge: new frontiers to actionable knowledge. In M. A. Rahim and R. T. Golembiewski (eds.), *Current Topics in Management*, Vol. 10 (pp. 39–50), New Brunswick, NJ: Transaction Publishers.

Li, M. and Gao, F. (2003). Why Nonaka highlights tacit knowledge: a critical review. *Journal of Knowledge Management*, 7(4), 6–14.

Lin, C. and Wu, C. (2005). A knowledge creation model for ISO 9001:2000. *Total Quality Management*, 16(5), 657–670.

Lowendahl, B. R. (1997). *Strategic Management of Professional Service Firms.* Copenhagen: Copenhagen Business School Press.

McAdam, R. and McCreedy, S. (2000). A critique of knowledge management: using a social constructionist model. *New Technology, Work and Employment*, 15(2), 155–168.

Newell, S., Robertson, M., Scarbrough, H. and Swan, J. (2002). *Managing Knowledge Work.* Basingstoke: Palgrave Macmillan.

Nonaka, I. (1991). The knowledge-creating company. *Harvard Business Review*, 69(6), 96–104.

Nonaka, I. (1994). A dynamic theory of organizational knowledge creation. *Organization Science*, 5(1), 14–37.

Nonaka, I. (1998). The knowledge-creating company. In *Harvard Business Review on Knowledge Management* (pp. 21–45), Boston, MA: Harvard Business School Press.

Nonaka, I. and Takeuchi, H. (1995). *The Knowledge-Creating Company: How Japanese Companies Create the Dynamics of Innovation.* Oxford: Oxford University Press.

Nonaka, I., Toyama, R. and Konno, N. (2000). SECI, *ba* and leadership: a unified model of dynamic knowledge creation. *Long Range Planning*, 33, 5–34.

Peña, I. (2002). Intellectual capital and business start-up success. *Journal of Intellectual Capital*, 3, 180–198.

Petrash, G. (1996). Dow's journey to a knowledge value management culture. *European Management Journal*, 14(4), 365–373.

Polanyi, M. (1958). *Personal Knowledge: Towards a Post-Critical Philosophy.* London: Routledge & Kegan Paul.

Polanyi, M. (1962). *Personal Knowledge: Towards a Post-Critical Philosophy.* Chicago, IL: University of Chicago Press.

Polanyi, M. (1966). *The Tacit Dimension.* London: Routledge.

Probst, G. (1998). Practical knowledge management: a model that works. *Prism*, Second Quarter, 17–29.

Serenko, A. and Bontis, N. (2004). Meta-review of knowledge management and intellectual capital literature: citation impact and research productivity rankings. *Knowledge and Process Management*, 11(3), 185–198.

Seufert, A., von Krogh, G. and Bach, A. (1999). Towards knowledge networking. *Journal of Knowledge Management*, 3(3), 180–190.

Spender, J. C. (1994). Organizational knowledge, collective practice and Penrose rents. *International Business Review*, 3(4), 353–367.

Spender, J. C. (1996). Making knowledge the basis of a dynamic theory of the firm. *Strategic Management Journal*, 17(Special Issue), 45–62.

Spender, J. C. (2002). Knowledge, uncertainty, and an emergency theory of the firm. In C. W. Choo and N. Bontis (eds.), *The Strategic Management of Intellectual Capital and Organizational Knowledge* (pp. 149–162), New York: Oxford University Press.

Sveiby, K. E. (1994). Towards a knowledge perspective on organization. Doctoral thesis, University of Stockholm, Stockholm.

Sveiby, K. E. (1996). Transfer of knowledge and the information processing professions. *European Management Journal*, 14(4), 379–388.

Sveiby, K. E. (1997). *The New Organizational Wealth: Managing and Measuring Knowledge-Based Assets.* San Francisco, CA: Berrett-Koehler Publishers.

Thomke, S. and von Hippel, E. (2002). Customers as innovators: a new way to create value. *Harvard Business Review*, 80(4), 74–81.

Tsoukas, H. (1996). The firm as a distributed knowledge system: a constructionist approach. *Strategic Management Journal*, 17(Special Issue), 11–25.

Uzzi, B. and Lancaster, R. (2003). Relational embeddedness and learning: the case of bank loan managers and their clients. *Management Science*, 49(4), 383–399.

Werr, A., Blomberg, J. and Löwstedt, J. (2009). Gaining external knowledge — boundaries in managers' knowledge relations. *Journal of Knowledge Management*, 13(6), 448–463.

Zuboff, S. (1988). *In the Age of the Smart Machine: The Future of Work and Power*. Oxford: Heinemann Professional.

Chapter 5

Organizations in the Knowledge-Based Economy

Knowledge Objectives

After studying this chapter, you should be able to:

- Identify the features of the knowledge-based economy;
- Differentiate agrarian, industrial and knowledge-based societies;
- Explain the typology of organizations in the knowledge-based society;
- Explore the various forms of knowledge-intensive firms; and
- Provide arguments for an organization to be claimed as a knowledge-based organization.

5.1 Introducing the Chapter

Since the 1990s, the concept of the knowledge-based economy has been brought up for a broader discussion in the management literature. Contemporary researchers argue that the society we live in is totally dependent on organizational knowledge, and so several scholars (e.g., Bell, 1979; Starbuck, 1992) have attempted to relabel the post-industrial society as the "knowledge-based society". Katsoulakos and Zevgolis (2004) argue that the knowledge economy (KE) has evolved out of the industrial society; Daniel Bell's (1973) seminal book,

The Coming of Post-Industrial Society, has inspired contemporary scholars (e.g., Toffler, 1990; Reich, 1991; Quinn, 1992; Nonaka and Takeuchi, 1995) to think about the knowledge-based society; while Drucker (1993) traces the roots of the knowledge society back to the period after the Second World War (cited in Bukh *et al.*, 2005).

It is noted that most developed countries are now being regarded as classic examples of a successfully restructured "services-oriented knowledge economy". Parallel to this, Ward (2002) contends that, in the post-industrial knowledge age, organizations have shifted their focus from being product-oriented to knowledge-oriented in the sense that organizations compete in processes and innovations rather than in products.

Bell (1979) claims that knowledge is the key resource of the post-industrial era. As a result, an emerging trend is observed showing the relative decline of capital- and labor-intensive organizations in favor of knowledge-intensive organizations (Starbuck, 1992). A World Bank (1998) report states that knowledge has become perhaps the most important factor in determining one's standard of living — more so than land, capital and labor. As the knowledge society unfolds, organizations are now starting to think seriously about knowledge, its value, and the way in which knowledge can be managed. Reflecting this view, Katsoulakos and Zevgolis (2004) argue that today we live in a global knowledge economy, meaning that value creation for an organization is predominantly based on its knowledge-driven activities (e.g., knowledge creation and exchange).

Some scholars (e.g., Porat, 1977; Earl, 1996; Hayes-Roth *et al.*, 1983) have reclassified employment categories to accommodate knowledge work, claiming that knowledge is a source whose refinement and reproduction create wealth, and that information technology (IT) is an enabler that turns knowledge into a valuable industrial product. In line with this, contemporary researchers (e.g., Jashapara, 2005; Bukh *et al.*, 2005) argue that the introduction of information technologies, such as computers and the Internet, has resulted in greater awareness of the importance of knowledge in the 21st-century economy. As Jashapara (2005) points out, "The rapid advance of information technology and telecommunications in the last decade and the relative decline of capital and labour-intensive industries has meant that many Western economies are emerging into knowledge economies".

In the early 1960s, Peter Drucker coined the terms "knowledge work" and "knowledge worker" (see Drucker, 1973). More recently, Starbuck (1992) similarly argued that there is now an emerging trend towards the displacement of routine work by knowledge work. Today, the majority of the global workforce is engaged in the knowledge-based service sector. In this regard, Drucker (1993, p. 4) suggests that knowledge work has become the "central resource of a developed economy"; and knowledge workers, "the central workforce". Knowledge workers form a vital part of the knowledge economy; however, the definition of knowledge worker varies greatly. The OECD (1996) defines the knowledge worker as belonging to the group of scientists, engineers, information and communication technology (ICT) specialists, and technicians who generate knowledge. Moreover, the OECD (1996) states that knowledge workers form the dominant sector of Western workforces. In fact, about 70% of the global workforce is now engaged in knowledge-based service activities.

It is observed that the majority of organizations are now engaged in knowledge management practices. This chapter will present an overview of the features of the knowledge economy (KE). Section 5.2 will explain the differences between agrarian, industrial and knowledge (post-industrial) economies. Next, the categories of organizations based on "knowledge intensity" will be elaborated in Section 5.3. There are scholars who view that the terms "knowledge-based organization", "knowledge-intensive firm", "professional service firm" and "knowledge-creating company" are synonymous; while others argue that these organizations are actually different, providing some interesting insights into the nature of these organizations. Section 5.4 will provide arguments in favor of the claim that all organizations in the knowledge society are knowledge-based organizations. Finally, the chapter will end with concluding remarks in Section 5.5.

5.2 The Notion of the Knowledge-Based Economy

Whenever the knowledge-based society is discussed, the notion of organizational knowledge is treated as a source of the highest-quality power. In this regard, scholars (e.g., Toffler, 1990; Drucker, 1993; Reich, 1991; Quinn, 1992; Nonaka and Takeuchi, 1995) actually talk about a society in which knowledge is the key strategic resource for an organization. This has coincided with the development of the "knowledge-based view of the firm", as postulated by Grant (1997). According to Grant (1997), the transition from an industrial society to a knowledge-based society has been driven by an increasing focus on knowledge as the most important component for organizations. This, then, begs the question: What is meant by the emerging knowledge economy, which is already referred to as the post-industrial society?

Hislop (2005) defines the knowledge-based economy as a society where knowledge-based goods and services have replaced manufactured goods as the main wealth generators for a firm. Reflecting this view, Jashapara (2005) mentions that there has been a relative decline in capital- and labor-intensive industries. Countries like the USA and the UK are considered as examples of services-oriented knowledge economies. In line with this, Lundvall and Borras (1998) observe that a "new view" of organizations has evolved that focuses on the way in which the traditional distinction between manufacturing and services is becoming increasingly blurred in the new economy. Likewise, Drucker (1993, p. 8) predicts that "[t]he basic economic resource … is and will be knowledge", whereby the uniqueness of the knowledge society is that knowledge "has become the resource, rather than a resource".

In the early years of the 21st century, the knowledge society has emerged as a tangible reality of the corporate landscape. Probst *et al.* (2000, p. 3) state that organizational knowledge is the critical factor in the present economy, as compared with land in the agrarian society and capital in the industrial society. There are several characteristics that constitute the knowledge society and help to differentiate it from the other two societies. These characteristics will be identified in turn.

5.2.1 *Features of the Agrarian, Industrial and Knowledge Societies*

Generally speaking, the agrarian and the industrial societies were characterized by an emphasis on land and capital, respectively. The knowledge society, however, is characterized by an emphasis on knowledge and ideas. Drucker (1992, p. 95), for example, asserts: "In this society, knowledge is the primary resource for individuals and for the economy overall. Land, labor, and capital — the economist's traditional factors of production — do not disappear, but they become secondary". In the contemporary world, the central value-adding activities are neither the allocation of capital to productive uses nor labor. To be sure, every organization requires knowledge in varying degrees. In this regard, the contrast between agricultural firms, the oil industry and the computer software development industry can help to illustrate the differences between these three societies.

There are a few studies (e.g., Sasser *et al.*, 1978; Fuchs, 1968; Mills and Moberg, 1982; Lowendahl *et al.*, 2001) that have led to two widely cited distinctions between service-oriented organizations and manufacturing enterprises:

- Differences in the underlying production processes, i.e., knowledge resource versus traditional factors of production (labor and capital); and
- Differences in the nature of outputs, i.e., intangible heterogeneous products (knowledge-based) versus tangible homogeneous products (manufactured).

In the knowledge society, the biggest sector is the service sector and the largest source of employment is the knowledge worker. As Drucker (1993) puts it: "Knowledge-intensive firms are the organizations in which knowledge workers have high levels of education and specialist skills and combine this expertise with the ability to identify and solve problems". Likewise, Alvesson (2001) describes knowledge-intensive firms as organizations where most work is said to be of an intellectual nature and where well-educated, qualified employees form the major part of the workforce in order to produce quality products and/or services. Contrarily, the farming sector dominated in the agrarian society and the agricultural worker was the biggest source of employment in that society; while in the industrial society, the manufacturing sector was the dominant sector and the industrial worker was the largest source of employment.

Rifkin (2000) argues that ownership of physical capital mattered most in the industrial society, while intellectual capital is treated as the driving force in the post-capitalist society. As mentioned previously, the key characteristic of the knowledge economy is knowledge. Unlike physical assets, knowledge can often be transferred and used for different purposes on a global scale. The main economic challenge of the knowledge society, therefore, is the productivity of knowledge work and knowledge workers. In this context, the argument of Mellahi *et al.* (2005), for example, is very relevant:

> In the oil industry, a company's wealth is largely determined by the physical control of oil fields, oil tankers, and petrol stations. In the software industry, a company's wealth is determined by the intellectual ownership of computer programs and the creativity of its staff. The physical location of oil fields and petrol stations plays a huge role, whereas a software programmer can work anywhere.

The differences between the agrarian, industrial and knowledge economies are summarized in Table 5.1.

The knowledge society has now become an accepted reality of the present-day business landscape. As a result, the knowledge economy has an impact on the way in which organizations operate. Against this backdrop, Drucker (1992) suggests that competing in the new knowledge society requires a new paradigm of management in order to enhance the effectiveness of knowledge work in knowledge-based organizations. Consequently, organizations need to take the following issues into account so as to ensure their survival and growth

Table 5.1 Salient Features of the Agrarian, Industrial and Knowledge Economies

Features	Agrarian Society	Industrial Society	Knowledge Society
Key production factor	Land	Capital	Knowledge
Wealth base of organizations	Ownership of land	Holding of capital and the latest technology	Possession of knowledge (particularly tacit)
Primary products	Anything extracted from farming, breeding and mining	Manufactured goods	Intangible products (e.g., software, corporate solutions)
Main sector	Agricultural sector	Manufacturing sector	Service sector
Main occupation	Farmer	Factory worker	Knowledge worker
Goals	Ensuring maximum production	Reaching economies of scale	Enhancing quality of service

(Katsoulakos and Zevgolis, 2004; Quinn, 1992; Probst *et al.*, 2000; Eisenhardt and Santos, 2002):

- *Knowledge-sharing and learning culture.* Several scholars (e.g., Katsoulakos and Zevgolis, 2004) suggest that the emergence of the knowledge-based economy requires some sort of training and learning for employees at all levels in knowledge-based organizations. Such training and learning sessions seem to help increase one's capability to manage knowledge-based activities (Quinn, 1992).
- *Adequate investment.* It is essential to make a huge investment in managing the knowledge assets of an organization. Organizations operating in the knowledge economy must invest more to manage organizational knowledge. Probst *et al.* (2000, p. 3) suggest that it is much more profitable for an organization to make a large investment in managing its knowledge assets than to spend the same amount on material assets.

- *Compatible organizational design.* The emerging knowledge economy itself is increasingly dynamic. In this scenario, organizations must be flexible and accommodative. Instead of focusing on their formal structure, organizations need to be more flexible and resilient so that they can cope with the rapid pace of change in the turbulent global environment. Resonating with this view, Eisenhardt and Santos (2002) argue that organizations in the knowledge economy need to generate dynamic capabilities which rely on combining internal competencies with the know-how of exogenous forces.

Arthur (1996, p. 100) provides a comprehensive picture to help us understand what the knowledge society is, further arguing that the knowledge-based society is moving:

- beyond bulk-material manufacturing to designing new technologies;
- beyond processing physical resources to processing knowledge; and
- beyond applying raw energy to applying ideas.

Although the majority of scholars believe in the existence of the knowledge-based society in the 21st century, the notion of the knowledge society is not totally free from criticism. In this regard, Hislop (2002, 2005) provides a long list of criticisms of the knowledge society, which are succinctly mentioned below:

- Knowledge work is merged with service-sector jobs; however, all service-sector employment cannot be knowledge-intensive work. While some service-sector work (such as consultancy, research, etc.) can be classified as being knowledge-intensive, other types of service work (such as security, office cleaning, fast food restaurant work, etc.) are low-skilled, repetitive and routine (Thompson *et al.*, 2001; Hislop, 2005).
- Hislop (2005) rejects the claim that employment growth has occurred mainly in knowledge-intensive occupations. The fact is that growth in professional occupations still only accounts for 20%

of all employment. Moreover, Thompson *et al.* (2001) add that employment growth has been equally significant in other routine, low-skilled occupations.

5.3 Organizations in the Knowledge Economy

As mentioned earlier, there has been an emerging trend towards the displacement of capital- and labor-intensive organizations by knowledge-intensive organizations, and of routine work by knowledge work (Starbuck, 1992; Jashapara, 2005). Accordingly, the growth of knowledge-based organizations in the global economy is visible (Windrum and Tomlinson, 1999; Lundvall and Borras, 1998). The involvement of the global workforce in knowledge-based service activities indicates the importance of knowledge-based organizations. In his book, *The Coming of Post-Industrial Society*, Bell (1973) argues that the expanding importance of knowledge-based organizations is essential to the vision of a knowledge-based society. Similarly, Binney (2001) contends that "becoming a knowledge-based organization is seen as an obligatory condition of success for organizations as they enter the era of the knowledge economy".

However, numerous contradictions in knowledge-based organizations are apparent in the relevant literature. The idea of the knowledge-intensive firm, for example, seems to overlap with the notion of other service organizations. It is found in the relevant literature that the term "knowledge-intensive firm" has been used interchangeably with "professional service firm", "knowledge-based organization", "human asset-intensive firm", "knowledge-creating company" and "knowledge-intensive business service". The fact is that there is no clear-cut single framework of organizations in the knowledge-based society. Nevertheless, it is important to have such a framework so as to explain what features a knowledge-creating company, for instance, possesses, and how it relates to other service-based knowledge organizations — namely, knowledge-intensive firms or professional service firms. The rest of this section will address the various forms of organizations in the knowledge-based society.

5.3.1 *Typology of Organizations Based on Knowledge Intensity*

In recent organizational studies and knowledge management literature, organizations have been labeled either as knowledge-based organizations (Alvesson, 2001; Winch and Schneider, 1993; Holsapple and Whinston, 1987; Blackler, 1995), knowledge-intensive firms (Starbuck, 1992), professional service firms (Empson, 2001; Morris, 2001), human asset-intensive firms (Coff, 1995), knowledge-intensive business services (Bettencourt *et al.*, 2002; Larsen, 2001) or knowledge-creating companies (Nonaka and Takeuchi, 1995; Choo, 1996). For example, while discussing the typology of organizational knowledge, Blackler (1995) sets out different types of organizations as follows:

- Expert-dependent organizations (professional bureaucracy such as a hospital);
- Knowledge-routinized organizations (machine bureaucracy such as a traditional factory);
- Communication-intensive organizations (adhocracy innovation-mediated production); and
- Symbolic-analyst-dependent organizations (knowledge-intensive firms such as a software consultancy).

As a useful starting point, the following subsections will attempt to explore whether the terms "knowledge-based organization", "knowledge-intensive firm", "professional service firm" and "knowledge-creating company" are synonymous or different, and provide some interesting insights into the nature of these organizations.

5.3.2 *Knowledge-Based Organization (KBO)*

Leading management theoreticians (e.g., Brown and Duguid, 1998) argue that all types of organizations — whether they be manufacturing or service-based — appear to be knowledge-based organizations, since they are involved to some degree in the acquisition, sharing, creation, storage, retrieval and utilization of relevant and actionable knowledge. Brown and Duguid (1998), for example, postulate that all organizations are in essence knowledge-based organizations.

The idea that all organizations and their employees at various levels use knowledge to some extent is becoming increasingly accepted; thus, employees can be considered as knowledge workers and their organizations as knowledge-based organizations. In this regard, Morris and Empson (1998) argue that professional service firms, such as accounting and consulting enterprises, can be thought of as classic examples of knowledge-based service organizations. However, it is not only consulting firms that can claim to be knowledge-based organizations. All other organizations also fall under the category of knowledge-based organizations, because each of them views knowledge as the most critical resource for the firm to survive and compete in the knowledge-based economy. Moreover, every organization needs to share knowledge more easily among its employees and also make stored knowledge more accessible throughout the organization (Jasimuddin, 2005); the advent of information and communication technology (ICT) has made this task possible and easier.

Although all organizations require knowledge in varying degrees, there are two widely cited distinctions between organizations in the industrial and knowledge societies: factors of production (i.e., traditional factors of production versus knowledge) and nature of products (i.e., homogeneous products versus heterogeneous outputs). Knowledge-based organizations encompass a vast array of different types of operations across service sectors. Organizations dealing with law, management consulting, accountancy and auditing, financial services, creative advertising and public relations, architectural and engineering consulting, research, media (newspapers, periodicals, television and radio), and software development are just a few examples of knowledge-based organizations.

5.3.3 *Knowledge-Intensive Firm (KIF)*

In the relevant literature, several contemporary management theorists (e.g., Empson, 2001; Morris, 2001; Alvesson, 2001; Winch and

Schneider, 1993; Coff, 1995; Nonaka and Takeuchi, 1995; Choo, 1996; Bettencourt *et al.*, 2002; Larsen, 2001) state that the term "knowledge-intensive firm" has been used interchangeably with "knowledge-based organization". In fact, knowledge-intensive firms are organizations in which knowledge is used to solve complex problems in order to provide a differentiated range of solutions to customers (Ekstedt, 1989; Hedberg, 1990).

Several researchers — most notably Hinings *et al.* (1991), Starbuck (1992), Winch and Schneider (1993), Alvesson (2001) and Nurmi (1998) — have attempted to define knowledge-intensive firms as a distinct category of organizations. Starbuck (1992), for instance, defines a knowledge-intensive firm as an entity where employees possess outstanding expertise that helps in making important contributions to enhance the competitive advantage of the firm. As Drucker (1993) puts it: "Knowledge-intensive firms are the organizations in which knowledge workers have high levels of education and specialist skills and combine this expertise with the ability to identify and solve problems".

Table 5.2 lists a sample of definitions of knowledge-intensive firms as provided by management scholars. It is evident from the table that there is no underlying definitional consensus in the usage of the term "knowledge-intensive firm". This is further supported by Newell *et al.* (2002, p. 26), who contend that "a precise definition of a knowledge-intensive firm is elusive and it is clear from the term itself that it is a socially constructed, broad-ranging and yet quite ambiguous concept".

Edvinsson and Sullivan (1996) emphasize the use of employees' knowledge as a source of an organization's competitive advantage. It appears that such a firm derives its profits from the commercialization of the knowledge created by its employees. Resonating with this view, Lowendahl (1997) argues that knowledge-intensive firms rely heavily on expert knowledge, embedded in intangible products and services, to compete. Likewise, Alvesson (2001) characterizes a knowledge-intensive firm as an organization where most work is said to be of an intellectual nature and where well-educated, qualified employees form the major part of the workforce in order to produce quality products and/or services.

Table 5.2 Knowledge-Intensive Firm Defined

Authors	Definitions
Alvesson (2001)	One that is said to be of an intellectual nature where well-educated, qualified employees form the major part of its workforce, which produces quality products and/or services
Drucker (1993)	One where knowledge workers have high levels of education and specialist skills, and have the ability to identify and solve problems
Edvinsson and Sullivan (1996)	One where knowledge is created by its employees and used as a source of competitive advantage; hence, its profits are derived from the commercialization of the knowledge
Empson (2001)	One that is primarily concerned with the application of specialist technical knowledge to create customized solutions to clients' problems
Lowendahl (1997)	One that relies heavily on expert knowledge to produce intangible products and services
Starbuck (1992)	One that requires the exceptional expertise of its members, whose knowledge makes important contributions
Winch and Schneider (1993)	One where the expertise of its staff is its sole trading asset in providing standardized intangible services and in trading independently with corporate clients

Source: adapted from Jasimuddin *et al.* (2005).

However, Newell *et al.* (2002) disagree with the claim that the skills and expertise required in all types of knowledge-intensive firms are necessarily acquired through formal education and qualifications. These scholars bring up the example of a software developer: in order to become a software developer or web designer, one does not need to have a degree in computer science. What is of most importance is that he or she is actually engaged in primary value-generating activities, which consist of the accumulation, creation, transfer, storage and use of knowledge, for the purpose of developing a customized service or product and to satisfy the existing and potential clients' needs (Bettencourt *et al.*, 2002; Davenport *et al.*, 1996; Starbuck, 1992).

Winch and Schneider (1993) suggest three criteria that must be fulfilled so as to treat an organization as a knowledge-intensive firm:

- The expertise of employees, which is regarded as the central asset that a knowledge-intensive firm needs to have for its business;
- The standardized intangibility of a knowledge-intensive firm's services that it renders to its clients; and
- The tendency of a knowledge-intensive firm to deal independently with potential corporate customers.

Similarly, Apostolou and Mentzas (1999) reinforce this point of view by suggesting that knowledge-intensive firms share some common characteristics, which include:

- Their "products" are intangible, i.e., they do not consist of goods but of complex problem-solving services;
- Their "production process" is non-standardized and highly dependent on teamwork;
- The majority of their employees are educated and creative people; and
- Their customers are treated individually.

Hence, the term "knowledge-intensive firm" is used to describe an organization that can produce outstanding results with the help of exceptional expertise. In other words, the knowledge worker is the core competency of such an organization. Knowledge-intensive firms are typically involved in a variety of activities, from law and accounting to architectural engineering, research and development (R&D), consulting (management and computer), advertising, and software design. In this context, Lowendahl (1997), for example, identifies three generic types of knowledge-intensive firms:

- Organizations premised on their strategic focus, i.e., client relations (e.g., law and accountancy practices);

Table 5.3 Key Elements of a Knowledge-Intensive Firm

Key Elements	Descriptions	Sources
Input (knowledge)	A knowledge-intensive firm requires the exceptional expertise of its employees.	Starbuck (1992), Drucker (1993), Winch and Schneider (1993), Edvinsson and Sullivan (1996), Lowendahl (1997), Lowendahl *et al.* (2001), Morris and Empson (1998), Empson (2001), Alvesson (2001)
Activities	A knowledge-intensive firm has the ability to identify and solve problems through processing knowledge with corporate clients. It effectively makes sense, creates knowledge and makes decisions.	Drucker (1993), Winch and Schneider (1993), Choo (1996), Edvinsson and Sullivan (1996)
Output	A knowledge-intensive firm delivers intangible solutions to clients' problems and derives its profits from the commercialization of knowledge.	Winch and Schneider (1993), Lowendahl (1997), Morris and Empson (1998), Alvesson (2001)

Source: adapted from Jasimuddin (2006).

- Organizations premised on creative, problem-solving innovations (e.g., advertising agencies, software development firms); and
- Organizations premised on the adaptation of ready solutions (e.g., large management consultancy firms).

Based on the views of researchers, the key issues with respect to the term "knowledge-intensive firm" can be extracted as shown in Table 5.3. Indeed, Table 5.3 reinforces Grant's (1997) argument regarding knowledge-based organizations.

5.3.4 *Professional Service Firm (PSF)*

Another important form of knowledge-based organizations is the professional service firm. According to Morris and Empson (1998, p. 610), the term "professional service firm" refers to an organization that trades mainly on the knowledge of its human capital (i.e., its employees) to develop and deliver intangible solutions to clients' problems. One can narrowly categorize professional service firms as a specific kind of knowledge-intensive firm.

In fact, the notion of the professional service firm seems to overlap with that of the various service organizations, especially the knowledge-intensive firm. In this regard, Empson (2001) highlights the application of specialist technical knowledge in professional service firms to the creation of customized solutions to clients' problems. Newell *et al.* (2002) reinforce this point of view by contending that professional service firms, such as law and accountancy firms, tend to be seen as a subset of knowledge-intensive firms. The very large, global consultancies, such as Accenture, IBM Business Consulting Services, Ernst & Young and KPMG, tend to resemble professional service firms.

Several other researchers (e.g., Maister, 1982; Greenwood *et al.*, 1990; Hinings *et al.*, 1991; Empson, 2001; Alvesson, 2001; Lowendahl *et al.*, 2001) have also devoted their attention to professional service firms, arguing that such firms emphasize the following properties ascribed to a profession (besides expertise):

- A code of ethics;
- Standardized education;
- A strong professional association;
- Cohesion;
- Monopolization of the labor market through entry restrictions; and
- Autonomy.

Whilst the various categories of knowledge-intensive firms may overlap, the above features ascribed to professions are not necessarily apparent in all knowledge-intensive firms. These requirements — codes of ethics, strong professional affiliations and specific educational entry requirements — lead to restricted access in professional service firms. However, these requirements need not, and do not, exist in many other knowledge-intensive firms. People working in management consulting and software engineering firms, for example, do not qualify as recognized professionals (Starbuck, 1992); on the other hand, law firms, accountancy practices, technical engineering firms and architectural practices are all good examples of professional service firms. Prospective employees need to qualify for professional certificates in order to work in such organizations. Therefore, it could be argued that professional service firms are actually a subset of knowledge-intensive firms. Starbuck (1992, p. 717) supports this argument, suggesting:

> An expert may not be a professional, and a KIF may not be a professional firm. Professionals have specialized expertise that they gain through training or experience, and KIFs may employ people who have specialized expertise. Thus, KIFs may be professional firms. Many KIFs are not professional firms, however. One reason is that not all experts belong to recognized professions.

5.3.5 *Knowledge-Creating Company (KCC)*

Knowledge-creating companies are an important subset of companies within the knowledge-intensive firm category. Hedberg (1990) contends that one of the striking factors of knowledge-intensive firms is their capacity to solve complex problems through creative and innovative solutions. Such knowledge-intensive firms were popularly labeled by Nonaka and Takeuchi (1995) as "knowledge-creating companies", which has since been widely used by other knowledge management scholars.

Since knowledge plays a great role in innovative organizations (Scarbrough, 1995), knowledge-creating companies tend to engage themselves in such a way to promote innovation and, in some instances, creativity. Thus, "innovative organizations" and "knowledge-creating companies" can be used synonymously. As Apostolou and Mentzas (1999) argue, knowledge-intensive firms create innovative solutions for potential customers by integrating the knowledge of their individuals. Reflecting this view, Civi (2000) argues that "a knowledge-creating company can find new and better ways to perform, work together in a team, share a vision, fill gaps of knowledge, increase productivity, satisfy customers and ultimately compete". Management consulting firms, research groups, media agencies and software development firms are all good examples of knowledge-creating companies. More specifically, Ernst & Young's Center for Business Innovation and IBM Hursley Laboratory are typical examples of knowledge-creating companies that always come up with new ideas, new knowledge and new ways of doing things.

According to Civi (2000), in the knowledge world there are two types of organizations: knowledge-intensive firms and knowledge-creating firms. However, other scholars tend to see knowledge-creating companies as a subset of knowledge-intensive firms. It is argued here that professional service firms and knowledge-creating companies are both specific kinds or subsets of knowledge-intensive firms, as shown in Figure 5.1.

Having discussed the various forms of knowledge-based organizations, I shall next provide arguments in favor of the claim that all organizations in the knowledge society are knowledge-based organizations.

5.4 Knowledge Intensity Continuum

As mentioned earlier, there is considerable variation in the descriptions of knowledge-based organizations. Some categories of knowledge-based organizations are broader in scope, while the features ascribed to a particular form of organization are not necessarily apparent in other forms of knowledge-based organizations. Nevertheless, one feature that all of the knowledge-based organizations have in common is knowledge (albeit in varying degrees). The fact is that knowledge ranks first in the hierarchy of a knowledge-based

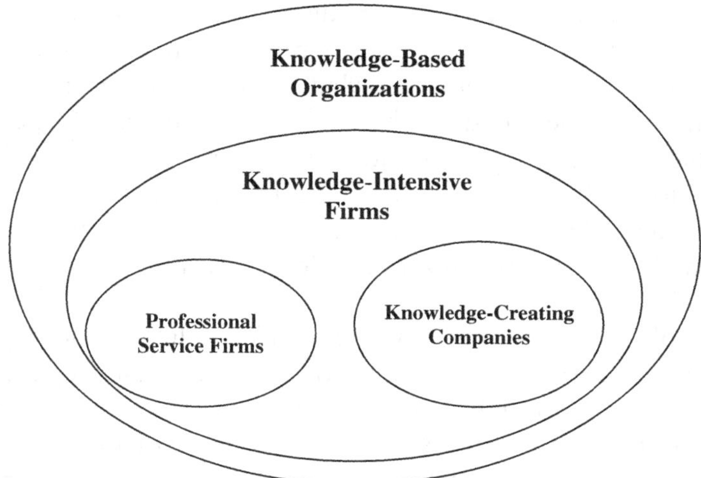

Figure 5.1 Categories of Firms Under Knowledge-Based Organizations
Source: adapted from Jasimuddin (2006).

organization's resources. In this context, the argument of Grant (1996), for example, is very relevant, in which he states that "the knowledge base of such organizations represents both an input in terms of the expertise residing in the organization and it is an output in the form of products or services generated to solve client problems".

In their influential book, *The Knowledge-Creating Company*, Nonaka and Takeuchi (1995) point out that the management of innovation is an ongoing process in which organizations create problems, define them, and then develop new knowledge for solutions. Reflecting this view, Nurmi (1998, p. 28) argues: "Creativity rather than automation is the key to productivity. ... Knowledge workers tend to believe that the organization serves as a springboard for their learning".

It should be mentioned that the notion of knowledge-based organizations was initially borrowed from the notion of service organizations and then reinterpreted in many ways, with the dimension of "knowledge intensity" positioned along a continuum.

Knowledge-based organizations are dedicated to innovation, creativity and the delivery of customized products to their customers. Among these organizations, knowledge-creating companies appear to be at the highest end of the "knowledge intensity" spectrum, given that their ability to innovate can often provide essentially new ways of doing things in relation to products, processes, people and technologies. Figure 5.2 depicts the placement of various forms of knowledge-based organizations along the knowledge intensity continuum.

By looking at Figure 5.2, we can conceptualize various forms of organizations based on the degree of possession and utilization of knowledge. Interestingly, there is another new concept in the emerging knowledge-based society that is also evolving as a powerful form of knowledge-based organizations. This form of organization is popularly termed "hybrid organization", which will be dealt with next.

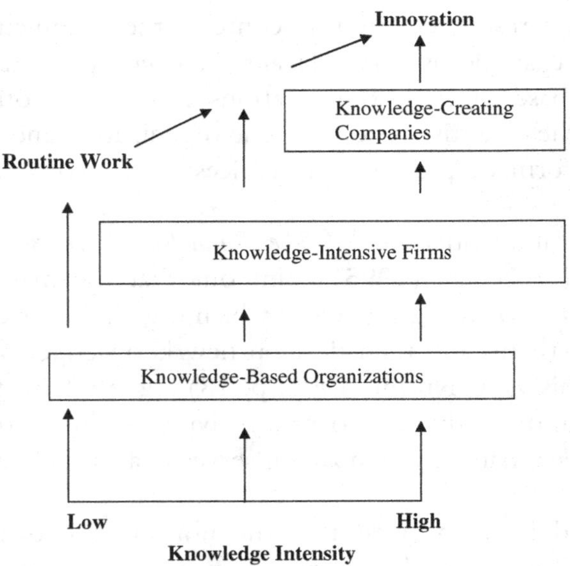

Figure 5.2 Organizations on the Knowledge Intensity Continuum

Source: adapted from Jasimuddin (2006).

5.4.1 *The Notion of Hybrid Organizations in the Knowledge Economy*

As noted earlier, knowledge ranks first in the hierarchy of resources in a knowledge-based organization. However, organizations in the knowledge-based society are so intertwined that sometimes it is difficult to separate one form of organization from another. Nonetheless, what is of more importance is that an organization must have, at the very least, basic attributes and capabilities that can be used to label it either as a knowledge-intensive firm or a knowledge-creating company. These basic attributes include the following:

- The critical asset of such an organization is knowledge;
- The employees of such an organization maintain face-to-face interaction with clients; and
- Such an organization provides intangible output.

It has already been noted that knowledge-intensive firms tend to be service-oriented organizations that often compete in their respective sectors based on their ability to solve complex problems and provide customized solutions. However, there are some manufacturing organizations that not only produce tangible products but also provide services by selling the knowledge, know-how and skills of their employees in the name of providing customized solutions. Such organizations are termed "hybrid organizations", or what Quinn (1992) calls "intelligent enterprises".

Hybrid organizations are initially established not as service-based organizations, but then eventually turn into knowledge-creating companies due to their enormous engagement in research and development (R&D) activities. Along with their usual routine work, innovation thus becomes a part of their tasks. As Clark *et al.* (1992) put it: "Innovation, which is a good example of knowledge work, is actually dependent on the creation and application of organizational knowledge that moves from initial awareness of new ideas to the implementation of it".

If the implementation of such ideas is found to be successful, then these can be utilized in the form of new products or services. Subsequently, these ideas are then used routinely throughout the organization, at which point they would no longer be referred to as innovation, as suggested by scholars such as Clark and Staunton (1989) and Rogers (1995). For instance, IBM, Buckman Laboratories, Nokia and Sharp are examples of hybrid organizations that rely heavily on physical capital as well as human capital (knowledge) to deliver their products and services. Figure 5.3 depicts the schematic representation of organizations in the knowledge economy.

It is evident that knowledge-based organizations perceive themselves as knowledge-intensive and fully recognize knowledge as a critical asset. Choo (1996) argues that knowledge-based organizations

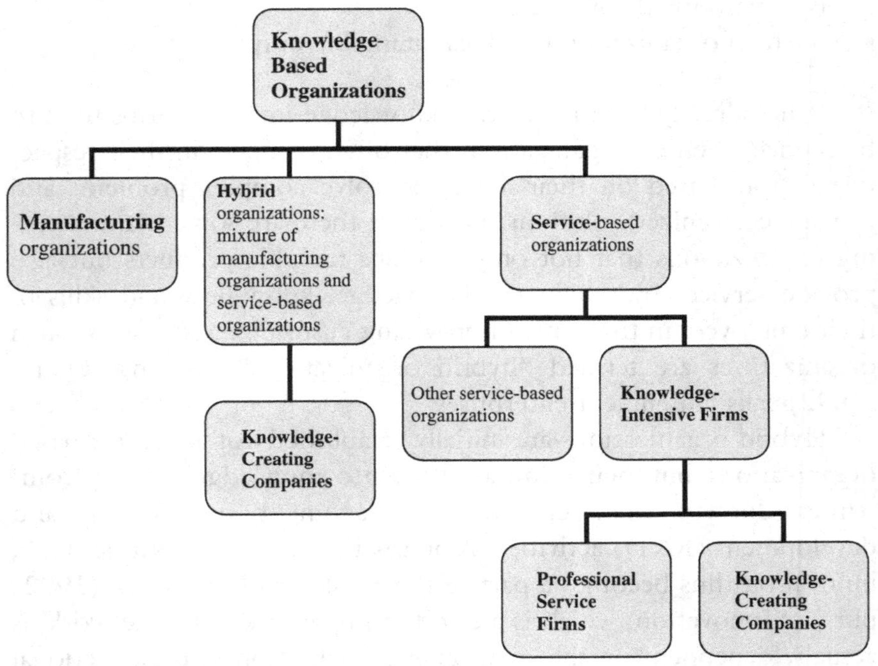

Figure 5.3 Organizations in the Knowledge-Based Society

Source: adapted from Jasimuddin (2006).

can effectively integrate sense making, knowledge creation and decision making, since they possess knowledge. The above discussion supports the claim that all organizations, be they in the service sector or the manufacturing sector, do possess some common features as far as managing knowledge is concerned. Hence, the notion of hybrid organization is thought to be an alternative form of knowledge-based organizations in the knowledge-driven economy.

5.5 Concluding Summary

As a useful starting point, this chapter has raised awareness of the existence of the knowledge-based society, presenting a discussion on the notion of the knowledge economy along with its features. The knowledge-based economy has become an accepted reality of the present-day business landscape. A key characteristic of the knowledge economy is organizational knowledge. Accordingly, knowledge workers form a vital part of the knowledge economy. Knowledge — rather than other factors of production — has become the critical resource, as knowledge workers provide the driving force for innovation and productivity improvements in goods and services.

There are various terms associated with knowledge-based organizations that have evolved in the knowledge-driven economy. It is observed that several scholars use the terms "knowledge-based organization", "knowledge-intensive firm", "professional service firm" and "knowledge-creating company" synonymously in the knowledge management literature. The existing literature provides some isolated descriptions where these terms seem to be, consciously or unconsciously, used interchangeably. This chapter has offered some interesting insights into the nature of these organizations. Some categories of knowledge-based organizations are broader in scope, while the features ascribed to a particular form of organization are not necessarily apparent in other forms of knowledge-based organizations.

Given that there are authors who view these organizations differently, and that the characteristics of the various knowledge-based organizations are quite different, there is therefore considerable variation in the descriptions of knowledge-based organizations. This chapter has sought to clarify whether these organizations are different or similar. However, the one common feature that all knowledge-based organizations possess is knowledge (albeit in varying degrees). Knowledge ranks first in the hierarchy of a knowledge-based organization's resources. Although the organizations in the knowledge-based society are so intertwined that it may be difficult to separate one form of organization from another, what is of more importance is that each organization must have at least some basic attributes and capabilities that can be used to label it as a knowledge-intensive firm or a knowledge-creating company. These basic attributes include the fact that the organization's critical asset is knowledge, it maintains face-to-face interaction with clients, and it provides intangible output.

Further Reading

Hansson, F. (2007). Science parks as knowledge organizations — the "ba" in action? *European Journal of Innovation Management*, 10(3), 348–366.

Jasimuddin, S. M. (2008). Is there a knowledge economy? Paper presented at the 15th Annual International Conference on Advances in Management, Boston, July.

Malhotra, N. and Morris, T. (2009). Heterogeneity in professional service firms. *Journal of Management Studies*, 46(6), September, 895–922.

Von Nordenflycht, A. (2010). What is a professional service firm? Toward a theory and taxonomy of knowledge-intensive firms. *Academy of Management Review*, 35(1), January, 155–174.

Woiceshyn, J. and Falkenberg, L. (2008). Value creation in knowledge-based firms: aligning problems and resources. *Academy of Management Perspectives*, 22(2), May, 85–99.

References

Alvesson, M. (2001). Knowledge work: ambiguity, image and identity. *Human Relations*, 54(7), 863–886.

Apostolou, D. and Mentzas, G. (1999). Managing corporate knowledge: a comparative analysis of experiences in consulting firms. Part 1. *Knowledge and Process Management*, 6(3), 129–138.

Arthur, W. B. (1996). Increasing returns and the new world of business. *Harvard Business Review*, 74(4), 100–109.

Bell, D. (1973). *The Coming of Post-Industrial Society*. Harmondsworth: Penguin.

Bell, D. (1979). Thinking ahead: communication technology — for better or for worse. *Harvard Business Review*, 57(3), May/June, 20–42.

Bettencourt, L. A., Ostrom, A. L., Brown, S. W. and Roundtree, R. I. (2002). Client co-production in knowledge-intensive business services. *California Management Review*, 44(4), 100–128.

Binney, D. (2001). The knowledge management spectrum — understanding the KM landscape. *Journal of Knowledge Management*, 5(1), 33–42.

Blackler, F. (1995). Knowledge, knowledge work and organizations: an overview and interpretation. *Organization Studies*, 16(6), 1021–1046.

Brown, J. and Duguid, P. (1998). Organizing knowledge. *California Management Review*, 40(3), 90–111.

Bukh, P. N., Christensen, K. S. and Mouritsen, J. (2005). New economy, new theory — or new practice? In P. N. Bukh, K. S. Christensen and J. Mouritsen (eds.), *Knowledge Management and Intellectual Capital: Establishing a Field of Practice* (pp. 1–14), Basingstoke: Palgrave Macmillan.

Choo, C. W. (1996). The knowing organization: how organizations use information to construct meaning, create knowledge and make decisions. *International Journal of Information Management*, 16(5), 329–340.

Civi, E. (2000). Knowledge management as a competitive asset: a review. *Marketing Intelligence & Planning*, 18(4), 166–174.

Clark, P., Bennett, D., Burcher, P., Newell, S., Swan, J. and Sharifi, S. (1992). The decision-episode framework and computer-aided production management (CAPM). *International Studies of Management and Organization*, 22, 69–80.

Clark, P. and Staunton, N. (1989). *Innovation in Technology and Organization*. London: Routledge.

Coff, R. W. (1995). Adapting to control dilemmas when acquiring human-asset-intensive firms: implications of the resource-based view. Paper presented at the Academy of Management Conference, Vancouver, British Columbia, Canada.

Davenport, T. H., Jarvenpaa, S. L. and Beers, M. C. (1996). Improving knowledge work processes. *Sloan Management Review*, Summer, 53–65.

Drucker, P. F. (1973). *Management: Tasks, Responsibilities, Practices*. New York: Harper & Row.

Drucker, P. F. (1992). The new society of organizations. *Harvard Business Review*, 70(5), 95–104.

Drucker, P. F. (1993). *Post-Capitalist Society*. New York: HarperCollins.

Earl, M. J. (1996). Knowledge strategies: propositions from two contrasting industries. In M. J. Earl (ed.), *Information Management: The Organizational Dimension* (pp. 36–51), Oxford: Oxford University Press.

Edvinsson, L. and Sullivan, P. (1996). Developing a model for managing intellectual capital. *European Management Journal*, 14(4), 356–364.

Eisenhardt, K. M. and Santos, F. M. (2002). Knowledge-based view: a new theory of strategy? In A. Pettigrew, H. Thomas and R. Whittington (eds.), *Handbook of Strategy and Management* (pp. 139–164), London: Sage.

Ekstedt, E. (1989). *Knowledge Renewal and Knowledge Companies*. Uppsala Papers in Economic History, Research Report No. 22. Department of Economic History, Uppsala University, Uppsala, Sweden.

Empson, L. (2001). Introduction: knowledge management in professional service firms. *Human Relations*, 54(7), 811–817.

Fuchs, V. (1968). *The Service Economy*. New York: Columbia University Press for the National Bureau of Economic Research.

Grant, R. M. (1996). Toward a knowledge-based theory of the firm. *Strategic Management Journal*, 17(Special Issue), 109–122.

Grant, R. M. (1997). The knowledge-based view of the firm: implications for management practice. *Long Range Planning*, 30(3), 450–454.

Greenwood, R., Hinings, C. R. and Brown, J. L. (1990). "P^2-form" strategic management: corporate practices in professional partnerships. *Academy of Management Journal*, 33(4), 725–755.

Hayes-Roth, F., Waterman, D. A. and Lenat, D. B. (1983). An overview of expert systems. In F. Hayes-Roth, D. A. Waterman and D. B. Lenat (eds.), *Building Expert Systems*, Reading, MA: Addison-Wesley.

Hedberg, B. (1990). Exit, voice, and loyalty in knowledge-intensive firms. Paper presented at the 10th Annual International Conference of the Strategic Management Society, Stockholm, September.

Hinings, C. R., Brown, J. L. and Greenwood, R. (1991). Change in an autonomous professional organization. *Journal of Management Studies*, 28(4), 375–393.

Hislop, D. (2002). Mission impossible? Communicating and sharing knowledge via information technology. *Journal of Information Technology*, 17, 165–177.

Hislop, D. (2005). *Knowledge Management in Organizations*. Oxford: Oxford University Press.

Holsapple, C. W. and Whinston, A. (1987). Knowledge-based organizations. *The Information Society*, 5(2), 77–90.

Jashapara, A. (2005). The emerging discourse of knowledge management: a new dawn for information science research? *Journal of Information Science*, 31(2), 136–148.

Jasimuddin, S. M. (2005). Storage of transferred knowledge or transfer of stored knowledge: Which direction? If both, then how? In *Proceedings of the 38th Hawaii International Conference on System Sciences*, Hawaii, January.

Jasimuddin, S. M. (2006). Organizations in the knowledge-based society. In M. A. Rahim (ed.), *Current Topics in Management*, Vol. 11 (pp. 53–67), New Brunswick, NJ: Transaction Publishers.

Jasimuddin, S. M., Klein, J. H. and Connell, C. (2005). Knowledge-intensive firms and other service-providing firms: how different are they, and how will their differences affect their management? Paper presented at the 12th Annual International Conference on Advances in Management, Washington, D.C., July.

Katsoulakos, P. and Zevgolis, D. (2004). Knowledge management review 2004. Available at http://www.kbos.net/.

Larsen, J. N. (2001). Knowledge, human resources and social practice: the knowledge-intensive business service firm as a distributed knowledge system. *The Service Industries Journal*, 21(1), 81–102.

Lowendahl, B. R. (1997). *Strategic Management of Professional Service Firms*. Copenhagen: Copenhagen Business School Press.

Lowendahl, B. R., Revang, O. and Fosstenlokken, S. M. (2001). Knowledge and value creation in professional service firms: a framework for analysis. *Human Relations*, 54(7), 911–931.

Lundvall, B. A. and Borras, S. (1998). *The Globalising Learning Economy: Implications for Innovation Policy*. European Commission, DG XII, TSER Report. Luxembourg: Office for Official Publications of the European Communities.

Maister, D. H. (1982). Balancing the professional service firm. *Sloan Management Review*, 24(1), 15–29.

Mellahi, K., Frynas, J. G. and Finlay, P. (2005). *Global Strategic Management*. Oxford: Oxford University Press.

Mills, P. K. and Moberg, D. J. (1982). Perspectives on the technology of service operations. *Academy of Management Review*, 7(3), 467–478.

Morris, T. (2001). Asserting property rights: knowledge codification in the professional service firm. *Human Relations*, 54(7), 819–838.

Morris, T. and Empson, L. (1998). Organisation and expertise: an exploration of knowledge bases and the management of accounting and consulting firms. *Accounting, Organizations and Society*, 23(5/6), 609–624.

Newell, S., Robertson, M., Scarbrough, H. and Swan, J. (2002). *Managing Knowledge Work*. Basingstoke: Palgrave Macmillan.

Nonaka, I. and Takeuchi, H. (1995). *The Knowledge-Creating Company: How Japanese Companies Create the Dynamics of Innovation*. Oxford: Oxford University Press.

Nurmi, R. (1998). Knowledge-intensive firms. *Business Horizons*, May/June, 26–32.

OECD (1996). *The Knowledge-Based Economy*. Paris: OECD.

Porat, M. (1977). *The Information Economy*. Washington, D.C.: US Government Printing Office.

Probst, G., Raub, S. and Romhardt, K. (2000). *Managing Knowledge: Building Blocks for Success*. Chichester: John Wiley & Sons Ltd.

Quinn, J. B. (1992). *Intelligent Enterprise: A Knowledge and Service Based Paradigm for Industry*. New York: The Free Press.

Reich, R. (1991). *The Work of Nations: Preparing Ourselves for 21st-Century Capitalism*. London: Simon & Schuster.

Rifkin, J. (2000). *The End of Work: The Decline of the Global Workforce and the Dawn of the Post-Market Era*. London: Penguin.

Rogers, E. (1995). *Diffusion of Innovations*, 4th ed. New York: Free Press.

Sasser, W. E., Olsen, R. P. and Wyckoff, D. D. (1978). *Management of Service Operations: Text, Cases, and Readings*. Boston: Allyn & Bacon.

Scarbrough, H. (1995). Blackboxes, hostages and prisoners. *Organization Studies*, 16(6), 991–1019.

Starbuck, W. H. (1992). Learning by knowledge-intensive firms. *Journal of Management Studies*, 29(6), 713–740.

Thompson, P., Warhurst, C. and Callaghan, G. (2001). Ignorant theory and knowledgeable workers: interrogating the connections between knowledge, skills and services. *Journal of Management Studies*, 38(7), 923–942.

Toffler, A. (1990). *Powershift: Knowledge, Wealth and Violence at the Edge of the 21st Century*. New York: Bantam Books.

Ward, R. C. (2002). Knowledge management, information management, or organizational learning: a comparative study of three states' approaches to knowledge management and information technology. Paper presented at the Southeastern Conference on Public Administration, Columbia, South Carolina, October.

Winch, G. and Schneider, E. (1993). Managing the knowledge-based organization: the case of architectural practice. *Journal of Management Studies*, 30(6), 923–937.

Windrum, P. and Tomlinson, M. (1999). Knowledge-intensive services and international competitiveness: a four country comparison. *Technology Analysis & Strategic Management*, 11(3), 391–408.

World Bank (1998). *World Development Report 1998/99: Knowledge for Development*. New York: Oxford University Press.

Chapter 6

Disciplinary Roots of Knowledge Management

Knowledge Objectives

After studying this chapter, you should be able to:

- Provide a basic idea about the origin of knowledge management;
- Find the disciplines on which knowledge management is exactly drawn; and
- Address who owns the knowledge management field.

6.1 Introducing the Chapter

The motivation for this chapter comes from the recognition that numerous scholars have raised the debate on the roots of the knowledge management field. As mentioned in Chapter 1, the concept of managing knowledge has been an issue affecting mankind for centuries, but popular use of the term "knowledge management" as such has only evolved in academic and business circles during the last 20 years. During this period, various areas of knowledge management have received much attention. Bukh *et al.* (2005) argue that only in recent years has knowledge management crystallized as a special field of practice. Knowledge management is turning into a key issue for organizations around the world. There are many reasons for the interest in organizational knowledge and knowledge management in practice, which are found in the relevant literature.

However, there are issues surrounding knowledge management that have yet to be explored. This is supported by several scholars (e.g., Raub and Ruling, 2001; Moffett *et al.*, 2003a; Gu, 2004; Hazlett *et al.*, 2005; Chae and Bloodgood, 2006), who argue that there are many areas within the knowledge management subject that remain undiscovered. This chapter will address one very important issue that has been found to be missing or relatively neglected: the disciplinary roots of knowledge management. Moffett *et al.* (2003a) support this view, stating, "One of such areas is the origin of knowledge management".

Despite a wide discussion surrounding knowledge management and the many benefits that are derived from such an initiative, there is much debate in the literature on whether it originates from a wide range of disciplines or a single discipline. It can be argued that the notion of knowledge management can hardly be understood by reference to its activities alone; rather, the field can be fully comprehended only when it is explored in line with its disciplinary roots. Unfortunately, only some isolated descriptions on the background or origin of knowledge management are available. In this chapter, a historical perspective on the development of knowledge management over the last 20 years will be given, and its disciplinary roots will be explained in detail. It is evident from the extant literature that various disciplines have contributed to the field. Resonating with this view, Loermans (2002) contends that several different disciplines have played a role in providing fresh insights into the subject.

This chapter is structured as follows. The origin of knowledge management is outlined in Section 6.2. Section 6.3 explains the argument that the knowledge management field is derived from a wide range of disciplines, and not from a single discipline. Academics and practitioners have borrowed theories and concepts from a mixture of disciplines such as organizational learning, strategic management, information systems, human resource management and economics, to name a few, in order to shape our understanding of knowledge management. Section 6.4 highlights the connections between the knowledge management discourse and other disciplines on which knowledge management is exactly drawn. Finally, the chapter ends with concluding remarks in Section 6.5.

6.2 Genesis of the Knowledge Management Field

The origin of the knowledge management field can be traced back to the end of the 20th century. Gu (2004), for example, argues that its roots can be found in the academic research of the mid-1970s. Gu (2004, pp. 171–172) also provides evidence by citing the works that were "authored by four pioneers respectively affiliated to institutions of higher learning in the United States, published in *Public Administration Review* Vol. 35, Iss. 6, 1975". These works could be thought of as the earliest contributions to the field.

However, other scholars (e.g., Beckman, 1999; Cooper, 2006; Jashapara, 2005) argue that the knowledge management topic has grown rapidly since the 1990s, driven by economic, technological and social trends in the knowledge-based economy. Garavelli *et al.* (2004), for example, observe: "The term knowledge management was coined at the beginning of the 1990s". In this regard, the research undertaken by Beckman (1999) suggests that Karl Wiig first coined the "knowledge management" concept in 1986 at a conference for the International Labour Organization (ILO) held in Switzerland. There is no doubt that Wiig was one of the first authors to reference knowledge management in his publications. In particular, Wiig (1997) addresses its history and demonstrates its chronological development. Parallel to this, Jashapara (2005) contends that "the start of the knowledge management discourse is normally attributed to around 1997", concluding that "the use of earlier time frames is unclear".

It is worth mentioning that a number of management theorists have contributed to its evolution. Among such pioneers are Peter Drucker, Karl Wiig, Paul Strassmann, Chris Argyris, Thomas Davenport, Laurence Prusak, Peter Senge, Tom Stewart and Dorothy Leonard-Barton, who stress the growing importance of organizational knowledge and knowledge management as strategic issues for organizations. The systems of managing knowledge, which were initially very much based on the work on artificial intelligence and expert systems in the 1980s, were given new labels such as "knowledge acquisition", "knowledge engineering", "knowledge-based systems" and "computer-based ontologies", and later on "knowledge management systems".

Knowledge management was popularized as a topic of research and practice among researchers when academics and practitioners started publishing their work on knowledge management in many different outlets. For instance, Tom Stewart (1991) introduced knowledge management in the popular press by writing an article, "Brainpower", in *Fortune* in 1991. Knowledge management received further attention among practitioners when Ikujiro Nonaka and Hirotaka Takeuchi (1995) wrote their classic book, *The Knowledge-Creating Company: How Japanese Companies Create the Dynamics of Innovation*, and T. H. Davenport and L. Prusak (1998) wrote *Working Knowledge: How Organizations Manage What They Know*.

It should be acknowledged that even today there are contradictory views regarding the origin of knowledge management. Reflecting this view, Jashapara (2005) demonstrates that its historical roots have come from an integration of organizational learning, strategy and information systems literatures. This has further brought out the controversy regarding its genesis. The next section will attempt to answer the question of which specific disciplines have contributed to the development of knowledge management.

6.3 Knowledge Management: An Offshoot of a Single Discipline or Many Disciplines?

It is evident in the relevant literature that part of the confusion that surrounds knowledge management can be attributed to its evolution. Many different disciplines have played a role in providing fresh insights into the emerging field of knowledge management. This is also underscored by Argote (2005), who contends that the conceptualization of knowledge management does not fall neatly into one discipline. Indeed, many of the terms used to describe knowledge management activities have been borrowed and adapted from other disciplines.

The wide variety of knowledge management definitions provided by scholars from many different disciplines reflects the fact that the knowledge management field is not derived from one single discipline. As evidenced in Chapter 2, such increased interest from across a wide variety of disciplines has also made it difficult to find a comprehensive definition of knowledge management. As Scarbrough (1996) comments, "The sprawling and eclectic literature and the ambiguity and definitional problems ... allow different groups to project their own interests and concerns onto it". Lopez *et al.* (2004) support this argument: "Defining the concept of knowledge management is difficult. This is due to the fact that this subject has been studied by several disciplines and from different approaches" (p. 94).

Prusak (2001), for instance, attempts to delve into the roots of knowledge management, and argues that its origins can be located in economics, sociology, philosophy and psychology. Jashapara (2005) maintains that the newly emerging discourse of knowledge management comes from a variety of disciplinary perspectives. Similarly, Argote (2005) observes that our understanding of knowledge management involves aspects of many subjects, including psychology, sociology, operations management, organizational behavior, strategic management, economics and information systems. In this regard, Nonaka and Takeuchi (1995) categorically state that the knowledge management discourse comes from a variety of disciplines such as psychology, management science, organizational science, sociology, strategy and production engineering. Awad and Ghaziri (2004, p. 2) argue that knowledge management is rooted in many disciplines, including business, economics, psychology and information management. Reflecting this view, Chae and Bloodgood (2006, p. 3) also assert: "Knowledge management has been approached from various angles, such as organizational theory, epistemology, cognitive science, management strategy, anthropology, and computer science, to name a few".

However, Hazlett *et al.* (2005) suggest that only two broad disciplines — information systems and management — have contributed to the knowledge management discourse. Furthermore, they reveal an apparent dichotomy between those researchers from an information systems background and those from a management background. Likewise, Sveiby (1999) acknowledges this implicitly when he divides research publications in the field into two categories:

- The first category consists of researchers who come from a computer science- and/or information science-oriented background. These researchers perceive knowledge to be an object and refer to knowledge management as the "management of information".
- The second category consists of researchers who come from a philosophy, psychology, sociology or business/management background. These scholars consider knowledge to be related to processes and view knowledge management as the "management of people".

There are some scholars (e.g., Gupta *et al.*, 2004; Garavelli *et al.*, 2004; Liebowitz and Beckman, 1998) with an information systems background who believe that knowledge management is derived from the application of expert systems, cognitive science and artificial intelligence. In this regard, several researchers — most notably Nissen *et al.* (2000), Swan *et al.* (1999), and Gamble and Blackwell (2001) — claim that knowledge management has its roots in a number of information technology systems and principles, including artificial intelligence, business process re-engineering (BPR), information systems, information management, expert systems and decision support systems, and data mining and data warehousing. Garavelli *et al.* (2004) support this view, stating, "The term knowledge management was coined at the beginning of the 1990s, a period characterized by the information and communication technology (ICT)". Ward (2002) also recognizes that, since the field of knowledge management emerged in the 1990s, new theoretical models have been developed that support a broader approach to data and information management within organizations. As Gupta *et al.* (2004, p. 9) put it:

> The 1980s also saw the development of systems for managing knowledge that relied on work done in artificial intelligence and expert

> systems, giving us such concepts as "knowledge acquisition," "knowledge engineering," "knowledge-based systems," and "computer-based ontologies". The phrase "knowledge management" finally came into being in the business community during this decade.

Moreover, Gamble and Blackwell (2001) provide a long list of disciplines from which knowledge management has drawn; this list includes cognitive science, expert systems and artificial intelligence, computer-supported collaborative work (CSCW), library and information science, technical writing, document management, decision support systems, semantic networks, relational and object databases, simulation, organizational science and network technology.

However, there is another group of scholars who believe that knowledge management has emerged from the subjects associated with organizational theory and management. For example, Styhre (2004) maintains that knowledge management is a special domain of organizational theory, and that the knowledge management literature is derived from a multiplicity of disciplines such as philosophy, psychology, organizational theory and sociology. Malhotra (1997) also argues that organizational models such as "inquiring system", "learning organization" and "double-loop learning organization" are now common references within the knowledge management literature in both the public and private sectors. Similarly, Chae and Bloodgood (2006) state that the emerging interdisciplinary discourse of knowledge management has been approached from various angles such as organizational theory, epistemology, cognitive science and management strategy.

Contrarily, there are several other academics who think that neither management nor information systems alone has contributed to the development of knowledge management. Rather, knowledge management initially borrowed contents from the information technology and information management literature as a means for developing the field; and subsequently, knowledge management moved the concepts of data and information from the field of information management to the field of organizational theory. Reflecting this view, therefore, such scholars (e.g., Raub and Ruling, 2001; Moffett *et al.*, 2003b; Gamble and Blackwell, 2001) concentrate on both management and information systems when exploring the roots of knowledge management. For example, Raub and Ruling (2001) suggest that the knowledge management discourse is derived from various subjects within broader areas of management, most specifically information systems, total quality management, organizational theory, human resource management and strategic management. Moffett *et al.* (2003b, p. 215) also observe that "knowledge management has its origins in a number of related areas, such as Human Resource Management, Total Quality Management, and Information Systems".

Although most authors agree that the development of knowledge management theory and practice continues to involve a wide range of disciplines, they fail to agree in mentioning one discipline that has exclusively contributed to the emerging knowledge management discourse. This indicates that the knowledge management field has evolved from a wide variety of disciplines, and not from a single discipline. Stated differently, scholars from other disciplines have brought their respective experiences and beliefs to popularize the subject. In a study based on a bibliometric analysis of global knowledge management research, Gu (2004) categorically contends that knowledge management has its origin in four different disciplines that are relatively independent. These disciplines are as follows:

- Organizational information processing;
- Business intelligence;
- Organizational cognition; and
- Organizational development.

Furthermore, Gu (2004) provides a comprehensive argument to show that knowledge management draws from a wide range of disciplines: "The first had its starting point in computer technology, the second on information services, the third on research on organizational innovation, learning, and sense making, and the fourth on business strategy and human resource management" (p. 181).

Having argued that knowledge management is multidisciplinary, scholars from a particular discipline cannot claim exclusive ownership of the field. Instead, the majority of authors now believe that knowledge management has grown from many roots. Table 6.1 illustrates that the knowledge management field stems from more than one discipline.

Table 6.1 Who Owns the Knowledge Management Field?

Authors	Disciplinary Roots
Argote (2005)	Psychology, sociology, operations management, organizational behavior, strategic management, economics, information systems
Awad and Ghaziri (2004)	Business, economics, psychology, information management
Chae and Bloodgood (2006)	Organizational theory, epistemology, cognitive science, management strategy, anthropology, computer science
Gamble and Blackwell (2001)	Cognitive science, expert systems and artificial intelligence, computer-supported collaborative work, library and information science, technical writing, document management, decision support systems, semantic networks, relational and object databases, simulation, organizational science, network technology
Gu (2004)	Computer technology; information services; organizational innovation, learning and sense making; business strategy and human resource management
Hazlett *et al.* (2005)	Information systems, management
Jashapara (2005)	Information systems, organizational learning, human resource management, strategic management
Lange (2006)	Organizational theory, management, management history, sociology of knowledge, economics
Moffett *et al.* (2003b)	Human resource management, total quality management, information systems
Nonaka and Takeuchi (1995)	Psychology, management science, organizational science, sociology, strategy, production engineering
Prusak (2001)	Management, economics, sociology, philosophy, psychology
Raub and Ruling (2001)	Management, information systems, total quality management, organizational theory, human resource management, strategic management
Styhre (2004)	Philosophy, psychology, organizational theory, sociology
Sveiby (1997)	Epistemology, computer science, cognitive psychology, pedagogy, information theory, brain research

6.4 Connections Between Knowledge Management and Other Disciplines

In light of the lingering debate over the roots of knowledge management, it is worth exploring the role played by established disciplines (such as information management and strategic management) in its development. The main disciplines that are widely believed to have a closer link to the topics surrounding knowledge management are information management, organizational learning, strategic management and innovation management. The relationship between knowledge management and these disciplines is far from being well-articulated in the academic literature; nevertheless, scholars from these four disciplines have undertaken research to explore their relationship. This section will briefly highlight the following questions so as to expand the discussion further in the subsequent chapters:

- Is knowledge management an offshoot of information management (see Chapter 7)?
- Are knowledge management and organizational learning similar to each other (see Chapter 8)?
- Is knowledge management closely linked to strategic management (see Chapter 9)?
- Does knowledge management facilitate innovation management (see Chapter 10)?

Information management. In the emerging knowledge-based economy, it is evident that knowledge rather than information has become the strategic resource. It is observed that knowledge management has evolved out of many different disciplines, including information management. It could even be argued that one of the most closely related fields of knowledge management is information management. In line with this, Kakabadse *et al.* (2001, p. 140) argue that information management is an important pillar of knowledge management. Kakabadse *et al.* (2001) further add that knowledge management encompasses broader issues such as the knowledge creation process, which allows organizational members to transform information into knowledge and, thereby, use it for organizational success.

It is revealed that knowledge management has borrowed some terminologies and technologies directly from the information management discipline. Koenig (1997) supports this, pointing out that many of the terms and techniques introduced in information management, such as knowledge mapping, are used in knowledge management. Birkinshaw (2001) also argues that, in many organizations, knowledge management has evolved out of information management; hence, knowledge and information are closely related concepts. Parallel to this, several scholars (e.g., Loermans, 2002; Nissen *et al.*, 2000; Swan *et al.*, 1999) contend that knowledge management has its roots in a number of information technology systems and principles, including:

- Artificial intelligence;
- Business process re-engineering (BPR);
- Information systems;
- Information management;
- Expert systems and decision support systems; and
- Data mining and data warehousing.

In this regard, Swan *et al.* (1999) argue that the origins of knowledge management can be clearly seen in information management. Many so-called information management tools have simply been rebadged and called "knowledge management" tools in an attempt by vendors to generate quick profits. As Blosch (2001, p. 39) reports, "much of literature on 'knowledge management' is almost identical in theme and content to that of 'information management'".

Wilson (2002) considers information management and knowledge management to be synonymous. However, the recent growing interest in organizational knowledge has prompted a shift in focus from information management to knowledge management. We will see in the next chapter that scholars possessing an information management background have contributed significantly to the development of knowledge management as an emerging discipline.

Organizational learning. Organizational learning is a mature discipline, as tremendous progress has occurred in this discipline over the last three decades. Many scholars (e.g., Choo, 1996; King *et al.*, 2008; Chae and Bloodgood, 2006; Gloet and Terziovski, 2004) argue that knowledge management has become a key issue in theoretical and empirical research in such disciplinary fields as organizational learning. In particular, Gloet and Terziovski (2004) state that contemporary knowledge management approaches appear to represent an extension of organizational learning, while King *et al.* (2008) contend that organizational learning is complementary to knowledge management. Parallel to this, Chae and Bloodgood (2006) acknowledge the fact that learning is a key concept of knowledge management studies. The linkage between knowledge management and organizational learning will be elaborated in Chapter 8.

Strategic management. Jasimuddin (2006) provides a comprehensive picture in addressing the roots of knowledge management, and argues that this discipline is derived from various subjects within broader areas of management, including strategic management. Several other scholars (Chae and Bloodgood, 2006; Barquin, 2001) maintain that the topic of knowledge management spans multiple disciplines, including strategy. For instance, Chae and Bloodgood (2006) point out that knowledge management is sweeping through several academic fields, such as organizational strategy and management strategy. Chapter 9 will focus more on the association between knowledge management and strategic management.

Innovation management. The knowledge-based economy is characterized by innovation, which is fundamentally linked to new knowledge. More specifically, innovation management deals with how the idea of innovation operates in organizations. The notion of organizational knowledge plays a large role in the innovation management process. Stated differently, innovation management discusses how best to create and use new knowledge and, thereby, innovate. As a result, there is a potential convergence between innovation management and knowledge management. Only recently have management scholars like Metaxiotis and Psarras (2006) begun to address the association between the two disciplines. Chapter 10 will review and assess the emerging research literature on knowledge management and innovation management by providing a theoretical account of the overlaps and complementarities existing between them. Such an effort will help to establish a theoretical link between these constructs.

Having reviewed the knowledge management literature in line with various related disciplines (see Table 6.2), there is an agreement among academics regarding its disciplinary roots. That is, the knowledge management discourse is not derived from one particular discipline; rather, there is a consensus among academics that the field draws from many different disciplines. Scholars (e.g., Chae and Bloodgood, 2006; Argote, 2005; Styhre, 2004; Moffett *et al.*, 2003b; Raub and Ruling, 2001; Prusak, 2001; Gamble and Blackwell, 2001) observe that the knowledge management discourse draws on multiple disciplines. This coincides with Drew (1999), who contends that the tree of knowledge management has developed from many different roots. Likewise, Jashapara (2005) observes that the newly emerging discourse of knowledge management comes from a variety of disciplinary perspectives, and that its future strength lies in its ability to adopt an integrated, interdisciplinary and strategic perspective. Lange (2006) also describes knowledge management as "essentially a hybrid academic discipline, grounded in the perspectives of Organization Theory, Management, Management History, the Sociology of Knowledge, and indeed Economics" (p. 15).

Although some scholars from a particular academic background may attempt to claim ownership of the knowledge management discourse, Table 6.1 provides evidence that the majority of authors from many different backgrounds believe that knowledge management has grown from many roots and disciplines. Hence, there is no scope to claim that only one particular discipline owns the knowledge management field. Instead, as Jashapara (2005) states, "Its historical roots have come from an integration of organizational learning,

Table 6.2 Association of Knowledge Management with Other Disciplines

Discipline	Focus	Sources
Information management	Knowledge management systems that support the identification and distribution of knowledge in organizations	Alavi and Leidner (1999, 2001), Argote (2005), Blumentritt and Johnston (1999), Boland and Tenkasi (1995), Chae and Bloodgood (2006), Hendriks (2001), Hislop (2002), Raub and Ruling (2001), Swan *et al.* (2000), Moffett *et al.* (2003a), Awad and Ghaziri (2004), Gupta *et al.* (2004), Garavelli *et al.* (2004), Liebowitz and Beckman (1998), Birkinshaw (2001), Loermans (2002), Nissen *et al.* (2000), Swan *et al.* (1999)
Organizational learning	Knowledge management for the transmission and absorption of knowledge in organizations	Argote (2005), Chae and Bloodgood (2006), Davenport and Prusak (1998), Nonaka and Takeuchi (1995), Probst *et al.* (2000), Raub and Ruling (2001), Swan and Scarbrough (2001), Styhre (2002)
Strategic management	Knowledge as an organizational resource of strategic significance	Argote (2005), Barney (1991), Chae and Bloodgood (2006), Grant (1996), Prahalad and Hamel (1990), Raub and Ruling (2001), Jasimuddin (2006), Spender (1996), Barquin (2001)
Innovation management	Knowledge management that facilitates innovation through the creation, utilization and diffusion of knowledge	Beesley and Cooper (2008), Darroch and McNaughton (2002), Gloet and Terziovski (2004), Hauschild *et al.* (2001), Lawson and Samson (2003), Metaxiotis and Psarras (2006), Nonaka and Takeuchi (1995)

strategy and information systems literatures". To reiterate this point, Lopez *et al.* (2004) contend that the knowledge management subject has been studied by several disciplines and from different approaches.

6.5 Concluding Summary

This chapter has focused on one very important issue of knowledge management: its disciplinary roots. In other words, this chapter has addressed the historical development of knowledge management. Given that scholars from several disciplines have attempted to claim ownership of the field, this chapter has also addressed the question of who owns knowledge management. Some scholars intend to establish it as an offshoot of an established discipline; however, it is proved that knowledge management is not derived from a single discipline. Rather, a wide range of subjects have contributed to evolve knowledge management as a well-established discipline. During the past two decades, academics and practitioners have borrowed ideas from various disciplines including organizational learning, strategic management, information systems, human resource management and economics, to name a few, in order to shape our understanding of the knowledge management field. In essence, knowledge management is a mixture of several different disciplines, and scholars from various disciplines are exploring the still-unexplored areas surrounding the field and exploiting them to fit into their own areas of study.

This chapter has presented an overview of the recent and rapidly growing literature on knowledge management so as to address whether it is an interdisciplinary field or grounded in a specific discipline. It is evident that knowledge management is a multidisciplinary paradigm and will eventually become a fully fledged discipline. However, there is as yet no consensus regarding the claim that knowledge management is a new field with its own research base. The next four chapters will expand the connection between knowledge management and other well-established disciplines, some of which have already contributed much to its development.

Further Reading

Jasimuddin, S. M., Connell, C. and Klein, J. H. (2008). Understanding organizational memory. In M. E. Jennex (ed.), *Knowledge Management: Concepts, Methodologies, Tools and Applications* (pp. 171–178), London: IGI Global.

Koenig, M. and Neveroski, K. (2008). The origins and development of knowledge management. *Journal of Information and Knowledge Management*, 7(4), 243–254.

References

Alavi, M. and Leidner, D. (1999). Knowledge management systems: emerging views and practices from the field. In *Proceedings of the 32nd Hawaii International Conference on System Sciences* (pp. 1–11).

Alavi, M. and Leidner, D. (2001). Knowledge management and knowledge management systems: conceptual foundations and research issues. *MIS Quarterly*, 25(1), 107–136.

Argote, L. (2005). Reflections on two views of managing learning and knowledge in organizations. *Journal of Management Inquiry*, 14, 43–48.

Awad, E. M. and Ghaziri, H. M. (2004). *Knowledge Management*. Singapore: Pearson.

Barney, J. B. (1991). Firm resources and sustained competitive advantage. *Journal of Management*, 17(1), 99–120.

Barquin, R. C. (2001). What is knowledge management? *Knowledge and Innovation: Journal of the KMCI*, 1(2), 127–143.

Beckman, T. J. (1999). The current state of knowledge management. In J. Liebowitz (ed.), *Knowledge Management Handbook* (pp. 1–22), Boca Raton, FL: CRC Press LLC.

Beesley, L. G. A. and Cooper, C. (2008). Defining knowledge management (KM) activities: towards consensus. *Journal of Knowledge Management*, 12(3), 48–62.

Birkinshaw, J. (2001). Why is knowledge management so difficult? *Business Strategy Review*, 12(1), 11–18.

Blosch, M. (2001). Pragmatism and organizational knowledge management. *Knowledge and Process Management*, 8(1), 39–47.

Blumentritt, R. and Johnston, R. (1999). Towards a strategy for knowledge management. *Technology Analysis & Strategic Management*, 11(3), 287–300.

Boland, R. J. Jr. and Tenkasi, R. V. (1995). Perspective making and perspective taking in communities of knowing. *Organization Science*, 6(4), 350–372.

Bukh, P. N., Christensen, K. S. and Mouritsen, J. (2005). New economy, new theory — or new practice? In P. N. Bukh, K. S. Christensen and J. Mouritsen (eds.), *Knowledge Management and Intellectual Capital: Establishing a Field of Practice* (pp. 1–14), Basingstoke: Palgrave Macmillan.

Chae, B. and Bloodgood, J. M. (2006). The paradoxes of knowledge management: an eastern philosophical perspective. *Information and Organization*, 16, 1–26.

Choo, C. W. (1996). The knowing organization: how organizations use information to construct meaning, create knowledge and make decisions. *International Journal of Information Management*, 16(5), 329–340.

Cooper, C. (2006). Knowledge management and tourism. *Annals of Tourism Research*, 33(1), 47–64.

Darroch, J. and McNaughton, R. (2002). Examining the link between knowledge management practices and types of innovation. In *Proceedings of the 7th World Congress on Intellectual Capital*, McMaster University, Hamilton, Ontario, Canada, January 16–18, 2002.

Davenport, T. H. and Prusak, L. (1998). *Working Knowledge: How Organizations Manage What They Know*. Boston, MA: Harvard Business School Press.

Drew, S. (1999). Building knowledge management into strategy: making sense of a new perspective. *Long Range Planning*, 32(1), 130–136.

Gamble, P. and Blackwell, J. (2001). *Knowledge Management: A State of the Art Guide*. London: Kogan Page.

Garavelli, C., Gorgoglione, M. and Scozzi, B. (2004). Knowledge management strategy and organization: a perspective of analysis. *Knowledge and Process Management*, 11, 273–282.

Gloet, M. and Terziovski, M. (2004). Exploring the relationship between knowledge management practices and innovation performance. *Journal of Manufacturing Technology Management*, 15(5), 402–409.

Grant, R. M. (1996). Prospering in dynamically-competitive environments: organizational capability as knowledge integration. *Organization Science*, 7, 375–387.

Gu, Y. (2004). Global knowledge management research: a bibliometric analysis. *Scientometrics*, 61, 171–190.

Gupta, J. N. D., Sharma, S. K. and Hsu, J. (2004). An overview of knowledge management. In J. N. D. Gupta and S. K. Sharma (eds.), *Creating Knowledge Based Organizations* (pp. 1–28), Hershey, PA: Idea Group Inc.

Hauschild, S., Licht, T. and Stein, W. (2001). Creating a knowledge culture. *McKinsey Quarterly*, 1, 74–81.

Hazlett, S., McAdam, R. and Gallagher, S. (2005). Theory building in knowledge management: in search of paradigms. *Journal of Management Inquiry*, 14(1), 31–42.

Hendriks, P. H. J. (2001). Many rivers to cross: from ICT to knowledge management systems. *Journal of Information Technology*, 16(2), 57–72.

Hislop, D. (2002). Mission impossible? Communicating and sharing knowledge via information technology. *Journal of Information Technology*, 17, 165–177.

Jashapara, A. (2005). The emerging discourse of knowledge management: a new dawn for information science research? *Journal of Information Science*, 31(2), 136–148.

Jasimuddin, S. M. (2006). Disciplinary roots of knowledge management: a theoretical review. *International Journal of Organizational Analysis*, 14(2), 171–180.

Kakabadse, N. K., Kouzmin, A. and Kakabadse, A. (2001). From tacit knowledge to knowledge management: leveraging invisible assets. *Knowledge and Process Management*, 8(3), 137–154.

King, W. R., Chung, T. R. and Haney, M. H. (2008). Editorial: knowledge management and organizational learning. *Omega*, 36, 167–172.

Koenig, M. E. D. (1997). Intellectual capital and how to leverage it. *The Bottom Line*, 10(3), 112–118.

Lange, T. (2006). The creation and management of knowledge: what can we learn from applying the principles of economics? *International Journal of Knowledge Management Studies*, 1(1/2), 7–17.

Lawson, B. and Samson, D. (2003). Developments in managing innovation, knowledge and e-business. In A. Gunasekaran, O. Khalil and S. M. Rahman (eds.), *Knowledge and Information Technology Management: Human and Social Perspectives* (pp. 1–13), Hershey, PA: Idea Group, Inc.

Liebowitz, J. and Beckman, T. (1998). *Knowledge Organizations: What Every Manager Should Know*. Boca Raton, FL: St. Lucie Press/CRC Press.

Loermans, J. (2002). Synergizing the learning organization and knowledge management. *Journal of Knowledge Management*, 6(3), 285–294.

Lopez, S. P., Peon, J. M. M. and Ordas, C. J. V. (2004). Managing knowledge: the link between culture and organizational learning. *Journal of Knowledge Management*, 8(6), 93–104.

Malhotra, Y. (1997). Knowledge management in inquiring organizations. In *Proceedings of the 3rd Americas Conference on Information Systems*, Indianapolis, IN.

Metaxiotis, K. and Psarras, J. (2006). Analysing the value of knowledge management leading to innovation. *International Journal of Knowledge Management Studies*, 1(1/2), 79–89.

Moffett, S., McAdam, R. and Parkinson, S. (2003a). An empirical analysis of knowledge management applications. *Journal of Knowledge Management*, 7(3), 6–26.

Moffett, S., McAdam, R. and Parkinson, S. (2003b). Technology and people factors in knowledge management: an empirical analysis. *Total Quality Management & Business Excellence*, 14(2), 215–224.

Nissen, M., Kamel, M. and Sengupta, K. (2000). Integrated analysis and design of knowledge systems and processes. *Information Resources Management Journal*, 13(1), 24–43.

Nonaka, I. and Takeuchi, H. (1995). *The Knowledge-Creating Company: How Japanese Companies Create the Dynamics of Innovation*. Oxford: Oxford University Press.

Prahalad, C. K. and Hamel, G. (1990). The core competition of the corporation. *Harvard Business Review*, 68(3), 79–91.

Probst, G., Raub, S. and Romhardt, K. (2000). *Managing Knowledge: Building Blocks for Success*. Chichester: John Wiley & Sons Ltd.

Prusak, L. (2001). Where did knowledge management come from? *IBM Systems Journal*, 40(4), 1002–1007.

Raub, S. and Ruling, C. (2001). The knowledge management tussle — speech communities and rhetorical strategies in the development of knowledge management. *Journal of Information Technology*, 16(2), 113–130.

Scarbrough, H. (1996). *The Management of Expertise*. London: Macmillan.

Spender, J. C. (1996). Making knowledge the basis of a dynamic theory of the firm. *Strategic Management Journal*, 17(Special Issue), 45–62.

Stewart, T. A. (1991). Brainpower: how intellectual capital is becoming America's most valuable asset. *Fortune*, June 3, 44–60.

Styhre, A. (2002). The knowledge-intensive company and the economy of sharing: rethinking utility and knowledge management. *Knowledge and Process Management*, 9(4), 228–236.

Styhre, A. (2004). Rethinking knowledge: a Bergsonian critique of the notion of tacit knowledge. *British Journal of Management*, 15, 177–188.

Sveiby, K. E. (1997). *The New Organizational Wealth: Managing and Measuring Knowledge-Based Assets.* San Francisco, CA: Berrett-Koehler Publishers.

Sveiby, K. E. (1999). Frequently asked questions about knowledge management. Available at http://www.sveiby.com.au/.

Swan, J., Newell, S. and Robertson, M. (2000). Limits of IT-driven knowledge management initiatives for interactive innovation processes: towards a community-based approach. In R. H. Sprague, Jr. (ed.), *Proceedings of the 33rd Hawaii International Conference on System Sciences (HICSS-33).*

Swan, J., Newell, S., Scarbrough, H. and Hislop, D. (1999). Knowledge management and innovation: networks and networking. *Journal of Knowledge Management*, 3, 262–275.

Swan, J. and Scarbrough, H. (2001). Editorial. *Journal of Information Technology*, 16(2), 49–55.

Ward, R. C. (2002). Knowledge management, information management, or organizational learning: a comparative study of three states' approaches to knowledge management and information technology. Paper presented at the Southeastern Conference on Public Administration, Columbia, South Carolina, October.

Wiig, K. M. (1997). Knowledge management: where did it come from and where will it go? *Expert Systems with Applications*, 13(1), 1–14.

Wilson, T. D. (2002). The nonsense of 'knowledge management'. *Information Research* (online journal), 8(1), available at http://informationr.net/ir/8-1/paper144.html/.

Chapter 7

Knowledge Management and Information Management

Knowledge Objectives

After studying this chapter, you should be able to:

- Provide a basic introduction of information management;
- Discuss the themes and concepts associated with information management;
- Explore the origin of information management;
- Explain the role of information management in organizations; and
- Evaluate the relationship between knowledge management and information management.

7.1 Introducing the Chapter

There is as yet no consensus regarding the claim that knowledge management is a new field with its own research base. However, there is evidence that well-established disciplines have played a significant role in the development of knowledge management. One of these disciplines is information management. This chapter will focus on the role that information management has played to popularize the knowledge management field. The chapter will also demonstrate that, although knowledge management is different from information management, the former has borrowed concepts from the latter.

In fact, this chapter aims to identify the issues that seem to clarify the concept of information management with respect to knowledge management, in order to provide fresh insights into the interdisciplinary field of knowledge management. The chapter starts with an overview of the recent literature on information management. Moreover, it will briefly look at the overlaps and synergies between knowledge management and information management, so as to address whether knowledge management is an offshoot of information management or is linked to information management.

As noted in the previous chapter, the information management discipline — along with other established subjects — has contributed significantly to position knowledge management as an emerging discipline. Thus far, limited research has explored the connection between information management and knowledge management. Several researchers (Mårtensson, 2000; Tsoukas and Vladimirou, 2001; Kakabadse *et al.*, 2001; Gourlay, 2000) acknowledge the lack of a clear distinction between knowledge management and information management in the relevant literature.

In the emerging knowledge-based economy, it is evident that knowledge rather than information has become the strategic resource. The recent growing interest in organizational knowledge has prompted a shift in focus from information management to knowledge management. In this regard, Jashapara (2005), for example, comments on the implications of the growth of knowledge management on information management, arguing that "the emerging discourse of knowledge management is creating a number of challenges for the information science discipline as we move towards a knowledge economy". The motivation for this chapter comes from the recognition that many scholars have debated the role of information management in the development of the knowledge management field. The distinction between knowledge management and information management is far from being well-articulated in the knowledge management literature, and this is compounded by the confusion around the concepts of knowledge and information. The present chapter will attempt to discuss this debate so as to establish the connection between knowledge management and information management.

The structure of this chapter is as follows. As a starting point, the themes and concepts associated with information management, including its strategic role in organizations, are elaborated in Section 7.2. Information management is a very well-established discipline, and research on information management in organizations has been conducted for quite a long time. In fact, its theory, research and practice have advanced substantially over the last 50 years. An understanding of the origin of information management is necessary in order to clarify the current status of information management concepts. Therefore, Section 7.3 discovers the origin of information management. In Section 7.4, scholars' views on the relationship between knowledge management and information management are reviewed. An identification of the factors associated with the two fields could shed some light on the nature of their association, as these factors can help to determine whether information management facilitates knowledge management. Or, put another way, information management is a forerunner of knowledge management. With this in mind, Section 7.5 explores the relationship between knowledge management and information management. The chapter ends with a concluding summary in Section 7.6.

7.2 The Notion of Information Management

I will first briefly discuss the various facets and relevant themes surrounding the information management field so as to understand its strategic importance. To begin with, it is important to define information management. There have been numerous attempts to define information management. Information management is the collection of information from various sources; the compiled information is then distributed to various audiences within and outside an organization, using many different routes, for their use. In short, information management entails the acquisition, organization, maintenance and retrieval of information. It is important to manage and categorize information so that people can find it easily. In the relevant literature, the terms "information management", "information resource management", "information systems" and "information technology" are used interchangeably.

It is noted that information management is more oriented toward the collection, control, preservation and retention of information. Cronin (1985) supports this, arguing that the major focus of information management initiatives seems to be to control systematically recorded information. Since the 1970s, this discipline has become popular in managing information for organizations. Indeed, information management processes strategic data that enable an organization to function effectively. This is largely due to the advent and wider use of information technology. It is very much visible that the storage of information has shifted to electronic means. By the late 1990s, a number of computer-driven technologies and tools were developed to support information management in contemporary organizations, be they public or private. Information is regularly exchanged and disseminated across computer networks using electronic means.

It is noticeable that the term "information management" itself is subject to many different definitions. Ciborra (2002), Albert (1998), van Beveren (2002) and Wilson (2002a), among others, have produced various definitions of information management. It is not surprising that there are diverse views of what information management is. As evidenced from Table 7.1, no consensus has emerged even on a core definition of information management.

7.3 The Origin of Information Management

The information management discipline has advanced substantially over the last 50 years. Eaton and Bawden (1991) mention that the idea of "information as a resource" underlies the discipline of information resource management. It is a well-established discipline that helps to make the right information available at the right time to use in the right place and, thereby, helps to enhance sustainable competitive advantage for firms. An understanding of the origins of information management is necessary in order to clarify the current status of information management concepts.

Table 7.1 Selected Definitions of Information Management

Authors	Definitions
Albert (1998)	The process of collecting, organizing, classifying and disseminating information throughout an organization, so as to make it purposeful to those who need it
Burk and Horton (1988)	The application of traditional management processes, particularly resource management principles, to the stewardship of an organization's information resources and assets
Ciborra (2002)	The study that deals with the deployment of information technology in organizations, institutions and society at large
Mallach (1994)	The storage, processing and communication of information
van Beveren (2002)	The core processes of critical data that enable a business to operate effectively
Wilson (1989)	The management of the information resources of an organization, which involves the management of information technology
Wilson (2002b)	The application of management principles to the acquisition, organization, control, dissemination and utilization of information relevant to the effective operation of organizations of all kinds

Although research on information management in organizations has been conducted for quite a long time, its theory, research and practice have evolved considerably over the past three decades in particular. Thus, information management has matured into a major field of management. Gallupe (2001) argues that the information management field has contributed greatly to what we know about planning, developing and using information systems. Daniels (1998) contends that information systems has now been positioned in the mainstream corporate landscape to the point where there is hardly an organization of any size that does not make use of the information management field for its operational success. Parallel to this, over the last 25 years many educational institutions, such as colleges and universities, across the world have been offering undergraduate and graduate programs in information management. Moreover, an increasing number of universities are setting up an independent department or school to concentrate academic programs and research exclusively in the area of information management.

It is noted that interest in the topics surrounding the information management field on the part of academics and practitioners has increased dramatically over the last few decades, as evidenced by the proliferation of books and journal articles published so far on the subject. Formal research in the information management area is observed in the continued publication of journals on information management. To be specific, over 50 peer-reviewed research journals have surfaced that address major aspects of information management as a primary focus. Table 7.2 provides a list of journals that are exclusively devoted to the concept of information management.

Historically, the study of information management originated as a subdiscipline of information systems, with an aim to manage information using technology both within and outside an organization. It is worth mentioning that information management overlaps with other science and managerial disciplines, such as computer science, engineering sciences, social sciences, business management and the recently emerging knowledge management. It is evident that information management has experienced a major transformation, especially during the past two decades. As Jashapara (2005) states, "Historically, this position in information systems strategy has arrived from a fixation on data processing in the 1960s, management information systems in the 1970s and 1980s and strategic information systems in the 1990s".

Ward (2002) also provides a comprehensive picture of the development of information management. He elaborates as follows:

- Over the past 40 years, the issue of management of data has come up to the forefront of the "information revolution". As data processing has matured, management of data has expanded to incorporate new tools such as data architecture, data structures and data warehouses. These emerging tools traditionally relate to

Table 7.2 A Selected List of Journals on Information Management

Journal Title	Year Launched	Frequency	Publisher
Behaviour & Information Technology	1982	Bimonthly	Taylor & Francis
Communications of the ACM	1958	Monthly	ACM
European Journal of Information Systems	1991	Bimonthly	Palgrave Macmillan
Information & Management	1977	8 issues per year	Elsevier
Information & Organization	1991	Quarterly	Elsevier
Information Resources Management Journal	1988	Quarterly	IGI Global
Information Systems Frontiers	1999	5 issues per year	SpringerLink
Information Systems Journal	1991	Bimonthly	Wiley-Blackwell
Information Systems Management	1984	Quarterly	Taylor & Francis
Information Systems Research	1990	Quarterly	INFORMS
Information Technology & People	1982	Quarterly	Emerald
International Journal of Information Management	1980	Bimonthly	Elsevier
Journal of Information Technology	1986	Quarterly	Palgrave Macmillan
Journal of Management Information Systems	1984	Quarterly	M.E. Sharpe
Journal of the ACM	1954	Bimonthly	ACM
Journal of the Association for Information Systems	2000	Monthly	AIS
MIS Quarterly	1977	Quarterly	AIS
New Technology, Work and Employment	1986	3 issues per year	Wiley-Blackwell
The Information Society	1981	5 issues per year	Taylor & Francis
The Journal of Strategic Information Systems	1991	Quarterly	Elsevier

an older concept of information management, and specifically to the application of information technology as a means of controlling access to data.

- Since the field of knowledge management emerged in the 1990s, new theoretical models have been developed that support a broader approach to data and information management within organizations. Knowledge management has entered both the information technology and management literature as a means for developing a knowledge-oriented culture within organizations, which involves the creation, sharing and application of knowledge. In many ways, knowledge management has moved the concepts of data and information from the field of information management to the field of organizational theory.

Scholars have different opinions on the linkage between knowledge management and information management. The next section will discuss scholars' diverse views on the linkage between the two disciplines.

7.4 Scholars' Views on the Connection Between Knowledge Management and Information Management

In general, knowledge management and information management are discussed independently in the relevant literature; they are rarely discussed together. In this section, the views of scholars on the relationship between knowledge management and information management will be expanded. As evident in the relevant literature, the existence of knowledge management still seems to be questioned when it is discussed from the information management perspective.

As mentioned in Chapter 6, knowledge management has evolved out of many different disciplines including information management. It is widely accepted that one of the most closely related fields of knowledge management is information management. In line with this, several authors (e.g., Loermans, 2002; Nissen *et al.*, 2000; Birkinshaw, 2001; Swan *et al.*, 1999) argue that knowledge management has its roots in a number of information technology systems and principles, such as artificial intelligence, information systems, information management, expert systems and decision support systems, and data mining and data warehousing.

Gloet and Terziovski (2004) rightly state that knowledge management appears to represent an extension of information systems. Similarly, Gu (2004, p. 181) claims that knowledge management draws from a wide range of disciplines, providing a comprehensive argument that it first had its starting point in computer technology and then in information services. It is true that knowledge management has borrowed terminologies and technologies from information management. As a result, there is a debate among academics and researchers on whether knowledge management and information management are two distinct disciplines or the same discipline.

7.4.1 *Knowledge Management as an Offshoot of Information Management*

Critics believe that knowledge management is nothing new. They treat the term "knowledge management" as a relabeled version of information management. Moreover, they argue that "knowledge management" is a catchy phrase that allows vendors to encourage their existing and prospective clients to implement knowledge management initiatives in their organizations, and thereby make money out of its use. Swan *et al.* (1999) support this, arguing that vendors attempt to simply rebadge information management tools as "knowledge management" tools in order to jump on the bandwagon of contemporary thinking.

Several scholars (e.g., Al-Hawamdeh, 2002; Blosch, 2001; Bouthillier and Shearer, 2002; Wilson, 2002a; Koenig, 1997; Broadbent, 1998; Streatfield and Wilson, 1999) wonder whether knowledge management really contains anything new. Bouthillier and Shearer (2002), for example, raise the debate on whether knowledge management is an emerging discipline or just a new label for information management. Parallel to this, scholars — most notably Lin and Wu (2005) and Nonaka *et al.* (2000) — observe that the idea of knowledge management as discussed by researchers and practitioners merely refers to the notion of information management. Similarly, Wilson (2002a) claims that there is little to distinguish knowledge management from information management. Moreover, Wilson (2002a) harbors reservations on even accepting knowledge management as an independent discipline. He holds an extremely critical stance, arguing that knowledge management is little more than a repackaged form of information management, viewing information and knowledge as synonymous.

On the other hand, Caldwell (2006) holds a moderate view, pointing out that knowledge management is an essential part of information management. It is also evident in the relevant literature that researchers in one field often fail to acknowledge the other field. Researchers in information management frequently exclude the term "knowledge" from their studies, and researchers in knowledge management are found to do the same with the term "information". In addition, other researchers tend to use the terms "information management" and "knowledge management" interchangeably. In this regard, Birkinshaw (2001, p. 14) argues that knowledge management emerged out of information management, for the obvious reason that knowledge and information are closely related concepts.

Based on the above views, it could apparently be argued that there is no need for knowledge management because it offers nothing new or different from information management. Looking back, this scenario is similar to the early development of information management, which evolved from data management. When information management first started to emerge as a paradigm, people at the time were still very much biased in favor of data management, and therefore were reluctant to accept information management as a new discourse. They thought that there was no need for information management, claiming that there was nothing new in it when data management was already out there. They strongly believed that data management could serve the purpose of what information management purported to serve.

There is clearly a strong argument that the knowledge management field has borrowed from the information management discipline. Koenig (1997) points out that many of the terms and techniques from information management are used in knowledge management, such as knowledge mapping. Jashapara (2005) argues that information science plays a large role in providing fresh insights into the development of the knowledge management discourse. Birkinshaw (2001, p. 14) contends that knowledge management in many organizations has evolved out of information management. Likewise, Kakabadse *et al.* (2001) argue that information management is an important pillar of knowledge management, adding that knowledge management encompasses broader issues which allow organizational members to transform information within the organization into knowledge and, thereby, use it for organizational success.

It should be acknowledged, as Gloet and Terziovski (2004) state, that knowledge management approaches tend to be driven predominantly by information technology. According to Vera and Crossan (2003), the rapid advancement of information technology and the Internet in the 1990s enabled the development of knowledge management tools. Malhotra (2000) also argues that recent advances in information technology, such as Lotus Notes, the Internet and the World Wide Web, offer the means to organize information into organizational "knowledge repositories". Andersen's "Knowledge Xchange", Booz Allen Hamilton's "Knowledge On-Line", Capgemini's "Knowledge Galaxy", Ernst & Young's Center for Business Knowledge and Monsanto's "Knowledge Management Architecture" are popular examples of such repositories.

7.4.2 *Information Management and Knowledge Management as Complementary to Each Other*

As mentioned in previous chapters, Karl Wiig first coined the concept of "knowledge management" in 1986. Many researchers (e.g., Bouthillier and Shearer, 2002) believe that information management and knowledge management are complementary. Gourlay (2000), for example, argues that, since knowledge management focuses mainly on knowledge representations rather than on knowledge itself, the distinction between information management and knowledge management becomes even more blurred. Similarly, Loughridge (1999, p. 245) states that many aspects of knowledge management practice bear a close resemblance to well-established practices in information management. Reflecting this view, Blosch (2001, p. 39) reports that "much of literature on 'knowledge management' is almost identical in theme and content to that of 'information management'".

Scholars, most notably Bouthillier and Shearer (2002), argue that information management and knowledge management are complementary because they are involved in various activities of a process surrounding information and knowledge, respectively. Against this backdrop, the interest in exploring the relationship between knowledge management and information management on the part of academics and practitioners has increased dramatically over the last few decades. This is evident from the proliferation of books and journal articles published so far on the subject. In fact, the topic of knowledge management is sweeping through several information management journals. King *et al.* (2008) believe that tremendous progress has occurred in knowledge management because scholars from the information management field have contributed much to popularize the subject over the last two decades.

Several recent special issues of journals illustrate the current interest in knowledge management in the information systems field alone. These include *Management Science* (Argote *et al.*, 2003), *MIS Quarterly* (Zmud, 2002; Sambamurthy and Subramani, 2005), *Journal of Management Information Systems* (Grover and Davenport, 2001), *Information Technology & People* (Gray and Meister, 2003) and *Information Systems Management* (Sharif and Al-Karaghouli, 2011). These journals indicate the combination of knowledge management and information management as an area of research.

As mentioned earlier, information management overlaps with the contemporary knowledge management discipline. In this respect, Firestone (2001, p. 25) addresses the question of what the difference is between knowledge management and information management: "[S]ince knowledge is a form of information it follows that KM [knowledge management] is a form of IM [information management]. KM is a more robust form of IM that provides management of activities not generally available in information management".

However, there is no concrete consensus regarding the claim that knowledge management and information management are the same thing. Several researchers (e.g., Mårtensson, 2000; Tsoukas and Vladimirou, 2001; Kakabadse *et al.*, 2001; Gourlay, 2000; Hildreth and Kimble, 2002) maintain that the lack of a clear distinction between information management and knowledge management is a critical issue within the knowledge management literature. Hildreth and Kimble (2002), for example, acknowledge the difficulty in distinguishing knowledge management from information management. Other authors (e.g., Bouthillier and Shearer, 2002; Gourlay, 2000; Loughridge, 1999; Blosch, 2001) argue that there is indeed a fine line between knowledge management and information management at both the conceptual and practical levels. The next section will go some way towards explaining the significant synergies between the two disciplines and how they overlap to a large extent.

7.5 The Intersection Between Knowledge Management and Information Management

As mentioned earlier, the aim of this chapter is to explore whether the terms "information management" and "knowledge management" are identical in theme and content. The fact is that there is no consensus among researchers regarding the claim that information management and knowledge management are the same thing. However, important opportunities for dialogue exist to understand the role that information management plays in the development of knowledge management, or vice versa. An extended examination of the association between the two disciplines could shed light on the nature of their linkage. This section will highlight the factors that may determine if knowledge management is a precursor of information management, or if knowledge management is shaped by information management. It is true that tremendous progress has occurred in knowledge management and information management independently over the last two decades, but there is still no agreement with respect to the claim that knowledge management is a part of information management or vice versa.

This section will attempt to clear up this conceptual confusion. More specifically, various factors will be used to explore the relationship between knowledge management and information management, and to provide a conceptual framework that integrates and establishes a theoretical link between these constructs. The recent interest in how to manage knowledge for an organization's benefit has prompted the use of information technology in managing knowledge. We will begin by defining the two constructs and acknowledging their distinct roots. Table 7.3 depicts the similarities and differences between these fields of research.

Working definition. It is important to define knowledge management and information management so as to demarcate their differences. The definitions of knowledge management and information management are briefly presented here to delineate their differences. In the beginning of this chapter and in Chapter 2, various definitions of information management and knowledge management, respectively, have been given. For example, Wilson (1989) defines information management as the management of an organization's information resources, which involves the management of information technology. Information management makes information available in a central repository (storage bin) so that employees of the organization can extract and use it when they really need it. Duffy (2001) states that one of the key objectives of information management is to ensure that information is stored and retrievable, arguing that information management is good in managing objects but not activities.

On the other hand, knowledge management is the strategic application of collective corporate knowledge and know-how. Knowledge assets are created through the collection, storage, sharing and linking of corporate knowledge pools using technology. Generally speaking, knowledge management attempts to capture the knowledge of an employee in order to make it available for use by other employees of the organization. Knowledge management refers to the identification and leveraging of an individual's knowledge and the collection of such knowledge in an organization so as

Table 7.3 Comparative Perspectives on Knowledge Management and Information Management

Attributes	Information Management	Knowledge Management
Disciplinary roots/ Conceptual origins	Organizational behavior, data management, organizational theory	Organizational theory, strategy, epistemology, cognitive science, information management
Perspective	Both inside and outside an organization	Both inside and outside an organization
Working definition	The process of collecting, selecting, organizing, sharing, distributing and using information with the help of technology	The study of strategy, process and technology to acquire, organize and share knowledge
Key input	Information	Knowledge
End result	Gaining the competitive advantage of an organization	Gaining the competitive advantage of an organization
Society	Information-based society	Knowledge-based society
Focus	Handling the information of an organization	Managing organizational knowledge
Type of organization	Information-based organization	Knowledge-based organization
Key processes	Identification of information needs, information acquisition, information organization and storage, information distribution, information use	Knowledge creation, knowledge sharing, knowledge dissemination, knowledge exploitation
Person in charge	Chief information officer	Chief knowledge officer

to support the organization's efforts at becoming more competitive (Davenport and Prusak, 1998; O'Dell and Grayson, 1998; Cross and Baird, 2000; Baird and Henderson, 2001).

In short, information management uses information systems to store, process and communicate information (see Mallach (1994), as cited in Sharratt and Usoro (2003)). Contrarily, knowledge management leverages an organization's knowledge to create additional value to business, using technology. The definition of the two constructs acknowledges their distinct roots.

Key input. As noted earlier, the distinction between knowledge management and information management is far from being well-articulated in the knowledge management literature, and this is compounded by the confusion around the concepts of knowledge and information. Hildreth and Kimble (2002) explain that, in order to clarify this distinction, it is necessary to understand how information and knowledge — which are grounded on data — relate to each other. Scholars (e.g., Bouthillier and Shearer, 2002; Shin *et al.*, 2001; Gourlay, 2006) argue that "information" and "knowledge" are often used interchangeably. However, in Chapter 1 a clear distinction was made between information and knowledge. Thus, one way to understand the prevailing disconnect between knowledge management and information management is to reflect upon the differences between knowledge and information. Bouthillier and Shearer (2002) support this, arguing that the distinctions drawn between the related concepts of information and knowledge need to be examined in order to differentiate information management from knowledge management. In line with this, Gallupe (2001) states that knowledge is considered as an extension of information in that knowledge is embedded with context. This makes knowledge more challenging than just information to manipulate and manage in a systematic manner.

Origin. Information management and knowledge management are two significant management paradigms, positioned comfortably within information systems and management theory, respectively. As mentioned earlier, the definition of the two constructs demonstrates their distinct roots. However, from a theoretical perspective, information management and knowledge management did not emerge from distinct disciplinary traditions. While knowledge management is claimed by many scholars to be an offshoot of information management, information management originated from information systems. As soon as information was considered as a critical resource for organizations, information management started to receive more attention than data management. Similarly, in the knowledge-based society, knowledge has become an increasingly critical resource for organizations; hence, knowledge management has evolved from many disciplines, including information management.

Society. Another way to understand the difference between information management and knowledge management is by looking at the society in which each field could be seen to be more useful. Since the beginning of the 21st century, the so-called information society has moved toward the knowledge-based society, highlighting the importance of knowledge (Jashapara, 2005). In the emerging knowledge economy, knowledge rather than information has become the critical resource as knowledge workers provide the driving force for innovation and productivity improvements in goods and services. As a result, this has prompted a rethink of information management and a shift in emphasis towards trying to manage knowledge rather than information.

Focus. Another basic difference between knowledge management and information management is their focus. Based on their definitions, it is observed that knowledge management focuses on managing organizational knowledge, while information management focuses on handling the information of an organization. In this context, several authors have explained the main focus of the two disciplines. According to Carlsson (2003), knowledge management is the process of exploring and exploiting organizational knowledge; whereas Place and Hyslop (1982) argue that information management focuses on the plans and activities that need to be performed to control an organization's records.

Firestone (2001, p. 25) argues that the basic focus of information management is on managing how information is produced and integrated into an organization, while knowledge management does the same with respect to knowledge. Al-Hawamdeh (2002, as cited in Caldwell, 2006) rightly comments that "while the focus in information management is mostly on explicit knowledge, knowledge management brings a new dimension, that is, the need to manage tacit knowledge by focusing on people and enhance their capability by improving communication, information transfer and collaboration".

Nature of knowledge. An understanding of the attributes of knowledge also helps to differentiate knowledge management from information management. Information management deals mostly with information, which several scholars also refer to as explicit knowledge. Contrarily, knowledge management handles both tacit and explicit knowledge, though more on the tacit component of knowledge. Duffy (2001) suggests that information management is good in managing objects; knowledge, however, is treated as an activity and not as an object. Interestingly, the minute an activity is transformed into an object, it should not be called knowledge but rather a piece of information. In this regard, Nonaka and Takeuchi (1995) conclude that knowledge management deals mainly with tacit and undocumented knowledge, while information management is responsible for managing information and explicit knowledge.

Processes involved. Another way to distinguish between knowledge management and information management is through understanding the steps involved in both disciplines. Bouthillier and Shearer (2002) rightly point out that "one way to distinguish between knowledge management and information management is to identify the processes or steps involved in both fields". As mentioned earlier, knowledge management and information management are involved in various activities surrounding knowledge and information, respectively. Information management is the process of managing the information resources of an organization. In this context, Choo (1996), for instance, identifies five basic steps of the information management process: identification of information needs, information acquisition, information organization and storage, information distribution, and information use.

On the other hand, the knowledge management process involves the acquisition, creation and exploitation of organizational knowledge. Jashapara (2004, p. 5) supports this, naming five activities of the knowledge management process, which include discovering, generating, evaluating, sharing and leveraging knowledge. Likewise, Siemieniuch and Sinclair (1999) state that the knowledge management process allows organizations to generate, disseminate and remove core knowledge requirements according to current and future needs. Moreover, Oluic-Vukovic (2001) outlines five steps in the knowledge processing chain — gathering, organizing, refining, representing and disseminating — that closely resemble the information lifecycle processes, suggesting again the interrelated aspects of knowledge management and information management.

Location. One other key distinction between knowledge management and information management is the location where knowledge and information reside. Information management works well in places with a strong emphasis on explicit knowledge. Duffy (2000) supports this, arguing that information management handles work-related objects well, which tend to be electronic and paper-based information.

In contrast, knowledge management is essentially about human beings who make an effort to create, share and store knowledge through interactions in their environment. Knowledge is housed in people's minds and brains, not in machines or documents. In this regard, Nonaka and Takeuchi (1995) emphasize in their book, *The Knowledge-Creating Company*, that only people can take the central role in knowledge creation, arguing that knowledge resides in an individual's subjective context of action based on information and that computers are merely tools. Resonating with this view, Marks *et al.* (2008) contend that knowledge resides in certain organizational members.

Required tools. The distinction between knowledge management tools and information management tools also helps to illustrate the difference between the two disciplines. We know that information management systems are good in managing objects but not activities, and that technology plays an important role in information management. Wilson (1989) supports this, arguing that information management is the management of the information resources of an organization and involves the management of information technology. Likewise, Duffy (2001) states that the focus for information management tools is on electronic and paper-based information. Although information technologies are very useful, they are not appropriate to deal with the richness and context of knowledge. It seems unlikely that knowledge can be managed by means of information technology alone (Vera and Crossan, 2003). Knowledge management systems extend beyond the traditional information systems, and touch upon the "context" of the information presented.

To be sure, knowledge management tools are related to information systems. As Gallupe (2001) contends, knowledge management systems (KMS), which are capable of handling and securing knowledge, do share many similarities with information systems. However, knowledge management is not all about technology; rather, technology enables the storage, transfer and dissemination of knowledge in a somewhat explicit form. Similarly, Ruggles (1997) states that knowledge management tools are technologies that enhance and enable knowledge generation, codification and transfer. Examples of some current computer-based systems that practitioners call knowledge management systems are some applications of Lotus Notes and "intranets" (Gallupe, 2001). Knowledge management incorporates the intelligent searching, categorization and accessing of data from disparate databases, e-mails and files (Willett and Copeland, 1998). According to Wilson (2002b), one of the key technologies driving knowledge management is collaborative technology. In particular, Web technology enables a company's professionals to work together and work virtually regardless of their geographical location.

To conclude, Wilson (2002b) argues that, while knowledge management systems include tools that also handle data and information, information management tools are not robust enough to truly facilitate knowledge management. The fact is that knowledge management is a key tool that organizes, stores and distributes knowledge in an organization, whenever it is required. In this context, Wilson (2002b) regards information management tools as a subset of knowledge management tools that allows organizations to generate, access, store and analyze data, usually in the form of facts and figures. It is important to put technology in its proper perspective in order to identify the most important connections between knowledge management and information management.

Role of people interaction. Information management deals with information resources, where information is more factual. Therefore, a high degree of human interaction is not necessary in order to manage information. Wilson (2002b) states that information management tools enable the manipulation of information. However, information generated by computer systems is not a very rich carrier of human interpretation for potential action. Information technologies are structured and numerically oriented, whereas knowledge technologies deal most often with text. Knowledge technologies are thus more likely to need human interaction than information technologies because the former involves fewer transactions.

According to Davenport and Prusak (1998), knowledge technologies deal most frequently with text, which is in relatively unstructured forms such as clauses, sentences, paragraphs or even stories. Knowledge technologies are more likely to be employed in an interactive and iterative manner by their users. As a result, the role of people in knowledge technologies is integral to their success; whereas in information management, human interaction is minimal. Reflecting this view, Al-Hawamdeh (2002) states that information management focuses on developing intelligent systems, while knowledge management tends to develop tools for intelligent people.

Leadership role. Another way to understand the difference between knowledge management and information management is through finding the person responsible for managing knowledge and information. The apparent distinction between knowledge management and information management has led to the creation of different leadership roles in organizations. A chief information officer (CIO) manages explicit knowledge and information, while a chief knowledge officer (CKO) encourages employees to exchange knowledge with other members of the organization as well as grab tacit knowledge and store explicit knowledge. Most of the giant companies already have a chief information officer (CIO), and have recently created the position of chief knowledge officer (CKO).

In this regard, Davenport and Prusak (1998, as cited in Girard, 2006) describe the role of information managers and knowledge managers. Information managers are responsible for creating information by transforming data, while knowledge managers are responsible for producing the end product of knowledge either from information or from data. Stated differently, information managers have a role in contexting, categorizing, calculating, connecting and condensing information; whereas knowledge managers have a role in comparing, connecting and communicating knowledge.

Results. Both knowledge management and information management contribute to organizational performance. In most cases, the key drivers are improving organizational efficiency, maximizing an organization's potential and enhancing competitive advantage. Three decades ago, information management was considered as the most important factor to help companies achieve competitive advantage.

In the knowledge-based society, however, knowledge rather than information has now become the critical resource. Accordingly, knowledge workers provide the driving force for innovation and productivity improvements in goods and services. Presently, knowledge management is seen as helping to enhance sustainable competitive advantage. While information management deals with critical data that enable businesses to operate effectively, knowledge management goes beyond the day-to-day operations and seeks to build the capability to improve the way businesses function. Bouthillier and Shearer (2002) support this, arguing that the goal of information management is to ensure that information is stored and easily retrievable, whereas knowledge management is more focused on organizational outcomes.

This section has attempted to explore whether the terms "knowledge management" and "information management" are synonymous. Some scholars hold the view that the two fields are really different. In contrast, other researchers believe that one field has evolved from the other. This section has highlighted the similarities and differences between information management and knowledge management by exploring the factors that establish a theoretical link between these constructs. I would like to make clear that the emergence of knowledge management is not due to the failure of information management; instead, information science has played a role, as Jashapara (2005) argues, in providing fresh insights into the emerging knowledge management interdisciplinary discourse. Choo (1998) contends that information management is required for knowledge creation and application in organizations. Many researchers (e.g., Bouthillier and Shearer, 2002) believe that information management and knowledge management are complementary, given that there are some common themes available in both fields that are complementary in nature. Interestingly, both knowledge management and information management are involved in various activities of a process surrounding knowledge and information, respectively.

Although information management has helped to shape the notion of knowledge management, information management is not an antecedent of knowledge management. Nevertheless, knowledge management appears to represent an extension of information management. In other words, information management and knowledge management fit together, as there are significant synergies between these disciplines. At the same time, they overlap to a large extent. Our examination of the relationship between the two fields has helped us to derive two situations that have emerged in terms of the relationship between knowledge management and information management:

- In situation I, there is a connection between information management and knowledge management. More specifically, there is a linkage in that information management facilitates knowledge management. Birkinshaw (2001) reinforces this, arguing that knowledge management emerged out of information management, for the obvious reason that knowledge and information are closely related concepts.
- In situation II, information management and knowledge management fit together. There are significant synergies between these disciplines. The two fields are equally jointly responsible for managing organizational information and knowledge so as to enhance the competitive advantage of an organization.

7.6 Concluding Summary

Over the last two decades, knowledge management has been sweeping through many different academic fields, including information management. It is observed that knowledge management has attracted much attention in both academic and practitioner circles, especially those from information management. Information management is the study of strategy, process and technology to collect, select, organize, share, distribute and use information, and itself draws from a wide range of disciplines as well. Although research has been conducted on many topics in information management, there has been relatively little focus on the relationship between information management and knowledge management. The motivation for this chapter comes from the recognition that too many scholars have attempted to use both fields synonymously.

Several researchers have illustrated that the two disciplines are linked, claiming that knowledge management is a part of information management or an offshoot of information management. The fact is that knowledge management is not an entirely different discipline to information management; instead, they are both interrelated. However, it is not simply about replacing the word "information" in "information management" with the word "knowledge" in "knowledge management".

This chapter has started by explaining the themes and concepts associated with information management. Its strategic role in organizations has been elaborated. Information management is a very well-established discipline with a long history of development. Research on information management in organizations has been conducted over the last 50 years. This chapter has also sought to understand the origins and clarify the current status of information management, as well as find its linkage with the knowledge management field. For obvious reasons, information management and knowledge management are closely related concepts. Scholars admit that many terminologies and techniques used in knowledge management have been borrowed from information management. This explains why there are critics of knowledge management who think that the field is nothing new, as most of its topics have been taken from information management. For example, Wilson (2002b) expresses his reservations even on the existence of knowledge management, arguing that knowledge management is little more than a repackaged form of information management.

Nowadays, however, a growing consensus seems to be emerging that differentiates knowledge management from information management. This chapter has argued that the terms "knowledge management" and "information management" are not synonymous; rather, they are different. It is noted that in the knowledge-based society an organization is not merely an information-processing machine, but an entity that creates knowledge through interactions among people. Organizational knowledge is now considered as the critical resource for firms, and so knowledge management has emerged as a new discourse over the last 20 years.

An attempt has been made to articulate some key factors in order to provide some interesting and important directions for comprehending the relationship between information management and knowledge management. Some authors acknowledge the critical significance of the connection between the two fields, whilst others do not seem to agree on combining them. This chapter has contributed to the lack of literature to date on the apparent synergies between them by addressing the question of how they fit together.

This chapter has provided a conceptual framework that defines and integrates knowledge management and information management, and that establishes a theoretical link between these subjects, hence clearing up the conceptual confusion. Regardless of the diverse opinions on information management and knowledge management as identified earlier in the literature, fostering and supporting information management is not dissimilar to managing knowledge at an organizational level. Although this chapter has contributed to our understanding of the relationship between the two disciplines, additional research is clearly needed to develop this link further.

Further Reading

Kyobe, M. (2010). A knowledge management approach to resolving the crises in the information systems discipline. *Journal of Systems and Information Technology*, 12(2), 161–173.

Maruster, L., Faber, N. R. and Peters, K. (2008). Sustainable information systems: a knowledge perspective. *Journal of Systems and Information Technology*, 10(3), 218–231.

References

Albert, S. (1998). Knowledge management: living up to the hype? *Midrange Systems*, 11(13), September, 52.

Al-Hawamdeh, S. (2002). Knowledge management: re-thinking information management and facing the challenge of managing tacit knowledge. *Information Research* (online journal), 8(1), available at http://informationr.net/ir/8-1/paper143.html/.

Argote, L., McEvily, B. and Reagans, R. (2003). Managing knowledge in organizations: an integrative framework and review of emerging themes. *Management Science*, 49(4), 571–582.

Baird, L. and Henderson, J. C. (2001). *The Knowledge Engine: How to Create Fast Cycles of Knowledge-to-Performance and Performance-to-Knowledge*. San Francisco, CA: Berrett-Koehler.

Birkinshaw, J. (2001). Why is knowledge management so difficult? *Business Strategy Review*, 12(1), 11–18.

Blosch, M. (2001). Pragmatism and organizational knowledge management. *Knowledge and Process Management*, 8(1), 39–47.

Bouthillier, F. and Shearer, K. (2002). Understanding knowledge management and information management: the need for an empirical perspective. *Information Research* (online journal), 8(1), available at http://informationr.net/ir/8-1/paper141.html/.

Broadbent, M. (1998). The phenomenon of knowledge management: what does it mean to the information professional? *Information Outlook*, 2(5), May, 23–36.

Burk, C. F. and Horton, F. W. (1988). *InfoMap: A Complete Guide to Discovering Corporate Information Resources*. Englewood Cliffs, NJ: Prentice Hall.

Caldwell, F. (2006). The new enterprise knowledge management. *VINE: The Journal of Information and Knowledge Management Systems*, 36(2), 182–185.

Carlsson, S. A. (2003). Knowledge managing and knowledge management systems in inter-organizational networks. *Knowledge and Process Management*, 10(3), 194–206.

Choo, C. W. (1996). The knowing organization: how organizations use information to construct meaning, create knowledge and make decisions. *International Journal of Information Management*, 16(5), 329–340.

Choo, C. W. (1998). *The Knowing Organization: How Organizations Use Information to Construct Meaning, Create Knowledge and Make Decisions.* New York: Oxford University Press.

Ciborra, C. (2002). *Labyrinths of Information.* Oxford: Oxford University Press.

Cronin, B. (1985). Introduction. In B. Cronin (ed.), *Information Management: From Strategies to Action* (pp. vii–ix), London: ASLIB.

Cross, R. and Baird, L. (2000). Technology is not enough: improving performance by building organizational memory. *Sloan Management Review*, 41(3), 69–78.

Daniels, S. (1998). The strategic use of information systems. *Work Study*, 47(5), 167–171.

Davenport, T. H. and Prusak, L. (1998). *Working Knowledge: How Organizations Manage What They Know.* Boston, MA: Harvard Business School Press.

Duffy, J. (2000). The KM technology infrastructure. *Information Management Journal*, 34(2), 62–66.

Duffy, J. (2001). The tools and technologies needed for knowledge management. *Information Management Journal*, 35(1), 64–67.

Eaton, J. J. and Bawden, D. (1991). What kind of resource is information? *International Journal of Information Management*, 11, 156–165.

Firestone, J. M. (2001). Key issues in knowledge management. *Knowledge and Innovation: Journal of the KMCI*, 1(3), 8–38.

Gallupe, B. (2001). Knowledge management systems: surveying the landscape. *International Journal of Management Reviews*, 3(1), 61–77.

Girard, J. P. (2006). Where is the knowledge we have lost in managers? *Journal of Knowledge Management*, 10(6), 22–38.

Gloet, M. and Terziovski, M. (2004). Exploring the relationship between knowledge management practices and innovation performance. *Journal of Manufacturing Technology Management*, 15(5), 402–409.

Gourlay, S. (2000). Frameworks for knowledge: a contribution towards conceptual clarity for knowledge management. Paper presented at the "Knowledge Management: Concepts and Controversies" Conference,

Warwick University, UK, February 10–11, 2000. Available at http://bprc.warwick.ac.uk/km013.pdf/.

Gourlay, S. (2006). Conceptualizing knowledge creation: a critique of Nonaka's theory. *Journal of Management Studies*, 43, 1415–1436.

Gray, P. H. and Meister, D. (2003). Introduction: fragmentation and integration in knowledge management research. *Information Technology & People*, 16(3), 259–265.

Grover, V. and Davenport, T. H. (2001). General perspectives on knowledge management: fostering a research agenda. *Journal of Management Information Systems*, 18(1), 5–21.

Gu, Y. (2004). Global knowledge management research: a bibliometric analysis. *Scientometrics*, 61, 171–190.

Hildreth, P. M. and Kimble, C. (2002). The duality of knowledge. *Information Research* (online journal), 8(1), available at http://informationr.net/ir/8-1/paper142.html/.

Jashapara, A. (2004). *Knowledge Management: An Integrated Approach*. Essex: Prentice Hall.

Jashapara, A. (2005). The emerging discourse of knowledge management: a new dawn for information science research? *Journal of Information Science*, 31(2), 136–148.

Kakabadse, N. K., Kouzmin, A. and Kakabadse, A. (2001). From tacit knowledge to knowledge management: leveraging invisible assets. *Knowledge and Process Management*, 8(3), 137–154.

King, W. R., Chung, T. R. and Haney, M. H. (2008). Editorial: knowledge management and organizational learning. *Omega*, 36, 167–172.

Koenig, M. E. D. (1997). Intellectual capital and how to leverage it. *The Bottom Line*, 10(3), 112–118.

Lin, C. and Wu, C. (2005). A knowledge creation model for ISO 9001:2000. *Total Quality Management*, 16(5), 657–670.

Loermans, J. (2002). Synergizing the learning organization and knowledge management. *Journal of Knowledge Management*, 6(3), 285–294.

Loughridge, B. (1999). Knowledge management, librarians and information managers: fad or future? *New Library World*, 100(6), 245–253.

Malhotra, Y. (2000). From information management to knowledge management: beyond the "hi-tech hidebound" systems. In T. K. Srikantaiah and M. E. D. Koenig (eds.), *Knowledge Management for the Information Professional* (pp. 37–61), Medford, NJ: Information Today, Inc.

Mallach, E. (1994). *Understanding Decision Support Systems and Expert Systems*. Burr Ridge, IL: Richard D. Irwin.

Marks, P., Polak, P., McCoy, S. and Galletta, D. (2008). Sharing knowledge. *Communications of the ACM*, 51(2), 60–65.

Mårtensson, M. (2000). A critical review of knowledge management as a management tool. *Journal of Knowledge Management*, 4(3), 204–216.

Nissen, M., Kamel, M. and Sengupta, K. (2000). Integrated analysis and design of knowledge systems and processes. *Information Resources Management Journal*, 13(1), 24–43.

Nonaka, I. and Takeuchi, H. (1995). *The Knowledge-Creating Company: How Japanese Companies Create the Dynamics of Innovation*. Oxford: Oxford University Press.

Nonaka, I., Toyama, R. and Konno, N. (2000). SECI, *ba* and leadership: a unified model of dynamic knowledge creation. *Long Range Planning*, 33, 5–34.

O'Dell, C. and Grayson, C. J. (1998). If only we knew what we know: identification and transfer of internal best practices. *California Management Review*, 40, 154–174.

Oluic-Vukovic, V. (2001). From information to knowledge: some reflections on the origin of the current shifting towards knowledge processing and further perspective. *Journal of the American Society for Information Science and Technology*, 52, 54–61.

Place, I. and Hyslop, D. J. (1982). *Records Management: Controlling Business Information*. Reston, VA: Reston Publishing Company.

Ruggles, R. (1997). *Knowledge Management Tools*. Boston, MA: Butterworth-Heinemann.

Sambamurthy, V. and Subramani, M. (2005). Special issue on information technology and knowledge management. *MIS Quarterly*, 29(1), 1–7.

Sharif, A. M. and Al-Karaghouli, W. (2011). Introduction: exploring the frontiers of knowledge management transfer in the public and private sector. *Information Systems Management*, 28(1), 2–4.

Sharratt, M. and Usoro, A. (2003). Understanding knowledge-sharing in online communities of practice. *Electronic Journal on Knowledge Management*, 1(2), 187–196.

Shin, M., Holden, T. and Schmidt, R. A. (2001). From knowledge theory to management practice: towards an integrated approach. *Information Processing and Management*, 37, 335–355.

Siemieniuch, C. E. and Sinclair, M. A. (1999). Organizational aspects of knowledge lifecycle management in manufacturing. *International Journal of Human-Computer Studies*, 51, 517–547.

Streatfield, D. and Wilson, T. (1999). Deconstructing knowledge management. *Aslib Proceedings*, 51(3), 67–71.

Swan, J., Newell, S., Scarbrough, H. and Hislop, D. (1999). Knowledge management and innovation: networks and networking. *Journal of Knowledge Management*, 3, 262–275.

Tsoukas, H. and Vladimirou, E. (2001). What is organizational knowledge? *Journal of Management Studies*, 38(7), 973–993.

van Beveren, J. (2002). A model of knowledge acquisition that refocuses knowledge management. *Journal of Knowledge Management*, 6(1), 18–22.

Vera, D. and Crossan, M. (2003). Organizational learning and knowledge management: toward an integrative framework. In M. Easterby-Smith and M. A. Lyles (eds.), *The Blackwell Handbook of Organizational Learning and Knowledge Management* (pp. 122–141), Oxford: Blackwell.

Ward, R. C. (2002). Knowledge management, information management, or organizational learning: a comparative study of three states' approaches to knowledge management and information technology. Paper presented at the Southeastern Conference on Public Administration, Columbia, South Carolina, October.

Willett, S. and Copeland, L. (1998). Knowledge management key to IBM's enterprise plan. *Computer Reseller News*, 800, July, 1–6.

Wilson, T. D. (1989). Towards an information management curriculum. *Journal of Information Science*, 15, 203–210.

Wilson, T. D. (2002a). *Knowledge Management Review: The Practitioner's Guide to Knowledge Management*. Chicago, IL: Melcrum Publishing.

Wilson, T. D. (2002b). The nonsense of 'knowledge management'. *Information Research* (online journal), 8(1), available at http://informationr.net/ir/8-1/paper144.html/.

Zmud, R. (2002). Special issue on redefining the organizational roles of information technology in the information age. *MIS Quarterly*, 26(3).

Chapter 8

Knowledge Management and Organizational Learning

Knowledge Objectives

After studying this chapter, you should be able to:

- Provide a basic introduction of organizational learning;
- Explore the origins of organizational learning;
- Discuss the notion of organizational learning from philosophical perspectives;
- Identify the properties of organizational learning;
- Describe the significance of learning in organizations; and
- Explain the linkage between organizational learning and knowledge management.

8.1 Introducing the Chapter

In today's turbulent global environment, the opportunity and capability to learn gives strength to organizations. As has been mentioned in previous chapters, an organization's competitive advantage depends very much on the capacity to manage its knowledge adequately. Resonating with this, several authors (e.g., de Geus, 1988; Vera and Crossan, 2003; Wick and Leon, 1993) contend that those organizations that have the ability to learn faster — and use knowledge immediately — than competing organizations seem to be more successful. Wick and Leon (1993, p. 19), for example, recognize the significance of organizational learning, commenting that organizations must either "learn or die". This chapter aims to identify and clarify the issues surrounding the concept of organizational learning with respect to knowledge management, in order to provide fresh insights into the interdisciplinary field of knowledge management.

Over the last three decades, the concept of organizational learning has received greater attention in the management literature (see Argyris and Schön, 1978, 1996; Bontis *et al.*, 2002; Cohen and Sproull, 1996; Crossan and Guatto, 1996; Crossan *et al.*, 1995, 1999; Daft and Huber, 1987; de Geus, 1988; Dodgson, 1993; Easterby-Smith, 1997; Fiol and Lyles, 1985; Huber, 1991; Jones, 1995; Levitt and March, 1988; Miner and Mezias, 1996; Senge, 1990; Shrivastava, 1983; Stata, 1989; Wick and Leon, 1993). Interest in the notion of organizational learning on the part of academics and practitioners has increased dramatically in recent decades, as evidenced by the proliferation of books and journal articles published so far on the subject. In particular, scholars like Chris Argyris, Nick Bontis, John Child, Michael Cohen, Mary Crossan, Richard Cyert, Richard Daft, Arie de Geus, Mark Easterby-Smith, C. Marlene Fiol, Tracy Guatto, George Huber, Barbara Levitt, Marjorie Lyles, James March, Donald Schön, Peter Senge, Paul Shrivastava and Lee Sproull have contributed much to develop and popularize the organizational learning field.

Formal research on organizational learning is observed in the launching of journals on the subject and in the devotion of special issues of several top scholarly journals to various aspects of organizational learning. Five peer-reviewed research journals have surfaced that address major issues of organizational learning as a primary focus (see Table 8.1). Furthermore, several special issues of management journals (e.g., *Organization Science*, 1999; *Organizational Dynamics*, 1993; *Accounting, Management and Information Technologies*, 1995; *Information and Organization*, 1995; *Omega*, 2008; *Organization Studies*, 1996; *Journal of Organizational Change Management*, 1996) are devoted to the concept of organizational learning.

Table 8.1 A List of Journals on Organizational Learning

Journal Title	Year Launched	Frequency	Publisher
International Journal of Innovation and Learning	2003	Bimonthly	Inderscience
International Journal of Knowledge and Learning	2005	Bimonthly	Inderscience
International Journal of Learning and Change	2005	Quarterly	Inderscience
International Journal of Learning and Intellectual Capital	2004	Quarterly	Inderscience
The Learning Organization	1994	Bimonthly	Emerald

Organizational learning is the process of improving an organization's capability to take effective actions through the use of organizational knowledge. Parallel interest in knowledge management and organizational learning has been sustained for the last two decades. Indeed, "organizational learning" and "knowledge management" are commonly used terms in today's management literature. However, there is a conceptual confusion between the two fields.

The literature on organizational learning and knowledge management is characterized by the use of very diverse terminologies. One could ask whether supporting organizational learning is the same thing as managing organizational knowledge. It is noted that there is limited research that jointly discusses the terms "knowledge management" and "organizational learning". Some argue that knowledge is an antecedent of learning, while others believe that knowledge is shaped by learning. Moreover, limited research examines the relationship between organizational learning and knowledge management. These fields are seldom discussed together. Vera and Crossan (2003) support this, contending that efforts to discuss and distinguish the fields of organizational learning and knowledge management are rare. Only recently, however, has research begun to address these constructs together. Resonating with this, Dimitriades (2005) states, "Until fairly recently, the terms 'organizational learning' and 'knowledge management' were often used interchangeably".

Against this backdrop, this chapter intends to fully address the similarities and differences between both fields of research. The purpose of this chapter is to provide a conceptual framework that defines organizational learning and then integrates it with knowledge management, thereby establishing a theoretical link between the two fields and reducing the conceptual confusion between them.

This chapter is organized in the following manner. First, I will briefly describe the definitions of organizational learning so as to clarify concepts in Section 8.2. As we know, organizational learning is the process through which employees share, generate, evaluate and combine knowledge. Early academic discussions about the concept of organizational learning date back to the 1960s. An understanding of its historical development is necessary in order to clarify its current status. With this aim, Section 8.3 discusses the origins of the organizational learning field. An organization's capability to learn is essential to enhance and sustain its competitive advantage. The organizational learning discipline has received attention among both academics and practitioners because it helps to improve organizational performance. Section 8.4 highlights the strategic importance of organizational learning. It is important to understand not only what organizational learning is, but also what its characteristics are so as to clarify the concepts associated with the organizational learning field. The properties of organizational learning are thus identified in Section 8.5. There are scholars who establish a positive link between organizational learning and knowledge management; contrarily, other authors do not see a direct relationship between these constructs. Section 8.6 furnishes the contradictory views of scholars on the question of whether knowledge management is a forerunner of organizational learning or vice versa. As we will see, learning has been increasingly defined in terms of knowledge processes. Section 8.7 addresses the similarities and differences between organizational learning and knowledge management, emphasizing the overlaps and synergies between these fields of research. Finally, the chapter ends with some concluding remarks in Section 8.8.

8.2 Organizational Learning Defined

As a starting point, it is important to understand what a learning organization is and what its characteristics are. This section will expand the notion of organizational learning, gathering definitions of the construct as well as giving a general overview of the organizational learning field from various perspectives. The fact is that it is difficult to define organizational learning. Numerous definitions of organizational learning have been provided by management theorists in the relevant literature. Most notably, Argote (1999), Argyris and Schön (1978), Cyert and March (1963), Huber (1991), Spender (2008), Levinthal and March (1993), Daft and Weick (1984), Fiol and Lyles (1985), Robey *et al.* (2000), Rahim (2002), and Lopez *et al.* (2004) have provided definitions of organizational learning that are widely cited in the extant literature.

Table 8.2 presents various organizational learning definitions as given by management scholars. Most organizational learning theorists (e.g., Argyris and Schön, 1978; Duncan and Weiss, 1979; Miller, 1996; Crossan *et al.*, 1995) conclude that the learning process encompasses both cognitive and behavioral change, and that individuals and groups learn by understanding and then by acting and interpreting. Parallel to this, Armstrong and Foley (2003, p. 74) agree that most definitions of organizational learning "concentrate on the observation and analysis of the processes involved in individual and collective learning inside organizations".

As evidenced from Table 8.2, no consensus has emerged on the definition of organizational learning. This is because various approaches and understandings surrounding organizational learning still remain in play (see Easterby-Smith *et al.*, 2000). However, it could be argued that learning has been increasingly defined in terms of knowledge processes. More specifically, several authors (e.g., Brown and Woodland, 1999; Wikstrom and Normann, 1994) claim that learning is the process of acquiring knowledge.

Here, I give a general overview of different perspectives of organizational learning. Hong *et al.* (2006) identify three broad streams of research in the organizational learning field: cognitive,

Table 8.2 Organizational Learning Definitions

Authors	Definitions
Addleson (1999)	The process of gaining knowledge and developing skills which empower organizational members to understand and thus to act effectively within social institutions (e.g., organizations)
Argote (1999)	The processes through which members share, generate, evaluate and combine knowledge
Argyris and Schön (1978)	A process of detecting and correcting errors
Cavaleri and Fearon (1996)	The purposeful creation of shared meanings derived from the common experiences of people in organizations
Crossan *et al.* (1995)	A process of change in cognition and behavior; it does not necessarily follow that these changes will directly enhance performance
Cyert and March (1963)	The adaptive processes of organizations
Daft and Weick (1984)	Knowledge about the interrelationships between an organization's actions and the environment
Day (1994)	A process that is comprised of open-minded inquiry, informed interpretations and accessible memory
Fiol and Lyles (1985)	The process of improving actions through better knowledge and understanding
Huber (1991)	A change in the range of an organization's potential behavior, which may or may not contribute to enhanced effectiveness
Kim (1993)	An increase in an organization's capability to take effective action
Lee *et al.* (1992)	A cyclical process in which individuals' actions lead to organizational interactions with the environment; environmental responses are then interpreted by individuals who learn by updating their beliefs about cause–effect relationships
Levinthal and March (1993)	A mechanism to cope with the problems of balancing the competing goals of developing new knowledge and exploiting current competencies in the face of dynamic tendencies to emphasize one or the other

(*Continued*)

Table 8.2 (*Continued*)

Authors	Definitions
Lopez *et al.* (2004)	A dynamic process of creation, acquisition and integration of knowledge aimed at the development of resources and capabilities that contribute to better organizational performance
Meyer-Dohm (1992)	The continuous testing and transforming of experience into shared knowledge, which an organization accesses and uses to achieve its core purpose
Miller (1996)	A process that increases organizational knowledge, unlike decision making which need not; learning may in fact occur long before, or long after, action is taken
Nadler *et al.* (1992)	A process that requires an environment in which the results of experiments are sought after, examined and disseminated throughout an organization
Rahim (2002)	The activities that involve knowledge acquisition, knowledge distribution, information interpretation, and organizational memorization for future access and use
Robey *et al.* (2000)	An organizational process, both intentional and unintentional, that enables the acquisition of, access to and revision of organizational memory, thereby providing direction for organizational action
Shrivastava (1983)	A process by which the organizational knowledge base is developed and shaped
Slater and Narver (1995)	The development of new knowledge or insights that have the potential to influence behavior
Spender (2008)	The study of the learning processes of and within organizations
Stata (1989)	The principal process by which innovation occurs; in fact, the rate at which individuals and organizations learn may become the only sustainable competitive advantage, especially in knowledge-intensive industries
Strach and Everett (2006)	A focused, time-framed activity aimed at developing a given set of skills or gaining a relatively narrowly targeted set of knowledge
Vera and Crossan (2003)	The process of change in individual and shared thought and action, which is affected by and embedded in the institutions of an organization

routine-oriented and social/contextual perspectives. Each of these perspectives has a role to play in explaining various aspects of organizational learning, as elaborated below:

- *Cognitive perspective.* The cognitive, or knowledge-oriented, perspective tends to view organizational learning as the process of acquiring, creating, accumulating, storing and disseminating the knowledge of an organization. Within this perspective, organizational learning is assumed to entail content updating of the various categories of organizational knowledge (technical, procedural or strategic, in explicit or tacit form) collected from various sources, be they endogenous or exogenous.
- *Routine-oriented perspective.* Such a stream of research tends to focus on the repetitive sequences of activities in organizations. That is, organizational routines are defined as formalized, habitual, collective organizational practices that give rise to a shared understanding through the generation, integration and dissemination of knowledge. The major assumption here is that continuous modification and upgrading of collective routines (e.g., mechanistic and heuristic) enable organizations to respond to their changing environments.
- *Social (contextual) perspective.* The social (contextual) perspective tends to focus on situated learning. Within this stream, organizational learning is assumed to entail active, day-to-day participation in the construction of social processes, subject to the influence of various contexts such as culture and history.

Apparently, the definitions of organizational learning vary in their description. As mentioned earlier, organizational learning has been defined in several different ways. However, most definitions share common issues relating to knowledge, which may be interpreted as processes of knowledge creation, knowledge transfer, and knowledge storage for present and future use in order to improve the competitive advantage of an organization. It is also important to understand the origins of organizational learning. This will be dealt with next.

8.3 Origins of Organizational Learning

An understanding of the origins of organizational learning is necessary in order to clarify the current status of organizational learning concepts (Loermans, 2002). Early academic discussions about the concept of organizational learning date back to the 1960s (Cangelosi and Dill, 1965). In line with this, research by Lyles and Easterby-Smith (2003) suggests that Cyert and March were the first authors to reference organizational learning in their 1963 publication:

> It was a little over ten years ago that a conference was held at Carnegie Mellon University to honour March and his contribution to the field of organizational learning. This conference brought together researchers to assist in defining the field, to discuss current theoretical development, and to identify the areas of research for the future. [Lyles and Easterby-Smith, 2003]

On the other hand, Robey *et al.* (2000) report that Argyris and Schön (1978) were the earliest proponents of organizational learning. In any case, the topics surrounding this field have noticeably captured the attention of managers and other practitioners; for instance, Senge (1990) attempts to make popular the concept of organizational learning in his book, *The Fifth Discipline*. In this regard, de Pablos (2002) draws a succint picture of the development of organizational learning: "Back in 1965, Cangelosi and Dill concluded that more empirical work was required in order to advance the field. Two decades later, Fiol and Lyles (1985) recognized that challenges have not been met yet. The field has been slow to evolve and even now there is a tremendous scarcity of empirical research in this field".

8.4 The Role of Organizational Learning

Despite the confusion that may emerge due to the diverse definitions of organizational learning as shown in Table 8.2, there seems to be a consensus that treats it as a process enabling the acquisition, creation, accumulation, storage and transfer of knowledge. Organizational learning provides direction for organizational action, which in turn directly contributes to better organizational performance. The definitions of organizational learning proposed by management theorists such as Argyris and Schön (1978), Huber (1991), Lopez *et al.* (2004), Crossan *et al.* (1995), Crossan and Hulland (1997), Meyer-Dohm (1992), Bontis *et al.* (2002), and Fiol and Lyles (1985) actually emphasize the contribution of learning to enhance organizational effectiveness and organizational performance.

The role of organizational learning for business survival has been increasingly discussed since the 1990s. As noted earlier, the organizational learning field has received attention among both academics and practitioners, because an organization's capability to learn is essential in order to enhance and sustain its competitive advantage. Although the relationship between learning and performance is complex, most scholars (e.g., Senge, 1990; Malhotra, 1996; Manasco, 1998; Sandelands, 1999) agree that organizational learning helps to improve organizational performance. Drawing from organizational learning theory, the assumption here is that effective acquisition and utilization of knowledge is a source of flexibility, adaptability and competitive advantage (Stata, 1989; Spicer and Sadler-Smith, 2006), and hence is associated with better organizational performance.

Researchers have similar views about the impact of learning and knowledge on firm performance. Several scholars (Cangelosi and Dill, 1965; Fiol and Lyles, 1985; Rayport and Sviokla, 1995) establish a positive link between these constructs. Cangelosi and Dill (1965), for example, mention that improved performance *is* learning. Furthermore, effective learning can increase the probability of improved performance (Bontis *et al.*, 2002; Crossan *et al.*, 1995; Crossan and Hulland, 1996). In this context, Bontis *et al.* (2002) empirically prove that there is a positive relationship between the stocks of learning at all levels of an organization and business performance.

Several other authors (e.g., Stata, 1989; Senge, 1990; Ulrich *et al.*, 1993; McGill and Slocum, 1993; Nevis *et al.*, 1995) believe that an organization's ability to learn and utilize the lessons it has learnt faster than its rivals is a strategic source of sustainable competitive advantage. Ulrich *et al.* (1993, p. 55), for instance, argue that a successful organization is one that can learn new knowledge and translate it into action quicker than rival organizations. Parallel to this, Senge (1990) contends, "The most successful corporation of the 1990s will be something called the learning organization and the ability to learn faster than your competitors may be the only sustainable means of achieving competitive advantage".

The notion of a learning organization and its properties will now be discussed in turn.

8.5 Properties of Organizational Learning

There are various concepts associated with the organizational learning field, such as individual learning, organizational learning and the learning organization. Writers (e.g., Sun and Scott, 2003; Easterby-Smith and Lyles, 2003; Pemberton and Stonehouse, 2000) often use the terms "organizational learning" and "learning organization" interchangeably. Pemberton and Stonehouse (2000) state that organizational learning is an integral feature of any learning organization. Nowadays, however, a growing consensus seems to be emerging that differentiates these constructs (Sun and Scott, 2003). Easterby-Smith and Lyles (2003) support this, stating that organizational learning and the learning organization are each quite different.

In this regard, scholars argue that the notion of the learning organization is increasingly relevant to 21st-century management research because of the greater complexity and uncertainty of the business environment, along with technological and market uncertainties in the turbulent global environment. As Loermans (2002) states, a learning organization generates new knowledge which helps to enhance and sustain its competitive advantage; at the same time, the learning organization must ensure that such new knowledge is properly codified, organized and made available for optimal use by all those who need it. In other words, a learning organization needs to effectively manage the knowledge that it creates so as to continue learning. It is, therefore, important to understand what a learning organization is and what the characteristics of a learning organization are.

Table 8.3 provides a list of definitions of a learning organization as given by organizational learning scholars. An organization needs to

Table 8.3 Learning Organization Definitions

Authors	Definitions
Akhavan and Jafari (2006)	An organization that creates, acquires and transfers competence, and that is able to change its behavior according to new knowledge and views
Garvin (1993)	An organization that is skilled in creating, acquiring and transferring knowledge, and at modifying its behavior to reflect new knowledge and insights
Huber (1991)	An entity that learns if, through its processing of information, the range of its potential behaviors is changed
Levitt and March (1988)	An organization that learns by encoding inferences from history into routines that guide behavior
Marquardt (1996)	An organization that learns powerfully and collectively, and that continually transforms itself to better collect, manage and use knowledge for success
Mills and Friesen (1992)	An organization that sustains internal innovation with the immediate goals of improving quality, enhancing customer or supplier relationships, and more effectively executing business strategy, and with the ultimate objective of sustaining profitability
Senge (1990)	A place where people continually expand their capacity of creating results they really want, where patterns of thinking are broadened and matured, where collective aspiration is free, and where people continually learn to learn
Strach and Everett (2006)	A problem-solving process targeted at filling the gaps between actual and potential performance

learn quickly while it works so that it can adapt quickly to make changes so as to adjust with the external environment. Garvin (1998) suggests that the building blocks of a learning organization include learning from past experience, learning from others and transferring knowledge. In Senge's (1990) book, *The Fifth Discipline*, he describes learning organizations as places where organizational members continually expand their capacity to produce the results they expect, where new patterns of thinking are nurtured, where collective aspiration is set free, and where members continually learn how to learn together. Senge (1990) establishes five disciplines associated with a learning organization:

- Systems thinking;
- Personal mastery;
- Mental models;
- Building of a shared vision; and
- Team learning.

These disciplines are considered necessary for an organization to be regarded as a learning organization.

Learning organizations are seen as intelligent enterprises that are capable of managing knowledge-based activities, which are the key to productivity and wealth generation (see Quinn, 1992, as cited in Katsoulakos and Zevgolis, 2004). In line with this, Lopez *et al.* (2004) review various studies on organizational learning and identify four constructs:

- *Acquisition of knowledge*, which is done through internal development or by extracting knowledge from external sources;
- *Distribution of knowledge*, which is transferred among organizational members;
- *Interpretation of knowledge*, which is done through sharing knowledge among organizational members; and
- *Organizational memory*, which is the storage of knowledge for future use.

Based on the above constructs, Lopez *et al.* (2004) go even further to identify the properties of organizational learning. They characterize the organizational learning process by a series of key features, as mentioned below:

- Learning is a *transformation* activity that is continuously created and recreated, and not an independent entity to be acquired or transferred.
- Learning is *cumulative* in that the amount of knowledge at a certain point in time is a function of the cumulated knowledge acquired up to that moment.

- Learning is a *process* whose goal is to improve an organization by means of new initiatives into the organization, and thereby impact organizational performance.
- Learning is a *system-level process*, which embraces the whole of the organization and not just a particular individual(s).

Several other scholars (e.g., Argyris and Schön, 1978; Crossan *et al.*, 1995; de Pablos, 2002; Strach and Everett, 2006) suggest different types of learning processes, including:

- *Single-loop learning*, which is manifested in cognitive and behavioral changes within the existing strategic paradigm;
- *Double-loop learning*, which involves changes through breaking out of the existing paradigm;
- *Incremental learning*, which is manifested in small changes in the observed pattern of behavior;
- *Radical learning*, which involves radical changes in the observed pattern of behavior;
- *Internal learning*, which is manifested by learning within the boundary of a firm; and
- *External learning*, which is all about learning from others who reside outside an organization's own boundary, such as alliance partners, competitors, suppliers, customers, etc.

It is important to understand not only what a learning organization is and what its characteristics are, but also how it relates to the emerging topic of knowledge management. This is due to the fact that a learning organization needs to effectively manage the knowledge that it creates so as to continue learning. This will be dealt with next.

8.6 Scholars' Views on the Connection Between Knowledge Management and Organizational Learning

As noted previously, organizational learning refers to the study of the learning processes of and within organizations. One could ask whether supporting organizational learning is the same thing as managing organizational knowledge. This section will contribute to this debate, and argue that a better understanding of the relationship between organizational learning and knowledge management can provide valuable insights into this linkage issue. The research examining the connection between the two fields is somewhat limited. Nevertheless, several scholars (e.g., Pemberton and Stonehouse, 2000; Argote *et al.*, 2003; Dimitriades, 2005; King *et al.*, 2008; Metaxiotis and Psarras, 2006; Easterby-Smith and Lyles, 2003) have attempted to contribute to the knowledge management and organizational learning literature by clarifying the concepts and presenting frameworks that appear to illustrate their relationship.

In the knowledge-based society, there is no doubt that knowledge and learning are the key sources of competitive advantage for organizations (Kleiner and Roth, 1998; Badaracco, 1991; Drucker, 1993; Senge, 1990; Sveiby, 1997; Boisot, 1998). Surprisingly, however, many researchers in the organizational learning field exclude the term "knowledge" from their literature, while authors from the knowledge management area often fail to acknowledge the term "learning" in their writings. For example, knowledge management scholars such as Davenport and Prusak (1998) and Sveiby (1997) do not mention "learning" in the relevant literature; while organizational learning scholars such as Senge (1990), Malhotra (1996) and Santosus (1996) rarely mention the term "knowledge". Similarly, scholars such as Davenport (1997), Davenport and Prusak (1998), Nonaka and Takeuchi (1995), and Swan *et al.* (1999) are not ready to accept any connection between organizational learning and knowledge management. Moreover, there are only a few discussions relating to organizational learning (e.g., Addleson, 1999; Schein, 1996) that briefly mention "knowledge" in passing, without expanding any further on the association between these constructs.

However, there are some scholars (e.g., King *et al.*, 2008; Choo, 1998; Kolb *et al.*, 1991; Lave, 1993; Coulson-Thomas, 1997) who recognize the linkage between organizational learning and knowledge management. The relationship between organizational learning and knowledge management is covered by a host of authors (Argote *et al.*, 2003; King *et al.*, 2008; Kolb *et al.*, 1991; Lave, 1993; Coulson-Thomas, 1997; Gloet and Terziovski, 2004; Allee, 1997; Cangelosi and Dill, 1965; Fiol and Lyles, 1985; Loermans, 2002; Scarbrough and Swan, 2001; Leonard and Sensiper, 1998; de Pablos, 2002; Sierhuis and Clancey, 1997; Revilla *et al.*, 2005; Moreno-Luzon and Lloria, 2008; Metaxiotis and Psarras, 2006; Figueroa and González, 2006). For instance, Choo (1998) argues that knowledge management has become a key issue in theoretical and empirical research in a wide variety of disciplinary fields, including organizational learning.

8.6.1 *Knowledge Management as an Outcome of Organizational Learning*

Many researchers (Bontis *et al.*, 2002; Revilla *et al.*, 2005; Strach and Everett, 2006) use the terms "learning" and "knowledge" interchangeably. Revilla *et al.* (2005), for example, suggest that learning and knowledge are closely linked, whereby knowledge is a critical output of learning. Gloet and Terziovski (2004) observe that contemporary knowledge management approaches appear to represent an extension of organizational learning.

In line with this, Antonacopoulou (2006) contends that knowledge is not just an antecedent of learning, but is also shaped by learning. Likewise, Strach and Everett (2006) argue that knowledge is often associated with learning. Pisano (1994) adds that supporting learning and managing knowledge at both individual and organizational levels play a central role in improving the competitive edge of firms. As Allee (1997) puts it, "In order to be a high-performing learning organization, work processes must incorporate conscious and deliberate attention to every aspect of knowledge".

The fact is that knowledge generation is believed to be the final outcome of the learning process. Conversely, learning occurs when the creation, exchange and application of organizational knowledge is discussed. Although its definitions as presented in Table 8.2 vary in their description, learning has been increasingly defined in terms of knowledge processes. Argote (1999), for example, defines learning as "knowledge acquisition". Wikstrom and Normann (1994) state that knowledge is achieved through learning, adding that everyday learning is a natural and continuous process and often leads to knowledge acquisition. According to Antonacopoulou (2006), the existing definitions of learning actually present knowledge as one of the outcomes of learning.

Knowledge is also seen as an important part of the learning process. In this context, several commentators (e.g., Revans, 1971; Klatt *et al.*, 1985) state that there are a few essential requirements to complete learning. These key requirements, all of which surround knowledge, include:

- The recognition of one's own need to learn;
- The search for the relevant knowledge; and
- The test of that new knowledge in practical action.

This is supported by Swan *et al.* (1999), who argue that "knowledge management is not a development of, but a divergence from, the literature on organizational learning".

8.6.2 *Knowledge Management and Organizational Learning as Two Distinct Disciplines*

Having reviewed the relevant literature, Antonacopoulou (2006) reports that in some cases organizational learning and knowledge management are treated as distinct entities. Several scholars (e.g., Easterby-Smith and Lyles, 2003; Antonacopoulou, 2006; Nonaka and Takeuchi, 1995; Davenport, 1997; Swan *et al.*, 1999; Davenport and Prusak, 1998) support this, treating them as distinct and thereby independent disciplines. Nonaka and Takeuchi (1995), for example, insist that organizational learning and knowledge management are two different concepts. Davenport (1997) also suggests that organizational learning is an entirely different discipline to knowledge management. Reflecting this view, Easterby-Smith and Lyles (2003) successfully map the two sets of literatures to show that organizational learning and knowledge management are each quite different. Several recent journal special issues as well as articles in regular academic journals illustrate the current interest in knowledge management by theorists in the organizational learning field alone.

8.6.3 *Knowledge Management and Organizational Learning as Complementary to Each Other*

Scarbrough and Swan (2001) assert that the conceptualization of knowledge management overlaps to some extent with other literatures, including that of the organizational learning field. Indeed, King *et al.* (2008) strongly view that organizational learning is complementary to knowledge management.

Not only are the terms "knowledge" and "learning" often used interchangeably (Bontis *et al.*, 2002), but there is also conceptual confusion between the terms "organizational learning" and "knowledge management". More specifically, one could ask whether fostering and supporting a learning organization is the same thing as managing organizational knowledge. In this regard, Metaxiotis and Psarras (2006) suggest that knowledge creation is now being explored as an increasingly critical factor that is needed to support organizational learning. Similarly, Pemberton and Stonehouse (2000, p. 186) state that successful learning organizations create an organizational environment that combines organizational learning with knowledge management.

Goh (2003, as cited in Dimitriades, 2005) contends that the current literature on organizational learning "uses a confusing variety of terms and concepts". As mentioned earlier, the terms "organizational learning" and "knowledge management" are often used interchangeably. Loermans (2002) adds that the discipline of knowledge management and the phenomenon of the learning organization are inextricably linked. Reflecting this view, Figueroa and González (2006) assert that the processes of knowledge management and organizational learning are intimately related.

As we have seen, most definitions of organizational learning share common issues relating to knowledge, which may be interpreted as processes of knowledge creation, knowledge transfer, and knowledge storage for future use in order to improve an organization's competitive advantage. According to Rahim (2002), the notion of organizational learning refers to the activities that involve knowledge acquisition, knowledge distribution, information interpretation, and organizational memorization for future access and use. This definition provides evidence that the terms "organizational learning" and "knowledge management" can be used interchangeably. Likewise, Jasimuddin (2005) states that "knowledge management involves activities related to capturing, utilizing, creating, transferring, and storing of organizational knowledge".

In this regard, Spender's (2008) comments on organizational learning and knowledge management are worth mentioning:

> In practice, the two literatures run curiously parallel and, worshiping at different altars, honor different high priests; March or Argyris and double loops, on the one hand, versus Polanyi and tacit knowledge, on the other. While the focus of organizational learning is mostly on managing the production or growth of the organization's knowledge, knowledge management is more puzzling. At times it seems to embrace learning, whereas at other times it suggests the more extensive agendas of the 'knowledge-based view' or the knowledge-based view of competitive advantage.

Based on the above discussion, it is evident that there are contradictory views regarding the relationship between knowledge management and organizational learning. On one side of this debate, there are scholars who believe that organizational learning and knowledge management are the same thing because organizational knowledge is right in the center of the organizational learning paradigm. In fact, the availability of knowledge is crucial in order to learn and then put it into action. Others do not see a direct relationship between these constructs, arguing that they are two distinct disciplines. Yet others tend to establish a positive link between these constructs. It can be argued that organizational learning and knowledge management are closely linked, and that the latter is a part of the former or vice versa. In this regard, Spender (2008) rightly states that knowledge is generated by manageable processes of organizational learning, with the outcome being managed in turn by the processes of knowledge management. Hence, these fields are complementary (Antal *et al.*, 2001). Significant improvements can only be achieved by organizations if synergies are generated between both of these processes through understanding their connection. The next section will discuss this in more detail.

8.7 Linkage Between Knowledge Management and Organizational Learning

Many terms have emerged in the relevant literature to describe and prescribe organizational learning and knowledge management. There are diverse opinions on the connection between the two fields. Argote *et al.* (2003) contend that interest in the issues surrounding the two disciplines on the part of academics and practitioners has increased dramatically in recent years, as evidenced by the proliferation of books and journal articles published on both subjects. It is, therefore, important to understand how organizational learning relates to the emerging knowledge management subject.

This section will fully address the similarities and differences between knowledge management and organizational learning, and thereby explore their relationship. Or, stated differently, this section will attempt to find the connection between both fields of research and discuss its applicability. As noted previously, a variety of perspectives have been used to look at organizational learning issues, whilst knowledge management scholars such as Allee (1997) suggest that each aspect of knowledge has a corresponding learning activity which supports it. Taking a broader view, knowledge management and organizational learning appear to have somewhat overlapping issues. At the same time, both disciplines are treated as sources of competitive advantage (Vera and Crossan, 2003).

It is revealed that knowledge management works well with organizational learning in an organizational setting. Nowadays, a growing consensus seems to be emerging that differentiates these constructs as follows:

- Effective knowledge management can create more successful organizational learning; and
- Organizational learning is crucial for knowledge management implementation.

In particular, this section will highlight several factors that explore the similarities and differences between organizational learning and knowledge management, and establish a theoretical link between these constructs. Indeed, knowledge management approaches appear to represent an extension of organizational learning (Gloet and Terziovski, 2004). The section will also go further to explain how organizational learning and knowledge management fit together. I will begin by defining the two constructs and acknowledging their distinct roots. Table 8.4 depicts the similarities and differences between these fields of research.

Similarity in definitions. Defining organizational learning and knowledge management will help us to determine whether the two fields are the same or different. According to Scarbrough and Swan (2001), knowledge management is "any process of creating, acquiring, capturing, sharing and using knowledge, wherever it resides, to enhance learning and performance in organizations"; while Argote (1999) defines organizational learning as the processes through which organizational members share, generate, evaluate and combine knowledge. It appears that the knowledge management definition has borrowed ideas from organizational learning. This argument is given more weight by Rahim (2002), who defines organizational learning as knowledge acquisition, knowledge distribution, information interpretation and organizational memorization. Therefore, it is evident that the definitions of organizational learning given by authors share common themes with that of knowledge management. More specifically, the definitions of organizational learning and knowledge management have in common the notion of organizational knowledge, which is captured and used (or turned into new knowledge) and

Table 8.4 Comparative Perspectives on Knowledge Management and Organizational Learning

Dimensions	Organizational Learning	Knowledge Management
Disciplinary roots/ Conceptual origins	Organizational behavior, organizational theory	Organizational theory, strategy, epistemology, cognitive science, information management
Perspective	Inside an organization	Both inside and outside an organization
Working definition	The processes through which knowledge is generated, shared and combined among organizational members	Any process of the creation, exchange, distribution and storage of knowledge in an organization
End result	Gaining the competitive advantage of an organization	Gaining the competitive advantage of an organization
Focus	The process of the knowledge (i.e., why and how to learn)	The content of the knowledge (i.e., how to manage knowledge)
Type of organization	Learning organization	Knowledge organization
Role of technology	Less important	Not a critical factor
Key processes	Knowledge acquisition, knowledge distribution, knowledge interpretation, organizational memory	Knowledge creation, knowledge sharing, knowledge dissemination, knowledge exploitation
Person in charge	Chief learning officer	Chief knowledge officer

then disseminated and stored for future use, in order to foster innovation through a spiral of organizational learning and hence improve competitive advantage (Nonaka, 1988, 1991a, 1991b, 1998; Nonaka and Takeuchi, 1995; Nonaka and Reinmoeller, 2000; de Pablos, 2001, 2002; von Krogh and Grand, 2002; Wiig, 1993).

Conceptual origins. One basic difference between organizational learning and knowledge management can be traced by looking at their disciplinary roots. As shown in Chapter 3, knowledge management has been approached from various angles and disciplines, including organizational learning. Since the field of knowledge management emerged in the 1990s, new theoretical models have been developed that support a broader approach to organizational learning within organizations. As Mukherjee (2003) states, "Following the footsteps of organisational learning, knowledge management came to the attention of management researchers in the early 1990s".

While exploring the genesis of the two fields, scholars such as Chae and Bloodgood (2006) acknowledge the distinct roots of each field. As mentioned in Section 8.3, organizational theory has contributed much to the organizational learning field. On the other hand, knowledge management has borrowed from different disciplines, including organizational theory, epistemology, cognitive science, strategy and organizational learning (Jasimuddin, 2005). Interestingly, many scholars — especially organizational learning theorists — still think that knowledge management is an offshoot of organizational learning. Gu (2004, p. 181) supports this, claiming that knowledge management draws from a wide range of disciplines, including organizational learning.

Major focus. Another basic difference between organizational learning and knowledge management is related to their focus. Easterby-Smith and Lyles (2003) assert that organizational learning tends to focus on the process of the knowledge that an organization acquires, creates, processes and eventually uses; whereas knowledge management tends to focus on the content of such knowledge. Similarly, Vera and Crossan (2003) state that organizational learning focuses on learning as a process of change, while knowledge management studies the processes of the discovery and deployment of knowledge.

Perspective. Yet another factor that differentiates organizational learning from knowledge management is their perspective. Organizational learning tends to operate within an organization so as to improve its capability to take effective actions through the use of organizational knowledge. It is true that, in today's turbulent global environment, the capability to learn provides an increasingly important benefit to organizations. Organizations are convinced that the faster an organization can learn, the quicker it can gain a competitive advantage over rival firms. On the other hand, knowledge management functions both within and outside an organization. Knowledge management implies access to a broad knowledge base from both internal and external sources. Indeed, it is widely recognized that knowledge existing outside a firm's boundaries is critical to organizational success.

Processes involved. One common feature in both knowledge management and organizational learning is the processes involved in these fields. Organizational learning is a process of change that involves the activities associated with knowledge acquisition, knowledge distribution, information interpretation, and knowledge storage for future access and use. Likewise, the knowledge management process involves activities related to capturing, utilizing, creating, transferring and storing organizational knowledge. There seems to be a consensus among scholars to treat both the processes of organizational learning and knowledge management as a strategic element that helps to improve an organization's capability to take effective actions through better knowledge creation and learning.

Role of technology. The use of technology is an important factor that differentiates organizational learning and knowledge management. Robey *et al.* (2000) assert that information technology is an enabler of organizational learning. The same thing is true when it comes to implementing knowledge management initiatives. In some cases, though, an over-reliance of technology is found in knowledge management, causing the human side of it to be ignored. Loermans (2002) argues that, although technology plays an important role in storing and disseminating knowledge, it has little or no role in creating new knowledge. Davenport (1997) adds that information technology has not solved the problem of managing knowledge. More specifically, Kleiner and Roth (1998) believe that technology is not a critical factor in knowledge management and is even less so in the learning process. Loermans (2002) supports this, confirming that technology is not an issue for the learning organization; it has, however, become a major issue for knowledge management.

Type of organization. Another factor that makes organizational learning and knowledge management somewhat different is the type of organization, wherein supporting learning and managing knowledge are respectively taken as the top corporate agenda. In the knowledge-based society, advocates of the organizational learning and knowledge management disciplines encourage organizations to claim themselves as learning organizations and knowledge organizations, respectively. According to Strach and Everett (2006), a learning organization transforms information into knowledge and then disseminates the knowledge across organizational units by means of a systematic self-organizing mechanism. The idea of the learning organization is a perpetual organizational philosophy, with principled learning being one of the key roles of the company (Senge, 1990). Pemberton and Stonehouse (2000, p. 184) see organizational learning as an integral feature of any learning organization, meaning such an organization effectively utilizes its knowledge resources to generate superior performance. In this regard, Loermans (2002) suggests that "the organization is only a learning organization if such knowledge is captured and systemized to the benefit of the entire organization".

On the other hand, almost all organizations — be they manufacturing or service-based — appear to be knowledge organizations, since they are involved to some degree in the acquisition, sharing, creation, storage, retrieval and use of knowledge. It is worth mentioning that employees of any organization at all levels use knowledge, so they can be considered knowledge workers. Brown and Duguid (1998) support this, postulating that all organizations are in essence knowledge-based organizations. Moreover, a knowledge organization needs to become a learning organization, thus accounting for Malhotra's (1997) finding that the learning organization is now a common reference within the knowledge management literature. Pemberton and Stonehouse (2000, p. 186) further add that successful learning organizations create an organizational environment that combines organizational learning with knowledge management.

Person in charge. The apparent distinction between organizational learning and knowledge management has led to the creation of different leadership roles in firms, namely, chief learning officers in learning organizations and chief knowledge officers in knowledge organizations. Stuller's (1998) comment is worth mentioning in differentiating the persons in charge: "Chief learning officers have a human resources focus and build on training, education, leadership development, and change management, while chief knowledge officers have an information technology focus and build on knowledge worker productivity, knowledge repositories, and networks".

End result. As mentioned earlier, the role of organizational learning for business survival has increased significantly since the 1970s (Rayport and Sviokla, 1995; Senge, 1990; Malhotra, 1996; Manasco, 1998; Sandelands, 1999). Likewise, knowledge management is purported to be essential to sustained competitive advantage and continued business success (Drucker, 1998; Davenport and Prusak, 1998; Fusaro, 1998; Stewart, 1997). Moreover, Scarbrough and Swan (2001) state that knowledge management enhances learning and performance in organizations. Crossan *et al.* (1995) also conclude that good performance is a sign of learning. Similarly, the knowledge-based view stresses a positive link between knowledge and performance. Ulrich *et al.* (1993, p. 55), for example, argue that a successful organization is one that can learn new knowledge and translate it into action quicker than rival organizations.

Recent empirical efforts have found support for the direct positive impact of both knowledge management and organizational learning on performance. Rayport and Sviokla (1995), for instance, argue that there exists a consensus among scholars and practitioners that knowledge and learning are two of the most strategic resources in gaining the competitive advantage of an organization. In this regard, Vera and Crossan (2003) conclude that the views of the impact of organizational learning and knowledge management on performance are not diverse: "While the learning organization literature presents an equivocal link between the learning process and performance, the knowledge management literature suggests that knowledge — if recognized as a source of competitive advantage — explains differences in performance".

Learning and knowledge are treated as antecedents of firm outcomes. Barney (1991) argues that knowledge which is valuable, rare, inimitable and non-substitutable could lead to competitive advantage. In this context, Vera and Crossan (2003) suggest that learning which is "effective" and knowledge which is "relevant" may have positive effects on performance. Since managing knowledge and supporting learning have become crucial tasks for an organization's survival, both knowledge management and organizational learning have emerged as full-fledged, distinct disciplines. Pisano (1994) reinforces this, arguing that supporting learning and managing knowledge at both individual and organizational levels play a central role in improving the competitive edge of firms.

The above discussion on the relationship between knowledge management and organizational learning provides some insight on the nature of their association. Chae and Bloodgood (2006) remark that learning is a key concept of knowledge management studies. Furthermore, Loermans (2002) sees a close relationship between the theories and practice of knowledge management and organizational learning, making an attempt to identify the synergies. DiBella (2001) proposes that there is a need "to bridge the divide" between knowledge management and organizational learning. Therefore, three situations have emerged in terms of the relationship between the two fields. These are mentioned below:

- In situation I, there is a connection between knowledge management and organizational learning in that organizational learning seems to be an antecedent of knowledge management. One of the key areas in contemporary organizational learning research is the management of knowledge in organizations.
- In situation II, there is an association between knowledge management and organizational learning in that knowledge management facilitates organizational learning. For example, Allee (1997) suggests that each aspect of knowledge management has a corresponding learning activity which supports it. In this context, Sierhuis and Clancey (1997) add that an important aspect of knowledge management is improving an organization's learning capability as well as its propensity to learn.
- In situation III, there is a close linkage between knowledge management and organizational learning, which are equally jointly responsible for developing a learning culture through the sharing

> of organizational knowledge. Put another way, both disciplines are mutually self-supporting: one concept simply cannot operate without the other. In this regard, Brown and Woodland (1999, as cited in Loermans, 2002) add further insight into the synergy between organizational learning and knowledge management by claiming that "it is impossible for an organisation to sustain competitive advantage without constantly learning and developing new knowledge".

There seems to be a consensus among scholars to treat both organizational learning and knowledge management as processes that help improve an organization's capability to take effective action through better knowledge creation and use. To be sure, the debate on the connection between organizational learning and knowledge management is far from over (Schein, 1996; Gourlay, 1999). Nevertheless, this section has contributed to this debate by providing valuable thoughts on the relationship between the two fields. As Robey *et al.* (2000) state, "Knowledge management and organizational learning go hand in hand".

8.8 Concluding Summary

Parallel interest in knowledge management and organizational learning has been sustained for decades. Only recently, however, has research begun to address these fields together. Given that scholars tend to use both terms interchangeably, this chapter has explored whether knowledge management and organizational learning are synonymous or different, or if one is evolved from the other. In doing so, some interesting insights have been gleaned on the nature of knowledge organizations and learning organizations.

This chapter has started by offering definitions of organizational learning so as to clarify its concepts and identify its properties. As we have seen, the organizational learning phenomenon has been defined in several different ways. For example, organizational learning is defined in some circles as the process through which employees share, generate, evaluate and combine knowledge. It is evident that most organizational learning definitions share common issues relating to knowledge, which may be interpreted as the creation of new knowledge through the processes of knowledge dissemination and transfer. There seems to be a consensus to treat organizational learning as a process enabling the acquisition, creation, accumulation, storage and dissemination of knowledge, so as to improve competitive advantage and meet prospective customers' changing needs in the turbulent and uncertain global environment.

The organizational learning discipline has received much attention among both academics and practitioners. Early academic discussions about the concept of organizational learning can be traced back to the 1960s, with Cyert and March being the first authors to reference organizational learning in their 1963 publication. The historical development of organizational learning has been briefly discussed here to understand the current status of organizational learning concepts.

The notion of organizational learning is popular because it helps to improve organizational performance. Although the relationship between learning and performance is complex, an organization's capability to learn is essential in order to enhance and sustain its competitive advantage. This chapter has also touched upon the strategic importance of organizational learning.

More importantly, this chapter has addressed how organizational learning relates to the emerging topic of knowledge management. Some scholars establish a positive link between organizational learning and knowledge management, whereas other authors do not see a direct relationship between the two constructs. The contradictory views of scholars on whether knowledge management is a forerunner of organizational learning or vice versa have been expanded in this chapter.

It is worth mentioning that learning has been increasingly defined in terms of knowledge processes. Although organizational learning and knowledge management are two distinct disciplines, they complement each other. Moreover, even though the relationship between knowledge management and organizational learning is complex, both fields have a similar impact on performance in that they both contribute to organizational performance. Robey *et al.* (2000) rightly state that knowledge management and organizational learning go hand in hand; while Crossan and Hulland (1997) use an analogy whereby organizational learning and knowledge management are comparable to the heart and lungs of a living organism, with both subjects being mutually self-supporting and critical to the well-being and survival of an organization.

Further Reading

Boateng, R. and Hinson, R. (2008). Information systems development: where does knowledge lie and how does learning occur? *Development and Learning in Organizations*, 22(3), 18–20.

Cavaleri, S. A. (2008). Are learning organizations pragmatic? *The Learning Organization*, 15(6), 474–485.

Easterby-Smith, M. and Prieto, I. M. (2008). Dynamic capabilities and knowledge management: an integrative role for learning. *British Journal of Management*, 19(3), 235–249.

Gherardi, S. (2009). Knowing and learning in practice-based studies: an introduction. *The Learning Organization*, 16(5), 352–359.

Ho, L.-A. (2008). What affects organizational performance?: The linking of learning and knowledge management. *Industrial Management & Data Systems*, 108(9), 1234–1254.

Hoe, S. L. and McShane, S. (2010). Structural and informal knowledge acquisition and dissemination in organizational learning: an exploratory analysis. *The Learning Organization*, 17(4), 364–386.

Peters, L. D., Johnston, W. J., Pressey, A. D. and Kendrick, T. (2010). Collaboration and collective learning: networks as learning organisations. *Journal of Business & Industrial Marketing*, 25(6), 478–484.

Sitzmann, T., Ely, K., Brown, K. G. and Bauer, K. N. (2010). Self-assessment of knowledge: a cognitive learning or affective measure? *Academy of Management Learning & Education*, 9(2), 169–191.

Walczak, S. (2008). Knowledge management and organizational learning: an international research perspective. *The Learning Organization*, 15(6), 486–494.

Yang, H., Phelps, C. and Steensma, H. K. (2010). Learning from what others have learned from you: the effects of knowledge spillovers on originating firms. *Academy of Management Journal*, 53(2), 371–389.

References

Addleson, M. (1999). What is a learning organization? Available at http://psol.gmu.edu/Home/perspectives.nsf/.

Akhavan, P. and Jafari, M. (2006). Critical issues for knowledge management implementation at a national level. *VINE: The Journal of Information and Knowledge Management Systems*, 36(1), 52–66.

Allee, V. (1997). *The Knowledge Evolution: Expanding Organizational Intelligence*. Boston, MA: Butterworth-Heinemann.

Antal, A. B., Dierkes, M., Child, J. and Nonaka, I. (2001). Introduction: finding paths through the handbook. In M. Dierkes, A. B. Antal, J. Child and I. Nonaka (eds.), *Handbook of Organizational Learning and Knowledge* (pp. 1–7), Oxford: Oxford University Press.

Antonacopoulou, E. P. (2006). Modes of knowing in practice: the relationship between knowledge and learning revisited. In B. Renzl, K. Matzler and H. Hinterhuber (eds.), *The Future of Knowledge Management* (pp. 7–28), Basingstoke: Palgrave Macmillan.

Argote, L. (1999). *Organizational Learning: Creating, Retaining and Transferring Knowledge*. Norwell, MA: Kluwer.

Argote, L., McEvily, B. and Reagans, R. (2003). Managing knowledge in organizations: an integrative framework and review of emerging themes. *Management Science*, 49(4), 571–582.

Argyris, C. and Schön, D. (1978). *Organizational Learning*. Reading, MA: Addison-Wesley.

Argyris, C. and Schön, D. (1996). *Organizational Learning II*. Reading, MA: Addison-Wesley.

Armstrong, A. and Foley, P. (2003). Foundations for a learning organization: organization learning mechanisms. *The Learning Organization*, 10(2), 74–82.

Badaracco, J. (1991). *The Knowledge Link: Competitive Advantage Through Strategic Alliances*. Boston, MA: Harvard Business School Press.

Barney, J. B. (1991). Firm resources and sustained competitive advantage. *Journal of Management*, 17(1), 99–120.

Boisot, M. H. (1998). *Knowledge Assets*. Oxford: Oxford University Press.

Bontis, N., Crossan, M. and Hulland, J. (2002). Managing an organizational learning system by aligning stocks and flows. *Journal of Management Studies*, 39(4), 437–469.

Brown, J. and Duguid, P. (1998). Organizing knowledge. *California Management Review*, 40(3), 90–111.

Brown, R. B. and Woodland, M. J. (1999). Managing knowledge wisely: a case study in organisational behaviour. *Journal of Applied Management Studies*, 8(2), 175–198.

Cangelosi, V. and Dill, W. (1965). Organizational learning: observations toward a theory. *Administrative Science Quarterly*, 10, 175–203.

Cavaleri, S. and Fearon, D. (1996). *Managing in Organizations That Learn*. Cambridge, MA: Blackwell Publishing.

Chae, B. and Bloodgood, J. M. (2006). The paradoxes of knowledge management: an eastern philosophical perspective. *Information and Organization*, 16, 1–26.

Choo, C. W. (1998). *The Knowing Organization: How Organizations Use Information to Construct Meaning, Create Knowledge and Make Decisions*. New York: Oxford University Press.

Cohen, M. and Sproull, L. (1996). *Organizational Learning*. London: Sage.

Coulson-Thomas, C. (1997). The future of the organization: selected knowledge management issues. *Journal of Knowledge Management*, 1(1), 15–26.

Crossan, M. and Guatto, T. (1996). Organizational learning research profile. *Journal of Organizational Change Management*, 9, 107–112.

Crossan, M. and Hulland, J. (1996). Measuring organizational learning. Working Paper No. 96-05, University of Western Ontario, London, Ontario, Canada.

Crossan, M. and Hulland, J. (1997). Measuring organizational learning. Ivey working paper, Presented to the Academy of Management, Boston, MA.

Crossan, M., Lane, H. and White, R. (1999). An organizational learning framework: from intuition to institution. *Academy of Management Review*, 24(3), 522–537.

Crossan, M., Lane, H., White, R. and Djurfeldt, L. (1995). Organizational learning: dimensions for a theory. *International Journal of Organizational Analysis*, 3(4), 337–360.

Cyert, R. M. and March, J. G. (1963). *A Behavioral Theory of the Firm*. Englewood Cliffs, NJ: Prentice Hall.

Daft, R. L. and Huber, G. P. (1987). How organizations learn: a communication framework. *Research in the Sociology of Organizations*, 5, 1–36.

Daft, R. L. and Weick, K. E. (1984). Toward a model of organizations as interpretation systems. *Academy of Management Review*, 9(2), 284–295.

Davenport, T. H. (1997). Ten principles of knowledge management and four case studies. *Knowledge and Process Management*, 4(3), 187–208.

Davenport, T. H. and Prusak, L. (1998). *Working Knowledge: How Organizations Manage What They Know*. Boston, MA: Harvard Business School Press.

Day, G. S. (1994). Continuous learning about markets. *California Management Review*, 36(4), 9–31.

de Geus, A. (1988). Planning as learning. *Harvard Business Review*, 66, March/April, 70–74.

de Pablos, P. O. (2001). Relevant experiences on measuring and reporting intellectual capital in European pioneering firms. In N. Bontis and C. Chong (eds.), *Organizational Intelligence: The Cutting Edge of Intellectual Capital and Knowledge Management*, New York: Butterworth-Heinemann.

de Pablos, P. O. (2002). Knowledge management and organizational learning: typologies of knowledge strategies in the Spanish manufacturing industry from 1995 to 1999. *Journal of Knowledge Management*, 6(1), 52–62.

DiBella, A. J. (2001). *Learning Practices: Assessment and Action for Organizational Improvement*. Upper Saddle River, NJ: Prentice Hall.

Dimitriades, Z. S. (2005). Creating strategic capabilities: organizational learning and knowledge management in the new economy. *European Business Review*, 17(4), 314–324.

Dodgson, M. (1993). Organizational learning: a review of some literatures. *Organization Studies*, 14(3), 375–394.

Drucker, P. F. (1993). *Post-Capitalist Society*. New York: HarperCollins.

Drucker, P. F. (1998). The coming of the new organization. In *Harvard Business Review on Knowledge Management* (pp. 1–19), Boston, MA: Harvard Business School Press.

Duncan, R. and Weiss, A. (1979). Organizational learning: implications for organizational design. *Research in Organizational Behavior*, 1, 75–123.

Easterby-Smith, M. (1997). Disciplines of organizational learning: contributions and critiques. *Human Relations*, 50(9), 1085–1113.

Easterby-Smith, M., Crossan, M. and Nicolini, D. (2000). Organizational learning: debates past, present and future. *Journal of Management Studies*, 37(6), 783–796.

Easterby-Smith, M. and Lyles, M. A. (eds.) (2003). *The Blackwell Handbook of Organizational Learning and Knowledge Management*. Oxford: Blackwell.

Figueroa, L. A. and González, A. B. (2006). Management of knowledge, information and organizational learning in university libraries. *Libri*, 56(3), 180–190.

Fiol, C. and Lyles, M. (1985). Organizational learning. *Academy of Management Review*, 10, 803–813.

Fusaro, R. (1998). Rating intangibles no easy task: Eli Lilly measures the value of knowledge management. *Computerworld*, 32(48), 8.

Garvin, D. A. (1993). Building a learning organization. *Harvard Business Review*, 71(4), 78–91.

Garvin, D. A. (1998). Building a learning organization. In *Harvard Business Review on Knowledge Management* (pp. 47–80), Boston, MA: Harvard Business School Press.

Gloet, M. and Terziovski, M. (2004). Exploring the relationship between knowledge management practices and innovation performance. *Journal of Manufacturing Technology Management*, 15(5), 402–409.

Goh, S. C. (2003). Improving organizational learning capability: lessons from two case studies. *The Learning Organization*, 10(4), 216–227.

Gourlay, M. J. (1999). Foundationalism: the problem of knowledge. Available at http://www.xs4all.nl/nexus/gourlay/found_prob.html/.

Gu, Y. (2004). Global knowledge management research: a bibliometric analysis. *Scientometrics*, 61, 171–190.

Hong, J. F. L., Easterby-Smith, M. and Snell, R. S. (2006). Transferring organizational learning systems to Japanese subsidiaries in China. *Journal of Management Studies*, 43(5), 1027–1058.

Huber, G. P. (1991). Organizational learning: the contributing processes and the literatures. *Organization Science*, 2(1), 88–115.

Jasimuddin, S. M. (2005). Knowledge of external sources' knowledge: new frontiers to actionable knowledge. In M. A. Rahim and R. T. Golembiewski (eds.), *Current Topics in Management*, Vol. 10 (pp. 39–50), New Brunswick, NJ: Transaction Publishers.

Jones, M. (1995). Organisational learning: collective mind or cognitivist metaphor? *Accounting, Management and Information Technologies*, 5(1), 61–77.

Katsoulakos, P. and Zevgolis, D. (2004). Knowledge management review 2004. Available at http://www.kbos.net/.

Kim, D. H. (1993). The link between individual and organizational learning. *Sloan Management Review*, Fall, 37–50.

King, W. R., Chung, T. R. and Haney, M. H. (2008). Editorial: knowledge management and organizational learning. *Omega*, 36, 167–172.

Klatt, L. A., Murdick, R. G. and Schuster, F. E. (1985). *Human Resource Management*. Columbus, OH: Charles E. Merrill/Bell & Howell.

Kleiner, A. and Roth, G. (1998). How to make experience your company's best teacher. In *Harvard Business Review on Knowledge Management* (pp. 137–151), Boston, MA: Harvard Business School Press.

Kolb, D. A., Lublin, S., Spoth, J. and Baker, R. (1991). Strategic management development: experiential learning and managerial competencies. In J. Henry (ed.), *Creative Management* (pp. 221–231), London: Sage.

Lave, J. (1993). The practice of learning. In S. Chaiklin and J. Lave (eds.), *Understanding Practice: Perspectives on Activity and Context* (pp. 3–32), Cambridge: Cambridge University Press.

Lee, S., Courtney, J. and O'Keefe, R. (1992). A system for organizational learning using cognitive maps. *Omega*, 20(1), 23–36.

Leonard, D. and Sensiper, S. (1998). The role of tacit knowledge in group innovation. *California Management Review*, 40, 112–132.

Levinthal, D. and March, J. (1993). The myopia of learning. *Strategic Management Journal*, 14, 95–112.

Levitt, B. and March, J. G. (1988). Organizational learning. *Annual Review of Sociology*, 14, 319–340.

Loermans, J. (2002). Synergizing the learning organization and knowledge management. *Journal of Knowledge Management*, 6(3), 285–294.

Lopez, S. P., Peon, J. M. M. and Ordas, C. J. V. (2004). Managing knowledge: the link between culture and organizational learning. *Journal of Knowledge Management*, 8(6), 93–104.

Lyles, M. A. and Easterby-Smith, M. (2003). Organizational learning and knowledge management: agendas for future research. In M. Easterby-Smith and M. A. Lyles (eds.), *The Blackwell Handbook of Organizational Learning and Knowledge Management* (pp. 639–652), Oxford: Blackwell.

Malhotra, Y. (1996). Organizational learning and learning organizations: an overview. Available at http://www.brint.com/papers/orglrng.htm/.

Malhotra, Y. (1997). Knowledge management in inquiring organizations. In *Proceedings of the 3rd Americas Conference on Information Systems*, Indianapolis, IN.

Manasco, B. (1998). Corporate knowledge nets and the learning imperative. Available at http://webcom.com/quantera/empires3.html/.

Marquardt, M. (1996). *Building the Learning Organization: A Systems Approach to Quantum Improvement and Global Success.* New York: McGraw-Hill.

McGill, M. E. and Slocum, J. W. (1993). Unlearning the organization. *Organizational Dynamics*, 22(2), 67–79.

Metaxiotis, K. and Psarras, J. (2006). Analysing the value of knowledge management leading to innovation. *International Journal of Knowledge Management Studies*, 1(1/2), 79–89.

Meyer-Dohm, P. (1992). Human resources 2020: structures of the learning company. In *Conference Proceedings: Human Resources in Europe at the Dawn of the 21st Century*, Luxembourg: Office for Official Publications of the European Communities.

Miller, D. (1996). A preliminary typology of organizational learning: synthesizing the literature. *Journal of Management*, 22(3), 485–505.

Mills, D. Q. and Friesen, B. (1992). The learning organization. *European Management Journal*, 10(2), 146–156.

Miner, A. S. and Mezias, S. J. (1996). Ugly duckling no more: pasts and futures of organizational learning research. *Organization Science*, 7(1), 88–99.

Moreno-Luzon, M. D. and Lloria, M. B. (2008). The role of non-structural and informal mechanisms of integration and coordination as forces in knowledge creation. *British Journal of Management*, 19, 250–276.

Mukherjee, A. (2003). Achieving knowledge management in construction: part I — a review of developments. *Construction Information Quarterly*, 5(3), 7–11.

Nadler, D., Gerstein, M. and Shaw, R. (1992). *Organizational Architecture: Designs for Changing Organizations.* San Francisco: Jossey-Bass.

Nevis, E. C., DiBella, A. J. and Gould, J. M. (1995). Understanding organizations as learning systems. *Sloan Management Review*, 36(2), 73–85.

Nonaka, I. (1988). Toward middle-up-down management: accelerating information creation. *Sloan Management Review*, 29(3), Spring, 9–18.

Nonaka, I. (1991a). The knowledge-creating company. *Harvard Business Review*, 69(6), 96–104.

Nonaka, I. (1991b). Managing the firm as an information creation process. In J. Meindl, R. L. Cardy and S. M. Puffer (eds.), *Advances in Information Processing in Organizations*, Vol. 4 (pp. 239–275), Greenwich, CT: JAI Press.

Nonaka, I. (1998). The knowledge-creating company. In *Harvard Business Review on Knowledge Management* (pp. 21–45), Boston, MA: Harvard Business School Press.

Nonaka, I. and Reinmoeller, P. (2000). Dynamic business systems for knowledge creation and utilization. In C. Despres and D. Chauvel (eds.), *Knowledge Horizons: The Present and the Promise of Knowledge Management* (pp. 89–112), Boston: Butterworth-Heinemann.

Nonaka, I. and Takeuchi, H. (1995). *The Knowledge-Creating Company: How Japanese Companies Create the Dynamics of Innovation.* Oxford: Oxford University Press.

Pemberton, J. D. and Stonehouse, G. H. (2000). Organisational learning and knowledge assets — an essential partnership. *The Learning Organization*, 7(4), 184–194.

Pisano, G. P. (1994). Knowledge, integration, and the locus of learning: an empirical analysis of process development. *Strategic Management Journal*, 15(S1), 85–100.

Quinn, J. B. (1992). Intelligent enterprise: a new paradigm. *Academy of Management Executive*, 6(4), 48–63.

Rahim, M. A. (2002). Toward a theory of managing organizational conflict. *International Journal of Conflict Management*, 13, 206–235.

Rayport, J. F. and Sviokla, J. J. (1995). Exploiting the virtual value chain. *Harvard Business Review*, 73(6), 75–85.

Revans, R. W. (1971). *Developing Effective Managers: A New Approach to Business Education.* New York: Praeger Publishers.

Revilla, E., Sarkis, J. and Acosta, J. (2005). Towards a knowledge management and learning taxonomy for research joint ventures. *Technovation*, 25, 1307–1316.

Robey, D., Boudreau, M. and Rose, G. M. (2000). Information technology and organizational learning: a review and assessment of research. *Accounting, Management and Information Technologies*, 10, 125–155.

Sandelands, E. (1999). Learning organizations: a review of the literature relating to strategies, building blocks and barriers. *Management Literature in Review*, 1(1), 1–10.

Santosus, M. (1996). The learning organization. *CIO Magazine*, June 1.

Scarbrough, H. and Swan, J. (2001). Explaining the diffusion of knowledge management: the role of fashion. *British Journal of Management*, 12(1), 3–12.

Schein, E. H. (1996). Organizational learning: what is new? Working paper, Society for Organizational Learning, MIT Sloan School of Management, Cambridge, MA.

Senge, P. M. (1990). *The Fifth Discipline: The Art and Practice of the Learning Organization.* New York: Doubleday.

Shrivastava, P. (1983). A typology of organizational learning systems. *Journal of Management Studies*, 20(1), 7–28.

Sierhuis, M. and Clancey, W. J. (1997). Knowledge, practice, activities and people. Available at http://ksi.cpsc.ucalgary.ca/AIKM97/sierhuis/sierhuis.html/.

Slater, S. F. and Narver, J. C. (1995). Market orientation and the learning organization. *Journal of Marketing*, 59(3), 63–74.

Spender, J. C. (2008). Organizational learning and knowledge management: whence and whither? *Management Learning*, 39(2), 159–176.

Spicer, D. P. and Sadler-Smith, E. (2006). Organizational learning in smaller manufacturing firms. *International Small Business Journal*, 24(2), 133–158.

Stata, R. (1989). Organizational learning — the key to management innovation. *Sloan Management Review*, 30, Spring, 63–74.

Stewart, T. A. (1997). *Intellectual Capital: The New Wealth of Organizations.* New York: Currency/Doubleday.

Strach, P. and Everett, A. E. (2006). Knowledge transfer within Japanese multinationals: building a theory. *Journal of Knowledge Management*, 10(1), 55–68.

Stuller, J. (1998). Chief of corporate smarts. *Training*, 35, 28–34.

Sun, P. Y. T. and Scott, J. L. (2003). Exploring the divide — organizational learning and learning organization. *The Learning Organization*, 10(4), 202–215.

Sveiby, K. E. (1997). *The New Organizational Wealth: Managing and Measuring Knowledge-Based Assets.* San Francisco, CA: Berrett-Koehler Publishers.

Swan, J., Newell, S., Scarbrough, H. and Hislop, D. (1999). Knowledge management and innovation: networks and networking. *Journal of Knowledge Management*, 3, 262–275.

Ulrich, D., von Glinow, M. A. and Jick, T. (1993). High-impact learning: building and diffusing learning capability. *Organizational Dynamics*, 22(2), 52–66.

Vera, D. and Crossan, M. (2003). Organizational learning and knowledge management: toward an integrative framework. In M. Easterby-Smith and M. A. Lyles (eds.), *The Blackwell Handbook of Organizational Learning and Knowledge Management* (pp. 122–141), Oxford: Blackwell.

von Krogh, G. and Grand, S. (2002). From economic theory toward a knowledge-based theory of the firm: conceptual building blocks. In C. W. Choo and N. Bontis (eds.), *The Strategic Management of Intellectual Capital and Organizational Knowledge* (pp. 163–184), New York: Oxford University Press.

Wick, C. W. and Leon, L. S. (1993). *The Learning Edge: How Smart Managers and Smart Companies Stay Ahead*. New York: McGraw-Hill.

Wiig, K. M. (1993). *Knowledge Management Foundations: Thinking About Thinking — How People and Organizations Create, Represent, and Use Knowledge*. Arlington, TX: Schema Press.

Wikstrom, S. and Normann, R. (1994). *Knowledge and Value: A New Perspective on Corporate Transformation*. London: Routledge.

Chapter 9

Knowledge Management and Strategic Management

Knowledge Objectives

After studying this chapter, you should be able to:

- Provide a basic introduction of strategic management with respect to knowledge management;
- Explore the origin of strategic management;
- Discuss the notion of strategic management from philosophical perspectives;
- Identify the key areas of strategic management;
- Describe the significance of strategic management in organizations; and
- Explain the linkage between strategic management and knowledge management.

9.1 Introducing the Chapter

The relevant literature on management and organizational studies provides an interdisciplinary treatment of knowledge management. As mentioned in previous chapters, knowledge management has been approached from various academic fields, including strategic management (Kogut and Zander, 1992; Spender and Grant, 1996; Zack, 1999a; Eisenhardt and Santos, 2002; Demsetz, 1991; Grant, 1996a;

Roberts, 1998; Grant and Baden-Fuller, 2004). In the emerging knowledge-based society, the knowledge-based view of the firm (Grant, 1996a) is one of the major areas of strategic management studies that encourages organizations to recognize knowledge as the primary productive factor. Organizational knowledge is treated as a strategic source of sustainable competitive advantage for organizations. Reflecting this view, Grant and Baden-Fuller (2004) postulate that the knowledge-based focus in strategic management research acknowledges the important role that organizational knowledge plays in achieving the competitive advantage of firms.

Given the increasing knowledge-based approach to strategy, organizations have started to look at the factors of production in an entirely new way. Parallel to this, Zack (1999a) contends that the need to better understand the role of knowledge in organizations has emerged as a central objective in theoretical and empirical research in well-established disciplinary fields like strategic management. As a result, the notion of organizational knowledge and how to manage knowledge in organizations has become a key strategic issue.

It is observed that a large number of books and journal articles on the topics surrounding strategic management have appeared over the past 25 years. During this period of time, several peer-reviewed research journals have surfaced to address major aspects of strategic management as a primary focus. A selective list of journals relating to strategic management is shown in Table 9.1. Moreover, formal research in the strategic management area can be seen in the devotion of special issues of several top scholarly journals to strategic management. One leading journal on strategic management, the *Strategic Management Journal*, is listed among the 30 journals used by the *Financial Times* to rank business schools in terms of their scholarly achievements. Indeed, the *Strategic Management Journal* is one of the most highly regarded and influential publications within the management discipline.

Academic research has been conducted in many different areas within the strategic management discipline. Despite this, however, there still remain a large number of under-researched topics. One such area that has received relatively little focus is the relationship

Table 9.1 A List of Journals on Strategic Management

Journal Title	Year Launched	Frequency	Publisher
Business Strategy and the Environment	1992	8 issues per year	Wiley-Blackwell
Business Strategy Review	1990	Quarterly	Wiley-Blackwell
Handbook of Business Strategy	2000	1 issue per year	Emerald
Journal of Economics & Management Strategy	1992	Quarterly	Wiley-Blackwell
Long Range Planning	1968	Bimonthly	Elsevier
Strategic Change	1992	8 issues per year	Wiley-Blackwell
Strategic Management Journal	1980	13 issues per year	Wiley-Blackwell
Strategic Organization	2003	Quarterly	Sage
Strategy & Leadership	1973	Bimonthly	Emerald
Technology Analysis & Strategic Management	1989	10 issues per year	Taylor & Francis

between knowledge management and strategic management. To be sure, the notion of knowledge management is being increasingly incorporated as a separate chapter in strategic management textbooks (e.g., Haberberg and Rieple, 2008 (Chapter 10); Huff *et al.*, 2009 (Chapter 11); Lynch, 2006 (Chapter 11); Peng, 2009 (Chapter 10); Stacey, 2007 (Chapter 4)), because knowledge management is considered to be an important component of the strategic management discipline. Furthermore, several management journal special issues illustrate the recent growing interest in knowledge management in strategic management research, such as *Strategic Management Journal*'s 1996 winter special issue on "knowledge and the firm" (Spender and Grant, 1996).

It is evident that the literature on strategic management and knowledge management is characterized by the use of very diverse terminologies, whereby concepts are often employed but rarely discussed together. However, research examining the relationship between the two fields is limited. Stated differently, little progress has occurred to investigate the linkage between these subjects. Since organizational knowledge is viewed as a key ingredient for the success of strategy formulation, the management of organizational knowledge can be regarded as an essential part of strategic management as well. Therefore, there is a rationale behind the argument that knowledge management is related to the various processes of strategic management.

The question of whether knowledge management is shaped by strategic management or vice versa is still up for debate. The emphasis placed on knowledge and strategy as sources of competitive advantage has motivated us to explore the connection between the two fields. An examination of the linkage between them will shed some light on the nature of their association. Thus, this chapter will help to determine whether strategic management is a precursor of knowledge management or not.

Whilst this book focuses on the interdisciplinary approach to knowledge management, this chapter will deal exclusively with the relationship between knowledge management and strategic management. Scholars recognize that no single overreaching framework is available to clear up the conceptual confusion. Against this backdrop, the purpose of this chapter is to contribute to the knowledge management and strategic management literatures by clarifying the concepts and presenting a framework illustrating their relationship. More specifically, this chapter will suggest a framework that integrates both subjects in order to establish a theoretical link between these constructs and their performance.

This chapter is organized in the following manner. The chapter begins by giving various definitions of strategic management in Section 9.2, emphasizing its role in organizations. This is followed by a discussion on the historical development of strategic management as an established discipline in Section 9.3. It is also important to understand the concepts and themes associated with strategic management. Section 9.4, therefore, elaborates on the key topics of strategic management research. A better understanding of the relationship between strategic management and knowledge management can provide valuable insights into this linkage issue. Some writers recognize the critical significance of the connection between them, while others do not seem to make any attempt to combine them.

The relevant scholars' views on their relationship are discussed in Section 9.5. There is great potential for the cross-fertilization of ideas between strategic management and knowledge management. Section 9.6 examines the relationship between these two fields, highlighting several factors that could shed some insight on the nature of their association. Finally, the chapter ends with some concluding remarks in Section 9.7.

9.2 Strategic Management Defined

Since the 1970s, strategic management has become popular among researchers and practitioners. In fact, strategic management is often discussed in the context of achieving an organizational goal. However, it is difficult to comprehend the concept of strategic management because there are numerous definitions of the construct in the relevant literature. Hence, this section will briefly discuss the various definitions of strategic management given by scholars in order to clarify the associated concepts and understand the notion of strategic management.

Generally speaking, strategic management is the process of formulating and implementing strategy so as to ensure the sustainable competitive advantage of an organization. Table 9.2 presents some definitions of strategic management as given by scholars. As evidenced from Table 9.2, no consensus has emerged even on a core definition of strategic management. There is no single, universally accepted definition of the term "strategic management". Nevertheless, the majority of authors agree on (i) the process in which it is used, and (ii) the purpose for which it is used. In particular, most strategic management definitions concentrate on the analysis of the processes involved in scanning internal resources and the external environment so as to equip an organization to successfully compete with its rivals. Resonating with this, it is observed that most strategic management theorists (i.e., Bowman *et al.*, 2002; Carpenter and Sanders, 2007; Faulkner and Campbell, 2006; Henry, 2008; Hill and Jones, 2004; Ireland *et al.*, 2009; Jeffs, 2008; Johnson *et al.*, 2008; Mellahi *et al.*, 2005; Parthasarthy,

Table 9.2 Selected Definitions of Strategic Management

Authors	Definitions
Barney and Hesterly (2008)	A sequential set of "analyses" and "choices" that can increase the likelihood that a firm will choose a good strategy, that is, a strategy that generates competitive advantages
Bowman *et al.* (2002)	A domain that is centered on problems relating to the creation and sustainability of competitive advantage, or the pursuit of rents
Bracker (1980)	The analysis of internal and external environments of firms to maximize the utilization of resources in relation to objectives
Carpenter and Sanders (2007)	A process by which a firm incorporates the tools and and frameworks for developing and implementing a strategy
Faulkner and Campbell (2006)	The process of charting how to achieve a company's objectives, and adjusting the direction and methods to take advantage of changing circumstances
Fredrickson (1990)	A process that is concerned with those issues faced by managers who run entire organizations, or their multifunctional units
Henry (2008)	A process that involves analyzing the situation facing a firm and, on the basis of this analysis, formulating a strategy and finally implementing that strategy; the end result is for the organization to achieve a competitive advantage over its rivals in the industry
Hill and Jones (2004)	The process by which managers choose a set of strategies for a company that will allow it to achieve superior performance
Hunger and Wheelen (2007)	That set of managerial decisions and actions that determines the long-run performance of a corporation; it includes environmental scanning (both external and internal), strategy formulation (strategic planning), strategy implementation, and evaluation and control
Ireland *et al.* (2009)	The full set of commitments, decisions and actions required for a firm to achieve strategic competitiveness and earn above-average returns

(*Continued*)

Table 9.2 **(*Continued*)**

Authors	Definitions
Jeffs (2008)	The process of identifying, evaluating and implementing strategies in order to meet organizational objectives
Jemison (1981)	The process by which general managers of complex organizations develop and use a strategy to co-align their organization's competencies and the opportunities and constraints in the environment
Johnson *et al.* (2008)	A set of activities that includes understanding the strategic position of an organization, strategic choices for the future and how to manage strategy in action
Learned *et al.* (1965)	The study of the functions and responsibilities of general management as well as the problems which affect the character and success of the total enterprise
Mellahi *et al.* (2005)	The process of strategic decision making, wherein a process is a systematic way of carrying out interrelated activities in order to obtain desired goals and objectives; the strategy-making process involves key decisions made for and on behalf of the entire organization
Parthasarthy (2007)	A series of long-term decisions and actions taken by managers, through which they select and implement strategies
Peng (2009)	A way of managing the firm from a strategic, "big picture" perspective
Rumelt *et al.* (1994)	A process that is about the direction of organizations (most often, business firms); it includes those subjects of primary concern to senior management, or to anyone seeking reasons for the success and failure of organizations
Schendel and Cool (1988)	Work associated with the term "entrepreneur" and his/her function of starting and, given the infinite life of corporations, renewing organizations
Schendel and Hofer (1979)	A process that deals with the entrepreneurial work of an organization, with organizational renewal and growth, and, more particularly, with developing and utilizing the strategy which will guide the organization's operations

(*Continued*)

Table 9.2 (*Continued*)

Authors	Definitions
Smircich and Stubbart (1985)	The process of organization making, i.e., to create and maintain systems of shared meaning that facilitate organized action
Teece (1990)	The formulation, implementation and evaluation of managerial actions that enhance the value of a business enterprise
Van Cauwenbergh and Cool (1982)	A process that deals with the formulation aspects (policy) and the implementation aspects (organization) of calculated behavior in new situations; it is the basis for future administration when repetition of circumstances occurs

2007; Peng, 2009) conclude that strategic management is all about scanning the internal and external environment to formulate several options, and then picking up and implementing one of them as a good strategy in order to gain a competitive advantage over other rival firms.

Over the last 30 years, strategic management has developed as a subject of study for understanding and responding to competitors' moves in the turbulent business environment. Based on an appraisal of current definitions of strategic management (see Table 9.2), we can define it as the process by which an organization incorporates the tools and frameworks — including the knowledge management framework — for environmental scanning (both external and internal), strategy formulation, strategy implementation, and evaluation and control, so as to generate sustainable competitive advantages over its rivals.

9.3 The Origins of Strategic Management

An understanding of the origins of the strategic management field is necessary in order to clarify its current status. The subject has advanced substantially over the last three decades due to the increased interest from both academics and practitioners. Its roots can be traced back as early as 500 BC. While describing its historical origins, Heracleous (2003, p. 3) reports that the term "strategy":

> ... was coined in Athens around 508–7 BC, where ten *strategoi* comprised the Athenian war council and yielded both political and military power. Etymologically, *strategos*, or general, derives from *stratos* (army) and *agein* (to lead). . . . Parallel developments in Asia included Sun Tzu's *Art of War*, dated to around the 5th century BC (Sawyer, 1996). Sun Tzu emphasized meticulous planning, the ideal of vanquishing the enemy indirectly without the need to fight, the qualities of effective generals, advice on managing the troops, and general principles and tactics of engaging with the enemy.

The development of the strategic management field in the last several decades has been dramatic (Hitt *et al.*, 2004). Mahoney and McGahan (2007) point out that this discipline emerged mainly during the 1970s and early 1980s from the social and administrative sciences. Early works such as Chandler's (1962) *Strategy and Structure*, Ansoff's (1965) *Corporate Strategy*, and Learned *et al.*'s (1965) *Business Policy: Text and Cases* took on a contingency perspective, which is all about the fit between strategy and structure. It is worth mentioning that one important antecedent field of strategic management is business policy. Resonating with this, Learned *et al.* (1965), for example, contend that business policy is a precursor of strategic management.

It could be argued that the roots of strategic management have been largely practice-oriented. However, Hoskisson *et al.* (1999) state that recent developments in the discipline are strongly theory-based, with substantial empirical research, and are very much eclectic in nature. Parallel to this, Hitt (2006) asserts that the field is now more concerned with how to apply strategic management, and that most research in the field is focused on why some organizations outperform other rival organizations.

One of the most significant contributions to the development of strategic management comes from the industrial organization (IO) approach to strategy (e.g., Porter, 1980), which was subsequently succeeded by the resource-based view of the firm (e.g., Rumelt, 1991; Prahalad and Hamel, 1990; Grant, 1991; Barney, 1991, 1997; Mahoney and Pandian, 1992) during the early 1990s. The central argument here is that the strategic resources of an enterprise are critical sources of sustainable competitive advantage if the resource is valuable (V), rare (R), inimitable (I) and non-substitutable (N) — hence, the VRIN framework, as postulated by Barney (1991). Furthermore, a resource-based framework focuses on an organization's internal strengths (S) and weaknesses (W) relative to its external opportunities (O) and threats (T) — popularly abbreviated as the SWOT framework.

9.4 Key Areas of Strategic Management Research

The various topics in the strategic management field help to explain why an organization outperforms other competing organizations. The fact is that this discipline has given more attention to topics such as competitive strategies (D'Aveni, 1994; Gimeno, 2004), the strategy process (Chakravarthy *et al.*, 2003; Floyd *et al.*, 2005), corporate governance (Daily *et al.*, 2003; Hoskisson *et al.*, 2002), cooperative strategies (Dyer and Singh, 1998; Gulati and Singh, 1998; Ireland *et al.*, 2002), and international strategies (Lu and Beamish, 2004; Penner-Hahn and Shaver, 2005; Tallman, 2001).

Furthermore, a few areas surrounding strategic management have recently emerged, and have been receiving much attention among academics and practitioners. These contemporary topics are mentioned below:

- Strategic leadership (e.g., Finkelstein and Hambrick, 1996; Hambrick and Cannella, 2004; Cannella and Hambrick, 1993; Kesner and Sebora, 1994);
- Dynamic capabilities (e.g., Helfat and Peteraf, 2003; Teece *et al.*, 1997; Winter, 2003);
- Strategic entrepreneurship (e.g., Amit and Zott, 2001; Hitt *et al.*, 2001; Hitt *et al.*, 2002); and
- The knowledge-based view of the firm (e.g., Kogut and Zander, 1992; Spender and Grant, 1996).

The rest of this section will elaborate on the most common sub-streams that have appeared in strategic management textbooks.

- *The resource-based view (RBV) of the firm.* The most important area of research in strategic management is the management of resources available within an organization. The resource-based view focuses on the internal resources and capabilities of a firm that are required at the time of the formulation of a strategy in order to assess its strengths. Moreover, the resource-based view also helps to identify which resources will be available during strategy implementation, thus helping to gain a competitive advantage in the relevant markets and industries. The resource-based view postulates that differences in organizational performance are most fundamentally driven by differences in firm resources and capabilities. By understanding this topic, an organization can assess its strengths and weaknesses, and then match them with the resources and capabilities at its disposal.
- *The strategy process.* Another important area of strategic management research is the strategy process. The strategy process is a crucial dimension of strategic management, as it is concerned with the "how", "who" and "when" of strategy (de Wit and Meyer, 2004). More specifically, the strategy process addresses questions such as how a strategy should be formulated, implemented and evaluated. This topic allows us to conceptualize the dynamics of strategic management.
- *The strategy context.* Another core topic in the strategic management field is the strategy context, that is, the set of circumstances under which the strategy process operates. The strategy context is concerned with the "where" of strategy. According to de Wit and Meyer (2004), the strategy context is all about addressing the question of where — i.e., the environment in which — the strategy process is actually embedded. Both scholars and practitioners believe that the analysis of a firm's strategic environment is a crucial topic of strategic management. Analyzing the environment (be it internal or external) of a firm has a great role to play, particularly in strategy planning. The analysis of the external

environment enables one to comprehend the opportunities available out there and the threats that may evolve. Resonating with this, Faulkner and Campbell (2006, p. 4) rightly state, "Strategy is about the future, which is unknown and unknowable; there are many paths that a firm could follow, and firms operate in dynamic competitive environments". Likewise, Pitkethly (2006) describes the role of the firm's external environment in strategy formulation. In essence, such a topic helps to identify an organization's dynamic characteristics with respect to its internal and external contexts for strategy and organizational performance.

- *Strategic choices.* One of the objectives of strategic management is to choose a strategy among alternatives (i.e., options) that seems to enhance the competitive advantage of an organization through its proper implementation. Figure 9.1 depicts a tree of strategic choices. From a broader perspective, the strategic choices that are available to a firm fall into two large categories: business strategies and corporate strategies. Business strategies are actions that a firm

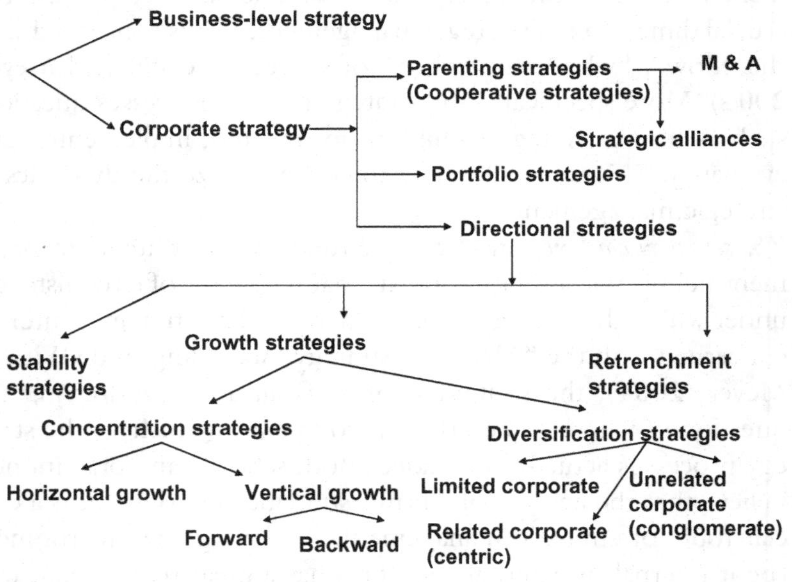

Figure 9.1 Strategy Tree

takes to gain competitive advantage by operating in a single market or industry. Two generic business strategies that are widely discussed are cost leadership strategy and product differentiation strategy (Barney and Hesterly, 2008), as mentioned below:

(i) Cost leadership strategy — Such a strategy provides a firm with an opportunity to generate competitive advantage by reducing its cost.
(ii) Product differentiation strategy — Such a strategy encourages a firm to gain competitive advantage by differentiating its product.
(iii) Combined strategy — Such a strategy is all about enhancing competitive advantage through the employment of both business strategies simultaneously.

- *Corporate strategies.* Corporate strategies are strategic actions that an organization takes to improve its competitive advantage by operating in many different unrelated markets or industries. A corporate strategy addresses interrelated questions such as in which areas a firm should compete, which modes and routes it should use to enter a new business, and what the rationale is behind competing in multiple businesses. Moreover, corporate strategy is also concerned with the relationship between the separate parts of a business and how the corporate "parent" adds value to these various parts. Such a topic helps to continue the debate regarding the arguments for and against concentrating a firm's resources and competing in just one industry or sector.
- *International strategies.* Another topic of increasing importance is the international strategy of an organization to enhance its strategic advantage through its global expansion. When a firm expands its business outside its home market, its strategy moves from a domestic phase to an international (global) strategy phase. There are many areas under the umbrella of international strategies, such as international market entry modes and international strategy configurations, which are widely covered nowadays in strategic management research.

- *Cooperative strategies.* Cooperative strategies are strategies in which organizations work together to achieve a shared objective. Popular forms of cooperative strategies include strategic alliances, joint ventures, and other types of corporate collaboration which entail voluntary agreements between firms involving the exchange, sharing or co-development of products, technologies or services (Gulati, 1995).
- *Corporate governance.* Corporate governance has become an increasingly important issue for organizations due to the recent wave of corporate scandals, especially since the late 1990s. Corporate governance refers to the set of mechanisms used to manage the relationship among stakeholders so as to determine and control the strategic direction, as well as monitor and assess the performance, of organizations (Lynall *et al.*, 2003). In other words, corporate governance is concerned with the structures and systems of control by which members of staff are held accountable for their performance and actions to those who have a legitimate stake in the organization. Corporate governance actually helps to protect the overall interests of stakeholders from wrongdoing by an employee, be they a technician or a chief executive officer. In fact, such a topic explains how corporate governance could be related to competitive advantage, how boards of directors are structured, and how they perform their roles to ensure corporate governance.
- *Strategic entrepreneurship.* One of the contemporary areas of strategic management research is strategic entrepreneurship, which refers to the taking of entrepreneurial actions using a strategic perspective. Strategic entrepreneurship has become an increasingly popular topic because it helps to create value for firms. When engaging in strategic entrepreneurship, an organization tends to focus on finding opportunities in its external environment that it can exploit later on through innovations. There are many areas under the umbrella of strategic entrepreneurship, such as innovation in a strategic context, entrepreneurial opportunities, and innovation through cooperative strategies. In recognition of the scholarly opportunities

presented by the entrepreneurship field, many journals have been published that focus on the notion of strategic entrepreneurship. Due to its popularity among academics and practitioners, the Strategic Management Society (SMS) introduced its first entrepreneurship journal — the *Strategic Entrepreneurship Journal* — in 2007.

- *Strategic leadership.* Another emerging topic that has become increasingly popular is the notion of strategic leadership. Strategic leadership refers to a manager's ability to articulate a strategic vision for the firm, and to motivate others to do things in an efficient and effective manner. Put simply, strategic leadership is concerned with managing the strategy-making process to increase the performance of an organization, thereby increasing its value. Such a topic helps to determine an organization's strategic direction.

  Strategic leaders are the people responsible for the design and execution of the strategic management process. Strategic leaders are typically top-level officials such as chief executive officers (CEOs), who are responsible for the overall performance of a corporation. These individuals manage the firm's resources, and have a large impact on firm performance through their experiential knowledge and wisdom. Therefore, the strategic leadership topic explains the roles that a strategic leader should play, directly and indirectly, in strategy formulation and implementation.
- *The knowledge-based view (KBV) of the firm.* In the strategic management literature (Kogut and Zander, 1992; Demsetz, 1991; Grant, 1996b; Roberts, 1998; Spender, 1996), the knowledge-based view of the firm posits that the primary rationale for a firm is the creation and application of knowledge, given that organizational knowledge is the strategic resource that seems to provide a sustainable competitive advantage. Hence, a firm's strategy formulation should focus primarily on the exploration and exploitation of organizational knowledge as well as the competitive capabilities derived from it (Leonard-Barton, 1995; Shariq, 1997). In this regard, Bierly and Chakrabarti (1996), for example, conclude that differences in organizational performance between firms are a result of their different knowledge bases and differing capabilities in developing and

deploying knowledge. Consequently, managing knowledge has been actively incorporated into the strategic management literature.

It is worth noting that the knowledge-based view (KBV) of the firm is actually an extension of the resource-based view (RBV) of the firm in that the former conceptualizes firms as knowledge-based organizations. Viewing firms from a knowledge-based perspective has sparked the need for knowledge management issues in the strategic management field. Indeed, more recent theoretical contributions in strategic management have been in the area of the knowledge-based view of the firm. By building on the notion of knowledge, the strategic management field helps to generate sustainable competitive advantages for organizations. Several scholars (e.g., Boisot, 1998; Spender, 1996; Nonaka and Teece, 2001) from the strategic management discipline also argue that a firm's competitive advantage flows from its unique knowledge and how it manages knowledge.

Cummings and Daellenbach (2009) conducted a survey in order to identify the themes that have received greater attention in the top-tier journal, *Long Range Planning*. By picking up keywords in titles of articles published in the journal over the past 40 years, the authors reported in their study that the following themes have received greater attention:

- Knowledge (and learning);
- Networks (relationships);
- Culture; and
- Corporate social responsibility (together with business ethics).

According to Cummings and Daellenbach (2009), knowledge (or learning) was the main subject for around 10% of all articles published in *Long Range Planning* over the last eight years (even without taking into account related terms like "intellectual capital"). This confirmation of the rise of knowledge as a key area of concern for strategists is reinforced by the fact that, of the ten most frequently cited articles published in the journal, eight articles are about knowledge. This also reflects the close connection between strategic management and knowledge management. The linkage between these fields will thus be explored in the next section.

9.5 Scholars' Views on the Connection Between Knowledge Management and Strategic Management

The emerging knowledge-based view of the firm, as prescribed by Grant (1996a), explains the importance of knowledge for an organization's success. It is noted that more recent theoretical contributions in strategic management have been in the area of the knowledge-based view of the firm. Hence, the recent rise of the knowledge-based view (KBV) of the organization provides a foundation for research on the linkage between strategic management and knowledge management. However, research exploring the connection between the two subjects is limited.

There is no doubt that strategic management and knowledge management are two significant management paradigms, being comfortably positioned within management theory and practice. From a theoretical perspective, both fields have emerged from distinct disciplinary traditions. The diverse origins of the two disciplines, as identified earlier, may have contributed to the lack of literature to date on the apparent linkage between these concepts. In addition, there are researchers who admit to the lack of a clear distinction between these subjects. Such a lack of established research to discuss the association between the two disciplines is treated as a critical issue within the relevant literature. This is due to the fact that the strategic management field generates sustainable competitive advantages for organizations, building on the notion of knowledge. Several authors — most notably Boisot (1998), Spender (1996), and Nonaka and Teece (2001) — also argue that a firm's competitive advantage flows from its unique knowledge and how it manages knowledge.

As mentioned earlier, viewing organizations from a knowledge-based perspective has sparked the need for a knowledge management framework in the strategic management field. In an attempt to establish a link between the two subjects, scholars from the strategic management discipline published a 1996 winter special issue of *Strategic Management Journal* on "knowledge and the firm" to demonstrate the role of organizational knowledge in particular and the knowledge management discipline in general within strategic management research and for organizational success.

Before discussing the various factors that help to identify the differences and similarities between strategic management and knowledge management, we will first look at scholars' views on their connection.

9.5.1 *Knowledge Management as a Key Element of Strategic Management*

In recent years, authors in the strategic management and knowledge management fields have started to develop the "business strategy" and "knowledge strategy" constructs. As a result, there are scholars who argue that knowledge management has evolved from strategic management. That is, such researchers believe that knowledge management is an offshoot of strategic management. However, the majority of strategic management theorists agree that one of its key components is the management of organizational knowledge. This is because the notion of knowledge management itself is essential for carrying out the strategic management process, especially when it comes to retrieving and utilizing knowledge so as to scan and analyze the environment. In this regard, Georgopoulos (2005) recognizes the critical significance of the relationship between strategy and knowledge in the e-business era, outlining that knowledge management is an integral part of strategic management. Similarly, Skyrme (1999) claims that knowledge is pervasive and strategic to any organization by identifying seven commonly used levers of strategies:

- Customer knowledge;
- Knowledge in products and services;
- Knowledge in people;
- Knowledge in processes;
- Organizational memory;

- Knowledge in relationships; and
- Knowledge assets.

One of the key strategic management processes of an organization is to analyze its environment in order to assess its own strengths and weaknesses in terms of its own resources and capabilities. The growing awareness of the strategic role that organizational knowledge plays in gaining competitive advantage has encouraged the top management of firms to look for ways to manage knowledge. Parallel to this, Bowman (2006) explains how a strategy is formulated for a firm, taking into account the firm's strategic assets, including organizational knowledge. Such a firm will thus be able to exploit the intellectual resources available at its disposal during strategy formulation. More specifically, business strategists find it useful to systematize knowledge through knowledge management implementation so that organizational knowledge is available at the time of strategy formulation.

It is evident from the extant literature that environmental analysis — a key element of strategy formulation — is very difficult (sometimes quite impossible) to carry out without the inclusion of internal and external sources of knowledge. In this context, Akhter (2003) states that, in the turbulent business environment, a firm needs to sustain its competitive advantage over its competitors through the exploration of knowledge from internal and external sources and its exploitation. Furthermore, Jasimuddin (2005) maintains that there is an alternative classification of knowledge based on the sources of knowledge, and that the interaction between both internal and external forces plays a role in gathering organizational knowledge which is then used to formulate a good strategy. While external knowledge resides outside a firm in customers, suppliers, competitors and other stakeholders, internal knowledge resides in the firm's own employees. Hence, gathering knowledge from both sources is essential to scan the internal and external environment of a corporation so as to formulate a strategy. In other words, knowledge management is helpful in gathering and using such organizational knowledge in strategic management.

In light of the increasing importance of knowledge processes as the principal activity of firms, knowledge management is frequently embedded in an organization's functional areas so as to derive a good business strategy. Senior management support is essential for knowledge management to be regarded as everyone's concern, not just the occupation of an isolated group or project (Liebowitz, 1999, 2003; Storey and Barnett, 2000). Moreover, it must be noted that strategy is not the outcome of an exclusively top-down process in a firm; rather, employees at lower and middle levels (many of whom are knowledge workers) need to be involved in strategy formulation as well in order to generate collective ownership of the process (Carlisle, 2002; Shaw and Edwards, 2005).

Organizations are always interested in exploring their knowledge base to exploit those aspects that are considered to be superior or distinctive in line with the VRIN framework (Barney, 1991), developing a suitable strategy and thereby gaining a competitive advantage. In this regard, Tissen *et al.* (1998) identify two major types of knowledge management:

- *Operational knowledge management*, which connects people to the system being used for the distribution and transfer of knowledge; and
- *Strategic knowledge management*, which links organizational knowledge with business strategy.

Zack (1999a) also discusses the concept of a knowledge strategy, arguing that such a strategy explicitly includes the notion of fit to an organization's business strategy. He suggests that a knowledge strategy describes the overall approach an organization intends to take to align its knowledge resources and capabilities with the intellectual requirements of business strategy.

9.5.2 *The Strategic Management Role for Knowledge Management Implementation*

There are scholars (e.g., Clarke, 2001; O'Dell and Grayson, 1998) who look at the role of strategic management for the successful implementation of knowledge management initiatives. Several scholars (e.g., Zand, 1997; Liebowitz and Beckman, 1998; Metaxiotis and Psarras, 2006; Koulopoulos and Frappaolo, 1999) suggest that one of the organizational elements that has the power to influence the success of knowledge management initiatives within an organization is through understanding knowledge management as a business strategy. For example, Clarke (2001) rightly contends that any knowledge management initiative is unlikely to be successful unless it is closely integrated with business strategy. Similarly, O'Dell and Grayson (1998) see knowledge management as a strategy to be developed in a firm to ensure that the right knowledge reaches the right people at the right time, and that those people share and use such knowledge to improve the organization's functioning.

Other scholars (e.g., du Plessis, 2007; Chait, 1999; Donoghue *et al.*, 1999; PricewaterhouseCoopers, 1999; Stadler and Stone, 2001; Clarke, 2001) also attempt to link knowledge management strategy to business strategy, arguing that the former should be tied to the latter and that managing knowledge can never be implemented in isolation. In this regard, Casselman and Samson (2007) utilize the concepts of good strategic management and the theory of the firm to place knowledge strategy on a more theoretically sound basis. Since knowledge management impacts upon most areas of the business, firms need to take a strategic approach to align knowledge management with business strategy (Zack, 1999a; Shaw *et al.*, 2007; McCann and Buckner, 2004; Snyman and Kruger, 2004).

One of the key issues that senior management has to address is how to manage knowledge so that it will be available for use. This means that managers have to formulate a strategy for managing knowledge. Several scholars (e.g., Hansen *et al.*, 1999; Jasimuddin, 2008) highlight the importance of developing an appropriate strategy for the smooth functioning of knowledge management. In line with this, Liebowitz (1999) contends that knowledge management *per se* is a key strategy that organizations are embracing to manage their organizational knowledge for strategic advantage. As noted earlier, there is a need to develop an appropriate strategy for the effective and efficient management of knowledge. Many scholars — most notably

Loermans (2002), Nissen *et al.* (2000) and Swan *et al.* (1999) — believe that strategic management plays a role in popularizing the notion of knowledge management. In a sense, knowledge management is clearly derived from strategic management, whereby many strategic management tools have simply been used to decide whether an organization needs to implement knowledge management practices.

Zack (1999a, 1999b) offers a framework that integrates knowledge strategy with business strategy: the SWOT (strengths, weaknesses, opportunities and threats) analysis. It is useful here to define what a knowledge strategy is. Bierly and Chakrabarti (1996) define a knowledge strategy as the set of strategic choices that shapes and directs an organization's learning process and determines the firm's knowledge base. Halawi *et al.* (2005) report that Zack's knowledge-based SWOT analysis can help to map a firm's knowledge-based resources and capabilities against strategic opportunities and threats so as to clearly understand its strengths and weaknesses. For this to happen, the firm needs to express its strategic intent and then explore the relevant knowledge in executing it.

9.5.3 *Strategic Management and Knowledge Management as Complementary to Each Other*

From the above discussion, it could be said that strategic management and knowledge management do complement each other. Tavakoli and Lawton (2005) suggest that knowledge management can have a significant role in increasing and improving strategic thinking, by drawing experiences and insights from all parts of an organization and making them available to points of strategic decision and action. The process of strategy formulation depends heavily on knowledge, be it internal or external.

Several scholars (e.g., Grant, 1996a; Zhang and Zhao, 2006; Tissen *et al.*, 1998; de Pablos, 2002; Cepeda-Carrion, 2006) conclude that knowledge management is a fundamental strategic process that facilitates the only sustainable competitive advantage for firms. Similarly, strategic management is a process that links organizational knowledge with business strategy. Snyman and Kruger (2004) illustrate the interdependency between the two subjects by developing a generic model, incorporating knowledge management with business strategy formulation. In line with this, Greiner *et al.* (2007) suggest a fit model that links business strategy with knowledge management, proposing a relationship between innovation and personalization on the one side and between efficiency and codification on the other side — hence, leading to improved business performance. Parallel to this, Cepeda-Carrion (2006) integrates both fields by taking a fine-grained look at the connection between knowledge resources and competitive advantage.

This section has gone some way towards explaining the significant synergies between strategic management and knowledge management, and how they overlap or fit together to a certain extent. However, there is also a definite consensus among researchers that the two disciplines are not the same thing. In fact, there is a fine line between these subjects at both conceptual and practical levels. This will be dealt with next.

9.6 Linkage Between Strategic Management and Knowledge Management

This section will briefly look at the issues that may help to explain the connection between knowledge management and strategic management. Although research has been conducted on many topics in strategic management, there has been relatively little focus on the relationship between strategic management and knowledge management. Drawing on the extant literature, this section will set out to explore their linkage in order to demonstrate that they are complementary fields of investigation. Knowledge management seems to work well with the subjective nature of strategy formulation in organizations. It is also important to clarify the degree of linkage between both disciplines. This section will highlight the factors that help to explore the similarities and differences between the two fields, and establish a theoretical link between them. I will begin by defining the two constructs and acknowledging their distinct roots. Table 9.3 shows the similarities and differences between these fields of research.

Table 9.3 Comparative Perspectives on Strategic Management and Knowledge Management

Dimensions	Strategic Management	Knowledge Management
Disciplinary roots/ Conceptual origins	Organizational behavior, organizational theory, business policy	Organizational theory, epistemology, cognitive science, strategic management
Perspective	Inside an organization	Both inside and outside an organization
Working definition	The process of analyzing the internal and external environment so as to formulate a firm's strategy	The study of strategy, process and technology to acquire, organize, share and use knowledge
End result	Gaining the competitive advantage of an organization	Gaining the competitive advantage of an organization
Focus	The formulation and implementation of strategy	The discovery and deployment of knowledge
Type of organization	An organization that intends to win over its rivals	Knowledge organization
Key processes	Environmental analysis, identification and evaluation of options, strategy selection and implementation	Knowledge creation, knowledge sharing, knowledge dissemination, knowledge exploitation
Person in charge	CEO and other members of a strategy team	Chief knowledge officer

Working definition. As a starting point, it is important to define knowledge management and strategic management so as to demarcate their differences. Generally speaking, knowledge management attempts to capture the knowledge of an employee with the aim to make it available in a central repository so that other employees can extract and use it when they really need it. While appraising the various definitions of knowledge management, Jashapara (2005) observes that some definitions come from a strong strategic management perspective. Zhang and Zhao (2006), for example, define knowledge management as the study of strategy, process and technology to acquire, select, organize, share and use business-critical information. Strategic management, on the other hand, is defined as the process by which a firm incorporates the relevant tools (including knowledge management frameworks) to scan both the external and internal environment in order to grab resources at the time of strategy formulation and implementation. Clearly, defining the knowledge management and strategic management concepts helps to differentiate one from the other.

Disciplinary roots. One way to understand the difference between knowledge management and strategic management is through a discussion of the conceptual origins of these fields. From a theoretical perspective, strategic management and knowledge management have emerged from distinct disciplinary traditions. Indeed, the diverse origins of the two subjects have contributed to the lack of literature to date on the apparent linkage between these concepts.

Several scholars maintain that strategic management actually draws from a wide range of disciplines such as organizational behavior, organizational theory and business policy. In contrast, knowledge management has been approached from various angles such as organizational theory, epistemology, cognitive science and strategic management (Chae and Bloodgood, 2006; Barquin, 2001; Eisenhardt and Santos, 2002; Jasimuddin, 2006). In particular, Barquin (2001) argues that the topic of knowledge management spans disciplines, including strategy. Likewise, Eisenhardt and Santos (2002, as cited in Chae and Bloodgood, 2006) point out that knowledge management is sweeping through several academic fields, including organizational strategy. Reflecting this view, Jasimuddin (2006) contends that knowledge management is derived from various subjects within broader areas of management, including strategic management.

Processes involved. Another way to understand the difference between knowledge management and strategic management is by looking at the processes through which these disciplines operate. As mentioned earlier, knowledge management is the process of exploring and exploiting organizational knowledge, which involves activities related to capturing, utilizing, transferring, creating and storing organizational knowledge. Siemieniuch and Sinclair (1999) postulate that the knowledge management process allows organizations to generate, share, disseminate and use core knowledge according to current and future requirements. On the other hand, the strategic management process involves analyzing the environment as well as identifying, evaluating and implementing strategies in order to meet organizational objectives. To this end, organizational knowledge plays a large role in the formulation and implementation of a business strategy.

Focus. An understanding of the basic focus of knowledge management and strategic management also allows us to differentiate the two concepts. Knowledge management deals mostly with managing and integrating knowledge into an organization; whereas strategic management focuses on the plans and activities that need to be performed in order to formulate a strategy through the analysis of the business environment, using organizational knowledge. It could be said that knowledge management focuses on managing a narrower set of activities than strategic management.

Leadership role. It is important to note that there are differences in leadership role in strategic management processes and knowledge management initiatives. Stated differently, another basic difference between knowledge management and strategic management can be found in the person(s) in charge — namely, those who are responsible for managing knowledge and formulating strategy, respectively. The apparent distinction between knowledge management and strategic management has led to the creation of different leadership roles in firms. The chief executive officer and other top management people working in a firm's strategy team are responsible for formulating and selecting a business strategy. On the other hand, the chief knowledge officer is in charge of managing knowledge and implementing knowledge management initiatives. Therefore, there is an important leadership role to be played in building and sustaining the momentum of any specific activity, whether it is associated with knowledge management or strategic management.

End result. Although knowledge management and strategic management can be distinguished in terms of their contribution to organizations, there are some common themes available in both fields that are somewhat complementary in nature. One such common theme is that both strategic management and knowledge management, independently of each other, help to enhance the competitive advantage of companies. The strategic management discipline helps us understand how to formulate and implement a strategy that will eventually generate a competitive advantage. Likewise, knowledge management explores and exploits organizational knowledge in order to ensure a sustainable competitive advantage for an organization. Therefore, the extant literature enables organizations to adopt a more integrated approach towards managing knowledge and strategy as sources of sustainable competitive advantage.

It has long been known that a firm's strategy can have a great impact on its competitive advantage. Moreover, there now exists a great awareness among researchers and practitioners that organizational knowledge and strategy play a large role in gaining and sustaining the competitive advantage of an enterprise. In fact, a central idea of strategic management is the notion of competitive advantages built on knowledge (Kirzner, 1979; Pavlovich and Corner, 2006).

Hence, from the strategic management perspective, we need to develop a knowledge strategy that helps to collect knowledge from a firm's employees (indigenous sources of knowledge) and also from other stakeholders (exogenous sources of knowledge), and subsequently store it in an organized manner so that the stored knowledge can easily be retrievable at the right time when needed, especially when scanning the internal and external environment and formulating a business strategy.

As seen in Table 9.3, there are some common dimensions in strategic management and knowledge management, leading both fields to be viewed as complementary. Concepts such as competitive advantage of companies, the role of top management, knowledge, the environment and strategy are found in both disciplines. Therefore, it can be argued that knowledge management needs to be employed in order to retrieve the right knowledge at the right time when formulating and implementing a business strategy. Similarly, we need strategic management to formulate a knowledge management strategy so that organizational knowledge can be explored and exploited efficiently. It is observed that the formulation of a strategy requires actionable knowledge, much like how the management of organizational knowledge needs an appropriate strategy.

Stated differently, strategic management has a role in the development of the knowledge management field, and in the successful implementation of knowledge management initiatives in an organizational context. Similarly, knowledge management has a role in strategic management research and practice so as to facilitate the strategy process. The strategic management discipline is required for the successful implementation of knowledge management, while knowledge management is important for the effective use of knowledge in strategy formulation. Thus, three situations have evolved in terms of the relationship between the two disciplines:

- In situation I, there is a linkage between knowledge management and strategic management in that knowledge management facilitates strategy formulation and implementation.
- In situation II, there is an association between knowledge management and strategic management in that knowledge management is clearly derived from strategic management. Many strategic management tools have been used to decide whether an organization needs to have knowledge management practices in place.
- In situation III, there is a close relationship between knowledge management and strategic management. This is due to the fact that both disciplines are equally jointly responsible for enhancing the competitive advantage of organizations.

9.7 Concluding Summary

The strategic management discipline, which has advanced substantially over the last 40 years, helps us understand how to formulate a strategy. The successful implementation of a strategy will eventually generate a competitive advantage for an organization. Similarly, knowledge management, which first emerged in the 1990s, is a fundamental strategic process that is widely regarded as the only source of sustainable competitive advantage for organizations.

This chapter has provided a conceptual framework that defines and integrates knowledge management and strategic management, and that establishes a theoretical link between the two constructs and their performance. The distinction between these subjects is far from being well-articulated in the management literature, and this is compounded by the confusion around the concepts of knowledge and strategy. Therefore, the chapter has explored whether the terms "knowledge" and "strategy" are closely related concepts in order to clear up this conceptual confusion.

This chapter has begun with a discussion on the definition and origin of strategic management. Strategic management is referred to as the process by which an organization incorporates the tools and frameworks for environmental scanning (both external and internal), strategy formulation (strategic planning), strategy implementation, and evaluation and control, so as to generate and enhance sustainable competitive advantages over its rivals. The development of the strategic management field has been particularly dramatic over the last several decades, having emerged mainly from the social and administrative sciences. For example, one important antecedent field of strategic management is business policy.

The strategic management field has given more attention to the topics that help an organization outperform other competing organizations. Key areas surrounding strategic management that have emerged and have been receiving attention among academics and practitioners include competitive strategy, the strategy process, corporate governance, cooperative strategies, international strategies, strategic leadership, dynamic capabilities, strategic entrepreneurship, and the knowledge-based view of the firm.

Scholars hold different views on the relationship between knowledge management and strategic management. Several authors argue that these fields are very different, whereas others argue that one is shaped by the other. From a theoretical perspective, the two subjects have emerged from distinct disciplinary traditions. Nowadays, a growing consensus seems to be emerging that differentiates these constructs. At the same time, it could be argued that there is great potential for the cross-fertilization of ideas between the fields.

The fact is that there is a need to have an integrated approach that recognizes the importance of organizational knowledge for business strategy formulation. Similarly, strategic management principles and concepts play a role in developing an appropriate strategy for knowledge management initiatives. It is also noted that the management of knowledge is regarded as an essential part of strategic management. That is, organizational knowledge is a key ingredient for the success of strategy formulation. Hence, it is important to understand how knowledge management is related to the various strategic management processes. This chapter has contributed toward reducing the confusion about strategy and knowledge issues by clarifying the concepts of strategic management and knowledge management in order to establish their relationship. Tiwana (2000, p. 103) reinforces this view, stating that "knowledge drives strategy and strategy drives knowledge management".

Further Reading

Jasimuddin, S. M. (2007). Exploring a linkage between knowledge management and strategic management. Paper presented at the 14th Annual International Conference on Advances in Management, Toronto, July.

Lasserre, P. (2007). *Global Strategic Management*, 2nd ed. Basingstoke: Palgrave Macmillan.

References

Akhter, S. H. (2003). Strategic planning, hypercompetition, and knowledge management. *Business Horizons*, 46(1), 19–24.

Amit, R. and Zott, C. (2001). Value creation in e-business. *Strategic Management Journal*, 22(6/7), 493–520.

Ansoff, H. I. (1965). *Corporate Strategy*. New York: McGraw-Hill.

Barney, J. B. (1991). Firm resources and sustained competitive advantage. *Journal of Management*, 17(1), 99–120.

Barney, J. B. (1997). *Gaining and Sustaining Competitive Advantage*. Reading, MA: Addison-Wesley.

Barney, J. B. and Hesterly, W. S. (2008). *Strategic Management and Competitive Advantage: Concepts and Cases*. Upper Saddle River, NJ: Prentice Hall.

Barquin, R. C. (2001). What is knowledge management? *Knowledge and Innovation: Journal of the KMCI*, 1(2), 127–143.

Bierly, P. and Chakrabarti, A. (1996). Generic knowledge strategies in the U.S. pharmaceutical industry. *Strategic Management Journal*, 17(Winter Special Issue), 123–135.

Boisot, M. H. (1998). *Knowledge Assets*. Oxford: Oxford University Press.

Bowman, C. (2006). Formulating strategy. In D. O. Faulkner and A. Campbell (eds.), *The Oxford Handbook of Strategy* (pp. 410–442), New York: Oxford University Press.

Bowman, E. H., Singh, H. and Thomas, H. (2002). The domain of strategic management: history and evolution. In A. Pettigrew, H. Thomas and R. Whittington (eds.), *Handbook of Strategy and Management* (pp. 31–51), London: Sage.

Bracker, J. (1980). The historical development of the strategic management concept. *Academy of Management Review*, 5(2), 219–224.

Cannella, A. A. Jr. and Hambrick, D. C. (1993). Effects of executive departures on the performance of acquired firms. *Strategic Management Journal*, 41(S1), 137–152.

Carlisle, Y. (2002). Strategic thinking and knowledge management. In S. Little, P. Quintas and T. Ray (eds.), *Managing Knowledge: An Essential Reader* (pp. 122–138), London: The Open University and Sage Publications.

Carpenter, M. A. and Sanders, W. G. (2007). *Strategic Management: A Dynamic Perspective — Concepts and Cases*. Upper Saddle River, NJ: Prentice Hall.

Casselman, R. M. and Samson, D. (2007). Aligning knowledge strategy and knowledge capabilities. *Technology Analysis & Strategic Management*, 19(1), 69–81.

Cepeda-Carrion, G. (2006). Understanding the link between knowledge management and firm performance: articulating and codifying critical knowledge areas. *International Journal of Knowledge and Learning*, 2(3/4), 238–262.

Chae, B. and Bloodgood, J. M. (2006). The paradoxes of knowledge management: an eastern philosophical perspective. *Information and Organization*, 16, 1–26.

Chait, L. P. (1999). Creating a successful knowledge management system. *Journal of Business Strategy*, 20(2), 23–26.

Chakravarthy, B., Mueller-Stewens, G., Lorange, P. and Lechner, C. (eds.) (2003). *Strategy Process: Shaping the Contours of the Field.* Oxford: Blackwell.

Chandler, A. D. (1962). *Strategy and Structure.* Cambridge, MA: MIT Press.

Clarke, T. (2001). The knowledge economy. *Education + Training*, 43(4/5), 189–196.

Cummings, S. and Daellenbach, U. (2009). A guide to the future of strategy? The history of *Long Range Planning*. *Long Range Planning*, 42, 234–263.

Daily, C. M., Dalton, D. R. and Rajagopalan, N. (2003). Governance through ownership: centuries of practice, decades of research. *Academy of Management Journal*, 46(2), 151–158.

D'Aveni, R. A. (1994). *Hypercompetition: Managing the Dynamics of Strategic Maneuvering.* New York: The Free Press.

de Pablos, P. O. (2002). Knowledge management and organizational learning: typologies of knowledge strategies in the Spanish manufacturing industry from 1995 to 1999. *Journal of Knowledge Management*, 6(1), 52–62.

de Wit, B. and Meyer, R. (2004). *Strategy: Process, Content, Context*, 3rd ed. London: Thomson Learning.

Demsetz, H. (1991). The theory of the firm revisited. In O. Williamson and S. Winter (eds.), *The Nature of the Firm* (pp. 159–178), New York: Oxford University Press.

Donoghue, L. P., Harris, J. G. and Weitzman, B. A. (1999). Knowledge management strategies that create value. *Outlook*, 1, 48–53.

du Plessis, M. (2007). Knowledge management: what makes complex implementations successful? *Journal of Knowledge Management*, 11(2), 91–101.

Dyer, J. H. and Singh, H. (1998). The relational view: cooperative strategy and sources of interorganizational competitive advantage. *Academy of Management Review*, 23(4), 660–679.

Eisenhardt, K. M. and Santos, F. M. (2002). Knowledge-based view: a new theory of strategy? In A. Pettigrew, H. Thomas and R. Whittington (eds.), *Handbook of Strategy and Management* (pp. 139–164), London: Sage.

Faulkner, D. O. and Campbell, A. (2006). Introduction. In D. O. Faulkner and A. Campbell (eds.), *The Oxford Handbook of Strategy* (pp. 1–26), New York: Oxford University Press.

Finkelstein, S. and Hambrick, D. (1996). *Strategic Leadership*. St. Paul, MN: West Educational Publishing Company.

Floyd, S. W., Roos, J., Jacobs, C. D. and Kellermanns, F. W. (eds.) (2005). *Innovating Strategy Processes*. Oxford: Blackwell.

Fredrickson, J. W. (1990). Introduction: the need for perspectives. In J. W. Fredrickson (ed.), *Perspectives on Strategic Management* (pp. 1–8), New York: Harper Business.

Georgopoulos, N. B. (2005). Knowledge management as an integral part of strategic management in e-business era. *International Journal of Knowledge and Learning*, 1(4), 373–387.

Gimeno, J. (2004). Competition within and between networks: the contingent effect of competitive embeddedness on alliance formation. *Academy of Management Journal*, 47(6), 820–842.

Grant, R. M. (1991). The resource-based theory of competitive advantage: implications for strategy formulation. *California Management Review*, 33(3), 114–135.

Grant, R. M. (1996a). Toward a knowledge-based theory of the firm. *Strategic Management Journal*, 17(Special Issue), 109–122.

Grant, R. M. (1996b). Prospering in dynamically-competitive environments: organizational capability as knowledge integration. *Organization Science*, 7, 375–387.

Grant, R. M. and Baden-Fuller, C. (2004). A knowledge accessing theory of strategic alliances. *Journal of Management Studies*, 41(1), 61–84.

Greiner, M. E., Böhmann, T. and Krcmar, H. (2007). A strategy for knowledge management. *Journal of Knowledge Management*, 11(6), 3–15.

Gulati, R. (1995). Does familiarity breed trust? The implications of repeated ties for contractual choice in alliances. *Academy of Management Journal*, 38, 85–112.

Gulati, R. and Singh, H. (1998). The architecture of cooperation: managing coordination costs and appropriation concerns in strategic alliances. *Administrative Science Quarterly*, 43(4), 781–814.

Haberberg, A. and Rieple, A. (2008). *Strategic Management: Theory and Application*. Oxford: Oxford University Press.

Halawi, L. A., Aronson, J. E. and McCarthy, R. V. (2005). Resource-based view of knowledge management for competitive advantage. *Electronic Journal of Knowledge Management*, 3(2), 75–86.

Hambrick, D. C. and Cannella, A. A. Jr. (2004). CEOs who have COOs: contingency analysis of an unexplored structural form. *Strategic Management Journal*, 25(10), 959–979.

Hansen, M. T., Nohria, N. and Tierney, T. (1999). What's your strategy for managing knowledge? *Harvard Business Review*, 77(2), 106–116.

Helfat, C. E. and Peteraf, M. A. (2003). The dynamic resource-based view: capability lifecycles. *Strategic Management Journal*, 24(10), 997–1010.

Henry, A. (2008). *Understanding Strategic Management*. Oxford: Oxford University Press.

Heracleous, L. (2003). *Strategy and Organization*. Cambridge: Cambridge University Press.

Hill, C. W. L. and Jones, G. R. (2004). *Strategic Management Theory: An Integrated Approach*, 6th ed. Boston, MA: Houghton Mifflin.

Hitt, M. A. (2006). Spotlight on strategic management. *Business Horizons*, 49, 349–352.

Hitt, M. A., Boyd, B. K. and Li, D. (2004). The state of strategic management research and a vision of the future. In D. Ketchen, Jr. and D. Bergh (eds.), *Research Methodology in Strategy and Management*, Vol. 1 (pp. 1–31), Amsterdam: Elsevier.

Hitt, M. A., Ireland, R. D., Camp, S. M. and Sexton, D. L. (2001). Strategic entrepreneurship: entrepreneurial strategies for wealth creation. *Strategic Management Journal*, 22(6/7), 479–491.

Hitt, M. A., Ireland, R. D., Camp, S. M. and Sexton, D. L. (eds.) (2002). *Strategic Entrepreneurship: Creating a New Mindset*. Oxford: Blackwell.

Hoskisson, R. E., Hitt, M. A., Johnson, R. A. and Grossman, W. (2002). Conflicting voices: the effects of institutional ownership heterogeneity and internal governance on corporate innovation strategies. *Academy of Management Journal*, 45(4), 697–716.

Hoskisson, R. E., Hitt, M. A., Wan, W. P. and Yiu, D. (1999). Theory and research in strategic management: swings of a pendulum. *Journal of Management*, 25(3), 417–456.

Huff, A. S., Floyd, S. W., Sherman, H. D. and Terjesen, S. (2009). *Strategic Management*. Hoboken, NJ: John Wiley & Sons.

Hunger, J. D. and Wheelen, T. L. (2007). *Essentials of Strategic Management*, 4th ed. Upper Saddle River, NJ: Prentice Hall.

Ireland, R. D., Hitt, M. A. and Vaidyanath, D. (2002). Managing strategic alliances to achieve a competitive advantage. *Journal of Management*, 28, 413–446.

Ireland, R. D., Hoskisson, R. E. and Hitt, M. A. (2009). *The Management of Strategy*, 8th ed. Mason, OH: South-Western/Cengage Learning.

Jashapara, A. (2005). The emerging discourse of knowledge management: a new dawn for information science research? *Journal of Information Science*, 31(2), 136–148.

Jasimuddin, S. M. (2005). Knowledge of external sources' knowledge: new frontiers to actionable knowledge. In M. A. Rahim and R. T. Golembiewski (eds.), *Current Topics in Management*, Vol. 10 (pp. 39–50), New Brunswick, NJ: Transaction Publishers.

Jasimuddin, S. M. (2006). Disciplinary roots of knowledge management: a theoretical review. *International Journal of Organizational Analysis*, 14(2), 171–180.

Jasimuddin, S. M. (2008). A holistic view of appropriate knowledge management strategy. *Journal of Knowledge Management*, 12(2), 57–66.

Jeffs, C. (2008). *Strategic Management*. Thousand Oaks, CA: Sage.

Jemison, D. B. (1981). The importance of an integrative approach to strategic management research. *Academy of Management Review*, 6(4), 601–608.

Johnson, G., Scholes, K. and Whittington, R. (2008). *Exploring Corporate Strategy: Text and Cases*, 8th ed. Harlow, Essex: FT Prentice Hall.

Kesner, I. F. and Sebora, T. C. (1994). Executive succession: past, present and future. *Journal of Management*, 20, 327–372.

Kirzner, I. (1979). *Perception, Opportunity, and Profit*. Chicago: University of Chicago Press.

Kogut, B. and Zander, U. (1992). Knowledge of the firm, combinative capabilities, and the replication of technology. *Organization Science*, 3(3), 383–397.

Koulopoulos, T. M. and Frappaolo, C. (1999). *Smart Things to Know About Knowledge Management*. Oxford: Capstone.

Learned, E., Christensen, C., Andrews, K. and Guth, W. (1965). *Business Policy: Text and Cases*. Homewood, IL: Irwin.

Leonard-Barton, D. (1995). *Wellsprings of Knowledge: Building and Sustaining the Sources of Innovation*. Boston, MA: Harvard Business School Press.

Liebowitz, J. (1999). Key ingredients to the success of an organization's knowledge management strategy. *Knowledge and Process Management*, 6(1), 37–40.

Liebowitz, J. (2003). Keynote paper: measuring the value of online communities, leading to innovation and learning. *International Journal of Innovation and Learning*, 1(1), 1–8.

Liebowitz, J. and Beckman, T. (1998). *Knowledge Organizations: What Every Manager Should Know*. Boca Raton, FL: St. Lucie Press/CRC Press.

Loermans, J. (2002). Synergizing the learning organization and knowledge management. *Journal of Knowledge Management*, 6(3), 285–294.

Lu, J. W. and Beamish, P. W. (2004). International diversification and firm performance: the S-curve hypothesis. *Academy of Management Journal*, 47(4), 598–609.

Lynall, M. D., Golden, B. R. and Hillman, A. J. (2003). Board composition from adolescence to maturity: a multitheoretic view. *Academy of Management Review*, 28(3), 416–431.

Lynch, R. (2006). *Corporate Strategy*, 4th ed. Harlow, Essex: FT Prentice Hall.

Mahoney, J. T. and McGahan, A. M. (2007). The field of strategic management within the evolving science of strategic organization. *Strategic Organization*, 5(1), 79–99.

Mahoney, J. T. and Pandian, J. R. (1992). The resource-based view within the conversation of strategic management. *Strategic Management Journal*, 13, 363–380.

McCann, J. E. and Buckner, M. (2004). Strategically integrating knowledge management initiatives. *Journal of Knowledge Management*, 8(1), 47–63.

Mellahi, K., Frynas, J. G. and Finlay, P. (2005). *Global Strategic Management*. Oxford: Oxford University Press.

Metaxiotis, K. and Psarras, J. (2006). Analysing the value of knowledge management leading to innovation. *International Journal of Knowledge Management Studies*, 1(1/2), 79–89.

Nissen, M., Kamel, M. and Sengupta, K. (2000). Integrated analysis and design of knowledge systems and processes. *Information Resources Management Journal*, 13(1), 24–43.

Nonaka, I. and Teece, D. J. (2001). Research directions for knowledge management. In I. Nonaka and D. J. Teece (eds.), *Managing Industrial Knowledge: Creation, Transfer and Utilization* (pp. 330–335), London: Sage.

O'Dell, C. and Grayson, C. J. (1998). If only we knew what we know: identification and transfer of internal best practices. *California Management Review*, 40, 154–174.

Parthasarthy, R. (2007). *Fundamentals of Strategic Management*. New York: Houghton Mifflin.

Pavlovich, K. and Corner, P. D. (2006). Knowledge creation through co-entrepreneurship. *International Journal of Knowledge Management Studies*, 1(1/2), 178–197.

Peng, M. W. (2009). *Global Strategic Management*. London: South-Western/Cengage Learning.

Penner-Hahn, J. and Shaver, J. M. (2005). Does international research and development increase patent output? An analysis of Japanese pharmaceutical firms. *Strategic Management Journal*, 26, 121–140.

Pitkethly, R. (2006). Analysing the environment. In D. O. Faulkner and A. Campbell (eds.), *The Oxford Handbook of Strategy* (pp. 231–266), New York: Oxford University Press.

Porter, M. E. (1980). *Competitive Strategy: Techniques for Analyzing Industries and Competitors*. New York: The Free Press.

Prahalad, C. K. and Hamel, G. (1990). The core competition of the corporation. *Harvard Business Review*, 68(3), 79–91.

PricewaterhouseCoopers (1999). KM business value: lessons learned from early adopters. *Global Enterprise Advisor*, 10, 7–8.

Roberts, H. (1998). The bottom-line of competence-based management: management accounting, control and performance measurement. Paper presented at the EAA Conference, Antwerp, Belgium.

Rumelt, R. (1991). How much does industry matter? *Strategic Management Journal*, 12(3), 167–185.

Rumelt, R., Schendel, D. and Teece, D. (1994). *Fundamental Issues in Strategy: A Research Agenda*. Boston, MA: Harvard Business School Press.

Sawyer, R. D. (1996). *The Complete Art of War*. Boulder, CO: Westview Press.

Schendel, D. and Cool, K. (1988). Development of the strategic management field: some accomplishments and challenges. In J. H. Grant (ed.), *Strategic Management Frontiers* (pp. 17–31), Greenwich, CT: JAI Press.

Schendel, D. and Hofer, C. W. (1979). *Strategic Management: A New View of Business Policy and Planning*. Boston, MA: Little, Brown and Company.

Shariq, S. Z. (1997). Knowledge management: an emerging discipline. *Journal of Knowledge Management*, 1(1), 75–82.

Shaw, D. and Edwards, J. S. (2005). Building user commitment to implementing a knowledge management strategy. *Information & Management*, 42(7), 977–988.

Shaw, D., Hall, M., Edwards, J. S. and Baker, B. (2007). Responding to crisis through strategic knowledge management. *Journal of Organizational Change Management*, 20(4), 559–578.

Siemieniuch, C. E. and Sinclair, M. A. (1999). Organizational aspects of knowledge lifecycle management in manufacturing. *International Journal of Human-Computer Studies*, 51, 517–547.

Skyrme, D. (1999). *Knowledge Networking: Creating the Collaborative Enterprise*. Oxford: Butterworth-Heinemann.

Smircich, L. and Stubbart, C. (1985). Strategic management in an enacted world. *Academy of Management Review*, 10(4), 724–736.

Snyman, R. and Kruger, C. J. (2004). The interdependency between strategic management and strategic knowledge management. *Journal of Knowledge Management*, 8(1), 5–19.

Spender, J. C. (1996). Making knowledge the basis of a dynamic theory of the firm. *Strategic Management Journal*, 17(Special Issue), 45–62.

Spender, J. C. and Grant, R. M. (1996). Knowledge and the firm: overview. *Strategic Management Journal*, 17(Winter Special Issue), 5–9.

Stacey, R. D. (2007). *Strategic Management and Organisational Dynamics: The Challenge of Complexity*, 5th ed. Harlow, Essex: FT Prentice Hall.

Stadler, C. and Stone, T. (2001). eBusiness: knowledge management's new killer application. In *Infosmart Africa 2001 Conference Proceedings*, The Dome at Northgate, Johannesburg, Gauteng, South Africa, July 10–12.

Storey, J. and Barnett, E. (2000). Knowledge management initiatives: learning from failure. *Journal of Knowledge Management*, 4(2), 145–156.

Swan, J., Newell, S., Scarbrough, H. and Hislop, D. (1999). Knowledge management and innovation: networks and networking. *Journal of Knowledge Management*, 3, 262–275.

Tallman, S. (2001). Global strategic management. In M. A. Hitt, R. E. Freeman and J. S. Harrison (eds.), *The Backwell Handbook of Strategic Management* (pp. 464–490), Oxford: Blackwell.

Tavakoli, I. and Lawton, J. (2005). Strategic thinking and knowledge management. *Handbook of Business Strategy*, 6(1), 155–160.

Teece, D. J. (1990). Contributions and impediments of economic analysis to the study of strategic management. In J. W. Fredrickson (ed.), *Perspectives on Strategic Management* (pp. 39–80), New York: Harper Business.

Teece, D. J., Pisano, G. and Shuen, A. (1997). Dynamic capabilities and strategic management. *Strategic Management Journal*, 18(7), 509–533.

Tissen, R., Andriessen, D. and Deprez, F. L. (1998). *Value-Based Knowledge Management — Creating the 21st Century Company: Knowledge Intensive, People Rich*. Amsterdam: Addison-Wesley Longman.

Tiwana, A. (2000). *The Knowledge Management Toolkit*. Englewood Cliffs, NJ: Prentice Hall.

Van Cauwenbergh, A. and Cool, K. (1982). Strategic management in a new framework. *Strategic Management Journal*, 3(3), 245–264.

Winter, S. G. (2003). Understanding dynamic capabilities. *Strategic Management Journal*, 24(10), 991–995.

Zack, M. H. (1999a). Developing a knowledge strategy. *California Management Review*, 41(3), 125–145.

Zack, M. H. (1999b). Managing codified knowledge. *Sloan Management Review*, 40(4), 45–58.

Zand, D. (1997). *The Leadership Triad: Knowledge, Trust, and Power*. New York: Oxford University Press.

Zhang, D. and Zhao, J. L. (2006). Preface — knowledge management in organizations. *Journal of Database Management*, 17(1), 1–8.

Chapter 10

Knowledge Management and Innovation Management

Knowledge Objectives

After studying this chapter, you should be able to:

- Provide a basic introduction of innovation management with respect to knowledge management;
- Explore the origin of innovation management;
- Discuss the notion of innovation management from philosophical perspectives;
- Explain the typologies of innovation;
- Identify the key areas of innovation management;
- Discuss the significance of innovation management in organizations; and
- Elaborate on the linkage between innovation management and knowledge management.

10.1 Introducing the Chapter

During the 1950s, innovation management was treated as an isolated development resulting from research conducted by academics. Nowadays, however, innovation is no longer thought of as a specific outcome of an individual action, but more as a discipline. Innovation is considered by researchers to be an important source of competitive advantage for organizations. As a result, innovation management has attracted the attention of practitioners. It is worth mentioning that, almost eight decades ago, the world-renowned economist Joseph Schumpeter (1934) contended that innovation was the main driver of a country's economic development.

The notion of innovation management has become increasingly important in the ever-changing global environment due to a greater awareness of the significance of innovation. In the 21st century, an organization's ability to innovate faster than its competitors is regarded as a powerful source of competitive advantage. Indeed, the idea of the innovative organization is becoming increasingly relevant to the contemporary corporate world. Consequently, innovation management has been established as an important issue for achieving an organization's sustainable competitive advantage, and understanding how to make an organization innovative has become crucial.

We know that organizational knowledge is at the heart of knowledge management. Similarly, the concept of organizational knowledge plays a great role in the innovation management process. Thus, it could be argued that there is a link between knowledge management and innovation management. However, this issue has not been fully articulated in the relevant literature. To be sure, tremendous progress has occurred in knowledge management and innovation management independently over the last two decades, but the literature shows definite gaps in the investigation of the two disciplines jointly (Pyka, 2002; Dvir and Pasher, 2004; Denning, 2005; Scozzi *et al.*, 2005). The linkage between these fields has only just begun to be explored.

The aim of this chapter is to clarify the concepts of innovation management and knowledge management in order to highlight their relationship. This chapter will provide a conceptual framework that defines and integrates the two concepts. An essential starting point is to understand what innovation management is, what its characteristics are, and how it relates to the emerging topic of knowledge management. Recent studies have tried to throw some light on the relationship between the two fields. This chapter will examine their close conceptual and practical links, and so shed some insight on the nature of their association. More specifically, the chapter will highlight the factors that help to explain whether innovation management is a precursor of knowledge management or whether innovation management is shaped by knowledge management.

I will start by critically explaining the innovation management construct, acknowledging its various definitions and distinct roots in Section 10.2. There are various terms surrounding the notion of innovation management that sometimes create confusion. Section 10.3 will attempt to reduce such confusion. The concept of innovation has been discussed from many different perspectives. Traditionally, innovation can be classified in terms of the nature of innovation and the form of innovation. Section 10.4 will discuss these typologies of innovation. The innovation management field has become increasingly important in the dynamic global environment. Section 10.5 will highlight the role that this field plays in enhancing the competitive advantage of an organization over its rivals. As with any other well-established discipline, there are various issues that are discussed in the innovation management research. Section 10.6 will identify some of the key areas surrounding it. Researchers and practitioners have many different views on the relationship between knowledge management and innovation management. Section 10.7 will concentrate on scholars' conflicting views regarding the connection or potential convergence between the two subjects. More importantly, there are several factors that can easily help to demarcate these fields, thus establishing a theoretical link between them. Section 10.8 will examine the overlaps and complementarities that exist between innovation management and knowledge management. Finally, a concluding summary will be presented in Section 10.9.

10.2 Innovation Management Defined

The concept of innovation has evolved significantly over the last 40 years (Hidalgo and Albors, 2008). Innovation management discusses how best to create and use new knowledge and, thereby, innovate.

Innovation management theories attempt to address the following three issues:

- The way in which the notion of innovation operates in an organization, be it private or public, commercial or non-commercial;
- The rationale behind an organization being more innovative than others; and
- The different strategies of an organization in terms of innovation.

Tinnesand (1973, as cited in Cumming, 1998) reviewed 188 publications which interpret the meaning of the word "innovation" as follows:

- The introduction of a new idea (36%);
- A new idea (16%);
- The introduction of an invention (14%);
- An idea different from existing ideas (14%);
- The introduction of an idea disrupting the prevailing behavior (11%); and
- An invention (9%).

Moreover, Cumming (1998, p. 22) reports that the meaning of the word "innovation" has subtly changed over the last 30 years. In the 1960s and 1970s, innovation was thought of as a process, as the introduction of change. Some scholars refer to innovation as simply the generation of a new idea. Nordfors (2004), for example, sees innovation as the introduction of something new. It is worth mentioning that the first and seminal definition of innovation was proposed by Schumpeter (1934, as cited in Hidalgo and Albors, 2008), who associated it to economic development and defined it as a new combination of productive resources, incorporating five specific cases as given below:

(i) Introduction of new products;
(ii) New production methods;
(iii) Exploration of new markets;

(iv) Conquering of new sources of supply; and
(v) New ways of organizing business.

Metaxiotis and Psarras (2006) observe that there are numerous definitions of innovation management in the existing literature. Haberberg and Rieple (2008) support this, stating that "there are probably hundreds of definitions of innovation". Management scholars such as Afuah (1998), Carnegie and Butlin (1993), Denning (2004), Drejer (2008), Drucker (1985), Haberberg and Rieple (2008), Hargadon and Fanelli (2002), Lawson and Samson (2003), Livingstone *et al.* (1998), Luecke and Katz (2003), Metaxiotis and Psarras (2006), Nordfors (2004), Roberts (1981), Schumpeter (1934), Thompson (1967), Udwadia (1990), Urabe (1988), West and Farr (1990), and Williams (1999) have produced definitions of innovation management that are widely cited by other researchers. Table 10.1 illustrates the many different perceptions of innovation management.

As an emerging science, the innovation management field has drawn from a wide range of established disciplines. As a result, there are often conflicting definitions (see Table 10.1), or a lack of consensus on what innovation management means. However, scholars such as Nyström (1990), Metaxiotis and Psarras (2006), and Edquist (1997) argue that most definitions of innovation management share common features with respect to the concept of organizational knowledge. That is, organizational knowledge is eventually turned into new products, processes or services, and hence into competitive advantage over competing organizations, meeting customers' changing needs. As Metaxiotis and Psarras (2006) suggest, "When we talk about innovation, we do not just mean product innovation". Reflecting this view, Lowe (1995) contends that innovation needs to be directed at products, processes, markets and production competencies.

10.3 Terminology Associated with Innovation Management

In the relevant literature, terms like "fashion", "creativity", "invention" and "innovation" are often used synonymously. Haberberg and

Table 10.1 Definitions of Innovation Management

Authors	Definitions
Afuah (1998)	The use of new technological and market knowledge to offer a new product or service to customers
Carnegie and Butlin (1993)	Something new or improved that is done by an enterprise to create significantly added value either directly for the enterprise or directly for its customers
Denning (2004)	The adoption of a new practice in a community
Drejer (2008)	The creation of new business for organizations; hence, it goes beyond creativity, invention and product development
Drucker (1985)	The specific tool of entrepreneurs, or the means by which they exploit change as an opportunity for a different business or service; it is capable of being presented as a discipline, capable of being learned and capable of being practiced
Haberberg and Rieple (2008)	The implementation of a significantly new idea in a specific context; this may apply to products, technologies or processes
Hargadon and Fanelli (2002)	The adaptation of existing knowledge into new activities; thus, existing knowledge serves as the base for building new ideas or reconfiguring existing ones
Lawson and Samson (2003)	The means by which knowledge is incorporated into economic activity
Livingstone *et al.* (1998)	New products or processes that increase value, including anything from patents and newly developed products to creative uses of information and effective human resource management systems
Luecke and Katz (2003)	The embodiment, combination or synthesis of knowledge in original, relevant, valued new products, processes or services
Metaxiotis and Psarras (2006)	A process of keeping ideas alive, imagining new uses for old ideas and putting promising concepts to the test; it depends heavily on knowledge, particularly since knowledge represents a realm far deeper than simply that of data, information and conventional logic

(*Continued*)

Table 10.1 (*Continued*)

Authors	Definitions
Nordfors (2004)	The introduction of something new
Roberts (1981)	Innovation = invention + commercialization
Schumpeter (1934)	The process of creating a commercial product from an invention
Thompson (1967)	The generation, acceptance and implementation of new ideas, processes, products or services
Udwadia (1990)	The successful creation, development and introduction of new products, processes or services
UK Department of Trade and Industry (DTI) (1998)	The process of taking new ideas effectively and profitably to satisfy customers
Urabe (1988)	The generation of a new idea and its implementation into a new product, process or service, leading to the dynamic growth of the national economy and the increase of employment as well as the creation of pure profit for the innovative business enterprise
West and Farr (1990)	The intentional introduction and application within a role, group or organization of ideas, processes, products or procedures, new to the relevant unit of adoption, designed to significantly benefit the individual, group, organization or wider society
Williams (1999)	The implementation of both discoveries and inventions and the process by which new outcomes, whether products, systems or processes, come into being

Rieple (2008), for instance, postulate that such terms are used interchangeably in some industries. Several scholars (e.g., D'Aveni, 1994; Dougherty and Hardy, 1996; Utterback, 1994; Lawson and Samson, 2003) view innovation as a mechanism by which organizations make an effort to produce the new products, processes and systems required for adapting to changing markets, technologies and modes of competition. There are scholars who use the terms "innovation" and "invention" interchangeably, while others commonly see innovation as synonymous to creativity. But in reality, the term "innovation" differs from "invention" and "creativity".

To start with, it is worth repeating Haberberg and Rieple's (2008) comment that "there are probably hundreds of definitions of innovation" — as there are of creativity. Several authors — most notably Kuhn (1985), Badawy (1988), Martins and Terblanche (2003), Davila *et al.* (2006), and Cumming (1998) — argue that the concepts of creativity and innovation are not synonymous. Creativity is treated as a component of generative learning, whereas innovation is the application of new and creative ideas. For example, Kuhn (1985) contends that creativity forms something from nothing, while innovation shapes that something into products and services. Reflecting this view, Badawy (1988) points out that creativity brings something new into being, while innovation brings something new into use. Likewise, Martins and Terblanche (2003) state that creativity focuses on the nature of thought processes and intellectual activity that are used to generate new insights or solutions to problems. Moreover, Davila *et al.* (2006, p. xvii) point out that "creativity implies coming up with ideas, [but] it's the 'bringing ideas to life' ... that makes innovation the distinct undertaking it is". Nevertheless, creativity and innovation can be regarded as overlapping constructs between two stages of the creative process, namely idea generation and idea implementation (Martins and Terblanche, 2003).

Another issue to address is whether the terms "innovation" and "invention" can be used interchangeably. According to Schumpeter (1961), there is a very clear distinction between invention and innovation. Invention refers to the discovery or creation of a new idea, product or process, whereas innovation is the process through which an invention obtains commercial value. For example, an invention may be the creation of a new computer software, a new computer design, a new method for painting a house, a new way of distributing and selling a product, a new academic module or degree scheme, or a new form of structure designed for an organization.

The fact is that the word "innovation" is used to mean new practices of new ideas. These ideas have no impact unless they are adopted into practice. Innovation is viewed as the implementation of an invention; as such, it is a business reality and an important source of competitive advantage. Reflecting this view, Twiss (1992) rightly remarks that "for an invention to become an innovation it must succeed in the marketplace".

According to Schumpeter (1961, p. 88), "As long as they are not carried into practice, inventions are economically irrelevant". Let us consider some of the most famous inventions, such as the vacuum cleaner and sewing machine. It is observed that the originators of these inventions are not remembered, whereas brand names like Hoover and Singer are widely known throughout the world. Only a few of us have heard of James Murray Spangler and Elias Howe, the inventor of the vacuum cleaner and sewing machine, respectively (Tidd *et al.*, 2001). In contrast, personalities like W. H. "Boss" Hoover, to whom Spangler sold his idea of the vacuum cleaner, and Isaac Merritt Singer, to whom Howe sold his idea of the sewing machine, are well known to all of us.

An invention becomes an innovation when an idea becomes a reality and has commercial value. As noted earlier, like the vacuum cleaner and sewing machine, a newly developed software has no value unless and until it is commercialized. Similarly, a new technology for painting a product can be said to be an innovation if it offers a more efficient system of painting to minimize costs and save time, along with meeting customers' needs; while the launching of a new degree scheme (say, a Master's in Knowledge Management) by a university may allow it to recruit new students who may be interested to pursue their studies in such an academic program. Therefore, it could be argued that the technical aspect is used to determine the success of an invention, whereas the commercial element is used to determine the success of an innovation.

In this regard, Denning (2004) draws a sharp distinction between innovation and invention. Invention means simply the creation of something new — an idea, an artifact, a device, a procedure. There is no guarantee that an idea or invention, no matter how clever, will become an innovation. Innovation requires attention to other people, specifically what they value and will adopt; invention, on the other hand, requires only attention to technology. To further clarify this point, Denning (2004) cites a classic example of the World Wide Web, which was invented by Tim Berners-Lee:

> Berners-Lee's invention was a Web browsing system on a NeXT computer circa 1990. This system included HTML, a new markup language for documents containing hyperlinks, HTTP, a new protocol for downloading an object designated by a hyperlink, URL, a scheme for global Internet names, and a graphical user interface. ... Some say this invention is not remarkable. What is remarkable is the innovation that came from it.

According to Tidd *et al.* (2001, p. 87), "Innovation is a process, not a single event, and needs to be managed. The influences on the process can be manipulated to affect the outcome — that is, it can be managed". Parallel to this, Goffin and Mitchell (2005, p. 2) state:

> [I]nnovation management is like competing in an event like the Olympic pentathlon; excellent performance in one discipline alone will not guarantee a gold medal. Too many companies have focused on just one area of innovation management — for example on improving new product development — when there are other aspects that are equally important. Leading companies take a broad view of innovation management, considering a range of issues from idea generation, to implementation, to business culture.

There are several other authors who argue that it is very difficult to demarcate innovation and invention. Haberberg and Rieple (2008) explain that it is almost impossible to separate invention from innovation in some industries; for example, in biotechnology, the development of a new gene modification technique happens through practical, applied development in the laboratory. Nevertheless, Haberberg and Rieple (2008) attempt to give comprehensive definitions of the following three concepts, thus making a distinction among them:

- *Creativity* is the production of novel or original ideas in a domain;
- *Invention* is the first occurrence of an idea for a new product or process; and

- *Innovation* is the implementation of a significantly new idea in a specific context.

As an emerging science, a multiplicity of terms are used interchangeably in the innovation management field. The lack of consistent definitions for the terms "innovation", "invention" and "creativity" makes rigorous discussions of innovation management difficult. However, there is at least a minimum consensus that innovation, invention and creativity are not the same thing.

10.4 Typologies of Innovation

The concept of innovation can be discussed from many different perspectives. Traditionally, innovation can be classified from two angles: the nature of innovation and the form of innovation. In particular, when we talk about the nature of innovation, a distinction of innovations can again be drawn between radical innovation and incremental innovation (Grøtnes, 2009). Moreover, innovations can appear in many different forms; that is, innovations can also be seen as product innovation or process innovation. This will be elaborated below.

10.4.1 *Typology of Innovation Based on the Nature of Innovation*

An innovation could be a full-fledged new product (or service). Alternatively, it could be an existing product with newly developed features that is claimed to be new in the market, and that is commercialized in some new way which opens up new uses for it. In line with this, scholars (e.g., Dewar and Dutton, 1986; Ettlie *et al.*, 1984; Freeman, 1982; Mansfield, 1968; McDermott and O'Dell, 2001; Mokyr, 1990; Zaltman *et al.*, 1973; Koen, 2005; Johannessen, 2008) argue that innovations can be seen as radical innovations, i.e., something qualitatively new, or incremental (continuous) innovations, i.e., small step-by-step improvements.

Radical innovations are innovations that initiate new directions in technology. Koen (2005) argues that in recent times these are discontinuous events that are usually the result of a research and development (R&D) activity in companies, universities and government laboratories, either isolatedly or jointly. Radical innovations usually bring about productive technological breakthroughs and create new knowledge. It is noted that radical innovations are revolutionary and nonlinear in nature. Such innovations often use new technologies to serve newly created markets. The development of the original personal computer (PC) is a classic example of a radical innovation, that is, the reinvention of the computer by developing a "new chip" that had the capability to process a trillion calculations per second.

In contrast to radical innovations, incremental innovations modify and improve an existing product or process. Koen (2005) contends that these are small-step innovations that occur more or less continuously in any business activity. Such an innovation is incremental in nature, building on existing knowledge bases and providing small improvements in the current product lines. In fact, the majority of innovations are incremental innovations, which are evolutionary and linear in nature. Companies launch more incremental innovations than radical innovations; therefore, most innovations are not major technological breakthroughs but modifications, often of a very minor nature.

Parallel to this, Christensen and Rosenbloom (1995) state that incremental innovations are innovations which progress along established paths. The incremental approach to innovation is successfully pursued in the manufacturing sector, for example, as reflected in car manufacturers which roll out new models at regular but short intervals. It is incremental innovation that makes any product's life short.

It is worth mentioning the case of Motorola, a Fortune 100 company with US$42.6 billion of sales in 2006. Since its inception as Galvin Manufacturing Corporation, Motorola has been known for its innovative products. For instance, it introduced the first car radios in 1930, followed by the development of handheld cellular telephones in 1984. The fact is that Motorola has been involved in both radical (e.g., handheld cellular telephone) and incremental (e.g., RAZR 2) innovations through its successful R&D activities.

10.4.2 *Typology of Innovation Based on the Form of Innovation*

Innovation management studies (e.g., Rogers, 1983; Urabe, 1988; Utterback, 1994; Afuah, 1998; Garcia and Calantone, 2002; McDermott and O'Connor, 2002; Pedersen and Dalum, 2004) have outlined other aspects of innovation that are more related to the final consumer of innovative goods or services as well as to the innovation process. In this regard, Schumpeter (1934) incorporates many forms of innovation, including new products, processes, markets, raw materials, and types of organization. More specifically, scholars such as Johannessen (2008), Dosi (1988), Teece (1989), and Utterback and Abernathy (1975) distinguish between product innovation and process innovation.

Product innovation is the development of a new product. Classic examples of product innovation include a new model of a car, a new form of insurance policy, or a restaurant offering a new vegetarian menu. Contrarily, process innovation is concerned with how the product is made or delivered to customers. The development of robots in the manufacturing industry, a new technology for painting a product, and a restaurant opening a self-service section (in addition to waiter-service operation) are examples of process innovation.

Johannessen (2008) argues that process innovations can in turn be divided into organization and technology. Process innovations with respect to organization refer to a new market organization or internal company organization, while process innovations with respect to technology refer to human artifacts. In this context, Gehlen (1980, p. 19) classifies technology in terms of three entities: instrument, machine, and automaton.

Furthermore, Metaxiotis and Psarras (2006) categorize the innovation process based on the level of an organization:

- Innovation of new products and services, including the creation of new consumption;
- Innovation of an operation's improvement, including the introduction of new methods and processes; and

- Innovation of ability improvement, such as developing workers' abilities, improving cooperation between units and stakeholders, and improving organizational culture.

In his classic work, Schumpeter (1934) states that companies are engaged in three types of innovative activity:

- *Invention* is the act of creating or developing a new product or process.
- *Innovation* is the process of creating a commercial product from an invention. Innovation begins after an invention is chosen for development. Thus, an invention brings something new into being, while an innovation brings something new into use.
- Finally, *imitation* is the adoption of a similar innovation by different organizations.

10.5 The Role of Innovation Management

As mentioned earlier, Schumpeter (1934) incorporates a wide variety of forms of innovation, including new products, processes, markets, raw materials, and types of organization. In the knowledge-based economy, successful innovation is viewed as a top priority within organizations, be they commercial or non-commercial. Presently, the organizational focus has shifted from being product-oriented to knowledge-oriented. As a result, organizations today compete more on the basis of processes than on products (Ward, 2002). Parallel to this, several scholars (e.g., Revilla *et al.*, 2005; Subramaniam and Venkatraman, 1999) argue that competition is becoming more knowledge-based and that the sources of competitive advantage are shifting away from physical assets to intellectual capabilities. Against this backdrop, Westland (2008) argues that innovation has become the industrial religion of the 21st century.

In line with this, there are researchers (e.g., Baumol *et al.*, 2007; Beesley and Cooper, 2008; Gloet and Terziovski, 2004; Lawson and Samson, 2003; Metaxiotis and Psarras, 2006; Snow *et al.*, 2009; Hult *et al.*, 2004; Jin *et al.*, 2004; Quinn *et al.*, 1997) who claim that innovation is a key source of competitive advantage and economic growth. Innovation is viewed as one of the most crucial tasks and has proved to be a celebrated component of corporate success, especially in turbulent and highly competitive environments. Organizations, irrespective of their size, consider innovation as a core competency.

It is evident that successful innovation is seen as a top priority within successful organizations (Revilla *et al.*, 2005). In a study published by Accenture and Talent Foundation (2002, as cited in Metaxiotis and Psarras, 2006), 96% of business leaders ranked innovation as one of the top ten items on their corporate agenda. This view is an extension of that of the Organisation for Economic Co-operation and Development (OECD) (2000), which recognizes the fact that encouraging innovation is high on the agendas of government policy makers as they make relentless efforts to create environments that support the activities needed to foster innovation. The governments of the developed world, in particular, are investing billions of dollars to attain or maintain supremacy in innovation.

In this regard, Denning (2004) postulates that innovation is the only way to assure marketplace strength for lean organizations. Organizations that institutionalize innovation and adopt an open and flexible attitude to change are better positioned in the competitive global market. Successful companies describe innovation as key to increasing their profits and expanding their share in the global market. It is observed that companies that invest more in innovation seem to achieve the highest returns.

This point is also underscored by Metaxiotis and Psarras (2006), who state that, in today's fierce business competition, innovation fuels organizational growth and is the engine that allows companies to sustain their viability. Similarly, Gloet and Terziovski (2004) assert that, in an ideal situation, the following benefits can be expected to be derived from innovation:

- Innovation has the capacity to improve the performance of a company;
- Innovation helps to solve existing problems; and

- Innovation creates value and thereby ensures sustainable competitive advantage for an organization.

Both academics and practitioners have given much attention to the innovation management research, seeing as innovation is a proven cornerstone of competitive advantage for organizations (Snow *et al.*, 2009). Educational institutions have also come forward to disseminate knowledge and understanding associated with innovation management. New courses and degree programs in innovation management, which exclusively focus on the role of innovation in business, are now being offered by business schools across universities.

Likewise, a large number of books and journals on topics associated with innovation management have appeared during the past 25 years. Many peer-reviewed research journals have surfaced that address major aspects of the field as a primary focus (see Table 10.2). Moreover, formal research in this subject can be observed in the devotion of special issues of several top scholarly journals to such topics. In fact, several leading innovation management journals are listed in the UK's Association of Business Schools (ABS) Academic Journal Quality Guide, and are used by the UK Research Assessment Exercise (RAE) to rank business schools in terms of their scholarly contributions.

Table 10.2 A Selected List of Journals on Innovation Management

Journal Title	Year Launched	Frequency	Publisher
Creativity and Innovation Management	1992	Quarterly	Wiley-Blackwell
European Journal of Innovation Management	1998	Quarterly	Emerald
Industry and Innovation	1993	8 issues per year	Taylor & Francis
International Journal of Innovation Management	1997	Bimonthly	World Scientific
Journal of Product Innovation Management	1984	Bimonthly	Wiley-Blackwell

Despite its importance for organizational growth and success, innovation is not an easy task to accomplish in organizations. Innovations are the work of a few gifted people, who can be labeled as "celebrity innovators". During the early 19th century, innovation was driven predominantly by immensely talented, creative and visionary individuals. For example, inventors like Thomas Edison, Alexander Bell and Henry Ford formed their own laboratories where they came up with their fantastic ideas; subsequently, they established business firms to transform those ideas into tangible products and eventually commercialized their product ideas.

Today, it is widely recognized that innovation is a significant source of competitive advantage. As a result, innovation management has emerged as a crucial area in the study of organizations. Bellini and Lo Storto (2006) reinforce this view, stating that there exists a diffused awareness among scholars that innovation has become one of the most important factors in establishing an organization's competitive advantage. Having discussed its role in the business context, the next section will focus on the emerging topics in innovation management.

10.6 Key Areas in Innovation Management

Innovation management as a discipline is a relatively young field; nonetheless, research in this domain has been growing at an impressive rate in recent decades. Most management scholars assert that innovation is critical for the competitive advantage of organizations, for it holds great promise. The notion of innovation management helps us understand how innovation, technology and strategy can be closely integrated so as to create the sustainable competitiveness of an organization. In our global environment, such a subject will allow us to develop skills in recognizing new technological trends and new innovations in an organization. By eventually integrating innovation, technology and strategy into the organization, innovation management will help us develop behaviors that create and implement innovation within the organization.

The evolution of innovation management over the last three decades has been dramatic. This section will highlight some of the major themes in the rapidly expanding literature on the subject. Academics are making a much-appreciated effort to foster innovation management in management education. Indeed, there has been a notable thrust in recent curriculum development in higher education that focuses on designing and offering modules and degree schemes centered on innovation management, in order to spread innovation management education.

Since its inception, the development of this area of study has been impressive. From its humble beginnings as limited content in such areas as new product development in production/operation management and technology management courses in the business school curriculum, innovation management is now a firmly established field in the study of business and organizations. A number of Master of Business Administration (MBA) programs have begun to focus on the area of innovation management. Within a relatively short period of time, this field has witnessed significant growth in the diversity of topics explored and the variety of research methods employed.

The majority of innovation management research focuses on why some firms are more innovative than others. One explanation is that innovative firms spend more time and money on innovations. On top of that, they have a full-fledged research and development (R&D) unit that is dedicated to innovation activities. Its footprints can also be found in the top management's corporate agenda. While the roots of innovation management have traditionally been in more applied areas, current topics of the discipline are strongly theory-based, with substantial empirical research.

It is noted that innovation management has traditionally focused on concepts associated with innovative activity that affect firm performance. Since the 1990s, rich streams and substreams of research have emerged in innovation management textbooks. Most recently, the field of innovation management has given more attention to open innovation. The key topics associated with innovation management are mentioned below:

- The notion of innovation;
- Innovation-supporting environments;

- Innovation and globalization;
- Building of the innovative organization;
- Innovation processes and systems;
- Innovation networks;
- National systems of innovation;
- Development of an innovation strategy;
- Entrepreneurship and innovation;
- Innovation in emerging economies;
- Corporate venturing;
- Open innovation; and
- Legal and ethical issues in innovation.

The greatest challenge — and at the same time the most interesting aspect — of innovation management as a scholarly discipline is the ever-evolving nature of its research. All of the issues related to the field must be integrated if organizations are really serious about sustaining their competitive advantage. The recent rise of the innovation activity, together with the two closely related content areas of open innovation and technological innovation, has attracted attention in the crucial research domain. During this period of early development, a number of scholars have made significant contributions to the field. Theoretically, its central premise addresses the fundamental question of why organizations are different in terms of innovation, and how organizations ensure innovative achievement and thereby achieve sustainable competitive advantage. Although academic research has been conducted on many different areas within innovation management, there still remain a large number of under-researched topics. One such area that has received less attention is the linkage between knowledge management and innovation management.

10.7 Scholars' Views on the Connection Between Knowledge Management and Innovation Management

Over the decades, innovation management has emerged as an area of interest in academia and organizational practice. Bellini and Lo Storto

(2006) state that the extant literature surrounding innovation management covers many different disciplines and areas of interest for academics and practitioners. Interestingly, the knowledge-based economy is characterized by innovation, which is fundamentally linked to new knowledge (Quinn *et al.*, 1997; Beesley and Cooper, 2008; Lawson and Samson, 2003). Stated differently, innovation is a key determinant of competitiveness in the knowledge-based economy. Reflecting this view, the UK Department for Education and Employment (DfEE) (2000, p. 4) asserts, "Knowledge is crucial because at the cutting edge of innovation in the new economy are knowledge producers: universities and businesses whose fundamental products are the ideas and research which provide the engine for change in goods and services".

As mentioned earlier, scholars such as Nyström (1990), Metaxiotis and Psarras (2006), and Edquist (1997) argue that most definitions of innovation management share common features associated with organizational knowledge. That is, organizational knowledge is eventually turned into new products, processes and services to meet customers' changing needs. The increasing importance of knowledge as an economic driver has major implications for innovation management. Revilla *et al.* (2005) view new knowledge (especially technological knowledge) as the foundation for innovation, change and sustainable competitive advantage.

The fact is that some of the features ascribed to knowledge-intensive firms are necessarily apparent in innovative organizations, since knowledge plays a great role in such organizations (Scarbrough, 1995). A knowledge-creating company tends to be involved in promoting innovation and, in some instances, creativity. The terms "innovative organization" and "knowledge-creating company" could even be used synonymously, as Apostolou and Mentzas (1999) claim that knowledge-intensive firms create innovative solutions for potential customers by integrating the knowledge of their individuals. Chapter 5 has discussed the concept of the knowledge-creating company in more detail.

One of the goals of knowledge management initiatives is to facilitate the product innovation of an organization. Thus, the question here is how knowledge management can help to create more successful innovations. This section will address this core issue. Quinn *et al.*

(1997) assert that knowledge creation and innovation are critical for the competitive advantage of firms. Reflecting this view, Clark *et al.* (1992) argue that innovation is a good example of knowledge work and is actually dependent on the creation and application of organizational knowledge, moving from the initial awareness of new ideas to the implementation of such ideas.

This section will analyze the value of effective knowledge management leading to innovation. Several scholars (e.g., D'Aveni, 1994; Dougherty and Hardy, 1996; Utterback, 1994; Lawson and Samson, 2003) point out that the innovation process requires the application of knowledge in some new or novel way. Therefore, it could be argued that there is a close link between knowledge management and innovation management. Likewise, referring to the importance of creating new knowledge, Nonaka (1998, p. 22) states:

> In an economy where the only certainty is uncertainty, the one sure source of lasting competitive advantage is knowledge. When markets shift, technologies proliferate, competitors multiply, and products become obsolete almost overnight, successful companies are those that consistently create new knowledge, disseminate it widely throughout the organization, and quickly embody it in new technologies and products. These activities define the "knowledge-creating" company, whose sole business is continuous innovation.

Parallel interest in knowledge management and innovation management as two separate disciplines has been sustained for decades. However, the linkage between knowledge management and innovation management has not been fully articulated in the literature. In this regard, having reviewed the existing literature, Asimakou (2009) reveals that in practice there is no crossover between the knowledge management and innovation management literatures, as innovation management scholars have been late to embrace the theoretical progress of the knowledge management field.

To be sure, there is isolated research (e.g., Johannessen, 2008; Asimakou, 2009; Metaxiotis and Psarras, 2006) that examines the relationship between innovation management and knowledge management. Only recently have management scholars begun to address the disciplines together. Johannessen (2008), for example, states that knowledge development and innovation strategies are closely linked so as to promote competitive advantages at the corporate level. Parallel to this, Metaxiotis and Psarras (2006) explore the relationship between knowledge management and innovation management, discussing the applicability of knowledge management concepts in innovation management.

As mentioned in Chapter 2, an important component of knowledge management is knowledge creation, which refers to the activities involved in developing and creating new ideas used for product or process development. Scholars such as Hauschild *et al.* (2001) and von Krogh (1998) observe that knowledge creation is the key source of innovation in an organization. This is due to the fact that innovation and the creation of knowledge are both closely tied to new processes, products and services. Hauschild *et al.* (2001), for example, state that knowledge management is an increasingly essential component of innovation and value creation. Gloet and Terziovski (2004) examine the relationship between knowledge management approaches and innovation performance through a preliminary study on manufacturing companies in Australia and New Zealand, finding that knowledge management contributes to innovation performance.

Metaxiotis and Psarras (2006) also investigate this relationship, showing that effective knowledge can lead an organization to successful innovation. In this context, Dobni (2006) argues that the basis of innovation is knowledge, and that innovation is realized through the ability to use knowledge in order to identify and pursue opportunities. Other researchers — most notably Marinova (2004) and Rodan and Galunic (2004) — contend that knowledge management drives the extent to which employees generate knowledge within their spheres of influence, and that the extent of shared knowledge greatly influences innovation.

Other authors (e.g., Cohen and Levinthal, 1990; Gloet and Terziovski, 2004; Lawson and Samson, 2003) also state that innovation depends heavily on the creation, utilization and diffusion of knowledge within companies and new product development processes. Lawson and Samson (2003), for example, argue that knowledge lies at the heart of the innovation process. Moreover, others (e.g., Darroch and McNaughton, 2002; Beesley and Cooper, 2008) posit that knowledge is widely recognized as a fundamental antecedent to innovation. Likewise, Nonaka and Takeuchi (1995) emphasize tacit knowledge as a main source of creating new knowledge and continuous innovation; especially in Japan, tacit knowledge is vital for the innovation process. More specifically, Nonaka and Takeuchi (1995) contend that the transfer and diffusion of organizational knowledge enables innovation: "Successful companies can create knowledge, disseminate it throughout the organization, and embody it in new technologies and products. These activities define a knowledge-creating company, whose sole business is continuous innovation".

Faniel and Majchrzak (2007) further contend that individuals' knowledge is likely to stimulate individuals' ability to generate new ideas for new products, processes and services, which eventually lead to innovations. The impact of knowledge management practices on innovation has also been analyzed in the European context. In this regard, the European Commission (2004a) examines how knowledge management can really succeed in the innovation process. There are a number of indicating relationships between knowledge management and innovation management that recognize the value of knowledge and that assimilate and apply it to commercial ends, which is critical to a firm's innovative capabilities. As Hutchings (1998) stresses, "knowledge capture is built into key business processes to ensure that knowledge assets are always kept up to date, leading to innovation".

The American Productivity and Quality Center (APQC) (2004) has carried out another study entitled "Using Knowledge Management to Drive Innovation". Their study investigates how some organizations create, manage and leverage their knowledge more effectively than others, concluding that better nurturing of knowledge helps to accelerate and enhance innovation. The way these organizations manage knowledge is part of the reason why they are so innovative. The actions of top professional service firms (PSFs) such as Procter & Gamble and Capgemini provide evidence of the linkage between knowledge management and innovation management, as shown below:

- Procter & Gamble has a successful history of its innovation processes. Using knowledge management initiatives in its "open innovation" strategy, it has come up with new ideas and opportunities (Addison, 2004).
- Capgemini uses knowledge management practices to capture and share knowledge in support of continuous innovation. Key to its success are "knowledge editors", who are the focal points for capturing and maintaining best-practice knowledge (Hutchings, 1998).

Having discussed scholars' views on the relationship between innovation management and knowledge management, there is still a debate on whether these subjects overlap. The next section will identify the factors that help to explore the similarities and differences between the two fields, and establish a theoretical link between these constructs.

10.8 Linkage Between Knowledge Management and Innovation Management

There is a reasonable consensus that knowledge and innovation make up the competitive strength needed for successful companies. In line with this, there are parallels between the literature on innovation management and knowledge management with respect to understanding and managing organizational knowledge. The concepts of innovation management and knowledge management have been shown to be closely related and mutually supporting, but are not the same.

In particular, knowledge management needs to be in place for the innovation process in an organization — which is the key area of innovation management — to work. With this aim in mind, this section will address how both subjects fit together. Organizations are still in the early stages of understanding the linkage between these disciplines. I will begin by defining the two constructs and acknowledging their distinct roots. Table 10.3 depicts the similarities and differences between these fields of research.

Definitions involved. Innovation management emphasizes the innovation activity, namely the creation and commercialization of new products or processes, thereby helping a firm to claim itself as innovative. On the other hand, knowledge management is the formalization of and access to the experience, knowledge and expertise required to create new capabilities, enable superior performance, encourage innovation and enhance customer value. In line with this, Liebowitz (2003) defines knowledge management as a "means creating value from an organisation's intangible assets" that deals with "how best to leverage knowledge internally

Table 10.3 Comparative Perspectives on Innovation Management and Knowledge Management

Dimensions	Innovation Management	Knowledge Management
Disciplinary roots/ Conceptual origins	Economics, entrepreneurship, sociology, engineering, technology	Organizational theory, epistemology, cognitive science, strategic management
Perspective	Inside an organization	Both inside and outside an organization
Working definition	The innovation activity, i.e., the creation and commercialization of new products or processes	The study of strategy, process and technology to collect, refine, create, share and use knowledge
End result	Gaining the competitive advantage of an organization	Gaining the competitive advantage of an organization
Focus	The creation of a commercial product from an invention	The exploration and exploitation of the content of the knowledge
Type of organization	Innovative organization	Knowledge organization
Key processes	Generation and innovation of new commercial products or services	Knowledge creation, knowledge sharing, knowledge dissemination, knowledge exploitation

and externally". The definitions of innovation management and knowledge management presented in Table 10.1 and Table 2.1, respectively, vary in their description. Although each phenomenon has been defined in several different ways, there seems to be a consensus that treats organizational knowledge as a process enabling innovation. Most of these definitions share a common view on organizational knowledge, which is turned into new knowledge (i.e., creation of knowledge) in order to help improve competitive advantage.

Processes involved. One way to distinguish between knowledge management and innovation management is by identifying the processes or steps involved in both fields. Siemieniuch and Sinclair (1999) postulate that the knowledge management process allows an organization to generate, disseminate and use its core knowledge; whereas the innovation management process is all about the creation and commercialization of a new process or product, which depends heavily on knowledge. The differences in their processes illustrate the difference between the two fields. In short, the innovation management process generates and innovates new commercial products or services, while the knowledge management process involves the creation and sharing of knowledge which is used for innovation purposes.

Main focus. Another basic difference between knowledge management and innovation management can be seen in terms of their focus. As we know, knowledge management focuses on the creation, acquisition, dissemination, transfer, storage and application of an organization's explicit and tacit knowledge. In contrast, the innovation management field emphasizes the innovative process, that is, the generation of new ideas using an organization's existing knowledge and the commercialization of such new knowledge. This means that the focus of innovation management goes beyond the generation and transformation of a new idea into many different forms of product, process and technology, for it incorporates the commercialization of the new product or process as well. In other words, the main focus of the knowledge management field is to provide inputs for the smooth functioning of innovation management.

Knowledge management entails the identification, capture, exchange, creation and application of knowledge (European Commission, 2004b). In order to create knowledge for innovation, firms need to organize the knowledge management process to make the knowledge actionable. However, such knowledge is difficult for the people involved to communicate and understand if it is very much tacit in nature.

Outcome. Tidd and Bessant (2009) suggest that successful innovation management requires the acquisition and use of knowledge, which is a key organizational asset and a major source of competitive advantage. In fact, the concepts of knowledge management and innovation management are commonly used in discussions that address how best to manage existing knowledge so as to create new knowledge, innovate something new and thereby commercialize the innovation, leading to the competitive advantage of a company. According to Metaxiotis and Psarras (2006), the relative contributions of both subjects are crucial to a firm's competitive advantage. Moreover, a fair percentage of senior managers believe that both knowledge management and innovation management can help organizations to become more innovative. Hence, the two disciplines should be integrated into the organizational knowledge strategy if organizations are really serious about sustaining their competitive advantage.

The conceptualization of knowledge management overlaps to some extent with other literatures, including that of innovation (Uhlaner *et al.*, 2007). In this section, I have mapped out the relationship between knowledge management and innovation management based primarily on the foregoing discussion. Interestingly, there are researchers (e.g., Hauschild *et al.*, 2001) who claim that the knowledge management and innovation management fields have acknowledged the importance of each other. In particular, the nature and evolution of innovation management can be described in terms of knowledge creation so as to ensure a firm's competitive advantage. This highlights the importance of the creation of new knowledge as a critical component of an organization's ability to innovate. At the same time, other researchers with a primary interest in knowledge processes have started to examine the conceptual links to innovation management, by empirically investigating how it can be facilitated by knowledge management.

This section has acknowledged the distinct roots of knowledge management and innovation management, identified boundaries, and proposed a relationship between the constructs associated with the two disciplines. Although knowledge management is not an antecedent of innovation management, it could be strongly argued that innovation management is shaped by knowledge management, give that knowledge management can successfully contribute to the enhancement of innovation in the knowledge-based economy. Moreover, knowledge management facilitates innovation management. The positive relationship between the processes of knowledge and innovation has been well documented.

Having discussed the relationship between the two subjects, it could be argued that there is no consensus regarding the claim that knowledge management is a part of innovation management or vice versa. Rather, three situations are said to have emerged in terms of the relationship between them:

- In situation I, there is a connection between the two disciplines in that organizational knowledge is a crucial component of innovation management. Although each phenomenon has been defined in several different ways, there seems to be a consensus that treats organizational knowledge as a process enabling innovation.
- In situation II, there is an association between the two fields in that knowledge management facilitates innovation management.
- In situation III, there is a close relationship between knowledge management and innovation management in that researchers of both disciplines have identified knowledge resources as being critical for achieving and sustaining competitiveness. In this manner, both disciplines jointly contribute to enhance the competitive advantage of an organization.

The linkage between knowledge management and innovation management continues to be a strong and viable research topic. There is a need to have a model that illustrates this connection. For example, Johannessen (2008) proposes a model to integrate the two subjects.

10.9 Concluding Summary

Almost eight decades ago, the world-renowned economist Joseph Schumpeter (1934) talked about innovation, arguing that it was the main driver of a country's economic development. Today, innovation management remains a scholarly young field. Over the last several decades, innovation management has developed as a field of study for the improvement of products and services, so as to allow an organization to lead and respond to competitors' moves as well as enjoy first-mover advantages in the turbulent business environment. This chapter has addressed these issues, clarifying the concepts of innovation management and knowledge management in order to highlight their relationship. In doing so, the chapter has provided a conceptual framework that defines and integrates — and thus reduces the confusion about — innovation and knowledge issues.

I have started by critically explaining the notion of innovation management. Innovation management is the implementation of both discoveries and inventions, that is, the process by which new products, systems or processes are commercialized. There are various constructs such as "invention", "creativity" and "innovation" that sometimes create confusion, as the lack of consistent definitions for these terms makes rigorous discussion of innovation management difficult. This chapter has reduced such confusion, arguing that in reality the concepts of invention, creativity and innovation are not synonymous.

The typology of innovation is explored from many different perspectives. This chapter has discussed two dimensions that help to classify innovation: the nature of innovation and the form of innovation. With respect to the nature of innovation, a distinction of innovations can be drawn between radical innovation and incremental innovation. As for the form of innovation, innovations can be seen as either product innovations or process innovations.

The innovation management field has become increasingly important in the ever-changing global environment, despite being a relatively new area of research. The notion of innovation is claimed to be a key source of competitive advantage; hence, innovation management as an emerging discipline has gained rapidly growing attention among academics and practitioners. The evolution of this field since its inception has been impressive. The discipline has matured tremendously over the past 30 years, as evidenced by the huge number of papers, books and websites on innovation management topics that have appeared.

This chapter has demonstrated and explained some of the major themes in the rapidly expanding literature on innovation management. The subject has received growing attention not only in the field of management studies, but also in the more practical domain of business. This chapter has highlighted the role of innovation management in enhancing the competitive advantage of an organization over its rivals. As a result, interest in and attention to the themes and issues surrounding innovation management have been growing at an impressive rate in recent decades. Various issues are discussed in the innovation management research; these include the notion of innovation, innovation-supporting environments, innovation networks, national systems of innovation, the development of an innovation strategy, innovation in emerging economies, open innovation, and ethical issues in innovation. Most recently, the field of innovation management has given more focus to open innovation. These topics help to explain why and how some firms are more innovative than other competing firms.

It is worth mentioning that researchers and practitioners have many different views on the relationship between knowledge management and innovation management. The fact is that companies must innovate or die; their ability to create, learn, adapt and change something is a core competency for survival. Therefore, most companies have begun to establish a common strategic goal of managing knowledge, which entails developing a knowledge cycle and making knowledge available company-wide. Knowledge management can successfully contribute to the enhancement of innovation in the knowledge-based economy. As the 21st century progresses, the breadth and depth of knowledge required to innovate is expected to increase considerably.

This chapter has examined the relationship between knowledge management and innovation management, shedding some light on the nature of their association. These disciplines go hand in hand. Most authors recognize and accept the linkage between the two subjects, while others are not ready to accept any connection between them. As a matter of fact, innovation management and knowledge management should be treated as distinct and, thereby, independent entities. There are several factors that can easily demarcate the knowledge management and innovation management fields.

The positive relationship between the processes of knowledge and innovation has been well documented. It is a fact that the transfer and diffusion of organizational knowledge enables innovation. Stated differently, the innovation process depends heavily on knowledge. This chapter has shown the potential convergence between the two fields, providing a theoretical account of the overlaps and complementarities that exist between them. Both disciplines share a common interest in knowledge for the benefit of organizations; as such, they are considered to have complementary rather than exclusive views.

The discussion presented in this chapter seems to clear up the conceptual confusion regarding the linkage between knowledge management and innovation management. Although innovation management and knowledge management are strongly connected and perhaps even interdependent, this chapter has argued that they are not completely overlapping fields of research. The issues related to these subjects need to be integrated if organizations are really serious about sustaining their competitive advantage. There is great potential for the cross-fertilization of ideas between the two fields, as well as important opportunities for dialogue for researchers who are interested in understanding the role and impact of both innovation management and knowledge management in firms.

Further Reading

Buganza, T. and Verganti, R. (2009). Open innovation process to inbound knowledge: collaboration with universities in four leading firms. *European Journal of Innovation Management*, 12(3), 306–325.

Cowan, R. and Jonard, N. (2009). Knowledge portfolios and the organization of innovation networks. *Academy of Management Review*, 34(2), 320–342.

Dasgupta, M., Sahay, A. and Gupta, R. K. (2009). The role of knowledge management in innovation. *Journal of Information and Knowledge Management*, 8(4), 317–330.

Jantunen, A., Puumalainen, K. and Hurmelinna-Laukkanen, P. (2008). Knowledge sharing and innovation performance. *Journal of Information and Knowledge Management*, 7(3), 187–195.

Kamasak, R. and Bulutlar, F. (2010). The influence of knowledge sharing on innovation. *European Business Review*, 22(3), 306–317.

Kyriazopoulos, P. and Samanta, I. (2009). Creating an innovation culture through knowledge management: the Greek firms. *International Journal of Knowledge and Learning*, 5(1), 81–95.

Lee, S. M., Olson, D. L. and Trimi, S. (2010). The impact of convergence on organizational innovation. *Organizational Dynamics*, 39(3), 218–225.

Shang, S. S. C., Lin, S.-F. and Wu, Y.-L. (2009). Service innovation through dynamic knowledge management. *Industrial Management & Data Systems*, 109(3), 322–337.

Taminiau, Y., Smit, W. and de Lange, A. (2009). Innovation in management consulting firms through informal knowledge sharing. *Journal of Knowledge Management*, 13(1), 42–55.

Tortoriello, M. and Krackhardt, D. (2010). Activating cross-boundary knowledge: the role of Simmelian ties in the generation of innovations. *Academy of Management Journal*, 53(1), 167–181.

von Hippel, E. (1994). "Sticky information" and the locus of problem solving: implications for innovation. *Management Science*, 40, 429–439.

Wallin, M. W. and von Krogh, G. (2010). Organizing for open innovation: focus on the integration of knowledge. *Organizational Dynamics*, 39(2), 145–154.

Xu, J., Houssin, R., Caillaud, E. and Gardoni, M. (2010). Macro process of knowledge management for continuous innovation. *Journal of Knowledge Management*, 14(4), 573–591.

Yang, J. and Rui, M. (2009). Turning knowledge into new product creativity: an empirical study. *Industrial Management & Data Systems*, 109(9), 1197–1210.

References

Accenture and Talent Foundation (2002). Innovation climbs corporate agenda. *Knowledge Management*, November 14.

Addison, M. (2004). Open innovation: the KM dimension. *Inside Knowledge*, 7(9), available at http://www.ikmagazine.com/xq/asp/txtSearch.CoP/exactphrase.1/sid.0/articleid.A2A35510-6B53-470A-A2DA-933A387C99E6/qx/display.htm/.

Afuah, A. (1998). *Innovation Management: Strategies, Implementation, and Profits.* New York: Oxford University Press.

American Productivity and Quality Center (2004). Linking knowledge to innovation and bottom line benefits. *Strategic Direction*, 20(2), 28–30.

Apostolou, D. and Mentzas, G. (1999). Managing corporate knowledge: a comparative analysis of experiences in consulting firms. Part 1. *Knowledge and Process Management*, 6(3), 129–138.

Asimakou, T. (2009). *Innovation, Knowledge and Power in Organizations.* Abingdon: Routledge.

Badawy, M. K. (1988). How to prevent creativity mismanagement. *IEEE Engineering Management Review*, 16(2), 63–68.

Baumol, W. J., Litan, R. E. and Schramm, C. J. (2007). *Good Capitalism, Bad Capitalism, and the Economics of Growth and Prosperity.* New Haven, CT: Yale University Press.

Beesley, L. G. A. and Cooper, C. (2008). Defining knowledge management (KM) activities: towards consensus. *Journal of Knowledge Management*, 12(3), 48–62.

Bellini, E. and Lo Storto, C. (2006). Growth strategy as practice in small firm as knowledge structure. *International Journal of Knowledge Management Studies*, 1(1/2), 133–159.

Carnegie, R. and Butlin, M. (1993). *Managing the Innovating Enterprise: Australian Companies Competing with the World's Best.* Melbourne: Business Council of Australia.

Christensen, C. M. and Rosenbloom, R. S. (1995). Explaining the attacker's advantage: technological paradigms, organizational dynamics, and the value network. *Research Policy*, 24(2), 233–257.

Clark, P., Bennett, D., Burcher, P., Newell, S., Swan, J. and Sharifi, S. (1992). The decision-episode framework and computer-aided production management (CAPM). *International Studies of Management and Organization*, 22, 69–80.

Cohen, W. M. and Levinthal, D. A. (1990). Absorptive capacity: a new perspective on learning and innovation. *Administrative Science Quarterly*, 35, 128–152.

Cumming, B. S. (1998). Innovation overview and future challenges. *European Journal of Innovation Management*, 1(1), 21–29.

Darroch, J. and McNaughton, R. (2002). Examining the link between knowledge management practices and types of innovation. In *Proceedings of the 7th World Congress on Intellectual Capital*, McMaster University, Hamilton, Ontario, Canada, January 16–18, 2002.

D'Aveni, R. A. (1994). *Hypercompetition: Managing the Dynamics of Strategic Maneuvering*. New York: The Free Press.

Davila, T., Epstein, M. J. and Shelton, R. (2006). *Making Innovation Work: How to Manage It, Measure It, and Profit from It*. Upper Saddle River, NJ: Pearson Education.

Denning, P. J. (2004). The social life of innovation. *Communications of the ACM*, 47(4), 15–19.

Denning, S. (2005). Why the best and brightest approaches don't solve the innovation dilemma. *Strategy & Leadership*, 33(1), 4–11.

Dewar, R. and Dutton, J. E. (1986). The adoption of radical and incremental innovations: an empirical analysis. *Management Science*, 32(11), 1422–1433.

Dobni, C. B. (2006). The innovation blueprint. *Business Horizons*, 49(4), 329–339.

Dosi, G. (1988). Sources, procedures and microeconomic effects of innovation. *Journal of Economic Literature*, 26, 1120–1171.

Dougherty, D. and Hardy, C. (1996). Sustained product innovation in large, mature organizations: overcoming innovation-to-organization problems. *Academy of Management Journal*, 39(5), 1120–1153.

Drejer, A. (2008). Are you innovative enough? *International Journal of Innovation and Learning*, 5(1), 1–17.

Drucker, P. F. (1985). *Innovation and Entrepreneurship*. New York: Harper & Row.

Dvir, R. and Pasher, E. (2004). Innovation engines for knowledge cities: an innovation ecology perspective. *Journal of Knowledge Management*, 8(5), 16–27.

Edquist, C. (ed.) (1997). *Systems of Innovation: Technologies, Institutions and Organizations*. London: Pinter.

Ettlie, J. E., Bridges, W. P. and O'Keefe, R. D. (1984). Organization strategy and structural differences for radical versus incremental innovation. *Management Science*, 30, 682–695.

European Commission (2004a). *Innovation Management and the Knowledge-Driven Economy*. Brussels: Directorate-General for Enterprise.

European Commission (2004b). Innovation through KM. *Knowledge Management*, March 8.

Faniel, I. M. and Majchrzak, A. (2007). Innovating by accessing knowledge across departments. *Decision Support Systems*, 43(4), 1684–1691.

Freeman, C. (1982). *The Economics of Industrial Innovation*. Cambridge, MA: MIT Press.

Garcia, R. and Calantone, R. (2002). A critical look at technological innovation typology and innovativeness terminology: a literature review. *Journal of Product Innovation Management*, 19(2), 110–132.

Gehlen, A. (1980). *Man in the Age of Technology*. New York: Columbia University Press.

Gloet, M. and Terziovski, M. (2004). Exploring the relationship between knowledge management practices and innovation performance. *Journal of Manufacturing Technology Management*, 15(5), 402–409.

Goffin, K. and Mitchell, R. (2005). *Innovation Management: Strategy and Implementation Using the Pentathlon Framework*. Basingstoke: Palgrave Macmillan.

Grøtnes, E. (2009). Standardization as open innovation: two cases from the mobile industry. *Information Technology & People*, 22(4), 367–381.

Haberberg, A. and Rieple, A. (2008). *Strategic Management: Theory and Application*. Oxford: Oxford University Press.

Hargadon, A. and Fanelli, A. (2002). Action and possibility: reconciling dual perspectives of knowledge in organizations. *Organization Science*, 13(3), 290–302.

Hauschild, S., Licht, T. and Stein, W. (2001). Creating a knowledge culture. *McKinsey Quarterly*, 1, 74–81.

Hidalgo, A. and Albors, J. (2008). Innovation management techniques and tools: a review from theory and practice. *R&D Management*, 38(2), 113–127.

Hult, G. T. M., Hurley, R. F. and Knight, G. A. (2004). Innovativeness: its antecedents and impact on business performance. *Industrial Marketing Management*, 33, 429–438.

Hutchings, G. (1998). Knowledge capture and sharing in support of continuous adaptation and innovation. *Knowledge Management*, 2(4).

Jin, Z., Hewitt-Dundas, N. and Thompson, N. J. (2004). Innovativeness and performance: evidence from manufacturing sectors. *Journal of Strategic Marketing*, 12, 255–266.

Johannessen, J. (2008). Organisational innovation as part of knowledge management. *International Journal of Information Management*, 28(5), 403–412.

Koen, C. I. (2005). *Comparative International Management*. Maidenhead: McGraw-Hill.

Kuhn, R. L. (1985). *Frontiers in Creative and Innovative Management*. Cambridge, MA: Ballinger.

Lawson, B. and Samson, D. (2003). Developments in managing innovation, knowledge and e-business. In A. Gunasekaran, O. Khalil and S. M. Rahman (eds.), *Knowledge and Information Technology Management: Human and Social Perspectives* (pp. 1–13), Hershey, PA: Idea Group, Inc.

Liebowitz, J. (2003). Keynote paper: measuring the value of online communities, leading to innovation and learning. *International Journal of Innovation and Learning*, 1(1), 1–8.

Livingstone, L., Palich, L. and Carini, G. (1998). Viewing strategic innovation through the logic of contradiction. *Competitiveness Review*, 8(1), 46–54.

Lowe, P. (1995). *The Management of Technology*. London: Chapman & Hall.

Luecke, R. and Katz, R. (2003). *Managing Creativity and Innovation*. Boston, MA: Harvard Business School Press.

Mansfield, E. (1968). *Industrial Research and Technological Innovation*. New York: Norton.

Marinova, D. (2004). Actualizing innovation effort: the impact of market knowledge diffusion in a dynamic system of competition. *Journal of Marketing*, 68(3), 1–20.

Martins, E. C. and Terblanche, F. (2003). Building organisational culture that stimulates creativity and innovation. *European Journal of Innovation Management*, 6(1), 64–74.

McDermott, C. M. and O'Connor, G. C. (2002). Managing radical innovation: an overview of emergent strategy issues. *Journal of Product Innovation Management*, 19(6), 424–438.

McDermott, R. and O'Dell, C. (2001). Overcoming cultural barriers to sharing knowledge. *Journal of Knowledge Management*, 5(1), 76–85.

Metaxiotis, K. and Psarras, J. (2006). Analysing the value of knowledge management leading to innovation. *International Journal of Knowledge Management Studies*, 1(1/2), 79–89.

Mokyr, J. (1990). *The Lever of Riches: Technological Creativity and Economic Progress*. Oxford: Oxford University Press.

Nonaka, I. (1998). The knowledge-creating company. In *Harvard Business Review on Knowledge Management* (pp. 21–45), Boston, MA: Harvard Business School Press.

Nonaka, I. and Takeuchi, H. (1995). *The Knowledge-Creating Company: How Japanese Companies Create the Dynamics of Innovation*. Oxford: Oxford University Press.

Nordfors, D. (2004). The role of journalism in innovation systems. *Innovation Journalism*, 1(7), 1–18.

Nyström, H. (1990). *Technological and Market Innovation: Strategies for Product and Company Development*. Chichester: John Wiley & Sons.

OECD (2000). *A New Economy? The Changing Role of Innovation and Information Technology in Growth*. Paris: OECD.

Pedersen, C. R. and Dalum, B. (2004). Incremental versus radical change: the case of the Digital North Denmark program. Paper presented at the DRUID Summer Conference 2004, Copenhagen, June 14–16.

Pyka, A. (2002). Innovation networks in economics: from the incentive-based to the knowledge-based approaches. *European Journal of Innovation Management*, 5(3), 152–163.

Quinn, J. B., Baruch, J. J. and Zien, K. A. (1997). *Innovation Explosion: Using Intellect and Software to Revolutionize Growth Strategies*. New York: The Free Press.

Revilla, E., Sarkis, J. and Acosta, J. (2005). Towards a knowledge management and learning taxonomy for research joint ventures. *Technovation*, 25, 1307–1316.

Roberts, E. B. (1981). *Generating Effective Corporate Innovation*. New York: The Free Press.

Rodan, S. and Galunic, C. (2004). More than network structure: how knowledge heterogeneity influences managerial performance and innovativeness. *Strategic Management Journal*, 25(6), 541–562.

Rogers, E. (1983). *Diffusion of Innovations*, 3rd ed. New York: Free Press.

Scarbrough, H. (1995). Blackboxes, hostages and prisoners. *Organization Studies*, 16(6), 991–1019.

Schumpeter, J. (1934). *The Theory of Economic Development*. Cambridge, MA: Harvard University Press.

Schumpeter, J. (1961). *The Theory of Economic Development.* Oxford: Oxford University Press.

Scozzi, B., Garavelli, C. and Crowston, K. (2005). Methods for modeling and supporting innovation processes in SMEs. *European Journal of Innovation Management*, 8(1), 120–137.

Siemieniuch, C. E. and Sinclair, M. A. (1999). Organizational aspects of knowledge lifecycle management in manufacturing. *International Journal of Human-Computer Studies*, 51, 517–547.

Snow, C. C., Strauss, D. R. and Culpan, R. (2009). Community of firms: a new collaborative paradigm for open innovation and an analysis of Blade.org. *International Journal of Strategic Business Alliances*, 1(1), 53–72.

Subramaniam, M. and Venkatraman, N. (1999). The influence of leveraging tacit overseas knowledge for global new product development capability: an empirical examination. In M. A. Hitt, P. G. Clifford, R. D. Nixon and K. P. Coyne (eds.), *Dynamic Strategic Resources* (pp. 373–401), Chichester: Wiley.

Teece, D. J. (1989). Inter-organizational requirements of the innovation process. *Managerial and Decision Economics*, 10(Special Issue), 35–42.

Thompson, J. D. (1967). *Organizations in Action.* New York: McGraw-Hill.

Tidd, J. and Bessant, J. (2009). *Managing Innovation: Integrating Technological, Market and Organizational Change*, 4th ed. Chichester: John Wiley & Sons.

Tidd, J., Bessant, J. and Pavitt, K. (2001). *Managing Innovation: Integrating Technological, Market and Organizational Change*, 2nd ed. Chichester: John Wiley & Sons.

Tinnesand, B. (1973). Towards a general theory of innovation. PhD thesis, University of Wisconsin–Madison, Madison, WI.

Twiss, B. (1992). *Managing Technological Innovation*, 4th ed. London: Pitman.

Udwadia, F. E. (1990). Creativity and innovation in organizations. *Technological Forecasting and Social Change*, 38(1), 65–80.

Uhlaner, L., van Stel, A., Meijaard, J. and Folkeringa, M. (2007). The relationship between knowledge management, innovation and firm performance: evidence from Dutch SMEs. Working paper, SCALES program, EIM Business & Policy Research, Zoetermeer, The Netherlands.

UK Department for Education and Employment (2000). *Opportunity for All: Skills for the New Economy.* London: DfEE.

UK Department of Trade and Industry (1998). *Our Competitive Future: Building the Knowledge Driven Economy.* Competitiveness White Paper, DTI, London.

Urabe, K. (1988). Innovation and the Japanese management system. In K. Urabe, J. Child and T. Kagono (eds.), *Innovation and Management: International Comparisons* (pp. 3–25), Berlin: Walter de Gruyter & Co.

Utterback, J. M. (1994). *Mastering the Dynamics of Innovation: How Companies Can Seize Opportunities in the Face of Technological Change.* Boston, MA: Harvard Business School Press.

Utterback, J. M. and Abernathy, W. J. (1975). A dynamic model of process and product innovation. *Omega*, 3(6), 639–656.

von Krogh, G. (1998). Care in knowledge creation. *California Management Review*, 40(3), 133–153.

Ward, R. C. (2002). Knowledge management, information management, or organizational learning: a comparative study of three states' approaches to knowledge management and information technology. Paper presented at the Southeastern Conference on Public Administration, Columbia, South Carolina, October.

West, M. A. and Farr, J. L. (1990). Innovation at work. In M. A. West and J. L. Farr (eds.), *Innovation and Creativity at Work: Psychological and Organizational Strategies* (pp. 3–13), Chichester: Wiley.

Westland, J. C. (2008). *Global Innovation Management.* New York: Palgrave Macmillan.

Williams, A. (1999). *Creativity, Invention and Innovation.* Sydney: Allen & Unwin.

Zaltman, G., Duncan, R. and Holbek, J. (1973). *Innovations and Organizations.* New York: Wiley.

Chapter 11

Knowledge Management Challenges

Knowledge Objectives

After studying this chapter, you should be able to:

- Provide an overview of the notion of knowledge management;
- Explain the challenges of knowledge management; and
- Offer suggestions for future work that may lead to additional progress.

11.1 Introducing the Chapter

Despite being a relatively young discipline, knowledge management has grown dramatically in size and influence over the last two decades. The notion of knowledge management has become a crucial corporate agenda for organizations around the world. Most organizations now claim themselves to be knowledge-based organizations, and allocate more time and money to introduce knowledge management initiatives in their organizations. As a matter of fact, the history of knowledge management shows a progression from a concern for research to a concern for practice, and from playing a crucial support function to performing a major business function. Meanwhile, organizations have been making efforts to develop a framework for assessing contextual information, taking into account more knowledge exchanges.

The main focus of knowledge management practice has been on how an organization discovers and deploys its knowledge. Thousands of companies across the world have incorporated knowledge management as part of their business function. Moreover, many organizations have established a full-fledged knowledge management department and created the position of chief knowledge officer (CKO), who is dedicated to ensuring the successful implementation of knowledge management initiatives.

11.2 A Brief Overview

There is no doubt that interest in and attention to knowledge management research has increased dramatically over time. As mentioned previously, more and more relevant journals are being launched jointly by academics and publishers to address knowledge management issues as a primary focus. Four leading knowledge management journals — *Journal of Information & Knowledge Management*, *Journal of Knowledge Management*, *Knowledge and Process Management*, and *Knowledge Management Research & Practice* — are listed in the Association of Business Schools (ABS) Academic Journal Quality Guide, which is used by the Research Assessment Exercise (RAE) to rank UK business schools in terms of their scholarly achievements. For example, since its introduction in 1997, the *Journal of Knowledge Management* has grown from a nascent outlet devoted to an emerging field of study to become one of the most highly regarded and influential publications within the management and information systems disciplines. Parallel to this, other world-class journals such as *Harvard Business Review*, *California Management Review*, *Academy of Management Journal*, *Academy of Management Review*, *British Journal of Management*, *Sloan Management Review*, *Journal of Management Studies* and *Management Science* have been regularly publishing articles associated with knowledge management.

Furthermore, a host of professional associations have been formed by academics and practitioners interested in knowledge management research and practice. The knowledge management theme has also received greater attention in several conference tracks, such as the "business policy and strategy" division, the "information systems" division and the "organizational learning" division of top-tier conferences like the Academy of Management (AOM) Conference, the British Academy of Management (BAM) Conference, the Strategic Management Society (SMS) Conference, the International Conference on Advances in Management (ICAM) and the Hawaii International Conference on System Sciences (HICSS). For example, the "knowledge and learning" track of the BAM Conference and the "knowledge management" track of the HICSS have expanded from a small set of scholars in the early 2000s to more than 200 members. In addition, a number of books written by such authors as Leonard-Barton (1995), Nonaka and Takeuchi (1995), and Davenport and Prusak (1998) have contributed significantly to further develop the subject.

In order to substantiate and sustain its popularity, academics are making a much-appreciated effort to foster knowledge management in management education. In line with this, there has been a notable thrust in recent curriculum development within the higher education environment that focuses on designing and offering modules and degree schemes centered on this subject, so as to spread knowledge management education.

It is noted that parallel interest in knowledge management and several related subjects surrounding management and information systems as separate disciplines has been sustained for decades. Indeed, interest in knowledge management has increased largely because its theories and ideas have been profoundly influenced and shaped by neighboring subject areas such as strategic management, organizational learning, human resource management, organizational theory, innovation management and information systems. The motivation for this book comes from the recognition that too many scholars from these fields have attempted to discuss and use knowledge management.

Throughout this book, the notion of knowledge management and its relationship with other related disciplines has been explored. There is as yet no consensus among researchers regarding the following claims:

- Whether knowledge management is an offshoot of information management;
- Whether organizational learning and knowledge management are the same thing;
- Whether knowledge management and strategic management are somewhat separate; and
- Whether innovation management and knowledge management perform fairly unrelated management tasks.

Hence, it cannot be said that knowledge management is an exclusive part or an offshoot of another discipline, or that they are entirely different disciplines. However, what could be said is that they are interrelated and sometimes complement each other. This book has examined the question of how knowledge management and the other related disciplines fit together. It can be argued that there is clearly a high potential for synergies between these disciplines, given the many interrelations and dependencies between these fields.

This final chapter will look into the future of knowledge management, taking a critical perspective of the way in which it is implemented. Becerra-Fernandez *et al.* (2004) argue that the future of knowledge management can be highlighted by three continuing trends:

(i) Knowledge management will benefit from its progress;
(ii) The field will continue the shift toward integrating knowledge from a variety of different perspectives; and
(iii) The discipline will continue to make trade-offs in numerous important areas.

The purpose of this chapter is to take stock of some of the major points raised in the preceding chapters. The intervening chapters have described and evaluated the nature and significance of organizational knowledge, the key developments in knowledge management, and the meanings and attributes of various established disciplines associated with management and information systems as well as their relationship with knowledge management. Knowledge management holds great promise, as described in this book; however, the story of its success in achieving its stated objectives varies. Birkinshaw (2001) reinforces this, stating that knowledge management promises much but often delivers very little, noting that its success rate is mixed.

One way of comprehending the future is to look at the past to identify trends and then envisage how these are likely to continue in the decades to come. While some companies have very successfully implemented knowledge management, others have yet to receive dividends out of its implementation. In this context, the widely cited result of the Gartner Group (1999) survey alerts us to a grim reality. Resonating with this, Birkinshaw (2001) contends that plenty of cases of knowledge management initiatives have not delivered the expected results. In fact, there are a lot of challenges and problems ahead. Thus, a reasonable and sensible question that could be asked is this: how are the most important issues evolving, and what of the future? It is essential to identify issues and challenges related to the notion of knowledge management, particularly its implementation.

11.3 The Challenges of Knowledge Management

This chapter will address certain challenges of knowledge management, and offer suggestions for future work that may lead to additional progress. Several scholars, most notably Beckman (1997) and Kalkan (2008), have categorically focused on its challenges for business. Beckman (1997, p. 19) sees several knowledge management challenges in its implementation in typical organizations, including:

- Knowledge is often hoarded rather than shared;
- Valuable knowledge developed by others is often ignored rather than applied in daily work situations;
- Knowledge and expertise are often not valued by the corporate culture, which fails to measure intellectual assets; and
- Employees who share knowledge and expertise are often considered naive, instead of being rewarded for their valuable organizational behavior.

Likewise, Kalkan (2008, p. 390) identifies six factors as the main knowledge management challenges faced by global business organizations today:

- Developing a working definition of knowledge;
- Dealing with tacit knowledge and utilizing information technology;
- Adapting to cultural complexity;
- Paying attention to human resources;
- Developing new organizational structures; and
- Coping with increased competition.

The fact is that the challenges we talk about in relation to knowledge management are basically the challenges and problems we face during its implementation. Several questions are now being raised by many concerned researchers (e.g., Chen and Chen, 2006; Fahey and Prusak, 1998), including whether it is really worthwhile to invest in knowledge management and whether its implementation has been a success. Resonating with this, Fahey and Prusak (1998) identify a set of pervasive errors which they call "the eleven deadliest sins of knowledge management" that impede its implementation. Desouza (2003) reports that most knowledge management initiatives fall short of their goals, implying an organizational failure to implement it properly. For example, the Gartner Group (1999, as cited in Desouza, 2003) showed that, out of 811 companies based in the US and Europe, 90% were aware of knowledge management and most of them had some activity under way. Similarly, Ruggles (1998) studied 431 North American and European companies with knowledge management initiatives under way, and found that only 13% of the respondents felt they were successful in transferring knowledge from one part of the organization to another, whereas only 46% ranked their companies high on the ability to generate new knowledge.

It is worth mentioning that the implementation of knowledge management is not an easy task. There are a variety of reasons for its failure. Before we can address what the future of knowledge management holds and how this will affect knowledge management implementation, it is essential to identify the current problems faced. An identification of the problems relating to the implementation of knowledge management will then help us find the remedies and, thereby, ensure its success. Both the problems and their possible remedies may be treated as challenges of knowledge management. Or, put another way, these challenges should be considered and encountered when striving for successful knowledge management implementation. The knowledge management challenges are discussed in detail below.

Understanding the notion of organizational knowledge and knowledge management. Although the potential benefits of knowledge management are apparent, one of the difficulties in dealing with knowledge management is the field itself. That is, knowledge management is yet to be structured. Resonating with this, Sauermann (2009) argues that one of the difficulties in dealing with knowledge management is that the field is ill-structured. In particular, the contributions to the knowledge management literature are scattered around a handful of specialized outlets and major journals in a variety of fields and disciplines.

The existing literature fails to agree on a unified definition, or even on the key concepts, behind the terms "organizational knowledge" and "knowledge management". Since the notion of knowledge management has very diverse academic and practical roots, practitioners find it difficult to understand what organizational knowledge and knowledge management are about. Accordingly, Kalkan (2008) argues that one of the main knowledge management challenges is developing a working definition of organizational knowledge. Several scholars still view knowledge as an inherently complex and confusing concept. In this regard, Adair (2004) contends that the definitions of knowledge are debatable. Reflecting this view, Chen and Chen (2006) claim that there is still a debate as to whether knowledge itself is a cognitive state, a process or an object. Nevertheless, researchers tend to agree that knowledge is multidimensional, arguing that knowledge is typically characterized by transdisciplinarity, complexity and heterogeneity.

Similarly, Chen and Chen (2006) state that a universally accepted definition of knowledge management does not yet exist. Hlupic *et al.* (2002) reinforce this, arguing that there is still confusion about what knowledge management really means. More specifically, Nonaka (1994, as cited in Jashapara, 2005) argues that the primary challenge in knowledge management is to develop our understanding of knowledge — especially tacit knowledge — and explore ways of articulating and sharing tacit knowledge across an organization. Parallel to this, De Long and Seemann (2000) believe that knowledge management is subject to considerable fuzzy thinking and misinterpretation, and identify two major sources of this conceptual confusion: the many dimensions of the concept of knowledge (see Chapter 1), and the different perspectives of knowledge management (see Chapter 3).

Clarifying and positioning the notion of knowledge management as an independent discipline. Another challenge of knowledge management as a scholarly discipline is the ever-evolving nature of its research. Knowledge management is a relatively young field, and its theories and ideas have been profoundly influenced by neighboring subject areas such as strategic management, organizational learning and information systems. Hence, there is no consensus regarding the claim that knowledge management is a new field with its own research base. As we have seen in Chapter 3, there are conflicts over the ownership of this field among researchers from various disciplinary backgrounds. Such divergent views on the genesis of knowledge management inevitably lead to differences of opinion about its ownership.

As noted earlier, parallel interest in knowledge management and other well-established subjects as separate disciplines has been sustained for decades. There are very diverse academic and practical roots of knowledge management. The linkage between knowledge management and other disciplines — most notably information management, organizational learning, strategic management and innovation management — has not been fully articulated in the literature. As a result, both academics and practitioners find it difficult to answer how the challenges faced can best be tackled. All of the issues related to knowledge management need to be integrated if organizations are really serious about sustaining their competitive advantage. Although this book has attempted to discover the linkage between knowledge management and these disciplines so as to exploit synergies, the relationship has yet to be fully understood and harnessed.

At the micro level, there is also a problem in positioning the knowledge management function in an organization. Some companies have introduced the knowledge management activity as a part of another business function. In such organizations, people who work in various functional departments — particularly the strategic team, information services and human resource department — tend to claim knowledge management as an important task of their own functional areas. Other organizations use a cross-functional team to develop and implement knowledge management, while in still others the chief executive officer (CEO) takes on a leading role.

Very recently, many organizations have opened an independent knowledge management unit instead of incorporating it as part of a functional area or team (e.g., strategy, human resources, innovation or learning). Moreover, some organizations have created a new position called a chief knowledge officer (CKO), who is assigned the responsibility for encouraging knowledge exchange and preserving stored knowledge so as to ensure that it is correct, relevant and current. However, the role of the CKO has not yet been fully understood or harnessed. Thus, the rationale behind the existence of a knowledge management department and a person who will be responsible for looking after the knowledge management task seems to be a key area of future research. The idea of the CKO will be elaborated later on in more detail.

Having sufficient resources. Implementing a knowledge management initiative is generally a formidable challenge, as it can be very expensive, time-consuming and resource-intensive. Accordingly, an effective knowledge management initiative requires money, technology and people. Stated differently, the organizational resources required for a knowledge management initiative include financial resources, committed people and time. As a result, such a high-cost proposition has a wider impact on the entire organization because it places tremendous demand on an organization's time and resources. It is evident that the implementation of a typical knowledge management initiative may take anywhere from one to two years.

The availability of abundant resources is a necessary but not sufficient condition for the smooth functioning of knowledge management. Plentiful financial resources cannot by themselves bring greater knowledge management success. Therefore, technical and motivated people may be more effective than bountiful resources to ensure the successful implementation of knowledge management.

Mitigating resistance to change. Resistance to any change is a common phenomenon in an organizational climate. When introducing a knowledge management initiative in an organizational setting, the resistance of employees is often observed. Various groups within an organization may resist its implementation. In line with this, Kalkan (2008, p. 390) identifies adaptation to cultural complexity as a knowledge management challenge that is faced by global businesses today. McKinlay (2002) warns that passive resistance is sufficient to limit the impact of knowledge management in practice. It could be argued that handling employees' resistance to knowledge management is another factor that is critical to its success.

Resonating with this, Beckman (1997) suggests that having a supportive culture is a prerequisite to enhance the chances of the successful implementation of knowledge management. Organizations need to develop a culture that helps to create awareness of such resistance, so that employees will voluntarily share their technical knowledge. An awareness of such resistance would enable organizations to take corrective action early and, thereby, deter this major obstacle to implementing knowledge management initiatives. A strong team of management support is often required to encourage employees to appreciate knowledge management initiatives and to develop a knowledge-sharing culture across the organization. Leadership and strong support of top management can thus also help to subdue such resistance, as will be discussed next.

Enjoying senior management support. One of the biggest hurdles of knowledge management is convincing top management to support activities relating to knowledge management initiatives. Widespread support for knowledge management from the top management is essential for its successful implementation. du Plessis (2007) supports this view, arguing that top management support is essential for the successful implementation of knowledge management, and that leaders have to share a vision on knowledge management and provide such a program with ongoing support.

Resonating with this, several scholars (e.g., Van Buren, 1998; Beckman, 1997, 1999; Greco, 1999; Dess and Picken, 2000; Ryan and Prybutok, 2001; Moffett *et al.*, 2003; Shah and Siddiqui, 2006; Hung *et al.*, 2005; Davenport *et al.*, 1998; Weber, 2007) argue that senior management leadership and commitment is widely considered to be a key success factor in the implementation of knowledge management. Beckman (1997), for example, suggests that leadership commitment is a prerequisite that needs to be considered so as to enhance the chances of success during its implementation. Otherwise, knowledge management projects may simply fail due to the lack of leadership support (Disterer, 2001; Weber, 2007).

There are cases where top management is least bothered about the knowledge-sharing issue. It is evident that many of them are reluctant to recognize the importance of knowledge management in their organizations. Consequently, there is a tendency to allocate (and spend) less money and time on launching knowledge management projects in their organizations. However, it is essential to gain consensus from senior management in advance so as to successfully operationalize the knowledge management process. Stated differently, top management commitment and support is crucial to help sustain funding for the entirety of any knowledge management initiative. Akhavan and Jafari (2006) reinforce this, commenting that good leadership and a strong support team can also help to build a firm-wide, shared vision for knowledge management solutions. In this regard, the top management should be carefully briefed about the aims of their knowledge management initiatives. Parallel to this, du Plessis (2007) suggests that leaders have to be continually briefed on the knowledge management program and what it entails, and how it is going to achieve the agreed knowledge management vision.

Balancing the use of technology and human resources. In some cases, an over-reliance of technology is found in knowledge management, ignoring the human side of it. Loermans (2002) argues that, although technology has an important role to play in the storage and dissemination of knowledge, it has little or no role in creating new knowledge. Davenport (1997) adds that information technology has not solved the problem of managing knowledge, whilst Kleiner and Roth (1998) believe that technology is not a critical factor in knowledge management.

In this regard, another challenge in knowledge management implementation is the role of technology and people. Birkinshaw (2001) argues that information technology is often regarded as a substitute for social interaction; as a result, knowledge management initiatives fail when they rely on inadequate technology. This point is also underscored by Fahey and Prusak (1998), who state that one of the sins of knowledge management that impedes its implementation is substituting technological contact for human interface. Similarly, Kalkan (2008) identifies dealing with tacit knowledge and utilizing information technology as one of the main knowledge management challenges.

It is a common question to ask whether knowledge management is about technology, people or both (Weeks, 2004). On the one hand, technology is an important element of knowledge management initiatives. There is no doubt that information technology plays a vital role as the crucial infrastructure of knowledge management implementation. Knowledge management tools such as search engines and portals are very much dependent on technology. Weeks (2004) reports that early efforts to implement knowledge management involve purchasing software such as Lotus Notes and building up other information technology infrastructure. In line with this, Laudon and Laudon (2000, as cited in Hlupic *et al.*, 2002) identify an array of technologies that support knowledge management, categorizing them into four groups:

(i) Tools that support knowledge sharing (e.g., groupware, intranets, the Internet);
(ii) Tools that support knowledge distribution (e.g., electronic calendars, desktop databases, desktop publishing);
(iii) Tools that support knowledge capture and codification (e.g., expert systems, neural networks, intelligent agents); and
(iv) Tools that support knowledge creation (e.g., investment workstations, computer-aided design (CAD), virtual reality).

On the other hand, although information technology is an important facilitator of data and information transmission and distribution, it can never be a substitute for rich interactivity, communication and learning. Knowledge is primarily a function and consequence of the meeting, dialogue and interaction of minds. Therefore, human intervention remains the only source of knowledge generation. Several scholars — most notably Nissen (2002) and Weber (2007) — believe that the tools mentioned above only deal with data and information; they are not capable of manipulating knowledge, as required in knowledge management approaches.

Against this backdrop, Desouza (2003) asserts that the biggest hurdle of knowledge management is not about handling technologies, but rather getting people to share their know-how. Technology can enable people to transcend distance and time barriers through the use of tools such as e-mail and group support systems, but it cannot motivate people to share knowledge since knowledge originates in the minds of individuals. Unless organizational members are motivated to share their knowledge, no amount of technology solutions can deliver the expected results. Moreover, Weeks (2004) states that the usefulness of a technology requires a high degree of human involvement to sort, index, codify and make sense of the data added to it.

Researchers and practitioners do not believe that technology can wholly replace people. In this regard, Armistead and Meakins (2002) contend that an effort needs to be made to achieve a balance between both factors, rather than relying exclusively on technology or human factors. Similarly, while proposing a knowledge management implementation framework, Wong and Aspinwall (2004) suggest a balanced view between technological and social perspectives.

According to Jashapara (2005), in order to redress the balance, there has been a marked shift in emphasis from technology towards people as the valuable resource. Although organizations initially followed a technological approach to managing knowledge, the focus has shifted recently and knowledge management is now more human-centered. This view is an extension of that of Armistead and Meakins (2002), who recognize that the majority of companies acknowledge the influential role of technology in knowledge management, but that it is ultimately a facilitator of human knowledge in an organization.

Measuring the performance of knowledge management initiatives. Drucker (1995) comments that knowledge, expertise, experience and patents are intangible, permanent assets, adding that the measurement of these assets is increasing in importance. Several researchers (e.g., Ernst & Young, 1999; Greco, 1999; Havens and Knapp, 1999; Mathi, 2004; KPMG, 1999, 2000; O'Dell and Grayson, 1999; du Plessis, 2007; PricewaterhouseCoopers, 1999; Torres, 1999; Jennex and Zakharova, 2005; Hung *et al.*, 2005; Martinez, 1998; Bassi and Van Buren, 1999; Pearson, 1999; Barsky and Marchant, 2000; Moffett *et al.*, 2003) argue that the measurement of knowledge management initiatives is essential. Jennex and Zakharova (2005), for example, suggest that knowledge management should be linked to the economic performance of an organization. Other scholars such as Chen and Chen (2006) wonder whether it is really worthwhile to invest in knowledge management.

However, one of the challenges of the knowledge management discipline is the calculation of the return on investment. Parallel to this, Fahey and Prusak (1998) believe that one of the 11 deadliest sins of knowledge management impeding its implementation is the development of a direct measure of knowledge. Hence, it is crucial to find a technique to measure the implications of knowledge management initiatives.

Reflecting this view, Fahey and Prusak (1998) raise the question of how to know whether knowledge management efforts are producing satisfactory results. This in turn leads to another question of how knowledge — which is usually seen as fuzzy and intangible — can be measured (Lang, 2001; Weeks, 2004). The existing literature (e.g., de Gooijer, 2000; American Productivity and Quality Center, 2000) shows that the measurement of knowledge management is possible but not simple: knowledge is an intangible asset, and therefore needs to be processed differently from other tangible business assets.

Measurement is important, for it helps to monitor the value of knowledge management initiatives and provides a link to the key performance indicators. Organizations need to use measurement yardsticks so as to assess whether the goals of knowledge management implementation have been achieved (Ahmed *et al.*, 1999; Lim *et al.*, 2000). Ernst & Young (1999, as cited in du Plessis, 2007) indicates that the overall performance of a knowledge management initiative needs to be measured. The performance measurement may include reviewing an organization's knowledge repository and giving visible rewards to those who show commitment to the knowledge management program. For example, Ernst & Young measures the amount of knowledge it uses in the form of proposals, presentations, deliverables, and the contributions of its knowledge repository to closing sales (Davenport *et al.*, 1998).

Creating a permanent position. A related challenge in knowledge management is finding a person in an organization who is well aware of the various aspects of knowledge management and the various locations of knowledge (including who knows what). Knowledge management initiatives should be administered by dedicated staff with a committed leader, known as the chief knowledge officer (CKO). Indeed, the creation of a permanent position to look after the smooth functioning of knowledge management is perhaps the most overlooked activity for knowledge management initiatives. Without a CKO, the program will probably never get the attention it deserves.

When an organization plans to introduce a knowledge management initiative, it needs to consider whether to create a leadership role to develop and drive the process. Many organizations have delegated the responsibility of managing knowledge by creating a new department and/or a new position. As mentioned previously, some organizations use a cross-functional team to develop knowledge management, while in others the chief executive officer (CEO) takes on a leading role. However, a growing number of companies have created the CKO position to administer knowledge management.

Several authors (e.g., du Plessis, 2007; KPMG, 2000; Reiss, 1999; Davenport and Prusak, 1998; Liebowitz, 1999; Earl and Scott, 1999; McKeen *et al.*, 2002) call for the creation and appointment of a chief knowledge officer. KPMG (2000), for instance, suggests creating knowledge centers with dedicated staff to ensure the consistent management of knowledge. Earl and Scott (1999) state that chief knowledge officers have an opportunity to become unique leaders in knowledge sharing and diffusion. Other scholars such as Haider (2009), Davenport (1996), Liebowitz and Beckman (1998), and Newman (1999) agree that this position is responsible for the smooth functioning of knowledge management. Haider (2009), for example, argues that the chief knowledge officer is an important figure whose prime objectives are as follows:

- To build a knowledge culture;
- To create a knowledge management infrastructure;
- To link the company's knowledge strategy to the company's business strategy; and
- To make it all pay off economically.

The importance of such a person is evidenced by the formal creation of the CKO position in Fortune 500 companies. Numerous corporations have set up new jobs for knowledge management specialists and chief knowledge officers. Desouza (2003) reports that more than 40% of Fortune 500 companies have a chief knowledge officer. Liebowitz and Beckman (1998) note that giant corporations such as Coca-Cola, Hewlett-Packard, and Coopers & Lybrand, to name a few, have established this new position within their organizations in order to manage knowledge.

All knowledge management activities represent a long-term commitment to building a knowledge culture. It is noted that developing a knowledge-sharing culture is by far the most difficult and time-consuming activity; thus, the chief knowledge officer can play a great role in this process. The chief knowledge officer has to be active in helping middle managers articulate the knowledge, and also should be involved in the creation of individual knowledge-related goals for managers and their subordinates.

Despite its importance, there has been relatively little serious academic research on the role of the chief knowledge officer. Al-Hawamdeh (2005) rightly comments that the role of such a person is critical, complex and multifaceted. The chief knowledge officer needs to know the owners of an individual document, not just the details of all the knowledge resources available in a database. Furthermore, Al-Hawamdeh (2005) suggests that a good chief knowledge officer combines an aptitude for technology-based knowledge (explicit) with a feel for the cultural and behavioral factors that impede or enable knowledge (implicit). There is still a question of whether such a role could be a full-time or part-time responsibility; future research may help to fill this gap.

Coping with Globalization. Another challenge of knowledge management is the impact of globalization of businesses on its implementation. In this regard, Kalkan (2008) states that one of the main knowledge management challenges faced by global businesses today is having to cope with the increased competition in the global landscape.

Despite the importance of knowledge management, there has been relatively little academic research into the impact of globalization on its implementation. In the corporate world, knowledge applies not only to techniques and physical sciences, but to all aspects of corporate behavior. Knowledge management enables international organizations to create, combine and share knowledge across the globe.

For giant companies doing business across the world, knowledge management creates both opportunities and constraints. The strength of a company depends upon its capability to create, combine and share knowledge across borders. On the other hand, there are constraints on knowledge management in global companies due to the differences in language and culture. Moreover, employees working in different countries may be reluctant to exchange knowledge due to a lack of trust between cross-border units. These factors need to be addressed for the effective application of knowledge management in an organization, which aims to spread its value-creation activities around the world.

11.4 Epilogue

In the discussion above, several knowledge management challenges have been identified that may impede its growth in the future as a scholarly discipline. Although the subject has emerged as an important area of research and practice, one of the greatest challenges — and at the same time one of the most interesting aspects — of knowledge management is the ever-evolving nature of its research. The controversies surrounding its origin have greatly improved our understanding of how various disciplines have contributed to its development, and have provided us with some conceptual depth.

However, these challenges need to be addressed so as to enable additional progress in the future. Birkinshaw (2001) rightly states that there are no simple solutions to the challenges of knowledge management. Kalkan (2008) suggests that the knowledge management challenges should be dealt with in a holistic manner, taking into account all internal and external factors influencing the knowledge management process. This chapter has given some insights into its future, and many of the ideas presented provide opportunities for future research.

Knowledge management has its share of problems and challenges. In particular, this chapter has identified issues and challenges related to the implementation of knowledge management — that is, what does the future hold, and how will this affect knowledge management implementation? Nevertheless, knowledge management research has advanced and been enriched by bringing diverse perspectives, concepts and topics of inquiry into the knowledge management field. The knowledge management discipline will certainly continue to grow and develop in the future.

Generally speaking, the arguments raised in this book project a vision of the future of knowledge management that is both promising and challenging. Davenport (1998) reinforces this, stating that knowledge management will never end because the nature of required knowledge is always changing. Things like new technologies, management approaches, regulatory issues, suppliers' ideas and customer concerns are always evolving. As a result, organizations keep changing their strategies, organizational structures, and products and services in line with the expectations of stakeholders and to compete with rivals. On top of that, new employees always need the existing knowledge of an organization to understand its dynamics and functional areas.

Due to its popularity, knowledge management is no longer a fad. Knowledge management is — and will be — a long-lasting phenomenon because academics and practitioners from various different disciplines, such as information systems, human resources, strategic management and organizational theory, are showing their interest through collaboration in terms of research and practice. Both practitioners and researchers alike recognize that knowledge management is an important area of management research and practice, arguing that it is a well-established area of academic debate. Hence, knowledge management will continue to expand as a scholarly discipline and have a bright future.

Further Reading

Chua, A. Y. K. (2009). The dark side of successful knowledge management initiatives. *Journal of Knowledge Management*, 13(4), 32–40.

Hildreth, P., Wright, P. and Kimble, C. (1999). Knowledge management: are we missing something? In *Proceedings of the 4th UKAIS Conference, York, UK* (pp. 347–356), Maidenhead: McGraw-Hill.

Jayasingam, S., Ansari, M. A. and Jantan, M. (2010). Influencing knowledge workers: the power of top management. *Industrial Management & Data Systems*, 110(1), 134–151.

Kambil, A. (2009). Obliterate knowledge management: everyone is a knowledge manager! *Journal of Business Strategy*, 30(6), 66–68.

Pillania, R. K. (2009). Demystifying knowledge management. *Business Strategy Series*, 10(2), 96–99.

Smith, H., McKeen, J. and Singh, S. (2010). Creating the KM mindset: why is it so difficult? *Knowledge Management Research & Practice*, 8(2), 112–120.

Streatfield, D. and Wilson, T. (1999). Deconstructing knowledge management. *Aslib Proceedings*, 51(3), 67–72.

References

Adair, K. (2004). Knowledge management: a misjudged instrument of strategic change? *Organization*, 11(4), 565–574.

Ahmed, P., Lim, K. and Zairi, M. (1999). Measurement practice for knowledge management. *Journal of Workplace Learning*, 11(8), 304–311.

Akhavan, P. and Jafari, M. (2006). Critical issues for knowledge management implementation at a national level. *VINE: The Journal of Information and Knowledge Management Systems*, 36(1), 52–66.

Al-Hawamdeh, S. (2005). Designing an interdisciplinary graduate program in knowledge management. *Journal of the American Society for Information Science and Technology*, 56(11), 1200–1206.

American Productivity and Quality Center (2000). *Successfully Implementing Knowledge Management*. Houston, TX: APQC International Benchmarking Clearinghouse.

Armistead, C. and Meakins, M. (2002). A framework for practising knowledge management. *Long Range Planning*, 35(1), 49–71.

Barsky, N. and Marchant, G. (2000). The most valuable resource: measuring and managing intellectual capital. *Strategic Finance*, 81(8), 58–62.

Bassi, L. and Van Buren, M. (1999). Valuing investments in intellectual capital. *International Journal of Technology Management*, 18(5/6/7/8), 414–432.

Becerra-Fernandez, I., Gonzalez, A. and Sabherwal, R. (2004). *Knowledge Management: Challenges, Solutions, and Technologies*. Upper Saddle River, NJ: Pearson/Prentice Hall.

Beckman, T. J. (1997). Implementing the knowledge organization in government. Paper presented at the 10th National Conference on Federal Quality, Washington, D.C.

Beckman, T. J. (1999). The current state of knowledge management. In J. Liebowitz (ed.), *Knowledge Management Handbook* (pp. 1–22), Boca Raton, FL: CRC Press LLC.

Birkinshaw, J. (2001). Why is knowledge management so difficult? *Business Strategy Review*, 12(1), 11–18.

Chen, M.-Y. and Chen, A.-P. (2006). Knowledge management performance evaluation: a decade review from 1995 to 2004. *Journal of Information Science*, 32(1), 17–38.

Davenport, T. H. (1996). Knowledge roles: the CKO and beyond. *CIO Magazine*, available at http://www.cio.com/archive/040196/davenport.html/.

Davenport, T. H. (1997). Ten principles of knowledge management and four case studies. *Knowledge and Process Management*, 4(3), 187–208.

Davenport, T. H. (1998). Knowledge management case study: knowledge management at Hewlett-Packard, early 1996. Available at http://www.bus.utexas.edu/kman/hpcase.htm/.

Davenport, T. H., De Long, D. W. and Beers, M. C. (1998). Successful knowledge management projects. *Sloan Management Review*, Winter, 43–57.

Davenport, T. H. and Prusak, L. (1998). *Working Knowledge: How Organizations Manage What They Know*. Boston, MA: Harvard Business School Press.

de Gooijer, J. (2000). Designing a knowledge management performance framework. *Journal of Knowledge Management*, 4(4), 303–310.

De Long, D. and Seemann, P. (2000). Confronting conceptual confusion and conflict in knowledge management. *Organizational Dynamics*, 29(1), 33–44.

Desouza, K. C. (2003). Knowledge management barriers: why the technology imperative seldom works. *Business Horizons*, 46(1), 25–29.

Dess, G. and Picken, J. (2000). Changing roles: leadership in the 21st century. *Organizational Dynamics*, 28(3), 18–34.

Disterer, G. (2001). Individual and social barriers to knowledge transfer. In *Proceedings of the 34th Hawaii International Conference on System Sciences (HICSS)*, Los Alamitos, CA: IEEE Computer Society Press.

Drucker, P. F. (1995). The network society. *Wall Street Journal*, March 29, p. A12.

du Plessis, M. (2007). Knowledge management: what makes complex implementations successful? *Journal of Knowledge Management*, 11(2), 91–101.

Earl, M. J. and Scott, I. (1999). Opinion: what is a chief knowledge officer? *Sloan Management Review*, 40(2), 29–38.

Ernst & Young (1999). Choosing your spots for knowledge management. Available at http://www.ey.com/global/gcr.nsf/international/international_home/.

Fahey, L. and Prusak, L. (1998). The eleven deadliest sins of knowledge management. *California Management Review*, 40(3), 265–276.

Gartner Group (1999). *The Knowledge Management Scenario: Trends and Directions for 1998–2003.* Gartner Group Strategic Analysis Report R-07-7706, March 18.

Greco, J. (1999). Knowledge is power. *Journal of Business Strategy*, 20(2), 19–22.

Haider, S. (2009). The organizational knowledge iceberg: an empirical investigation. *Knowledge and Process Management*, 16(2), 74–84.

Havens, C. and Knapp, E. (1999). Easing into knowledge management. *Strategy & Leadership*, 27(2), 4–9.

Hlupic, V., Pouloudi, A. and Rzevski, G. (2002). Towards an integrated approach to knowledge management: 'hard', 'soft' and 'abstract' issues. *Knowledge and Process Management*, 9(2), 90–102.

Hung, Y.-C., Huang, S.-M., Lin, Q.-P. and Tsai, M.-L. (2005). Critical factors in adopting a knowledge management system for the pharmaceutical industry. *Industrial Management & Data Systems*, 105(2), 164–183.

Jashapara, A. (2005). The emerging discourse of knowledge management: a new dawn for information science research? *Journal of Information Science*, 31(2), 136–148.

Jennex, M. E. and Zakharova, I. (2005). Knowledge management critical success factors. Available at http://www.management.com.ua/strategy/str110.html/.

Kalkan, V. D. (2008). An overall view of knowledge management challenges for global business. *Business Process Management Journal*, 14(3), 390–400.

Kleiner, A. and Roth, G. (1998). How to make experience your company's best teacher. In *Harvard Business Review on Knowledge Management* (pp. 137–151), Boston, MA: Harvard Business School Press.

KPMG (1999). *The Power of Knowledge — A Business Guide to Knowledge Management.* London: KPMG Consulting.

KPMG (2000). *Knowledge Management Research Report 2000.* London: KPMG Consulting.

Lang, J. C. (2001). Managerial concerns in knowledge management. *Journal of Knowledge Management*, 5(1), 43–59.

Laudon, K. C. and Laudon, J. P. (2000). *Management Information Systems: Organization and Technology in the Networked Enterprise*, 6th ed. Englewood Cliffs, NJ: Prentice Hall.

Leonard-Barton, D. (1995). *Wellsprings of Knowledge: Building and Sustaining the Sources of Innovation.* Boston, MA: Harvard Business School Press.

Liebowitz, J. (1999). Key ingredients to the success of an organization's knowledge management strategy. *Knowledge and Process Management*, 6(1), 37–40.

Liebowitz, J. and Beckman, T. (1998). *Knowledge Organizations: What Every Manager Should Know*. Boca Raton, FL: St. Lucie Press/CRC Press.

Lim, K., Ahmed, P. and Zairi, M. (2000). The role of sharing knowledge in management initiatives. Working Paper No. 0005, Bradford University School of Management, Bradford, UK.

Loermans, J. (2002). Synergizing the learning organization and knowledge management. *Journal of Knowledge Management*, 6(3), 285–294.

Martinez, M. (1998). The collective power of employee knowledge. *HR Magazine*, 43(2), 88–94.

Mathi, K. (2004). Key success factors for knowledge management. Available at http://www.knowledgeboard.com/download/2087/KSFsforKnowledgeManagement.pdf/.

McKeen, J., Staples, S. and Cohen, D. (2002). Examining knowledge managers. *KM Review*, 5(1), 9–10.

McKinlay, A. (2002). The limits of knowledge management. *New Technology, Work and Employment*, 17(2), 76–88.

Moffett, S., McAdam, R. and Parkinson, S. (2003). An empirical analysis of knowledge management applications. *Journal of Knowledge Management*, 7(3), 6–26.

Newman, A. (1999). Knowledge management. Info-line series, Issue 9903.

Nissen, M. (2002). An extended model of knowledge-flow dynamics. *Communications of the Association for Information Systems*, 8, 251–266.

Nonaka, I. (1994). A dynamic theory of organizational knowledge creation. *Organization Science*, 5(1), 14–37.

Nonaka, I. and Takeuchi, H. (1995). *The Knowledge-Creating Company: How Japanese Companies Create the Dynamics of Innovation*. Oxford: Oxford University Press.

O'Dell, C. and Grayson, C. J. Jr. (1999). Knowledge transfer: discover your value proposition. *Strategy & Leadership*, 27(2), 10–15.

Pearson, T. (1999). Measurements and the knowledge revolution. *Quality Progress*, 32(9), 31–37.

PricewaterhouseCoopers (1999). KM business value: lessons learned from early adopters. *Global Enterprise Advisor*, 10, 7–8.

Reiss, D. A. (1999). Companies need to learn how to leverage knowledge to sustain competitive advantage. Available at http://www.ey.com/global/gcr.nsf/US/Knowledge/.

Ruggles, R. (1998). The state of the notion: knowledge management in practice. *California Management Review*, 40(3), 80–89.

Ryan, S. D. and Prybutok, V. R. (2001). Factors affecting the adoption of knowledge management technologies: a discriminative approach. *Journal of Computer Information Systems*, 41(4), 31–37.

Sauermann, H. (2009). Book review. *Human Resource Management*, 48(3), 465–467.

Shah, M. H. and Siddiqui, F. A. (2006). Organisational critical success factors in adoption of e-banking at the Woolwich bank. *International Journal of Information Management*, 26, 442–456.

Torres, A. (1999). Unlocking the value of intellectual assets. *McKinsey Quarterly*, 4, 28–37.

Van Buren, M. (1998). Virtual coffee klatch. *Technical Training*, 9(5), 42–46.

Weber, R. O. (2007). Addressing failure factors in knowledge management. *Electronic Journal of Knowledge Management*, 5(3), 333–346.

Weeks, M. (2004). Knowledge management in the wild. *Business Horizons*, 47(6), 15–24.

Wong, K. Y. and Aspinwall, E. (2004). Knowledge management implementation frameworks: a review. *Knowledge and Process Management*, 11(2), 93–104.

Bibliography

Abrahamson, E. (1996). Management fashion. *Academy of Management Review*, 21(1), 254–285.

Accenture and Talent Foundation (2002). Innovation climbs corporate agenda. *Knowledge Management*, November 14.

Adair, K. (2004). Knowledge management: a misjudged instrument of strategic change? *Organization*, 11(4), 565–574.

Addison, M. (2004). Open innovation: the KM dimension. *Inside Knowledge*, 7(9), available at http://www.ikmagazine.com/xq/asp/txtSearch.CoP/exactphrase.1/sid.0/articleid.A2A35510-6B53-470A-A2DA-933A387C99E6/qx/display.htm/.

Addleson, M. (1999). What is a learning organization? Available at http://psol.gmu.edu/Home/perspectives.nsf/.

Afuah, A. (1998). *Innovation Management: Strategies, Implementation, and Profits.* New York: Oxford University Press.

Ahmed, P., Lim, K. and Zairi, M. (1999). Measurement practice for knowledge management. *Journal of Workplace Learning*, 11(8), 304–311.

Akhavan, P. and Jafari, M. (2006). Critical issues for knowledge management implementation at a national level. *VINE: The Journal of Information and Knowledge Management Systems*, 36(1), 52–66.

Akhter, S. H. (2003). Strategic planning, hypercompetition, and knowledge management. *Business Horizons*, 46(1), 19–24.

Alavi, M. (1997). *KPMG Peat Marwick U.S.: One Giant Brain.* Boston, MA: Harvard Business School.

Alavi, M. and Leidner, D. (1999). Knowledge management systems: emerging views and practices from the field. In *Proceedings of the 32nd Hawaii International Conference on System Sciences* (pp. 1–11).

Alavi, M. and Leidner, D. (2001). Knowledge management and knowledge management systems: conceptual foundations and research issues. *MIS Quarterly*, 25(1), 107–136.

Albert, S. (1998). Knowledge management: living up to the hype? *Midrange Systems*, 11(13), September, 52.

Albino, V., Garavelli, A. C. and Schiuma, G. (1998). Knowledge transfer and interfirm relationships in industrial districts: the role of the leader firm. *Technovation*, 19, 53–63.

Al-Hawamdeh, S. (2002). Knowledge management: re-thinking information management and facing the challenge of managing tacit knowledge. *Information Research* (online journal), 8(1), available at http://informationr.net/ir/8-1/paper143.html/.

Al-Hawamdeh, S. (2003). *Knowledge Management: Cultivating Knowledge Professionals*. Oxford: Chandos Publishing.

Al-Hawamdeh, S. (2005). Designing an interdisciplinary graduate program in knowledge management. *Journal of the American Society for Information Science and Technology*, 56(11), 1200–1206.

Allee, V. (1997). *The Knowledge Evolution: Expanding Organizational Intelligence*. Boston, MA: Butterworth-Heinemann.

Alter, S. (1996). *Information Systems: A Management Perspective*, 2nd ed. Menlo Park, CA: Benjamin/Cummings Publishing.

Alvesson, M. (2001). Knowledge work: ambiguity, image and identity. *Human Relations*, 54(7), 863–886.

Alvesson, M. and Karreman, D. (2001). Odd couple: making sense of the curious concept of knowledge management. *Journal of Management Studies*, 38(7), 995–1018.

American Productivity and Quality Center (1996). *Knowledge Management: Consortium Benchmarking Study Final Report*. Houston, TX: APQC International Benchmarking Clearinghouse.

American Productivity and Quality Center (2000). *Successfully Implementing Knowledge Management*. Houston, TX: APQC International Benchmarking Clearinghouse.

American Productivity and Quality Center (2004). Linking knowledge to innovation and bottom line benefits. *Strategic Direction*, 20(2), 28–30.

Amit, R. and Zott, C. (2001). Value creation in e-business. *Strategic Management Journal*, 22(6/7), 493–520.

Anand, V., Manz, C. and Glick, W. H. (1998). An organizational memory approach to information management. *Academy of Management Review*, 23(4), 796–809.

Andreu, R. and Sieber, S. (2006). External and internal knowledge in organizations. In D. G. Schwartz (ed.), *Encyclopedia of Knowledge Management* (pp. 173–179), Hershey, PA: Idea Group Reference.

Ansoff, H. I. (1965). *Corporate Strategy*. New York: McGraw-Hill.

Antal, A. B., Dierkes, M., Child, J. and Nonaka, I. (2001). Introduction: finding paths through the handbook. In M. Dierkes, A. B. Antal, J. Child and I. Nonaka (eds.), *Handbook of Organizational Learning and Knowledge* (pp. 1–7), Oxford: Oxford University Press.

Antonacopoulou, E. P. (2006). Modes of knowing in practice: the relationship between knowledge and learning revisited. In B. Renzl, K. Matzler and H. Hinterhuber (eds.), *The Future of Knowledge Management* (pp. 7–28), Basingstoke: Palgrave Macmillan.

Apostolou, D. and Mentzas, G. (1999). Managing corporate knowledge: a comparative analysis of experiences in consulting firms. Part 1. *Knowledge and Process Management*, 6(3), 129–138.

Argote, L. (1999). *Organizational Learning: Creating, Retaining and Transferring Knowledge*. Norwell, MA: Kluwer.

Argote, L. (2005). Reflections on two views of managing learning and knowledge in organizations. *Journal of Management Inquiry*, 14, 43–48.

Argote, L. and Ingram, P. (2000). Knowledge transfer: a basis for competitive advantage in firms. *Organizational Behavior and Human Decision Processes*, 82(1), 150–169.

Argote, L., Ingram, P., Levine, J. M. and Moreland, L. (2000). Knowledge transfer in organizations: learning from the experience of others. *Organizational Behavior and Human Decision Processes*, 82(1), 1–8.

Argote, L., McEvily, B. and Reagans, R. (2003). Managing knowledge in organizations: an integrative framework and review of emerging themes. *Management Science*, 49(4), 571–582.

Argyris, C. and Schön, D. (1978). *Organizational Learning*. Reading, MA: Addison-Wesley.

Argyris, C. and Schön, D. (1996). *Organizational Learning II*. Reading, MA: Addison-Wesley.

Aristotle (1998). *The Metaphysics*. H. Lawson-Tancred, trans. London: Penguin Books.

Armistead, C. and Meakins, M. (2002). A framework for practising knowledge management. *Long Range Planning*, 35(1), 49–71.

Armstrong, A. and Foley, P. (2003). Foundations for a learning organization: organization learning mechanisms. *The Learning Organization*, 10(2), 74–82.

Arthur, W. B. (1996). Increasing returns and the new world of business. *Harvard Business Review*, 74(4), 100–109.

Asimakou, T. (2009). *Innovation, Knowledge and Power in Organizations.* Abingdon: Routledge.

Awad, E. M. and Ghaziri, H. M. (2004). *Knowledge Management.* Singapore: Pearson.

Badaracco, J. (1991). *The Knowledge Link: Competitive Advantage Through Strategic Alliances.* Boston, MA: Harvard Business School Press.

Badawy, M. K. (1988). How to prevent creativity mismanagement. *IEEE Engineering Management Review*, 16(2), 63–68.

Baden-Fuller, C. and Pitt, M. (1996). The nature of innovating strategic management. In C. Baden-Fuller and M. Pitt (eds.), *Strategic Innovation* (pp. 3–42), London: Routledge.

Bailey, C. and Clarke, M. (2001). Managing knowledge for personal and organisational benefit. *Journal of Knowledge Management*, 5(1), 58–68.

Baird, L. and Henderson, J. C. (2001). *The Knowledge Engine: How to Create Fast Cycles of Knowledge-to-Performance and Performance-to-Knowledge.* San Francisco, CA: Berrett-Koehler.

Balogun, J. and Jenkins, M. (2003). Re-conceiving change management: a knowledge-based perspective. *European Management Journal*, 21(2), 247–257.

Barachini, F. (2009). Cultural and social issues for knowledge sharing. *Journal of Knowledge Management*, 13(1), 98–110.

Barney, J. B. (1991). Firm resources and sustained competitive advantage. *Journal of Management*, 17(1), 99–120.

Barney, J. B. (1997). *Gaining and Sustaining Competitive Advantage.* Reading, MA: Addison-Wesley.

Barney, J. B. and Hesterly, W. S. (2008). *Strategic Management and Competitive Advantage: Concepts and Cases.* Upper Saddle River, NJ: Prentice Hall.

Barquin, R. C. (2001). What is knowledge management? *Knowledge and Innovation: Journal of the KMCI*, 1(2), 127–143.

Barrett, M., Cappleman, S., Shoib, G. and Walsham, G. (2004). Learning in knowledge communities: managing technology and context. *European Management Journal*, 22(1), 1–11.

Barsky, N. and Marchant, G. (2000). The most valuable resource: measuring and managing intellectual capital. *Strategic Finance*, 81(8), 58–62.

Bassi, L. (1997). Harnessing the power of intellectual capital. *Training & Development*, 51(12), 25–30.

Bassi, L. and Van Buren, M. (1999). Valuing investments in intellectual capital. *International Journal of Technology Management*, 18(5/6/7/8), 414–432.

Baumol, W. J., Litan, R. E. and Schramm, C. J. (2007). *Good Capitalism, Bad Capitalism, and the Economics of Growth and Prosperity*. New Haven, CT: Yale University Press.

Becerra-Fernandez, I., Gonzalez, A. and Sabherwal, R. (2004). *Knowledge Management: Challenges, Solutions, and Technologies*. Upper Saddle River, NJ: Pearson/Prentice Hall.

Beckman, T. J. (1997). Implementing the knowledge organization in government. Paper presented at the 10th National Conference on Federal Quality, Washington, D.C.

Beckman, T. J. (1999). The current state of knowledge management. In J. Liebowitz (ed.), *Knowledge Management Handbook* (pp. 1–22), Boca Raton, FL: CRC Press LLC.

Beesley, L. G. (2004). Multi-level complexity in the management of knowledge networks. *Journal of Knowledge Management*, 8(3), 71–100.

Beesley, L. G. A. and Cooper, C. (2008). Defining knowledge management (KM) activities: towards consensus. *Journal of Knowledge Management*, 12(3), 48–62.

Beijerse, R. (1999). Questions in knowledge management: defining and conceptualising a phenomenon. *Journal of Knowledge Management*, 3(2), 94–109.

Bell, D. (1973). *The Coming of Post-Industrial Society*. Harmondsworth: Penguin.

Bell, D. (1979). Thinking ahead: communication technology — for better or for worse. *Harvard Business Review*, 57(3), May/June, 20–42.

Bellini, E. and Lo Storto, C. (2006). Growth strategy as practice in small firm as knowledge structure. *International Journal of Knowledge Management Studies*, 1(1/2), 133–159.

Bender, S. and Fish, A. (2000). The transfer of knowledge and the retention of expertise: the continuing need for global assignments. *Journal of Knowledge Management*, 4(2), 125–137.

Bergeron, B. (2003). *Essentials of Knowledge Management*. Hoboken, NJ: John Wiley & Sons.

Bettencourt, L. A., Ostrom, A. L., Brown, S. W. and Roundtree, R. I. (2002). Client co-production in knowledge-intensive business services. *California Management Review*, 44(4), 100–128.

Bhagat, R., Kedia, B., Harverston, P. and Triandis, H. (2002). Cultural variations in the cross-border transfer of organizational knowledge: an integrative framework. *Academy of Management Review*, 27(2), 204–221.

Bhatt, G. D. (2001). Knowledge management in organizations: examining the interaction between technologies, techniques, and people. *Journal of Knowledge Management*, 5(1), 68–75.

Bierly, P. and Chakrabarti, A. (1996). Generic knowledge strategies in the U.S. pharmaceutical industry. *Strategic Management Journal*, 17(Winter Special Issue), 123–135.

Binney, D. (2001). The knowledge management spectrum — understanding the KM landscape. *Journal of Knowledge Management*, 5(1), 33–42.

Birkinshaw, J. (2001). Why is knowledge management so difficult? *Business Strategy Review*, 12(1), 11–18.

Blackler, F. (1995). Knowledge, knowledge work and organizations: an overview and interpretation. *Organization Studies*, 16(6), 1021–1046.

Blosch, M. (2001). Pragmatism and organizational knowledge management. *Knowledge and Process Management*, 8(1), 39–47.

Blumentritt, R. and Johnston, R. (1999). Towards a strategy for knowledge management. *Technology Analysis & Strategic Management*, 11(3), 287–300.

Boiral, O. (2002). Tacit knowledge and environmental management. *Long Range Planning*, 35, 291–317.

Boisot, M. H. (1998). *Knowledge Assets*. Oxford: Oxford University Press.

Boland, R. J. Jr. and Tenkasi, R. V. (1995). Perspective making and perspective taking in communities of knowing. *Organization Science*, 6(4), 350–372.

Bontis, N., Crossan, M. and Hulland, J. (2002). Managing an organizational learning system by aligning stocks and flows. *Journal of Management Studies*, 39(4), 437–469.

Bounfour, A. (2003). The IC-dVAL approach. *Journal of Intellectual Capital*, 4(3), 396–413.

Bourdreau, A. and Couillard, G. (1999). Systems integration and knowledge management. *Information Systems Management*, 16(4), 24–32.

Bouthillier, F. and Shearer, K. (2002). Understanding knowledge management and information management: the need for an empirical perspective. *Information Research* (online journal), 8(1), available at http://informationr.net/ir/8-1/paper141.html/.

Bowman, C. (2006). Formulating strategy. In D. O. Faulkner and A. Campbell (eds.), *The Oxford Handbook of Strategy* (pp. 410–442), New York: Oxford University Press.

Bowman, E. H., Singh, H. and Thomas, H. (2002). The domain of strategic management: history and evolution. In A. Pettigrew, H. Thomas and R. Whittington (eds.), *Handbook of Strategy and Management* (pp. 31–51), London: Sage.

Boyett, J. H. and Boyett, J. T. (2001). *The Guru Guide to the Knowledge Economy*. New York: Wiley.

Bracker, J. (1980). The historical development of the strategic management concept. *Academy of Management Review*, 5(2), 219–224.

Broadbent, M. (1998). The phenomenon of knowledge management: what does it mean to the information professional? *Information Outlook*, 2(5), May, 23–36.

Broendsted, J. and Elkjaer, B. (2001). Information technology as a fellow player in organizational learning. In *Proceedings of the 9th European Conference on Information Systems (ECIS 2001)*, June 27–29, Bled, Slovenia.

Brooking, A. (1997). The management of intellectual capital. *Long Range Planning*, 30(3), 364–365.

Brown, J. and Duguid, P. (1998). Organizing knowledge. *California Management Review*, 40(3), 90–111.

Brown, R. B. and Woodland, M. J. (1999). Managing knowledge wisely: a case study in organisational behaviour. *Journal of Applied Management Studies*, 8(2), 175–198.

Brusoni, S., Prencipe, A. and Pavitt, K. (2001). Knowledge specialization, organizational coupling, and the boundaries of the firm: why do firms know more than they make? *Administrative Science Quarterly*, 46(4), 597–621.

Buckley, P. J. and Carter, M. J. (2000). Knowledge management in global technology markets: applying theory to practice. *Long Range Planning*, 33, 55–71.

Bukh, P. N., Christensen, K. S. and Mouritsen, J. (2005). New economy, new theory — or new practice? In P. N. Bukh, K. S. Christensen and J. Mouritsen (eds.), *Knowledge Management and Intellectual Capital: Establishing a Field of Practice* (pp. 1–14), Basingstoke: Palgrave Macmillan.

Burden, P. R. (2000). *Knowledge Management: The Bibliography*. Medford, NJ: Information Today, Inc.

Burk, C. F. and Horton, F. W. (1988). *InfoMap: A Complete Guide to Discovering Corporate Information Resources*. Englewood Cliffs, NJ: Prentice Hall.

Bushko, D. and Raynor, M. (1998). Knowledge management: new directions for IT (and other) consultants. *Journal of Management Consulting*, 10(2), November, 67–68.

Cabrera, A. and Cabrera, E. F. (2002). Knowledge-sharing dilemmas. *Organization Studies*, 23(5), 687–710.

Caldwell, F. (2006). The new enterprise knowledge management. *VINE: The Journal of Information and Knowledge Management Systems*, 36(2), 182–185.

Cangelosi, V. and Dill, W. (1965). Organizational learning: observations toward a theory. *Administrative Science Quarterly*, 10, 175–203.

Cannella, A. A. Jr. and Hambrick, D. C. (1993). Effects of executive departures on the performance of acquired firms. *Strategic Management Journal*, 41(S1), 137–152.

Carbonara, N. (2005). Information and communication technology and geographical clusters: opportunities and spread. *Technovation*, 25(3), 213–222.

Carlisle, Y. (2002). Strategic thinking and knowledge management. In S. Little, P. Quintas and T. Ray (eds.), *Managing Knowledge: An Essential Reader* (pp. 122–138), London: The Open University and Sage Publications.

Carlsson, S. A. (2003). Knowledge managing and knowledge management systems in inter-organizational networks. *Knowledge and Process Management*, 10(3), 194–206.

Carnegie, R. and Butlin, M. (1993). *Managing the Innovating Enterprise: Australian Companies Competing with the World's Best.* Melbourne: Business Council of Australia.

Carpenter, M. A. and Sanders, W. G. (2007). *Strategic Management: A Dynamic Perspective — Concepts and Cases.* Upper Saddle River, NJ: Prentice Hall.

Casselman, R. M. and Samson, D. (2007). Aligning knowledge strategy and knowledge capabilities. *Technology Analysis & Strategic Management*, 19(1), 69–81.

Cavaleri, S. and Fearon, D. (1996). *Managing in Organizations That Learn.* Cambridge, MA: Blackwell Publishing.

Cepeda-Carrion, G. (2006). Understanding the link between knowledge management and firm performance: articulating and codifying critical knowledge areas. *International Journal of Knowledge and Learning*, 2(3/4), 238–262.

Chae, B. and Bloodgood, J. M. (2006). The paradoxes of knowledge management: an eastern philosophical perspective. *Information and Organization*, 16, 1–26.

Chait, L. P. (1999). Creating a successful knowledge management system. *Journal of Business Strategy*, 20(2), 23–26.

Chakravarthy, B., Mueller-Stewens, G., Lorange, P. and Lechner, C. (eds.) (2003). *Strategy Process: Shaping the Contours of the Field*. Oxford: Blackwell.

Chandler, A. D. (1962). *Strategy and Structure*. Cambridge, MA: MIT Press.

Chase, R. (1997). The knowledge-based organization: an international survey. *Journal of Knowledge Management*, 1(1), 38–49.

Chase, R. (2006). A decade of knowledge management. *Journal of Knowledge Management*, 10(1), 1–6.

Chauvel, D. and Despres, C. (2002). A review of survey research in knowledge management: 1997–2001. *Journal of Knowledge Management*, 6(3), 207–223.

Chen, M.-Y. and Chen, A.-P. (2006). Knowledge management performance evaluation: a decade review from 1995 to 2004. *Journal of Information Science*, 32(1), 17–38.

Choo, C. W. (1996). The knowing organization: how organizations use information to construct meaning, create knowledge and make decisions. *International Journal of Information Management*, 16(5), 329–340.

Choo, C. W. (1998). *The Knowing Organization: How Organizations Use Information to Construct Meaning, Create Knowledge and Make Decisions*. New York: Oxford University Press.

Christensen, C. M. and Rosenbloom, R. S. (1995). Explaining the attacker's advantage: technological paradigms, organizational dynamics, and the value network. *Research Policy*, 24(2), 233–257.

Ciborra, C. (2002). *Labyrinths of Information*. Oxford: Oxford University Press.

Civi, E. (2000). Knowledge management as a competitive asset: a review. *Marketing Intelligence & Planning*, 18(4), 166–174.

Clark, P., Bennett, D., Burcher, P., Newell, S., Swan, J. and Sharifi, S. (1992). The decision-episode framework and computer-aided production management (CAPM). *International Studies of Management and Organization*, 22, 69–80.

Clark, P. and Staunton, N. (1989). *Innovation in Technology and Organization*. London: Routledge.

Clarke, T. (2001). The knowledge economy. *Education + Training*, 43(4/5), 189–196.

Coff, R. W. (1995). Adapting to control dilemmas when acquiring human-asset-intensive firms: implications of the resource-based view. Paper presented at the Academy of Management Conference, Vancouver, British Columbia, Canada.

Cohen, M. and Sproull, L. (1996). *Organizational Learning*. London: Sage.

Cohen, W. M. and Levinthal, D. A. (1990). Absorptive capacity: a new perspective on learning and innovation. *Administrative Science Quarterly*, 35, 128–152.

Collins English Dictionary (2000). Glasgow: HarperCollins Publishers.

Connell, N. A. D., Klein, J. H. and Powell, P. L. (2003). It's tacit knowledge but not as we know it: redirecting the search for knowledge. *Journal of the Operational Research Society*, 54, 140–152.

Cooper, C. (2006). Knowledge management and tourism. *Annals of Tourism Research*, 33(1), 47–64.

Coulson-Thomas, C. (1997). The future of the organization: selected knowledge management issues. *Journal of Knowledge Management*, 1(1), 15–26.

Court, A. W. (1997). The relationship between information and personal knowledge in new product development. *International Journal of Information Management*, 17(2), 123–138.

Cronin, B. (1985). Introduction. In B. Cronin (ed.), *Information Management: From Strategies to Action* (pp. vii–ix), London: ASLIB.

Cross, R. and Baird, L. (2000). Technology is not enough: improving performance by building organizational memory. *Sloan Management Review*, 41(3), 69–78.

Crossan, M. and Guatto, T. (1996). Organizational learning research profile. *Journal of Organizational Change Management*, 9, 107–112.

Crossan, M. and Hulland, J. (1996). Measuring organizational learning. Working Paper No. 96-05, University of Western Ontario, London, Ontario, Canada.

Crossan, M. and Hulland, J. (1997). Measuring organizational learning. Ivey working paper, Presented to the Academy of Management, Boston, MA.

Crossan, M., Lane, H. and White, R. (1999). An organizational learning framework: from intuition to institution. *Academy of Management Review*, 24(3), 522–537.

Crossan, M., Lane, H., White, R. and Djurfeldt, L. (1995). Organizational learning: dimensions for a theory. *International Journal of Organizational Analysis*, 3(4), 337–360.

Cumming, B. S. (1998). Innovation overview and future challenges. *European Journal of Innovation Management*, 1(1), 21–29.

Cummings, S. and Daellenbach, U. (2009). A guide to the future of strategy? The history of *Long Range Planning*. *Long Range Planning*, 42, 234–263.

Cyert, R. M. and March, J. G. (1963). *A Behavioral Theory of the Firm*. Englewood Cliffs, NJ: Prentice Hall.

Daft, R. L. and Huber, G. P. (1987). How organizations learn: a communication framework. *Research in the Sociology of Organizations*, 5, 1–36.

Daft, R. L. and Weick, K. E. (1984). Toward a model of organizations as interpretation systems. *Academy of Management Review*, 9(2), 284–295.

Daily, C. M., Dalton, D. R. and Rajagopalan, N. (2003). Governance through ownership: centuries of practice, decades of research. *Academy of Management Journal*, 46(2), 151–158.

Daniels, S. (1998). The strategic use of information systems. *Work Study*, 47(5), 167–171.

Darr, E. D. and Kurtzberg, T. R. (2000). An investigation of partner similarity dimensions on knowledge transfer. *Organizational Behavior and Human Decision Processes*, 82(1), 28–44.

Darroch, J. and McNaughton, R. (2002). Examining the link between knowledge management practices and types of innovation. In *Proceedings of the 7th World Congress on Intellectual Capital*, McMaster University, Hamilton, Ontario, Canada, January 16–18, 2002.

D'Aveni, R. A. (1994). *Hypercompetition: Managing the Dynamics of Strategic Maneuvering*. New York: The Free Press.

Davenport, T. H. (1996). Knowledge roles: the CKO and beyond. *CIO Magazine*, available at http://www.cio.com/archive/040196/davenport.html/.

Davenport, T. H. (1997). Ten principles of knowledge management and four case studies. *Knowledge and Process Management*, 4(3), 187–208.

Davenport, T. H. (1998). Knowledge management case study: knowledge management at Hewlett-Packard, early 1996. Available at http://www.bus.utexas.edu/kman/hpcase.htm/.

Davenport, T. H., De Long, D. W. and Beers, M. C. (1998). Successful knowledge management projects. *Sloan Management Review*, Winter, 43–57.

Davenport, T. H. and Grover, V. (2001). Special issue: knowledge management. *Journal of Management Information Systems*, 18(1), 3–4.

Davenport, T. H., Jarvenpaa, S. L. and Beers, M. C. (1996). Improving knowledge work processes. *Sloan Management Review*, Summer, 53–65.

Davenport, T. H. and Prusak, L. (1998). *Working Knowledge: How Organizations Manage What They Know*. Boston, MA: Harvard Business School Press.

Davila, T., Epstein, M. J. and Shelton, R. (2006). *Making Innovation Work: How to Manage It, Measure It, and Profit from It.* Upper Saddle River, NJ: Pearson Education.

Dawson, R. (2000). *Developing Knowledge-Based Client Relationships: The Future of Professional Services.* Boston: Butterworth-Heinemann.

Day, G. S. (1994). Continuous learning about markets. *California Management Review*, 36(4), 9–31.

de Geus, A. (1988). Planning as learning. *Harvard Business Review*, 66, March/April, 70–74.

de Gooijer, J. (2000). Designing a knowledge management performance framework. *Journal of Knowledge Management*, 4(4), 303–310.

De Long, D. and Seemann, P. (2000). Confronting conceptual confusion and conflict in knowledge management. *Organizational Dynamics*, 29(1), 33–44.

de Pablos, P. O. (2001). Relevant experiences on measuring and reporting intellectual capital in European pioneering firms. In N. Bontis and C. Chong (eds.), *Organizational Intelligence: The Cutting Edge of Intellectual Capital and Knowledge Management*, New York: Butterworth-Heinemann.

de Pablos, P. O. (2002). Knowledge management and organizational learning: typologies of knowledge strategies in the Spanish manufacturing industry from 1995 to 1999. *Journal of Knowledge Management*, 6(1), 52–62.

de Wit, B. and Meyer, R. (2004). *Strategy: Process, Content, Context*, 3rd ed. London: Thomson Learning.

DeJarnett, L. (1996). Knowledge the latest thing. *Information Strategy: The Executive's Journal*, 12(2), 3–5.

Demsetz, H. (1991). The theory of the firm revisited. In O. Williamson and S. Winter (eds.), *The Nature of the Firm* (pp. 159–178), New York: Oxford University Press.

Denning, P. J. (2004). The social life of innovation. *Communications of the ACM*, 47(4), 15–19.

Denning, S. (2005). Why the best and brightest approaches don't solve the innovation dilemma. *Strategy & Leadership*, 33(1), 4–11.

Descartes, R. (1996). *Meditations on First Philosophy*. J. Cottingham, ed. and trans. Cambridge: Cambridge University Press.

Desouza, K. C. (2003). Knowledge management barriers: why the technology imperative seldom works. *Business Horizons*, 46(1), 25–29.

Desouza, K. C. (ed.) (2005). *New Frontiers of Knowledge Management*. Basingstoke: Palgrave Macmillan.

Desouza, K. C., Awazu, Y. and Jasimuddin, S. M. (2005). Utilizing external sources of knowledge. *Knowledge Management Review*, 8(1), 16–19.

Desouza, K. C. and Evaristo, J. R. (2003). Global knowledge management strategies. *European Management Journal*, 21(1), 62–67.

Despres, C. and Chauvel, D. (eds.) (2000). *Knowledge Horizons: The Present and the Promise of Knowledge Management*. Woburn, MA: Butterworth-Heinemann.

Despres, C. and Hiltrop, J. M. (1995). Human resource management in the knowledge age: current practice and perspectives on the future. *Employee Relations*, 17(1), 9–23.

Dess, G. and Picken, J. (2000). Changing roles: leadership in the 21st century. *Organizational Dynamics*, 28(3), 18–34.

Dewar, R. and Dutton, J. E. (1986). The adoption of radical and incremental innovations: an empirical analysis. *Management Science*, 32(11), 1422–1433.

DiBella, A. J. (2001). *Learning Practices: Assessment and Action for Organizational Improvement*. Upper Saddle River, NJ: Prentice Hall.

Dierkes, M., Antal, A. B., Child, J. and Nonaka, I. (eds.) (2001). *Handbook of Organizational Learning and Knowledge*. Oxford: Oxford University Press.

Dimitriades, Z. S. (2005). Creating strategic capabilities: organizational learning and knowledge management in the new economy. *European Business Review*, 17(4), 314–324.

Disterer, G. (2001). Individual and social barriers to knowledge transfer. In *Proceedings of the 34th Hawaii International Conference on System Sciences (HICSS)*, Los Alamitos, CA: IEEE Computer Society Press.

Dixon, N. (2000). *Common Knowledge: How Companies Thrive by Sharing What They Know*. Boston, MA: Harvard Business School Press.

Dobni, C. B. (2006). The innovation blueprint. *Business Horizons*, 49(4), 329–339.

Dodgson, M. (1993). Organizational learning: a review of some literatures. *Organization Studies*, 14(3), 375–394.

Donoghue, L. P., Harris, J. G. and Weitzman, B. A. (1999). Knowledge management strategies that create value. *Outlook*, 1, 48–53.

Dosi, G. (1988). Sources, procedures and microeconomic effects of innovation. *Journal of Economic Literature*, 26, 1120–1171.

Dougherty, D. and Hardy, C. (1996). Sustained product innovation in large, mature organizations: overcoming innovation-to-organization problems. *Academy of Management Journal*, 39(5), 1120–1153.

Douglas, P. H. (2002). Information technology is out — knowledge sharing is in. *Journal of Corporate Accounting and Finance*, 13(4), 73–77.

Drejer, A. (2008). Are you innovative enough? *International Journal of Innovation and Learning*, 5(1), 1–17.

Drew, S. (1999). Building knowledge management into strategy: making sense of a new perspective. *Long Range Planning*, 32(1), 130–136.

Drucker, P. F. (1973). *Management: Tasks, Responsibilities, Practices.* New York: Harper & Row.

Drucker, P. F. (1985). *Innovation and Entrepreneurship.* New York: Harper & Row.

Drucker, P. F. (1992). The new society of organizations. *Harvard Business Review*, 70(5), 95–104.

Drucker, P. F. (1993). *Post-Capitalist Society.* New York: HarperCollins.

Drucker, P. F. (1995). The network society. *Wall Street Journal*, March 29, p. A12.

Drucker, P. F. (1998). The coming of the new organization. In *Harvard Business Review on Knowledge Management* (pp. 1–19), Boston, MA: Harvard Business School Press.

Drucker, P. F. (1999). *Management Challenges for the 21st Century.* Oxford: Butterworth-Heinemann.

du Plessis, M. (2007). Knowledge management: what makes complex implementations successful? *Journal of Knowledge Management*, 11(2), 91–101.

Duffy, J. (2000). The KM technology infrastructure. *Information Management Journal*, 34(2), 62–66.

Duffy, J. (2001). The tools and technologies needed for knowledge management. *Information Management Journal*, 35(1), 64–67.

Duncan, R. and Weiss, A. (1979). Organizational learning: implications for organizational design. *Research in Organizational Behavior*, 1, 75–123.

Dvir, R. and Pasher, E. (2004). Innovation engines for knowledge cities: an innovation ecology perspective. *Journal of Knowledge Management*, 8(5), 16–27.

Dyer, J. H. and Singh, H. (1998). The relational view: cooperative strategy and sources of interorganizational competitive advantage. *Academy of Management Review*, 23(4), 660–679.

Earl, M. J. (1994). Knowledge as strategy: reflections on Skandia International and Shorko Films. In C. Ciborra and T. Jelassi (eds.), *Strategic Information Systems: A European Perspective* (pp. 53–69), Chichester: John Wiley & Sons Ltd.

Earl, M. J. (1996). Knowledge strategies: propositions from two contrasting industries. In M. J. Earl (ed.), *Information Management: The Organizational Dimension* (pp. 36–51), Oxford: Oxford University Press.

Earl, M. J. (2001). Knowledge management strategies: toward a taxonomy. *Journal of Management Information Systems*, 18(1), 215–233.

Earl, M. J. and Scott, I. (1999). Opinion: what is a chief knowledge officer? *Sloan Management Review*, 40(2), 29–38.

Easterby-Smith, M. (1997). Disciplines of organizational learning: contributions and critiques. *Human Relations*, 50(9), 1085–1113.

Easterby-Smith, M., Crossan, M. and Nicolini, D. (2000). Organizational learning: debates past, present and future. *Journal of Management Studies*, 37(6), 783–796.

Easterby-Smith, M. and Lyles, M. A. (eds.) (2003). *The Blackwell Handbook of Organizational Learning and Knowledge Management.* Oxford: Blackwell.

Easterby-Smith, M., Lyles, M. A. and Tsang, E. W. K. (2008). Interorganizational knowledge transfer: current themes and future prospects. *Journal of Management Studies*, 45(4), 677–690.

Eaton, J. J. and Bawden, D. (1991). What kind of resource is information? *International Journal of Information Management*, 11, 156–165.

Edquist, C. (ed.) (1997). *Systems of Innovation: Technologies, Institutions and Organizations.* London: Pinter.

Edvinsson, L. and Sullivan, P. (1996). Developing a model for managing intellectual capital. *European Management Journal*, 14(4), 356–364.

Eisenhardt, K. M. and Santos, F. M. (2002). Knowledge-based view: a new theory of strategy? In A. Pettigrew, H. Thomas and R. Whittington (eds.), *Handbook of Strategy and Management* (pp. 139–164), London: Sage.

Ekstedt, E. (1989). *Knowledge Renewal and Knowledge Companies.* Uppsala Papers in Economic History, Research Report No. 22. Department of Economic History, Uppsala University, Uppsala, Sweden.

Empson, L. (1999). Books — knowledge management: in search of the philosophers' stone. *Business Strategy Review*, 10(2), 67–71.

Empson, L. (2001a). Introduction: knowledge management in professional service firms. *Human Relations*, 54(7), 811–817.

Empson, L. (2001b). Fear of exploitation and fear of contamination: impediments to knowledge transfer in mergers between professional service firms. *Human Relations*, 54(7), 839–862.

Ernst & Young (1999). Choosing your spots for knowledge management. Available at http://www.ey.com/global/gcr.nsf/international/international_home/.

Ettlie, J. E., Bridges, W. P. and O'Keefe, R. D. (1984). Organization strategy and structural differences for radical versus incremental innovation. *Management Science*, 30, 682–695.

European Commission (2004a). *Innovation Management and the Knowledge-Driven Economy*. Brussels: Directorate-General for Enterprise.

European Commission (2004b). Innovation through KM. *Knowledge Management*, March 8.

Fahey, L. and Prusak, L. (1998). The eleven deadliest sins of knowledge management. *California Management Review*, 40(3), 265–276.

Faniel, I. M. and Majchrzak, A. (2007). Innovating by accessing knowledge across departments. *Decision Support Systems*, 43(4), 1684–1691.

Faulkner, D. O. and Campbell, A. (2006). Introduction. In D. O. Faulkner and A. Campbell (eds.), *The Oxford Handbook of Strategy* (pp. 1–26), New York: Oxford University Press.

Figueroa, L. A. and González, A. B. (2006). Management of knowledge, information and organizational learning in university libraries. *Libri*, 56(3), 180–190.

Finkelstein, S. and Hambrick, D. (1996). *Strategic Leadership*. St. Paul, MN: West Educational Publishing Company.

Fiol, C. and Lyles, M. (1985). Organizational learning. *Academy of Management Review*, 10, 803–813.

Firestone, J. M. (2001). Key issues in knowledge management. *Knowledge and Innovation: Journal of the KMCI*, 1(3), 8–38.

Floyd, S. W., Roos, J., Jacobs, C. D. and Kellermanns, F. W. (eds.) (2005). *Innovating Strategy Processes*. Oxford: Blackwell.

Frappaolo, C. (1997). Finding what's in it. *Document World*, 2(5), September/October, 23–30.

Frappaolo, C. and Toms, W. (1999). Knowledge management: from terra incognita to terra firma. In J. W. Cortada and J. A. Woods (eds.), *The Knowledge Management Yearbook 1999–2000* (pp. 381–388), Boston, MA: Butterworth-Heinemann.

Fredrickson, J. W. (1990). Introduction: the need for perspectives. In J. W. Fredrickson (ed.), *Perspectives on Strategic Management* (pp. 1–8), New York: Harper Business.

Freeman, C. (1982). *The Economics of Industrial Innovation.* Cambridge, MA: MIT Press.

Fuchs, V. (1968). *The Service Economy.* New York: Columbia University Press for the National Bureau of Economic Research.

Fusaro, R. (1998). Rating intangibles no easy task: Eli Lilly measures the value of knowledge management. *Computerworld*, 32(48), 8.

Gallupe, B. (2001). Knowledge management systems: surveying the landscape. *International Journal of Management Reviews*, 3(1), 61–77.

Galup, S. D., Dattero, R. and Hicks, R. C. (2002). Knowledge management systems: an architecture for active and passive knowledge. *Information Resources Management Journal*, 15(1), 22–27.

Gamble, P. and Blackwell, J. (2001). *Knowledge Management: A State of the Art Guide.* London: Kogan Page.

Gao, F., Li, M. and Clarke, S. (2008). Knowledge, management, and knowledge management in business operations. *Journal of Knowledge Management*, 12(2), 3–17.

Garavelli, C., Gorgoglione, M. and Scozzi, B. (2004). Knowledge management strategy and organization: a perspective of analysis. *Knowledge and Process Management*, 11, 273–282.

Garcia, R. and Calantone, R. (2002). A critical look at technological innovation typology and innovativeness terminology: a literature review. *Journal of Product Innovation Management*, 19(2), 110–132.

Gartner Group (1999). *The Knowledge Management Scenario: Trends and Directions for 1998–2003.* Gartner Group Strategic Analysis Report R-07-7706, March 18.

Garvin, D. A. (1993). Building a learning organization. *Harvard Business Review*, 71(4), 78–91.

Garvin, D. A. (1998). Building a learning organization. In *Harvard Business Review on Knowledge Management* (pp. 47–80), Boston, MA: Harvard Business School Press.

Gehlen, A. (1980). *Man in the Age of Technology.* New York: Columbia University Press.

Georgopoulos, N. B. (2005). Knowledge management as an integral part of strategic management in e-business era. *International Journal of Knowledge and Learning*, 1(4), 373–387.

Gettier, E. L. (1963). Is justified true belief knowledge? *Analysis*, 23(6), 121–123.

Gilbert, M. and Cordey-Hayes, M. (1996). Understanding the process of knowledge transfer to achieve successful technological innovation. *Technovation*, 16(6), 301–312.

Gimeno, J. (2004). Competition within and between networks: the contingent effect of competitive embeddedness on alliance formation. *Academy of Management Journal*, 47(6), 820–842.

Girard, J. P. (2006). Where is the knowledge we have lost in managers? *Journal of Knowledge Management*, 10(6), 22–38.

Gloet, M. and Terziovski, M. (2004). Exploring the relationship between knowledge management practices and innovation performance. *Journal of Manufacturing Technology Management*, 15(5), 402–409.

Goffin, K. and Mitchell, R. (2005). *Innovation Management: Strategy and Implementation Using the Pentathlon Framework*. Basingstoke: Palgrave Macmillan.

Goh, S. C. (2003). Improving organizational learning capability: lessons from two case studies. *The Learning Organization*, 10(4), 216–227.

Gourlay, M. J. (1999). Foundationalism: the problem of knowledge. Available at http://www.xs4all.nl/nexus/gourlay/found_prob.html/.

Gourlay, S. (2000). Frameworks for knowledge: a contribution towards conceptual clarity for knowledge management. Paper presented at the "Knowledge Management: Concepts and Controversies" Conference, Warwick University, UK, February 10–11, 2000. Available at http://bprc.warwick.ac.uk/km013.pdf/.

Gourlay, S. (2006). Conceptualizing knowledge creation: a critique of Nonaka's theory. *Journal of Management Studies*, 43, 1415–1436.

Grant, R. M. (1991). The resource-based theory of competitive advantage: implications for strategy formulation. *California Management Review*, 33(3), 114–135.

Grant, R. M. (1996a). Toward a knowledge-based theory of the firm. *Strategic Management Journal*, 17(Special Issue), 109–122.

Grant, R. M. (1996b). Prospering in dynamically-competitive environments: organizational capability as knowledge integration. *Organization Science*, 7, 375–387.

Grant, R. M. (1997). The knowledge-based view of the firm: implications for management practice. *Long Range Planning*, 30(3), 450–454.

Grant, R. M. (2006). The knowledge-based view of the firm. In D. O. Faulkner and A. Campbell (eds.), *The Oxford Handbook of Strategy* (pp. 203–231), New York: Oxford University Press.

Grant, R. M. and Baden-Fuller, C. (2004). A knowledge accessing theory of strategic alliances. *Journal of Management Studies*, 41(1), 61–84.

Gray, P. H. and Chan, Y. E. (2000). Integrating knowledge management practices through a problem-solving framework. Working Paper WP 00-03, Queen's Centre for Knowledge-Based Enterprises, Kingston, Ontario, Canada.

Gray, P. H. and Meister, D. (2003). Introduction: fragmentation and integration in knowledge management research. *Information Technology & People*, 16(3), 259–265.

Greco, J. (1999). Knowledge is power. *Journal of Business Strategy*, 20(2), 19–22.

Greenwood, R., Hinings, C. R. and Brown, J. L. (1990). "P^2-form" strategic management: corporate practices in professional partnerships. *Academy of Management Journal*, 33(4), 725–755.

Greiner, M. E., Böhmann, T. and Krcmar, H. (2007). A strategy for knowledge management. *Journal of Knowledge Management*, 11(6), 3–15.

Grøtnes, E. (2009). Standardization as open innovation: two cases from the mobile industry. *Information Technology & People*, 22(4), 367–381.

Grover, V. and Davenport, T. H. (2001). General perspectives on knowledge management: fostering a research agenda. *Journal of Management Information Systems*, 18(1), 5–21.

Gu, Y. (2004). Global knowledge management research: a bibliometric analysis. *Scientometrics*, 61, 171–190.

Gulati, R. (1995). Does familiarity breed trust? The implications of repeated ties for contractual choice in alliances. *Academy of Management Journal*, 38, 85–112.

Gulati, R. (1999). Network location and learning: the influence of network resources and firm capabilities on alliance formation. *Strategic Management Journal*, 20(5), 397–420.

Gulati, R. and Singh, H. (1998). The architecture of cooperation: managing coordination costs and appropriation concerns in strategic alliances. *Administrative Science Quarterly*, 43(4), 781–814.

Gupta, A. K. and Govindarajan, V. (2000). Knowledge management's social dimension: lessons from Nucor Steel. *Sloan Management Review*, Fall, 71–80.

Gupta, J. N. D., Sharma, S. K. and Hsu, J. (2004). An overview of knowledge management. In J. N. D. Gupta and S. K. Sharma (eds.), *Creating Knowledge Based Organizations* (pp. 1–28), Hershey, PA: Idea Group Inc.

Haberberg, A. and Rieple, A. (2008). *Strategic Management: Theory and Application*. Oxford: Oxford University Press.

Haider, S. (2009). The organizational knowledge iceberg: an empirical investigation. *Knowledge and Process Management*, 16(2), 74–84.

Halawi, L. A., Aronson, J. E. and McCarthy, R. V. (2005). Resource-based view of knowledge management for competitive advantage. *Electronic Journal of Knowledge Management*, 3(2), 75–86.

Haldin-Herrgard, T. (2000). Difficulties in diffusion of tacit knowledge in organizations. *Journal of Intellectual Capital*, 1(4), 357–365.

Hambrick, D. C. and Cannella, A. A. Jr. (2004). CEOs who have COOs: contingency analysis of an unexplored structural form. *Strategic Management Journal*, 25(10), 959–979.

Hamel, G. and Prahalad, C. K. (1991). Corporate imagination and expeditionary marketing. *Harvard Business Review*, 69(4), 81–92.

Hammer, M. and Champy, J. (1993). *Reengineering the Corporation*. New York: HarperBusiness.

Hansen, M. T. (1999). The search–transfer problem: the role of weak ties in sharing knowledge across organizational subunits. *Administrative Science Quarterly*, 44(1), 82–111.

Hansen, M. T., Nohria, N. and Tierney, T. (1999). What's your strategy for managing knowledge? *Harvard Business Review*, 77(2), 106–116.

Hargadon, A. and Fanelli, A. (2002). Action and possibility: reconciling dual perspectives of knowledge in organizations. *Organization Science*, 13(3), 290–302.

Hauschild, S., Licht, T. and Stein, W. (2001). Creating a knowledge culture. *McKinsey Quarterly*, 1, 74–81.

Havens, C. and Knapp, E. (1999). Easing into knowledge management. *Strategy & Leadership*, 27(2), 4–9.

Hawryszkiewycz, I. (2009). *Knowledge Management*. Basingstoke: Palgrave Macmillan.

Hayes-Roth, F., Waterman, D. A. and Lenat, D. B. (1983). An overview of expert systems. In F. Hayes-Roth, D. A. Waterman and D. B. Lenat (eds.), *Building Expert Systems*, Reading, MA: Addison-Wesley.

Hazlett, S., McAdam, R. and Gallagher, S. (2005). Theory building in knowledge management: in search of paradigms. *Journal of Management Inquiry*, 14(1), 31–42.

Heavin, C. and Neville, K. (2006). Mentoring knowledge workers. In D. G. Schwartz (ed.), *Encyclopedia of Knowledge Management* (pp. 621–626), Hershey, PA: Idea Group Reference.

Hedberg, B. (1990). Exit, voice, and loyalty in knowledge-intensive firms. Paper presented at the 10th Annual International Conference of the Strategic Management Society, Stockholm, September.

Hegel, G. W. F. (1997). *On Art, Religion, and the History of Philosophy*. J. G. Gray, ed. Cambridge, MA: Hackett Publishing.

Heidegger, M. (1962). *Being and Time*. J. Macquarrie and E. Robinson, trans. New York: Harper & Row.

Helfat, C. E. and Peteraf, M. A. (2003). The dynamic resource-based view: capability lifecycles. *Strategic Management Journal*, 24(10), 997–1010.

Hendriks, P. (1999). Why share knowledge? The influence of ICT on the motivation for knowledge sharing. *Knowledge and Process Management*, 6(2), 91–100.

Hendriks, P. H. J. (2001). Many rivers to cross: from ICT to knowledge management systems. *Journal of Information Technology*, 16(2), 57–72.

Henry, A. (2008). *Understanding Strategic Management*. Oxford: Oxford University Press.

Heracleous, L. (2003). *Strategy and Organization*. Cambridge: Cambridge University Press.

Hibbard, J. (1997). Knowing what we know. *InformationWeek*, 653, October 20, 46–64.

Hicks, R. C., Dattero, R. and Galup, S. D. (2006). The five-tier knowledge management hierarchy. *Journal of Knowledge Management*, 10(1), 19–31.

Hidalgo, A. and Albors, J. (2008). Innovation management techniques and tools: a review from theory and practice. *R&D Management*, 38(2), 113–127.

Hildreth, P. M. and Kimble, C. (2002). The duality of knowledge. *Information Research* (online journal), 8(1), available at http://informationr.net/ir/8-1/paper142.html/.

Hill, C. W. L. and Jones, G. R. (2004). *Strategic Management Theory: An Integrated Approach*, 6th ed. Boston, MA: Houghton Mifflin.

Hinings, C. R., Brown, J. L. and Greenwood, R. (1991). Change in an autonomous professional organization. *Journal of Management Studies*, 28(4), 375–393.

Hislop, D. (2002). Mission impossible? Communicating and sharing knowledge via information technology. *Journal of Information Technology*, 17, 165–177.

Hislop, D. (2005). *Knowledge Management in Organizations*. Oxford: Oxford University Press.

Hitt, M. A. (2006). Spotlight on strategic management. *Business Horizons*, 49, 349–352.

Hitt, M. A., Boyd, B. K. and Li, D. (2004). The state of strategic management research and a vision of the future. In D. Ketchen, Jr. and D. Bergh (eds.), *Research Methodology in Strategy and Management*, Vol. 1 (pp. 1–31), Amsterdam: Elsevier.

Hitt, M. A., Ireland, R. D., Camp, S. M. and Sexton, D. L. (2001). Strategic entrepreneurship: entrepreneurial strategies for wealth creation. *Strategic Management Journal*, 22(6/7), 479–491.

Hitt, M. A., Ireland, R. D., Camp, S. M. and Sexton, D. L. (eds.) (2002). *Strategic Entrepreneurship: Creating a New Mindset*. Oxford: Blackwell.

Hlupic, V., Pouloudi, A. and Rzevski, G. (2002). Towards an integrated approach to knowledge management: 'hard', 'soft' and 'abstract' issues. *Knowledge and Process Management*, 9(2), 90–102.

Hoerem, T., von Krogh, G. and Roos, J. (1996). Knowledge-based strategic change. In G. von Krogh and J. Roos (eds.), *Managing Knowledge: Perspectives on Cooperation and Competition* (pp. 116–136), London: Sage.

Hofer-Alfeis, J. and van der Spek, R. (2002). The knowledge strategy process — an instrument for business owners. In T. H. Davenport and G. J. B. Probst (eds.), *Knowledge Management Case Book*, 2nd ed. (pp. 24–39), Erlangen, Germany: Publicis/Wiley.

Holsapple, C. W. (ed.) (2003). *Handbook on Knowledge Management*. Berlin: Springer.

Holsapple, C. W. and Jones, K. (2004). Exploring primary activities of the knowledge chain. *Knowledge and Process Management*, 11(3), 155–174.

Holsapple, C. W. and Whinston, A. (1987). Knowledge-based organizations. *The Information Society*, 5(2), 77–90.

Holtshouse, D. (1998). Knowledge research issues. *California Management Review*, 40(3), 277–280.

Hong, J. F. L., Easterby-Smith, M. and Snell, R. S. (2006). Transferring organizational learning systems to Japanese subsidiaries in China. *Journal of Management Studies*, 43(5), 1027–1058.

Hoskisson, R. E., Hitt, M. A., Johnson, R. A. and Grossman, W. (2002). Conflicting voices: the effects of institutional ownership heterogeneity and internal governance on corporate innovation strategies. *Academy of Management Journal*, 45(4), 697–716.

Hoskisson, R. E., Hitt, M. A., Wan, W. P. and Yiu, D. (1999). Theory and research in strategic management: swings of a pendulum. *Journal of Management*, 25(3), 417–456.

Hsieh, P. J., Lin, B. and Lin, C. (2009). The construction and application of knowledge navigator model (KNM): an evaluation of knowledge management maturity. *Expert Systems with Applications*, 36(2), Part 2, 4087–4100.

Huber, G. P. (1991). Organizational learning: the contributing processes and the literatures. *Organization Science*, 2(1), 88–115.

Huber, G. P. (2001). Transfer of knowledge in knowledge management systems: unexplored issues and suggested studies. *European Journal of Information Systems*, 10, 72–79.

Huff, A. S., Floyd, S. W., Sherman, H. D. and Terjesen, S. (2009). *Strategic Management*. Hoboken, NJ: John Wiley & Sons.

Hull, R. (2000). Knowledge management and the conduct of expert labour. In C. Prichard *et al.* (eds.), *Managing Knowledge* (pp. 49–68), Basingstoke: Macmillan Press Ltd.

Hult, G. T. M. (2003). An integration of thoughts on knowledge management. *Decision Sciences*, 34(2), 189–195.

Hult, G. T. M., Hurley, R. F. and Knight, G. A. (2004). Innovativeness: its antecedents and impact on business performance. *Industrial Marketing Management*, 33, 429–438.

Hung, Y.-C., Huang, S.-M., Lin, Q.-P. and Tsai, M.-L. (2005). Critical factors in adopting a knowledge management system for the pharmaceutical industry. *Industrial Management & Data Systems*, 105(2), 164–183.

Hunger, J. D. and Wheelen, T. L. (2007). *Essentials of Strategic Management*, 4th ed. Upper Saddle River, NJ: Prentice Hall.

Hutchings, G. (1998). Knowledge capture and sharing in support of continuous adaptation and innovation. *Knowledge Management*, 2(4).

Huysman, M. and de Wit, D. (2000). Knowledge management in practice. In J. Edwards and J. Kidd (eds.), *Proceedings of the Knowledge Management Conference (KMAC 2000)*, July 17–18, Birmingham, UK.

Inkpen, A. (1996). Creating knowledge through collaboration. *California Management Review*, 39(1), 123–140.

Inkpen, A. (1998). Learning and knowledge acquisition through international strategic alliances. *Academy of Management Executive*, 12(4), 69–80.

Inkpen, A. (2000). Learning through joint ventures: a framework of knowledge acquisition. *Journal of Management Studies*, 37(7), 1019–1043.

Ireland, R. D., Hitt, M. A. and Vaidyanath, D. (2002). Managing strategic alliances to achieve a competitive advantage. *Journal of Management*, 28, 413–446.

Ireland, R. D., Hoskisson, R. E. and Hitt, M. A. (2009). *The Management of Strategy*, 8th ed. Mason, OH: South-Western/Cengage Learning.

Jakubik, M. (2007). Exploring the knowledge landscape: four emerging views of knowledge. *Journal of Knowledge Management*, 11(4), 6–19.

Jashapara, A. (2004). *Knowledge Management: An Integrated Approach*. Essex: Prentice Hall.

Jashapara, A. (2005). The emerging discourse of knowledge management: a new dawn for information science research? *Journal of Information Science*, 31(2), 136–148.

Jasimuddin, S. M. (2004). Critical assessments of emerging theories of organizational knowledge. Paper presented at the Academy of Management (AOM) Conference, New Orleans, August.

Jasimuddin, S. M. (2005a). Knowledge of external sources' knowledge: new frontiers to actionable knowledge. In M. A. Rahim and R. T. Golembiewski (eds.), *Current Topics in Management*, Vol. 10 (pp. 39–50), New Brunswick, NJ: Transaction Publishers.

Jasimuddin, S. M. (2005b). Storage of transferred knowledge or transfer of stored knowledge: Which direction? If both, then how? In *Proceedings of the 38th Hawaii International Conference on System Sciences*, Hawaii, January.

Jasimuddin, S. M. (2006a). Knowledge transfer: a review to explore conceptual foundations and research agenda. In L. Moutinho, G. Hutcheson and P. Rita (eds.), *Advances in Doctoral Research in Management*, Vol. 1 (pp. 3–20), Singapore: World Scientific.

Jasimuddin, S. M. (2006b). Organizations in the knowledge-based society. In M. A. Rahim (ed.), *Current Topics in Management*, Vol. 11 (pp. 53–67), New Brunswick, NJ: Transaction Publishers.

Jasimuddin, S. M. (2006c). Disciplinary roots of knowledge management: a theoretical review. *International Journal of Organizational Analysis*, 14(2), 171–180.

Jasimuddin, S. M. (2006d). Towards an integrated framework of knowledge transfer. Unpublished PhD dissertation, University of Southampton, Southampton, UK.

Jasimuddin, S. M. (2008). A holistic view of appropriate knowledge management strategy. *Journal of Knowledge Management*, 12(2), 57–66.

Jasimuddin, S. M., Connell, C. and Klein, J. H. (2006). Understanding organizational memory. In D. G. Schwartz (ed.), *Encyclopedia of Knowledge Management* (pp. 870–875), Hershey, PA: Idea Group Reference.

Jasimuddin, S. M., Connell, C. and Klein, J. H. (2005a). The challenges of navigating a topic to a prospective researcher: the case of knowledge management research. *Management Research News*, 28, 62–76.

Jasimuddin, S. M., Klein, J. H. and Connell, C. (2005b). The paradox of using tacit and explicit knowledge: strategies to face dilemmas. *Management Decision*, 43(1), 102–112.

Jasimuddin, S. M., Klein, J. H. and Connell, C. (2005c). Knowledge-intensive firms and other service-providing firms: how different are they, and how will their differences affect their management? Paper presented at the 12th Annual International Conference on Advances in Management, Washington, D.C., July.

Jeffs, C. (2008). *Strategic Management*. Thousand Oaks, CA: Sage.

Jemison, D. B. (1981). The importance of an integrative approach to strategic management research. *Academy of Management Review*, 6(4), 601–608.

Jennex, M. E. and Zakharova, I. (2005). Knowledge management critical success factors. Available at http://www.management.com.ua/strategy/str110.html/.

Jin, Z., Hewitt-Dundas, N. and Thompson, N. J. (2004). Innovativeness and performance: evidence from manufacturing sectors. *Journal of Strategic Marketing*, 12, 255–266.

Johannessen, J. (2008). Organisational innovation as part of knowledge management. *International Journal of Information Management*, 28(5), 403–412.

Johnson, G., Scholes, K. and Whittington, R. (2008). *Exploring Corporate Strategy: Text and Cases*, 8th ed. Harlow, Essex: FT Prentice Hall.

Jones, D. (2003). Knowledge management and technical communication: a convergence of ideas and skills. Available at https://faculty.washington.edu/markh/tc400/.

Jones, M. (1995). Organisational learning: collective mind or cognitivist metaphor? *Accounting, Management and Information Technologies*, 5(1), 61–77.

Kakabadse, N. K., Kouzmin, A. and Kakabadse, A. (2001). From tacit knowledge to knowledge management: leveraging invisible assets. *Knowledge and Process Management*, 8(3), 137–154.

Kalkan, V. D. (2008). An overall view of knowledge management challenges for global business. *Business Process Management Journal*, 14(3), 390–400.

Kalling, T. (2003). Organization-internal transfer of knowledge and the role of motivation: a qualitative case study. *Knowledge and Process Management*, 10(2), 115–126.

Kant, I. (1999). *Critique of Pure Reason*. P. Guyer and A. W. Wood, eds. and trans. Cambridge: Cambridge University Press.

Kanter, J. (1999). Knowledge management, practically speaking. *Information Systems Management*, 16(4), Fall, 7–15.

Katsoulakos, P. and Zevgolis, D. (2004). Knowledge management review 2004. Available at http://www.kbos.net/.

Kesner, I. F. and Sebora, T. C. (1994). Executive succession: past, present and future. *Journal of Management*, 20, 327–372.

Kim, D. H. (1993). The link between individual and organizational learning. *Sloan Management Review*, Fall, 37–50.

King, W. R., Chung, T. R. and Haney, M. H. (2008). Editorial: knowledge management and organizational learning. *Omega*, 36, 167–172.

Kirzner, I. (1979). *Perception, Opportunity, and Profit*. Chicago: University of Chicago Press.

Klatt, L. A., Murdick, R. G. and Schuster, F. E. (1985). *Human Resource Management*. Columbus, OH: Charles E. Merrill/Bell & Howell.

Kleiner, A. and Roth, G. (1998). How to make experience your company's best teacher. In *Harvard Business Review on Knowledge Management* (pp. 137–151), Boston, MA: Harvard Business School Press.

Koen, C. I. (2005). *Comparative International Management*. Maidenhead: McGraw-Hill.

Koenig, M. E. D. (1997). Intellectual capital and how to leverage it. *The Bottom Line*, 10(3), 112–118.

Kogut, B. (1988). Joint ventures: theoretical and empirical perspectives. *Strategic Management Journal*, 9, 319–332.

Kogut, B. and Zander, U. (1992). Knowledge of the firm, combinative capabilities, and the replication of technology. *Organization Science*, 3(3), 383–397.

Kolb, D. A., Lublin, S., Spoth, J. and Baker, R. (1991). Strategic management development: experiential learning and managerial competencies. In J. Henry (ed.), *Creative Management* (pp. 221–231), London: Sage.

Koulopoulos, T. M. and Frappaolo, C. (1999). *Smart Things to Know About Knowledge Management*. Oxford: Capstone.

KPMG (1998). *Knowledge Management Research Report 1998*. London: KPMG Consulting.

KPMG (1999). *The Power of Knowledge — A Business Guide to Knowledge Management.* London: KPMG Consulting.

KPMG (2000). *Knowledge Management Research Report 2000.* London: KPMG Consulting.

Kuhn, R. L. (1985). *Frontiers in Creative and Innovative Management.* Cambridge, MA: Ballinger.

Lam, A. (1997). Embedded firms, embedded knowledge: problems in collaboration and knowledge transfer in global cooperative ventures. *Organization Studies,* 21(3), 487–513.

Lang, J. C. (2001). Managerial concerns in knowledge management. *Journal of Knowledge Management,* 5(1), 43–59.

Lange, T. (2006). The creation and management of knowledge: what can we learn from applying the principles of economics? *International Journal of Knowledge Management Studies,* 1(1/2), 7–17.

Larsen, J. N. (2001). Knowledge, human resources and social practice: the knowledge-intensive business service firm as a distributed knowledge system. *The Service Industries Journal,* 21(1), 81–102.

Laudon, K. C. and Laudon, J. P. (2000). *Management Information Systems: Organization and Technology in the Networked Enterprise,* 6th ed. Englewood Cliffs, NJ: Prentice Hall.

Lave, J. (1993). The practice of learning. In S. Chaiklin and J. Lave (eds.), *Understanding Practice: Perspectives on Activity and Context* (pp. 3–32), Cambridge: Cambridge University Press.

Lave, J. and Wenger, E. (1991). *Situated Learning: Legitimate Peripheral Participation.* Cambridge: Cambridge University Press.

Lawson, B. and Samson, D. (2003). Developments in managing innovation, knowledge and e-business. In A. Gunasekaran, O. Khalil and S. M. Rahman (eds.), *Knowledge and Information Technology Management: Human and Social Perspectives* (pp. 1–13), Hershey, PA: Idea Group, Inc.

Learned, E., Christensen, C., Andrews, K. and Guth, W. (1965). *Business Policy: Text and Cases.* Homewood, IL: Irwin.

Lee, S., Courtney, J. and O'Keefe, R. (1992). A system for organizational learning using cognitive maps. *Omega,* 20(1), 23–36.

Lehaney, B., Clarke, S., Coakes, E. and Jack, G. (2004). *Beyond Knowledge Management.* London: Idea Group Inc.

Leonard, D. and Sensiper, S. (1998). The role of tacit knowledge in group innovation. *California Management Review,* 40, 112–132.

Leonard-Barton, D. (1995). *Wellsprings of Knowledge: Building and Sustaining the Sources of Innovation.* Boston, MA: Harvard Business School Press.

Levinthal, D. and March, J. (1993). The myopia of learning. *Strategic Management Journal*, 14, 95–112.

Levitt, B. and March, J. G. (1988). Organizational learning. *Annual Review of Sociology*, 14, 319–340.

Li, M. and Gao, F. (2003). Why Nonaka highlights tacit knowledge: a critical review. *Journal of Knowledge Management*, 7(4), 6–14.

Liebowitz, J. (1999a). Key ingredients to the success of an organization's knowledge management strategy. *Knowledge and Process Management*, 6(1), 37–40.

Liebowitz, J. (ed.) (1999b). *Knowledge Management Handbook.* Boca Raton, FL: CRC Press LLC.

Liebowitz, J. (2003). Keynote paper: measuring the value of online communities, leading to innovation and learning. *International Journal of Innovation and Learning*, 1(1), 1–8.

Liebowitz, J. and Beckman, T. (1998). *Knowledge Organizations: What Every Manager Should Know.* Boca Raton, FL: St. Lucie Press/CRC Press.

Liebowitz, J. and Wilcox, L. (eds.) (1997). *Knowledge Management and Its Integrative Elements.* Boca Raton, FL: CRC Press.

Lim, K., Ahmed, P. and Zairi, M. (2000). The role of sharing knowledge in management initiatives. Working Paper No. 0005, Bradford University School of Management, Bradford, UK.

Lin, C. and Wu, C. (2005). A knowledge creation model for ISO 9001:2000. *Total Quality Management*, 16(5), 657–670.

Livingstone, L., Palich, L. and Carini, G. (1998). Viewing strategic innovation through the logic of contradiction. *Competitiveness Review*, 8(1), 46–54.

Locke, J. (1998). *An Essay Concerning Human Understanding.* A. S. Pringle-Pattison and D. Collinson, eds. Ware, Hertfordshire: Wordsworth Editions Ltd.

Loeb, K. A., Rai, A., Ramaprasad, A. and Sharma, S. (1998). Design, development and implementation of a global information warehouse: a case study at IBM. *Information Systems Journal*, 8, 291–311.

Loermans, J. (2002). Synergizing the learning organization and knowledge management. *Journal of Knowledge Management*, 6(3), 285–294.

Lopez, S. P., Peon, J. M. M. and Ordas, C. J. V. (2004). Managing knowledge: the link between culture and organizational learning. *Journal of Knowledge Management*, 8(6), 93–104.

Loughridge, B. (1999). Knowledge management, librarians and information managers: fad or future? *New Library World*, 100(6), 245–253.

Lowe, P. (1995). *The Management of Technology*. London: Chapman & Hall.

Lowendahl, B. R. (1997). *Strategic Management of Professional Service Firms*. Copenhagen: Copenhagen Business School Press.

Lowendahl, B. R., Revang, O. and Fosstenlokken, S. M. (2001). Knowledge and value creation in professional service firms: a framework for analysis. *Human Relations*, 54(7), 911–931.

Lu, J. W. and Beamish, P. W. (2004). International diversification and firm performance: the S-curve hypothesis. *Academy of Management Journal*, 47(4), 598–609.

Luecke, R. and Katz, R. (2003). *Managing Creativity and Innovation*. Boston, MA: Harvard Business School Press.

Luen, T. W. and Al-Hawamdeh, S. (2001). Knowledge management in the public sector: principles and practices in police work. *Journal of Information Science*, 27, 311–318.

Lundvall, B. A. and Borras, S. (1998). *The Globalising Learning Economy: Implications for Innovation Policy*. European Commission, DG XII, TSER Report. Luxembourg: Office for Official Publications of the European Communities.

Lyles, M. A. and Easterby-Smith, M. (2003). Organizational learning and knowledge management: agendas for future research. In M. Easterby-Smith and M. A. Lyles (eds.), *The Blackwell Handbook of Organizational Learning and Knowledge Management* (pp. 639–652), Oxford: Blackwell.

Lynall, M. D., Golden, B. R. and Hillman, A. J. (2003). Board composition from adolescence to maturity: a multitheoretic view. *Academy of Management Review*, 28(3), 416–431.

Lynch, R. (2006). *Corporate Strategy*, 4th ed. Harlow, Essex: FT Prentice Hall.

MacGillivray, A. (2003). Knowledge management education at Royal Roads University. *Competitive Intelligence Magazine*, 6(4), 37–40.

Machlup, F. (1980). *Knowledge: Its Creation, Distribution, and Economic Significance*. Princeton, NJ: Princeton University Press.

Macintosh, A. (1996). Position paper on knowledge asset management. Artificial Intelligence Applications Institute, University of Edinburgh, Scotland.

Mahlitta, J. (1996). Smarten up! *Computerworld*, 29(23), 84–87.

Mahoney, J. T. and McGahan, A. M. (2007). The field of strategic management within the evolving science of strategic organization. *Strategic Organization*, 5(1), 79–99.

Mahoney, J. T. and Pandian, J. R. (1992). The resource-based view within the conversation of strategic management. *Strategic Management Journal*, 13, 363–380.

Maister, D. H. (1982). Balancing the professional service firm. *Sloan Management Review*, 24(1), 15–29.

Malhotra, Y. (1996). Organizational learning and learning organizations: an overview. Available at http://www.brint.com/papers/orglrng.htm/.

Malhotra, Y. (1997). Knowledge management in inquiring organizations. In *Proceedings of the 3rd Americas Conference on Information Systems*, Indianapolis, IN.

Malhotra, Y. (1998). Business process redesign: an overview. *IEEE Engineering Management Review*, 26(3), Fall, 27–31.

Malhotra, Y. (2000a). From information management to knowledge management: beyond the "hi-tech hidebound" systems. In T. K. Srikantaiah and M. E. D. Koenig (eds.), *Knowledge Management for the Information Professional* (pp. 37–61), Medford, NJ: Information Today, Inc.

Malhotra, Y. (ed.) (2000b). *Knowledge Management and Virtual Organizations*. Hershey, PA: Idea Group Publishing.

Mallach, E. (1994). *Understanding Decision Support Systems and Expert Systems*. Burr Ridge, IL: Richard D. Irwin.

Manasco, B. (1998). Corporate knowledge nets and the learning imperative. Available at http://webcom.com/quantera/empires3.html/.

Mansfield, E. (1968). *Industrial Research and Technological Innovation*. New York: Norton.

Marinova, D. (2004). Actualizing innovation effort: the impact of market knowledge diffusion in a dynamic system of competition. *Journal of Marketing*, 68(3), 1–20.

Marks, P., Polak, P., McCoy, S. and Galletta, D. (2008). Sharing knowledge. *Communications of the ACM*, 51(2), 60–65.

Markus, M. L. (2000). Knowledge management. Presented at the Warwick Business School Seminar Series, University of Warwick, Coventry, UK.

Marquardt, M. (1996). *Building the Learning Organization: A Systems Approach to Quantum Improvement and Global Success*. New York: McGraw-Hill.

Marr, B., Gray, D. and Neely, A. (2003). Why do firms measure their intellectual capital? *Journal of Intellectual Capital*, 4, 441–464.

Marsh, C. H. and Morris, E. C. (2001). Corporate memory and technical communicators: a relationship with a new urgency. In *Proceedings of the IEEE International Professional Communication Conference 2001 (IPCC 2001)* (pp. 379–389).

Mårtensson, M. (2000). A critical review of knowledge management as a management tool. *Journal of Knowledge Management*, 4(3), 204–216.

Martinez, M. (1998). The collective power of employee knowledge. *HR Magazine*, 43(2), 88–94.

Martins, E. C. and Terblanche, F. (2003). Building organisational culture that stimulates creativity and innovation. *European Journal of Innovation Management*, 6(1), 64–74.

Martiny, M. (1998). Knowledge management at HP Consulting. *Organizational Dynamics*, 27(2), 71–78.

Mathi, K. (2004). Key success factors for knowledge management. Available at http://www.knowledgeboard.com/download/2087/KSFsforKnowledgeManagement.pdf/.

McAdam, R. and McCreedy, S. (2000). A critique of knowledge management: using a social constructionist model. *New Technology, Work and Employment*, 15(2), 155–168.

McCall, H., Arnold, V. and Sutton, S. G. (2008). Use of knowledge management systems and the impact on the acquisition of explicit knowledge. *Journal of Information Systems*, 22(2), Fall, 77–101.

McCann, J. E. and Buckner, M. (2004). Strategically integrating knowledge management initiatives. *Journal of Knowledge Management*, 8(1), 47–63.

McDermott, C. M. and O'Connor, G. C. (2002). Managing radical innovation: an overview of emergent strategy issues. *Journal of Product Innovation Management*, 19(6), 424–438.

McDermott, R. and O'Dell, C. (2001). Overcoming cultural barriers to sharing knowledge. *Journal of Knowledge Management*, 5(1), 76–85.

McEvily, B. and Zaheer, A. (1999). Bridging ties: a source of firm heterogeneity in competitive capabilities. *Strategic Management Journal*, 20, 1133–1156.

McGill, M. E. and Slocum, J. W. (1993). Unlearning the organization. *Organizational Dynamics*, 22(2), 67–79.

McKeen, J., Staples, S. and Cohen, D. (2002). Examining knowledge managers. *KM Review*, 5(1), 9–10.

McKinlay, A. (2002). The limits of knowledge management. *New Technology, Work and Employment*, 17(2), 76–88.

McNabb, D. E. (2007). *Knowledge Management in the Public Sector — A Blueprint for Innovation in Government*. New York: M.E. Sharpe.

Mellahi, K., Frynas, J. G. and Finlay, P. (2005). *Global Strategic Management*. Oxford: Oxford University Press.

Mertins, K., Heisig, P. and Vorbeck, J. (eds.) (2003). *Knowledge Management: Concepts and Best Practices*, 2nd ed. Berlin: Springer-Verlag.

Metaxiotis, K. and Psarras, J. (2006). Analysing the value of knowledge management leading to innovation. *International Journal of Knowledge Management Studies*, 1(1/2), 79–89.

Meyer-Dohm, P. (1992). Human resources 2020: structures of the learning company. In *Conference Proceedings: Human Resources in Europe at the Dawn of the 21st Century*, Luxembourg: Office for Official Publications of the European Communities.

Miller, D. (1996). A preliminary typology of organizational learning: synthesizing the literature. *Journal of Management*, 22(3), 485–505.

Mills, D. Q. and Friesen, B. (1992). The learning organization. *European Management Journal*, 10(2), 146–156.

Mills, P. K. and Moberg, D. J. (1982). Perspectives on the technology of service operations. *Academy of Management Review*, 7(3), 467–478.

Miner, A. S. and Mezias, S. J. (1996). Ugly duckling no more: pasts and futures of organizational learning research. *Organization Science*, 7(1), 88–99.

Moffett, S., McAdam, R. and Parkinson, S. (2003a). An empirical analysis of knowledge management applications. *Journal of Knowledge Management*, 7(3), 6–26.

Moffett, S., McAdam, R. and Parkinson, S. (2003b). Technology and people factors in knowledge management: an empirical analysis. *Total Quality Management & Business Excellence*, 14(2), 215–224.

Mokyr, J. (1990). *The Lever of Riches: Technological Creativity and Economic Progress*. Oxford: Oxford University Press.

Moreno-Luzon, M. D. and Lloria, M. B. (2008). The role of non-structural and informal mechanisms of integration and coordination as forces in knowledge creation. *British Journal of Management*, 19, 250–276.

Morey, D., Maybury, M. and Thuraisingham, B. (eds.) (2002). *Knowledge Management: Classic and Contemporary Works*. Cambridge, MA: MIT Press.

Morris, T. (2001). Asserting property rights: knowledge codification in the professional service firm. *Human Relations*, 54(7), 819–838.

Morris, T. and Empson, L. (1998). Organisation and expertise: an exploration of knowledge bases and the management of accounting and consulting firms. *Accounting, Organizations and Society*, 23(5/6), 609–624.

Mukherjee, A. (2003). Achieving knowledge management in construction: part I — a review of developments. *Construction Information Quarterly*, 5(3), 7–11.

Nadler, D., Gerstein, M. and Shaw, R. (1992). *Organizational Architecture: Designs for Changing Organizations.* San Francisco: Jossey-Bass.

Neef, D. (1999). Making the case for knowledge management: the bigger picture. *Management Decision*, 37(1), 72–78.

Nevis, E. C., DiBella, A. J. and Gould, J. M. (1995). Understanding organizations as learning systems. *Sloan Management Review*, 36(2), 73–85.

Newell, S., Robertson, M., Scarbrough, H. and Swan, J. (2002). *Managing Knowledge Work.* Basingstoke: Palgrave Macmillan.

Newell, S., Swan, J., Galliers, R. and Scarbrough, H. (1999). The intranet as a knowledge management tool? Creating new electronic fences. In M. Khosrowpour (ed.), *Proceedings of the Information Resources Management Association International Conference, "Managing Information Technology Resources in Organizations in the Next Millennium".*

Newman, A. (1999). Knowledge management. Info-line series, Issue 9903.

Newman, B. and Conrad, K. W. (2000). A framework for characterizing knowledge management methods, practices, and technologies. The Knowledge Management Theory Papers, Knowledge Management Forum, West Richland, WA.

Nissen, M. (2002). An extended model of knowledge-flow dynamics. *Communications of the Association for Information Systems*, 8, 251–266.

Nissen, M., Kamel, M. and Sengupta, K. (2000). Integrated analysis and design of knowledge systems and processes. *Information Resources Management Journal*, 13(1), 24–43.

Nonaka, I. (1988). Toward middle-up-down management: accelerating information creation. *Sloan Management Review*, 29(3), Spring, 9–18.

Nonaka, I. (1991a). The knowledge-creating company. *Harvard Business Review*, 69(6), 96–104.

Nonaka, I. (1991b). Managing the firm as an information creation process. In J. Meindl, R. L. Cardy and S. M. Puffer (eds.), *Advances in Information Processing in Organizations*, Vol. 4 (pp. 239–275), Greenwich, CT: JAI Press.

Nonaka, I. (1994). A dynamic theory of organizational knowledge creation. *Organization Science*, 5(1), 14–37.

Nonaka, I. (1998). The knowledge-creating company. In *Harvard Business Review on Knowledge Management* (pp. 21–45), Boston, MA: Harvard Business School Press.

Nonaka, I. and Konno, N. (1998). The concept of 'ba': building a foundation for knowledge creation. *California Management Review*, 40(3), 40–54.

Nonaka, I. and Reinmoeller, P. (2000). Dynamic business systems for knowledge creation and utilization. In C. Despres and D. Chauvel (eds.), *Knowledge Horizons: The Present and the Promise of Knowledge Management* (pp. 89–112), Boston: Butterworth-Heinemann.

Nonaka, I. and Takeuchi, H. (1995). *The Knowledge-Creating Company: How Japanese Companies Create the Dynamics of Innovation.* Oxford: Oxford University Press.

Nonaka, I. and Teece, D. J. (2001). Research directions for knowledge management. In I. Nonaka and D. J. Teece (eds.), *Managing Industrial Knowledge: Creation, Transfer and Utilization* (pp. 330–335), London: Sage.

Nonaka, I., Toyama, R. and Konno, N. (2000). SECI, *ba* and leadership: a unified model of dynamic knowledge creation. *Long Range Planning*, 33, 5–34.

Nordfors, D. (2004). The role of journalism in innovation systems. *Innovation Journalism*, 1(7), 1–18.

Nurmi, R. (1998). Knowledge-intensive firms. *Business Horizons*, May/June, 26–32.

Nyström, H. (1990). *Technological and Market Innovation: Strategies for Product and Company Development.* Chichester: John Wiley & Sons.

O'Dell, C. (1997). A current review of knowledge management best practices. Presented at the "Conference on Knowledge Management and the Transfer of Best Practices", Business Intelligence, London.

O'Dell, C. and Grayson, C. J. (1998). If only we knew what we know: identification and transfer of internal best practices. *California Management Review*, 40, 154–174.

O'Dell, C. and Grayson, C. J. Jr. (1999). Knowledge transfer: discover your value proposition. *Strategy & Leadership*, 27(2), 10–15.

OECD (1996). *The Knowledge-Based Economy.* Paris: OECD.

OECD (2000). *A New Economy? The Changing Role of Innovation and Information Technology in Growth.* Paris: OECD.

O'Leary, D. (1998). Knowledge management systems: converting and connecting. *IEEE Intelligent Systems and Their Applications*, 13(3), 30–33.

Olivera, F. (2000). Memory systems in organizations: an empirical investigation of mechanisms for knowledge collection, storage and access. *Journal of Management Studies*, 37(6), 811–832.

Oluic-Vukovic, V. (2001). From information to knowledge: some reflections on the origin of the current shifting towards knowledge processing and further perspective. *Journal of the American Society for Information Science and Technology*, 52, 54–61.

Osterloh, M. and Frey, B. S. (2000). Motivation, knowledge transfer, and organizational forms. *Organization Science*, 11(5), 538–550.

Pan, S. L. and Scarbrough, H. (1999). Knowledge management in practice: an exploratory case study. *Technology Analysis & Strategic Management*, 11(3), 359–374.

Parthasarthy, R. (2007). *Fundamentals of Strategic Management*. New York: Houghton Mifflin.

Pavlovich, K. and Corner, P. D. (2006). Knowledge creation through co-entrepreneurship. *International Journal of Knowledge Management Studies*, 1(1/2), 178–197.

Pearson, T. (1999). Measurements and the knowledge revolution. *Quality Progress*, 32(9), 31–37.

Pedersen, C. R. and Dalum, B. (2004). Incremental versus radical change: the case of the Digital North Denmark program. Paper presented at the DRUID Summer Conference 2004, Copenhagen, June 14–16.

Pemberton, J. D. and Stonehouse, G. H. (2000). Organisational learning and knowledge assets — an essential partnership. *The Learning Organization*, 7(4), 184–194.

Peña, I. (2002). Intellectual capital and business start-up success. *Journal of Intellectual Capital*, 3, 180–198.

Peng, M. W. (2009). *Global Strategic Management*. London: South-Western/Cengage Learning.

Penner-Hahn, J. and Shaver, J. M. (2005). Does international research and development increase patent output? An analysis of Japanese pharmaceutical firms. *Strategic Management Journal*, 26, 121–140.

Petrash, G. (1996). Dow's journey to a knowledge value management culture. *European Management Journal*, 14(4), 365–373.

Phillips, N. and Patrick, K. (2000). Knowledge management perspectives, organizational character and cognitive style. In J. Edwards and J. Kidd (eds.), *Proceedings of the Knowledge Management Conference (KMAC 2000)*, July 17–18, Birmingham, UK.

Pisano, G. P. (1994). Knowledge, integration, and the locus of learning: an empirical analysis of process development. *Strategic Management Journal*, 15(S1), 85–100.

Pitkethly, R. (2006). Analysing the environment. In D. O. Faulkner and A. Campbell (eds.), *The Oxford Handbook of Strategy* (pp. 231–266), New York: Oxford University Press.

Place, I. and Hyslop, D. J. (1982). *Records Management: Controlling Business Information*. Reston, VA: Reston Publishing Company.

Plato (1992). *Theaetetus.* B. Williams, ed., M. J. Levett, trans. and M. Burnyeat, rev. Cambridge, MA: Hackett Publishing.

Polanyi, M. (1958). *Personal Knowledge: Towards a Post-Critical Philosophy.* London: Routledge & Kegan Paul.

Polanyi, M. (1962). *Personal Knowledge: Towards a Post-Critical Philosophy.* Chicago, IL: University of Chicago Press.

Polanyi, M. (1966). *The Tacit Dimension.* London: Routledge.

Ponzi, L. and Koenig, M. E. D. (2002). Knowledge management: another management fad? *Information Research* (online journal), 8(1), available at http://informationr.net/ir/8-1/paper145.html/.

Porat, M. (1977). *The Information Economy.* Washington, D.C.: US Government Printing Office.

Porter, M. E. (1980). *Competitive Strategy: Techniques for Analyzing Industries and Competitors.* New York: The Free Press.

Powell, W. W., Koput, K. W. and Smith-Doerr, L. (1996). Interorganizational collaboration and the locus of innovation: networks of learning in biotechnology. *Administrative Science Quarterly*, 41(1), 116–145.

Prahalad, C. K. and Hamel, G. (1990). The core competition of the corporation. *Harvard Business Review*, 68(3), 79–91.

PricewaterhouseCoopers (1999). KM business value: lessons learned from early adopters. *Global Enterprise Advisor*, 10, 7–8.

Probst, G. (1998). Practical knowledge management: a model that works. *Prism*, Second Quarter, 17–29.

Probst, G., Raub, S. and Romhardt, K. (2000). *Managing Knowledge: Building Blocks for Success.* Chichester: John Wiley & Sons Ltd.

Prusak, L. (2001). Where did knowledge management come from? *IBM Systems Journal*, 40(4), 1002–1007.

Pyka, A. (2002). Innovation networks in economics: from the incentive-based to the knowledge-based approaches. *European Journal of Innovation Management*, 5(3), 152–163.

Quinn, J. B. (1992a). Intelligent enterprise: a new paradigm. *Academy of Management Executive*, 6(4), 48–63.

Quinn, J. B. (1992b). *Intelligent Enterprise: A Knowledge and Service Based Paradigm for Industry.* New York: The Free Press.

Quinn, J. B., Baruch, J. J. and Zien, K. A. (1997). *Innovation Explosion: Using Intellect and Software to Revolutionize Growth Strategies.* New York: The Free Press.

Quintas, P., Lefrere, P. and Jones, G. (1997). Knowledge management: a strategic agenda. *Long Range Planning*, 30(3), 385–391.

Rahim, M. A. (2002). Toward a theory of managing organizational conflict. *International Journal of Conflict Management*, 13, 206–235.

Raub, S. and Ruling, C. (2001). The knowledge management tussle — speech communities and rhetorical strategies in the development of knowledge management. *Journal of Information Technology*, 16(2), 113–130.

Rayport, J. F. and Sviokla, J. J. (1995). Exploiting the virtual value chain. *Harvard Business Review*, 73(6), 75–85.

Reich, R. (1991). *The Work of Nations: Preparing Ourselves for 21st-Century Capitalism*. London: Simon & Schuster.

Reiss, D. A. (1999). Companies need to learn how to leverage knowledge to sustain competitive advantage. Available at http://www.ey.com/global/gcr.nsf/US/Knowledge/.

Revans, R. W. (1971). *Developing Effective Managers: A New Approach to Business Education*. New York: Praeger Publishers.

Revilla, E., Sarkis, J. and Acosta, J. (2005). Towards a knowledge management and learning taxonomy for research joint ventures. *Technovation*, 25, 1307–1316.

Rifkin, J. (2000). *The End of Work: The Decline of the Global Workforce and the Dawn of the Post-Market Era*. London: Penguin.

Roberts, E. B. (1981). *Generating Effective Corporate Innovation*. New York: The Free Press.

Roberts, H. (1998). The bottom-line of competence-based management: management accounting, control and performance measurement. Paper presented at the EAA Conference, Antwerp, Belgium.

Roberts, J. (2000). From know-how to show-how? Questioning the role of information and communication technologies in knowledge transfer. *Technology Analysis & Strategic Management*, 12(4), 429–443.

Robey, D., Boudreau, M. and Rose, G. M. (2000). Information technology and organizational learning: a review and assessment of research. *Accounting, Management and Information Technologies*, 10, 125–155.

Rodan, S. and Galunic, C. (2004). More than network structure: how knowledge heterogeneity influences managerial performance and innovativeness. *Strategic Management Journal*, 25(6), 541–562.

Rogers, E. (1983). *Diffusion of Innovations*, 3rd ed. New York: Free Press.

Rogers, E. (1995). *Diffusion of Innovations*, 4th ed. New York: Free Press.

Rowe, G. and Wright, G. (1999). The Delphi technique as a forecasting tool: issues and analysis. *International Journal of Forecasting*, 15, 353–375.

Ruggles, R. (1997). *Knowledge Management Tools*. Boston, MA: Butterworth-Heinemann.

Ruggles, R. (1998). The state of the notion: knowledge management in practice. *California Management Review*, 40(3), 80–89.

Rumelt, R. (1991). How much does industry matter? *Strategic Management Journal*, 12(3), 167–185.

Rumelt, R., Schendel, D. and Teece, D. J. (1994). *Fundamental Issues in Strategy: A Research Agenda*. Boston, MA: Harvard Business School Press.

Ryan, S. D. and Prybutok, V. R. (2001). Factors affecting the adoption of knowledge management technologies: a discriminative approach. *Journal of Computer Information Systems*, 41(4), 31–37.

Sambamurthy, V. and Subramani, M. (2005). Special issue on information technology and knowledge management. *MIS Quarterly*, 29(1), 1–7.

Sanchez, R. and Heene, A. (1997). Reinventing strategic management: new theory and practice for competence-based competition. *European Management Journal*, 15(3), 303–317.

Sandelands, E. (1999). Learning organizations: a review of the literature relating to strategies, building blocks and barriers. *Management Literature in Review*, 1(1), 1–10.

Santosus, M. (1996). The learning organization. *CIO Magazine*, June 1.

Sasser, W. E., Olsen, R. P. and Wyckoff, D. D. (1978). *Management of Service Operations: Text, Cases, and Readings*. Boston: Allyn & Bacon.

Sauermann, H. (2009). Book review. *Human Resource Management*, 48(3), 465–467.

Sawyer, R. D. (1996). *The Complete Art of War*. Boulder, CO: Westview Press.

Scarbrough, H. (1995). Blackboxes, hostages and prisoners. *Organization Studies*, 16(6), 991–1019.

Scarbrough, H. (1996). *The Management of Expertise*. London: Macmillan.

Scarbrough, H. (1999). Knowledge as work: conflicts in the management of knowledge workers. *Technology Analysis and Strategic Management*, 11(1), 5–16.

Scarbrough, H. and Swan, J. (2001). Explaining the diffusion of knowledge management: the role of fashion. *British Journal of Management*, 12(1), 3–12.

Scarbrough, H., Swan, J. and Preston, J. (1999). *Knowledge Management: A Literature Review*. London: Institute of Personnel and Development.

Schein, E. H. (1996). Organizational learning: what is new? Working paper, Society for Organizational Learning, MIT Sloan School of Management, Cambridge, MA.

Schendel, D. and Cool, K. (1988). Development of the strategic management field: some accomplishments and challenges. In J. H. Grant (ed.), *Strategic Management Frontiers* (pp. 17–31), Greenwich, CT: JAI Press.

Schendel, D. and Hofer, C. W. (1979). *Strategic Management: A New View of Business Policy and Planning*. Boston, MA: Little, Brown and Company.

Schumpeter, J. (1934). *The Theory of Economic Development*. Cambridge, MA: Harvard University Press.

Schumpeter, J. (1961). *The Theory of Economic Development*. Oxford: Oxford University Press.

Schwartz, D. G. (2006a). Preface: knowledge management as a layered multi-disciplinary pursuit. In D. G. Schwartz (ed.), *Encyclopedia of Knowledge Management* (pp. 1–4), Hershey, PA: Idea Group Reference.

Schwartz, D. G. (ed.) (2006b). *Encyclopedia of Knowledge Management*. Hershey, PA: Idea Group Reference.

Scozzi, B., Garavelli, C. and Crowston, K. (2005). Methods for modeling and supporting innovation processes in SMEs. *European Journal of Innovation Management*, 8(1), 120–137.

Senge, P. M. (1990). *The Fifth Discipline: The Art and Practice of the Learning Organization*. New York: Doubleday.

Serenko, A. and Bontis, N. (2004). Meta-review of knowledge management and intellectual capital literature: citation impact and research productivity rankings. *Knowledge and Process Management*, 11(3), 185–198.

Seufert, A., von Krogh, G. and Bach, A. (1999). Towards knowledge networking. *Journal of Knowledge Management*, 3(3), 180–190.

Shah, M. H. and Siddiqui, F. A. (2006). Organisational critical success factors in adoption of e-banking at the Woolwich bank. *International Journal of Information Management*, 26, 442–456.

Sharif, A. M. and Al-Karaghouli, W. (2011). Introduction: exploring the frontiers of knowledge management transfer in the public and private sector. *Information Systems Management*, 28(1), 2–4.

Shariq, S. Z. (1997). Knowledge management: an emerging discipline. *Journal of Knowledge Management*, 1(1), 75–82.

Sharratt, M. and Usoro, A. (2003). Understanding knowledge-sharing in online communities of practice. *Electronic Journal on Knowledge Management*, 1(2), 187–196.

Shaw, D. and Edwards, J. S. (2005). Building user commitment to implementing a knowledge management strategy. *Information & Management*, 42(7), 977–988.

Shaw, D., Hall, M., Edwards, J. S. and Baker, B. (2007). Responding to crisis through strategic knowledge management. *Journal of Organizational Change Management*, 20(4), 559–578.

Sherif, K. (2002). Barriers to adoption of organizational memories: lessons from industry. In S. Barnes (ed.), *Knowledge Management Systems* (pp. 210–221), London: Thomson Learning.

Shin, M., Holden, T. and Schmidt, R. A. (2001). From knowledge theory to management practice: towards an integrated approach. *Information Processing and Management*, 37, 335–355.

Shrivastava, P. (1983). A typology of organizational learning systems. *Journal of Management Studies*, 20(1), 7–28.

Siemieniuch, C. E. and Sinclair, M. A. (1999). Organizational aspects of knowledge lifecycle management in manufacturing. *International Journal of Human-Computer Studies*, 51, 517–547.

Sierhuis, M. and Clancey, W. J. (1997). Knowledge, practice, activities and people. Available at http://ksi.cpsc.ucalgary.ca/AIKM97/sierhuis/sierhuis.html/.

Singh, M. D., Kant, R. and Narain, R. (2008). Knowledge management practices: a sectoral analysis. *International Journal of Innovation and Learning*, 5(6), 683–710.

Skyrme, D. (1999). *Knowledge Networking: Creating the Collaborative Enterprise*. Oxford: Butterworth-Heinemann.

Slater, S. F. and Narver, J. C. (1995). Market orientation and the learning organization. *Journal of Marketing*, 59(3), 63–74.

Smircich, L. and Stubbart, C. (1985). Strategic management in an enacted world. *Academy of Management Review*, 10(4), 724–736.

Smith, H. A. and McKeen, J. D. (2003a). Instilling a knowledge-sharing culture. Working Paper WP 03-11, Queen's Centre for Knowledge-Based Enterprises, Kingston, Ontario, Canada.

Snow, C. C., Strauss, D. R. and Culpan, R. (2009). Community of firms: a new collaborative paradigm for open innovation and an analysis of Blade.org. *International Journal of Strategic Business Alliances*, 1(1), 53–72.

Snowden, D. (1999). A framework for creating a sustainable knowledge management program. In J. W. Cortada and J. A. Woods (eds.), *The Knowledge Management Yearbook 1999–2000* (pp. 52–64), Boston, MA: Butterworth-Heinemann.

Snyman, R. and Kruger, C. J. (2004). The interdependency between strategic management and strategic knowledge management. *Journal of Knowledge Management*, 8(1), 5–19.

Sorensen, C. and Lundh-Snis, U. (2001). Innovation through knowledge codification. *Journal of Information Technology*, 16, 83–97.

Spender, J. C. (1994). Organizational knowledge, collective practice and Penrose rents. *International Business Review*, 3(4), 353–367.

Spender, J. C. (1996). Making knowledge the basis of a dynamic theory of the firm. *Strategic Management Journal*, 17(Special Issue), 45–62.

Spender, J. C. (2002). Knowledge, uncertainty, and an emergency theory of the firm. In C. W. Choo and N. Bontis (eds.), *The Strategic Management of Intellectual Capital and Organizational Knowledge* (pp. 149–162), New York: Oxford University Press.

Spender, J. C. (2008). Organizational learning and knowledge management: whence and whither? *Management Learning*, 39(2), 159–176.

Spender, J. C. and Grant, R. M. (1996). Knowledge and the firm: overview. *Strategic Management Journal*, 17(Winter Special Issue), 5–9.

Spicer, D. P. and Sadler-Smith, E. (2006). Organizational learning in smaller manufacturing firms. *International Small Business Journal*, 24(2), 133–158.

Stacey, R. D. (2007). *Strategic Management and Organisational Dynamics: The Challenge of Complexity*, 5th ed. Harlow, Essex: FT Prentice Hall.

Stadler, C. and Stone, T. (2001). eBusiness: knowledge management's new killer application. In *Infosmart Africa 2001 Conference Proceedings*, The Dome at Northgate, Johannesburg, Gauteng, South Africa, July 10–12.

Stankosky, M. A. (ed.) (2005). *Creating the Discipline of Knowledge Management: The Latest in University Research*. Oxford: Elsevier Butterworth-Heinemann.

Starbuck, W. H. (1992). Learning by knowledge-intensive firms. *Journal of Management Studies*, 29(6), 713–740.

Stata, R. (1989). Organizational learning — the key to management innovation. *Sloan Management Review*, 30, Spring, 63–74.

Steensma, H. K. (1996). Acquiring technological competencies through inter-organizational collaboration: an organizational learning perspective. *Journal of Engineering and Technology Management*, 12, 267–286.

Stein, E. W. (1995). Organization memory: review of concepts and recommendations for management. *International Journal of Information Management*, 15(1), 17–32.

Stein, E. W. and Zwass, V. (1995). Actualizing organizational memory with information systems. *Information Systems Research*, 6, 85–117.

Stenmark, D. (2000). Turning tacit knowledge tangible. In *Proceedings of the 33rd Hawaii International Conference on System Sciences (HICSS)*, Hawaii.

Stewart, T. A. (1991). Brainpower: how intellectual capital is becoming America's most valuable asset. *Fortune*, June 3, 44–60.

Stewart, T. A. (1997). *Intellectual Capital: The New Wealth of Organizations*. New York: Currency/Doubleday.

Storey, J. and Barnett, E. (2000). Knowledge management initiatives: learning from failure. *Journal of Knowledge Management*, 4(2), 145–156.

Strach, P. and Everett, A. E. (2006). Knowledge transfer within Japanese multinationals: building a theory. *Journal of Knowledge Management*, 10(1), 55–68.

Straker, I., Ison, S., Humphreys, I. and Francis, G. (2009). A case study of functional benchmarking as a source of knowledge for car parking strategies. *Benchmarking*, 16(1), 30–46.

Streatfield, D. and Wilson, T. (1999). Deconstructing knowledge management. *Aslib Proceedings*, 51(3), 67–71.

Stuller, J. (1998). Chief of corporate smarts. *Training*, 35, 28–34.

Styhre, A. (2002). The knowledge-intensive company and the economy of sharing: rethinking utility and knowledge management. *Knowledge and Process Management*, 9(4), 228–236.

Styhre, A. (2004). Rethinking knowledge: a Bergsonian critique of the notion of tacit knowledge. *British Journal of Management*, 15, 177–188.

Subramaniam, M. and Venkatraman, N. (1999). The influence of leveraging tacit overseas knowledge for global new product development capability: an empirical examination. In M. A. Hitt, P. G. Clifford, R. D. Nixon and K. P. Coyne (eds.), *Dynamic Strategic Resources* (pp. 373–401), Chichester: Wiley.

Sun, P. Y. T. and Scott, J. L. (2003). Exploring the divide — organizational learning and learning organization. *The Learning Organization*, 10(4), 202–215.

Sutton, D. C. (2001). What is knowledge and can it be managed? *European Journal of Information Systems*, 10, 80–88.

Sveiby, K. E. (1994). Towards a knowledge perspective on organization. Doctoral thesis, University of Stockholm, Stockholm.

Sveiby, K. E. (1996). Transfer of knowledge and the information processing professions. *European Management Journal*, 14(4), 379–388.

Sveiby, K. E. (1997). *The New Organizational Wealth: Managing and Measuring Knowledge-Based Assets*. San Francisco, CA: Berrett-Koehler Publishers.

Sveiby, K. E. (1999). Frequently asked questions about knowledge management. Available at http://www.sveiby.com.au/.

Swan, J., Newell, S. and Robertson, M. (2000). Limits of IT-driven knowledge management initiatives for interactive innovation processes: towards a community-based approach. In R. H. Sprague, Jr. (ed.), *Proceedings of the 33rd Hawaii International Conference on System Sciences (HICSS-33)*.

Swan, J., Newell, S., Scarbrough, H. and Hislop, D. (1999). Knowledge management and innovation: networks and networking. *Journal of Knowledge Management*, 3, 262–275.

Swan, J. and Scarbrough, H. (2001). Editorial. *Journal of Information Technology*, 16(2), 49–55.

Szulanski, G. (1996). Exploring internal stickiness: impediments to the transfer of best practice within the firm. *Strategic Management Journal*, 17, 27–43.

Szulanski, G. (2000). The process of knowledge transfer: a diachronic analysis of stickiness. *Organizational Behavior and Human Decision Processes*, 82(1), 9–27.

Tallman, S. (2001). Global strategic management. In M. A. Hitt, R. E. Freeman and J. S. Harrison (eds.), *The Blackwell Handbook of Strategic Management* (pp. 464–490), Oxford: Blackwell.

Tavakoli, I. and Lawton, J. (2005). Strategic thinking and knowledge management. *Handbook of Business Strategy*, 6(1), 155–160.

Teece, D. J. (1989). Inter-organizational requirements of the innovation process. *Managerial and Decision Economics*, 10(Special Issue), 35–42.

Teece, D. J. (1990). Contributions and impediments of economic analysis to the study of strategic management. In J. W. Fredrickson (ed.), *Perspectives on Strategic Management* (pp. 39–80), New York: Harper Business.

Teece, D. J., Pisano, G. and Shuen, A. (1997). Dynamic capabilities and strategic management. *Strategic Management Journal*, 18(7), 509–533.

Thomke, S. and von Hippel, E. (2002). Customers as innovators: a new way to create value. *Harvard Business Review*, 80(4), 74–81.

Thompson, J. D. (1967). *Organizations in Action*. New York: McGraw-Hill.

Thompson, P., Warhurst, C. and Callaghan, G. (2001). Ignorant theory and knowledgeable workers: interrogating the connections between knowledge, skills and services. *Journal of Management Studies*, 38(7), 923–942.

Tidd, J. and Bessant, J. (2009). *Managing Innovation: Integrating Technological, Market and Organizational Change*, 4th ed. Chichester: John Wiley & Sons.

Tidd, J., Bessant, J. and Pavitt, K. (2001). *Managing Innovation: Integrating Technological, Market and Organizational Change*, 2nd ed. Chichester: John Wiley & Sons.

Tinnesand, B. (1973). Towards a general theory of innovation. PhD thesis, University of Wisconsin–Madison, Madison, WI.

Tissen, R., Andriessen, D. and Deprez, F. L. (1998). *Value-Based Knowledge Management — Creating the 21st Century Company: Knowledge Intensive, People Rich.* Amsterdam: Addison-Wesley Longman.

Tiwana, A. (2000). *The Knowledge Management Toolkit.* Englewood Cliffs, NJ: Prentice Hall.

Tiwana, A. (2001). *Knowledge Management: E-Business and Customer Relationship Management Applications.* Upper Saddle River, NJ: Prentice Hall.

Tiwana, A. (2002). *The Knowledge Management Toolkit: Orchestrating IT, Strategy and Knowledge Platforms*, 2nd ed. Upper Saddle River, NJ: Prentice Hall.

Tobin, D. (1996). *Transformational Learning: Renewing Your Company Through Knowledge and Skills.* New York: John Wiley & Sons.

Toffler, A. (1990). *Powershift: Knowledge, Wealth and Violence at the Edge of the 21st Century.* New York: Bantam Books.

Torres, A. (1999). Unlocking the value of intellectual assets. *McKinsey Quarterly*, 4, 28–37.

Tsoukas, H. (1996). The firm as a distributed knowledge system: a constructionist approach. *Strategic Management Journal*, 17(Special Issue), 11–25.

Tsoukas, H. and Vladimirou, E. (2001). What is organizational knowledge? *Journal of Management Studies*, 38(7), 973–993.

Tuomi, I. (1999). Data is more than knowledge: implications of the reversed knowledge hierarchy for knowledge management and organizational memory. *Journal of Management Information Systems*, 16(3), 103–117.

Tversky, A. and Kahneman, D. (1981). The framing of decisions and the psychology of choice. *Science*, 211, 453–458.

Twiss, B. (1992). *Managing Technological Innovation*, 4th ed. London: Pitman.

Udwadia, F. E. (1990). Creativity and innovation in organizations. *Technological Forecasting and Social Change*, 38(1), 65–80.

Uhlaner, L., van Stel, A., Meijaard, J. and Folkeringa, M. (2007). The relationship between knowledge management, innovation and firm performance: evidence from Dutch SMEs. Working paper, SCALES program, EIM Business & Policy Research, Zoetermeer, The Netherlands.

UK Department for Education and Employment (2000). *Opportunity for All: Skills for the New Economy*. London: DfEE.

UK Department of Trade and Industry (1998). *Our Competitive Future: Building the Knowledge Driven Economy*. Competitiveness White Paper, DTI, London.

Ulrich, D., von Glinow, M. A. and Jick, T. (1993). High-impact learning: building and diffusing learning capability. *Organizational Dynamics*, 22(2), 52–66.

Urabe, K. (1988). Innovation and the Japanese management system. In K. Urabe, J. Child and T. Kagono (eds.), *Innovation and Management: International Comparisons* (pp. 3–25), Berlin: Walter de Gruyter & Co.

Utterback, J. M. (1994). *Mastering the Dynamics of Innovation: How Companies Can Seize Opportunities in the Face of Technological Change*. Boston, MA: Harvard Business School Press.

Utterback, J. M. and Abernathy, W. J. (1975). A dynamic model of process and product innovation. *Omega*, 3(6), 639–656.

Uzzi, B. and Lancaster, R. (2003). Relational embeddedness and learning: the case of bank loan managers and their clients. *Management Science*, 49(4), 383–399.

Vail, E. F. (1999). Mapping organizational knowledge. *Knowledge Management Review*, 8(May/June), 10–15.

van Beveren, J. (2002). A model of knowledge acquisition that refocuses knowledge management. *Journal of Knowledge Management*, 6(1), 18–22.

Van Buren, M. (1998). Virtual coffee klatch. *Technical Training*, 9(5), 42–46.

Van Cauwenbergh, A. and Cool, K. (1982). Strategic management in a new framework. *Strategic Management Journal*, 3(3), 245–264.

van den Hooff, B. and van Weenen, F. D. L. (2004). Committed to share: commitment and CMC use as antecedents of knowledge sharing. *Knowledge and Process Management*, 11(1), 13–24.

van der Spek, R. and Spijkervet, A. (1997). Knowledge management: dealing intelligently with knowledge. In J. Liebowitz and L. Wilcox (eds.), *Knowledge Management and Its Integrative Elements* (pp. 31–60), Boca Raton, FL: CRC Press.

van Wijk, R., Jansen, J. J. P. and Lyles, M. A. (2008). Inter- and intra-organizational knowledge transfer: a meta-analytic review and assessment of its antecedents and consequences. *Journal of Management Studies*, 45(4), 830–853.

Vera, D. and Crossan, M. (2003). Organizational learning and knowledge management: toward an integrative framework. In M. Easterby-Smith and M. A. Lyles (eds.), *The Blackwell Handbook of Organizational Learning and Knowledge Management* (pp. 122–141), Oxford: Blackwell.

von Krogh, G. (1998). Care in knowledge creation. *California Management Review*, 40(3), 133–153.

von Krogh, G. and Grand, S. (2002). From economic theory toward a knowledge-based theory of the firm: conceptual building blocks. In C. W. Choo and N. Bontis (eds.), *The Strategic Management of Intellectual Capital and Organizational Knowledge* (pp. 163–184), New York: Oxford University Press.

von Krogh, G., Ichijo, K. and Nonaka, I. (2000). *Enabling Knowledge Creation: How to Unlock the Mystery of Tacit Knowledge and Release the Power of Innovation*. New York: Oxford University Press.

Walsh, J. P. and Ungson, G. R. (1991). Organizational memory. *Academy of Management Review*, 16(1), 57–91.

Walters, D. (2000). Virtual organisations: new lamps for old. *Management Decision*, 38(6), 420–436.

Wang-Cowham, C. (2008). HR structure and HR knowledge transfer between subsidiaries in China. *The Learning Organization*, 15(1), 26–44.

Ward, R. C. (2002). Knowledge management, information management, or organizational learning: a comparative study of three states' approaches to knowledge management and information technology. Paper presented at the Southeastern Conference on Public Administration, Columbia, South Carolina, October.

Watson, I. (2003). *Applying Knowledge Management: Techniques for Building Corporate Memories*. San Francisco, CA: Morgan Kaufmann.

Webb, S. P. (1998). *Knowledge Management: Linchpin of Change — Some Practical Guidelines*. London: ASLIB.

Weber, R. O. (2007). Addressing failure factors in knowledge management. *Electronic Journal of Knowledge Management*, 5(3), 333–346.

Weeks, M. (2004). Knowledge management in the wild. *Business Horizons*, 47(6), 15–24.

Werr, A., Blomberg, J. and Löwstedt, J. (2009). Gaining external knowledge — boundaries in managers' knowledge relations. *Journal of Knowledge Management*, 13(6), 448–463.

West, M. A. and Farr, J. L. (1990). Innovation at work. In M. A. West and J. L. Farr (eds.), *Innovation and Creativity at Work: Psychological and Organizational Strategies* (pp. 3–13), Chichester: Wiley.

Westland, J. C. (2008). *Global Innovation Management*. New York: Palgrave Macmillan.

Wick, C. W. and Leon, L. S. (1993). *The Learning Edge: How Smart Managers and Smart Companies Stay Ahead*. New York: McGraw-Hill.

Wiig, K. M. (1993). *Knowledge Management Foundations: Thinking About Thinking — How People and Organizations Create, Represent, and Use Knowledge*. Arlington, TX: Schema Press.

Wiig, K. M. (1997). Knowledge management: where did it come from and where will it go? *Expert Systems with Applications*, 13(1), 1–14.

Wikstrom, S. and Normann, R. (1994). *Knowledge and Value: A New Perspective on Corporate Transformation*. London: Routledge.

Willett, S. and Copeland, L. (1998). Knowledge management key to IBM's enterprise plan. *Computer Reseller News*, 800, July, 1–6.

Williams, A. (1999). *Creativity, Invention and Innovation*. Sydney: Allen & Unwin.

Wilson, D. A. (1996). *Managing Knowledge*. Oxford: Butterworth-Heinemann.

Wilson, T. D. (1989). Towards an information management curriculum. *Journal of Information Science*, 15, 203–210.

Wilson, T. D. (2002a). *Knowledge Management Review: The Practitioner's Guide to Knowledge Management*. Chicago, IL: Melcrum Publishing.

Wilson, T. D. (2002b). The nonsense of 'knowledge management'. *Information Research* (online journal), 8(1), available at http://informationr.net/ir/8-1/paper144.html/.

Winch, G. and Schneider, E. (1993). Managing the knowledge-based organization: the case of architectural practice. *Journal of Management Studies*, 30(6), 923–937.

Windrum, P. and Tomlinson, M. (1999). Knowledge-intensive services and international competitiveness: a four country comparison. *Technology Analysis & Strategic Management*, 11(3), 391–408.

Winter, S. G. (2003). Understanding dynamic capabilities. *Strategic Management Journal*, 24(10), 991–995.

Wittgenstein, L. (1953). *Philosophical Investigations*. G. E. M. Anscombe, trans. Oxford: Basil Blackwell.

Wong, K. Y. and Aspinwall, E. (2004). Knowledge management implementation frameworks: a review. *Knowledge and Process Management*, 11(2), 93–104.

World Bank (1998). *World Development Report 1998/99: Knowledge for Development*. New York: Oxford University Press.

Zack, M. H. (1999a). Developing a knowledge strategy. *California Management Review*, 41(3), 125–145.

Zack, M. H. (1999b). Managing codified knowledge. *Sloan Management Review*, 40(4), 45–58.

Zaltman, G., Duncan, R. and Holbek, J. (1973). *Innovations and Organizations*. New York: Wiley.

Zand, D. (1997). *The Leadership Triad: Knowledge, Trust, and Power*. New York: Oxford University Press.

Zhang, D. and Zhao, J. L. (2006). Preface — knowledge management in organizations. *Journal of Database Management*, 17(1), 1–8.

Zins, C. (2006). Redefining information science: from "information science" to "knowledge science". *Journal of Documentation*, 62(4), 447–461.

Zmud, R. (2002). Special issue on redefining the organizational roles of information technology in the information age. *MIS Quarterly*, 26(3).

Zuboff, S. (1988). *In the Age of the Smart Machine: The Future of Work and Power*. Oxford: Heinemann Professional.

Zuckerman, A. and Buell, H. (1998). Is the world ready for knowledge management? *Quality Progress*, 31(6), 81–84.

Index